S0-AHG-654

WORKING WITH
ACTIVE
SERVER PAGES

QUE®

WORKING WITH
ACTIVE
SERVER PAGES

Written by

Michael Corning • Steve Elfanbaum • David Melnick

Working with Active Server Pages

Copyright© 1997 by Que® Corporation.

All rights reserved. Printed in the United States of America. No part of this book may be used or reproduced in any form or by any means, or stored in a database or retrieval system, without prior written permission of the publisher except in the case of brief quotations embodied in critical articles and reviews. Making copies of any part of this book for any purpose other than your own personal use is a violation of United States copyright laws. For information, address Que Corporation, 201 W. 103rd Street, Indianapolis, IN 46290. You may reach Que's direct sales line by calling 1-800-428-5331.

Library of Congress Catalog No.: 96-72211

ISBN: 0-7897-1115-x

This book is sold *as is*, without warranty of any kind, either express or implied, respecting the contents of this book, including but not limited to implied warranties for the book's quality, performance, merchantability, or fitness for any particular purpose. Neither Que Corporation nor its dealers or distributors shall be liable to the purchaser or any other person or entity with respect to any liability, loss, or damage caused or alleged to have been caused directly or indirectly by this book.

99 98 97   6 5 4 3 2

Interpretation of the printing code: the rightmost double-digit number is the year of the book's printing; the rightmost single-digit number, the number of the book's printing. For example, a printing code of 97-2 shows that the second printing of the book occurred in 1997.

All terms mentioned in this book that are known to be trademarks or service marks have been appropriately capitalized. Que cannot attest to the accuracy of this information. Use of a term in this book should not be regarded as affecting the validity of any trademark or service mark.

Screen reproductions in this book were created using Collage Plus from Inner Media, Inc., Hollis, NH.

Credits

PRESIDENT
Roland Elgey

PUBLISHER
Joseph B. Wikert

PUBLISHING MANAGER
Fred Slone

EDITORIAL SERVICES DIRECTOR
Elizabeth Keaffaber

MANAGING EDITOR
Sandy Doell

DIRECTOR OF MARKETING
Lynn E. Zingraf

ACQUISITIONS EDITOR
Christopher Booher

PRODUCTION EDITOR
Juliet MacLean

EDITORS
Jim Bowie
Sean Dixon
Susan Moore
Jeannie Smith

PRODUCT MARKETING MANAGER
Kristine Ankney

ASSISTANT PRODUCT MARKETING MANAGERS
Karen Hagen
Christy M. Miller

STRATEGIC MARKETING MANAGER
Barry Pruett

TECHNICAL EDITOR
Ramesh Chandak

TECHNICAL SUPPORT SPECIALIST
Nadeem Muhammed

ACQUISITIONS COORDINATOR
Carmen Krikorian

SOFTWARE RELATIONS COORDINATOR
Susan D. Gallagher

EDITORIAL ASSISTANTS
Jennifer L. Condon
Andrea Duvall

BOOK DESIGNER
Ruth Harvey

COVER DESIGNER
Nathan Clement

PRODUCTION TEAM
Michael Beaty
Debra Bolhuis
Marcia Brizendine
Wil Cruz
DiMonique Ford
Jason Hand
Tony McDonald
Steph Mineart
Erich Richter
Laura Robbins
Marvin Van Tiem

INDEXER
Sandy Henselmeier

Composed in *Century Old Style* and *ITC Franklin Gothic* by Que Corporation.

To Katy: a first book is like a first baby; only this time, I was in labor. Your support and patience kept me going, but your loving me back to health was the fun part.

—MC

To Holly, whose love, patience, encouragement, and understanding made this effort possible.

—SE

To my parents, Michael and Patty, whose nurturing support gave me the confidence to take on this book.

—DM

About the Authors

Michael Corning is a database developer living in Portland, Oregon. He holds an M.B.A. from Portland State University where he has also taught finance management. He began his computer career at Arthur Andersen & Company, fresh out of graduate school. He earned a license to practice as a CPA but found that he was much happier with spreadsheets than ledger sheets and retired from the profession. For the last five years, using Microsoft Access, he has been developing a comprehensive financial planning system for Chuck Jones & Associates, Inc. With the advent of Active Server Pages, he is porting all of that old-fashioned code to ASP.

Corning is a busy Webmaster for a wide range of interests from the *Conscious Investing* home page at **http://investing.com/** to the Web site, *Blueprint for a Vision* hosted by the Oregon Adoptive Rights Association at **http://oara.org/**. His other intellectual passion is his *Fractal Market Analysis* Web site at **http://oara.org/mpc/fma/** (a site that augments the books on chaos theory in finance written by Edgar E. Peters).

Corning is hopelessly in love with his wife, Katy, and tries to be the best loving father he can to his three sons, Christian, Seth, and Casey.

Steve Elfanbaum was born and raised in St. Louis, Missouri. After graduating from the University of Missouri with a degree in finance, he had a number of jobs, ranging from carpentry to sales. For the past seven years, he has held a number of IS positions within GE Capital. After completing General Electric's two-year Information Systems Management program, he took a team leader position in Stamford, developing and implementing client/server, imaging, and enterprise applications for a number of divisions within GE Capital. He currently lives and works in St. Louis with his wife, two boys, and dog.

David Melnick, who is currently consulting on Electronic Commerce for the Deloitte and Touche LLP Solutions Group, has over six years of experience in applying technology to support process re-engineering, with a special focus on implementing database-driven Internet/intranet-based applications for business.

He holds both an M.B.A. from the Anderson School at UCLA and the Microsoft Certified Professional status, providing him with both the technical and business skills to address the opportunities that businesses face in leveraging advanced technologies.

David has implemented Microsoft's premiere Internet Backoffice technologies, including Active Server and Merchant Server into production applications for Fortune 500 clients, providing integrated inventory management, order fulfillment, and online authorization capabilities over the Internet.

Acknowledgments

Writing a book about software while it is still in beta form is a harrowing experience. Under those circumstances one factor can make or break both the software and the book written about it: teamwork. I have been in my fair share of beta programs over the years, and none of them can hold a candle to the one that matured Active Server Pages. There are three reasons for this: the finest group of Microsoft people I have ever worked for, the Internet, and the unbelievable group of people connected together from all over this planet by the mailing group and the newsgroup. If the Internet had hands, I would recommend everyone involved pat themselves and each other on the back. The authors of this book are forever in your debt.

Specifically, our Microsoft cohorts, Paul Enfield and Mike Hedley, deserve my personal thanks. They consistently went beyond the call of duty for me and indulged both my ignorance and my over-exuberance during this project. Leo Artalejo, Denali Evangelist without peer, was incredible when it came to special requests (he even managed to fulfill them while traveling in Europe!) Guys, you were memorable; thank you.

On the mailing group and newsgroup I found even more patience and caring from my friend, Steve Boyce, in Great Britain, and from the New Zealand contingent, Chris Woodrow and Rod Drury. Gentlemen, you saved my bacon on more than one occasion, and I thank you. All of us put long hours into the beta phase of Denali (as many of us still prefer to call her—truly, one of the great code names ever given to a piece of software, don't you think?), and this makes their generosity all the more precious to me.

Of those not officially on the Denali team, my special gratitude must go to Kyle Geiger. Kyle's guidance through the most obscure part of ADO and ODBC were priceless in the time he saved me and the quality of information I was able to convey in this book. Any errors in the ADO section are my responsibility alone; Kyle couldn't have been more clear, thorough, and thoughtful. I trust, sir, you will find your influence all through the section on ADO, and that I got it mostly right.

For all the other "Denali Dilettantes" (you know who you are), it was an honor to serve with you. As I have said publicly, sometimes too passionately, and always when given even half a chance, I believe we Denali developers had a rare opportunity to be a part of history. For I am convinced that's where we all stand. Denali is going to make a difference in this world, and we three authors hope you, the reader, will get what C. S. Lewis called "the good infection" by the time you progress through the next 600 pages of this book.

A special thank-you goes out to Chris and Tammy Deardorff. As I was working on the last chapters of this book on the weekend after Christmas, most of Portland was without power for three days. Chris and Tammy welcomed Katy and me into their home and let me set up shop. Those three days turned out to be very important. Thanks, Chris and Tammy!

And finally, to our tireless and ever-patient editors, beginning with our lead cheerleader and motivational speaker, Christopher Booher. The conference calls were a blast. And to Juliet MacLean and Mike McKelvy, thanks for helping make me a better writer. I was unaccustomed to writing a book in the fashion that circumstances dictated, so if this thing works, it works because you know exactly what you're doing. Thank you all.

As I have said before, in the next millenium, imagination will be a key strategic advantage in business. Few things on the Internet today are more productive than Active Server Pages when it comes to turning that imagination into reality. May this book help you activate your dreams.

Michael Corning
michael@oara.org

I would like to thank Christopher Booher for his gentle insistance, which kept us on track, and Juliet MacLean, who continues to put up with our inability to comprehend deadlines. I would also like to thank my parents, Alan and Lois, for their continuing support and encouragement of my many endeavors over the years. Mostly, I want to thank my family, Holly, Danny, and Joey, for putting up with my spending so much time in my office, writing, in what has come to be known as the "Pit of Despair."

Steve Elfanbaum
selfanbaum@worldnet.att.net

To my parents, Michael and Patty, whose nurturing support gave me the confidence to take on this book. Michael, my father and business partner for the past three years, set the stage for my involvement in this book by continuously challenging me to explore new technologies that led to my participation in the May 1996 design preview in Redmond for what's now Active Server. And, to my beloved wife, Kerri, who helped me finish this book with her enduring patience, understanding, and keen ability to make fun of me, which allowed me to maintain my sanity during the intensive book-writing process.

I'd also like to acknowledge the unstoppable persistence of Christopher Booher and the Que team for their drive in keeping this project on track to actually get this book completed. To anyone that hasn't written a book before, without the continuous support of the editors you would only hear the disorganized ramblings of technology-loving fools like myself.

Also to Jim Tiedeman, the programmer who basically wrote and tested most of the case study illustrated here while I ran off writing about it.

David Melnick
davidm@melnick.com
http://www.melnick.com

We'd Like to Hear from You!

As part of our continuing effort to produce books of the highest possible quality, Que would like to hear your comments. To stay competitive, we *really* want you, as a computer book reader and user, to let us know what you like or dislike most about this book or other Que products.

You can mail comments, ideas, or suggestions for improving future editions to the address below, or send us a fax at (317) 581-4663. For the online inclined, Macmillan Computer Publishing has a forum on CompuServe (type **GO QUEBOOKS** at any prompt) through which our staff and authors are available for questions and comments. The address of our Internet site is **http://www.quecorp.com** (World Wide Web).

In addition to exploring our forum, please feel free to contact us personally to discuss your opinions of this book: We're **72410,2077** on CompuServe and **eu@que.mcp.com** on the Internet.

Thanks in advance—your comments will help us to continue publishing the best books available on computer topics in today's market.

Que Corporation
201 W. 103rd Street
Indianapolis, Indiana 46290
USA

N O T E Although we cannot provide general technical support, we're happy to help you resolve problems you encounter related to our books, disks, or other products. If you need such assistance, please contact our Tech Support department at 800-545-5914, ext. 3833.

To order other Que or Macmillan Computer Publishing books or products, please call our Customer Service department at (317) 581-3833.

Contents at a Glance

Table of Contents

III | Working with Active Server Objects and Components

IV | Database Management with Active Server Pages

15 Introducing ActiveX Data Objects   289

V | Appendixes

Introduction

One sure sign of the significance of Active Server Pages is that they are often confused with Internet Information Server 3.0. That is, many people think that they are synonymous. In reality, ASP is a single ISAPI filter that has been *added* to IIS 3.0. In almost everyone's mind, however, ASP has evidently supplanted the Microsoft Web server.

The second sign of the significance of ASP is much more subtle, and far more profound. The purpose of this book is to bring this level of significance into the open. In a word, ASP is the key to understanding everything else Microsoft is doing.

For years, many people have assumed that Bill Gates's famous phrase, "Information at Your Fingertips," was merely the sanitized propaganda of a Redmond software hegemony. In this interpretation, the "information" at your fingertips was a function of the Microsoft application you were using. The implication was that the more Microsoft products you used, the more information would be at your fingertips. This interpretation was reinforced by another (earlier) war cry, "A PC on every desktop, all running Microsoft programs."

With ASP, a new interpretation of Microsoft strategy is now possible. This interpretation is not grounded in speculation, but in direct experience. Each one of us can experience this new interpretation for ourselves when we first use an ASP application that uses ActiveX Data Objects (ADO), for ADO is based on a technology that is based on a premise that has far reaching implications for society. The technology is OLEDB, and the premise is "universal access, not universal storage."

What Microsoft means by this is that the key to "Information at Your Fingertips" is *not* realized by relying on local storage (and so, is not strictly a function of owning Microsoft programs). Fingertip information comes by *going* to the data, by knowing where it is and how to access it. In the same way that the Open Database Connectivity (ODBC) initiative enables SQL databases to communicate seamlessly with each other, OLEDB promises the same for data stored in all formats and on all servers attached to the Internet.

If you ponder the true nature and purpose of the Internet, HTML, and open standards, you begin to see that they are the public infrastructure counterpart to the private initiative that can only be adequately collected under the rubric of Active Server Pages. That is, only ASP gathers everything Microsoft needs—ActiveX controls, database access, the Component Object Model, the Distributed Component Object Model, and the Internet Information Server 3.0—into one coherent system. That public infrastructure and that private initiative are inseparable. What ASP does is make things easier for you—the developer—by bringing everything together under one umbrella or as you say into one coherent system.

The key is to recognize the *coherence* of this strategy. Few strategies have held together so well intrinsically and extrinsically, privately and publicly: IIS 3.0, without ASP, is just another Web server; with it, Microsoft has the last puzzle piece in place. In the same way, tightly integrating ADO into ASP conjoins everything else. Either one without the other is much less than half of both. ADO can be used in all Microsoft programming languages, but then it's restricted to the local file system. ASP without ADO, on the other hand, is no more than HTML. ASP without the Internet is doomed to isolation on the world's intranets. With the Internet and Active Server Pages, "Information at Your Fingertips" becomes a global reality and not one reserved only for the Microsoft faithful.

Whether this serves humanity or not is not up to Microsoft; it's up to us. ■

Transforming Internet/Intranet-Based Application Development

In his book, *The Road Ahead*, Bill Gates likens the Information Superhighway to the building of the national highway system in the United States, where the Internet represents the starting point in the construction of a new order of networked communication. We share his vision of the importance of this evolving communications infrastructure. And with this beginning, like the auto industry that blossomed with the expansion of well-developed roads, the production of software applications to leverage this new network infrastructure will be the blossoming industry as we move into the twenty-first century.

Before the marketing manager, CEO, or general consumer can appreciate the transformational value of this new superhighway, software applications that make the transition beyond the simple display of hypertext documents must become widely available. The development of these software applications will determine the long-term success or failure of this rapidly evolving set of global networks.

This superhighway, with its widely adopted standards and explosively expanding network connectivity, has launched a new era for software developers. Application developers working in groups, ranging from commercial software companies to corporate MIS teams, are discovering the capability to rapidly implement applications that extend and surpass even the most progressive groupware and client/server implementations currently in place.

Amidst this incredible excitement, however, developers building these applications quickly come to understand the immaturity of the development tools currently available. Until recently, most Internet developers found themselves working in first generation programming languages with the development environment consisting of little more than a text editor. This has been the primary drawback for developers, especially ones who have become spoiled in mature, graphical development environments. At this point, we hope to amaze and delight you with the power and ease of Web-based programming with Active Server Pages.

A New Era in Application Development

Active Server Pages represent a fundamental transition point for developers. If the Internet ushered in a new era in communication and network connectivity, Active Server Pages represent the first step in the beginning of an application development revolution. Unlike the client-specific processing associated with client side VBScript and ActiveX (OCX), Active Server Pages process at the Server and open the door to using other server services and function libraries in your application development process. Active Server Pages provide the building blocks that Microsoft has used in the creation of portions of its Commercial Internet System, and this environment already has become the foundation for its rapidly evolving platform of Internet development tools. Active Server Pages provide the key to leveraging the rapidly evolving standards as well as the existing ones including:

- Internet networking standards
- Web browser client standards
- Windows NT's evolving distributed computing architecture
- Open database connectivity standards

Active Server Pages bring the widely used Visual Basic programming environment to developers as the glue to integrate both new and existing server applications and services. By providing a means to build applications, utilizing the evolving OLE technologies, Active Server Pages bridge the gap between current Internet development and more traditional client/server development.

This book explores all of the key building blocks to deliver a Web-based application with Active Server Pages, from an appendix offering a quick tour of HTML to an introduction to COM and DCOM objects. This book offers an implementation-oriented guide to Internet/intranet development, exploring the key technologies including:

- HyperText Markup Language (HTML)
- Visual Basic scripting (VBScripting)
- Active Server objects
- Active Server components (bundled OLE applications)
- Custom OLE application development (components)
- Windows NT security, networking, and monitoring

By taking a hands-on look at all of the pieces of the Web-based application puzzle and then tying them together in a case study application, located in the appendixes, this book provides a complete guide to creating either your first or your best Web-based application. By organizing the sections and chapters of this book into stand-alone modules, this book provides a working tool for both beginning programmers and advanced developers making the transition into the best of the evolving Web-based application development environments.

Who Should Read This Book

The core of this book focuses on developing Active Server Pages-based applications. Although we address networking and business issues, we give primary attention to the programmer responsible for design, development, and implementation of an application, including the database connectivity and user interface requirements. Within the programming community, we have paid special attention to programmers with four core backgrounds:

- Microsoft C++ and Visual Basic programmers
- Web developers, building HTML and/or CGI programs
- Professional programmers transitioning to Web-based development
- Team and Project leaders beginning new Inter/intranet projects

For the Microsoft Programmer

If you have a background in application development based on any of Microsoft's BASIC languages, you will find Active Server Pages to be a painless transition to the Web development world. The writing team came from backgrounds in Visual Basic, C++, and Access Basic, and at first glance we saw Web programming as some black box. How does the Web browser talk to the Web server, and how does the Web server invoke our programs? And in the beginning, trying to understand the mechanics of the Common Gateway Interface (CGI) was very confusing. Fortunately, those days have left us, and the Active Server Pages development tools have made the process much easier to understand and work with.

Almost all of the application development techniques and constructs you've used in Visual Basic will partially or completely port to the Web world. In fact, as you will see demonstrated, the Visual Basic code you might have written to open a recordset from an ODBC datasource can in some cases be plugged directly into an Active Server Page. Although you need to take some time to understand the differences between VBScript and the full Visual Basic environment, you can actually use any version of Visual Basic to write VBScript code.

Without making it sound too simple, you will need to spend a little time to understand the client/server programming model of the Web. But with the lessons delivered in this book, you will rapidly be able to prototype applications within this environment. In fact, we even have a section to help you make sure your NT Server with the Internet Information Web Server is set up correctly. And to complete your Web programming jump-start—aside from the actual development of code—we hope to provide you with a good working knowledge of other Web-specific issues, ranging from security to network monitoring.

For the Web Developer

If you have written your own CGI programs in PERL, or if you have only used HTML in the past, this book provides you a key reference to leverage the power delivered in Microsoft's evolving generation of the Web-based application development tools. If you have working experience in HTML, you will quickly be able to integrate Visual Basic code into HTML pages for server-side processing. This technology provides a server-side, not client-side, approach to application development, which like CGI, enables you to deliver browser-independent applications. You can still invoke CGI applications from Active Server Pages, but you will quickly appreciate the reduced need to rely on CGI programs and will also begin to leverage the newly evolving market for COM objects, which offer a more efficient and flexible approach to accomplishing the same tasks.

As a CGI programmer you already have the knowledge and skills to build Internet applications, but you will be amazed by the efficiency and added value that Active Server Pages brings to the table. Although you will have to learn some Visual Basic, your core skills will translate rapidly into this environment. Windows NT and its interoperability between applications will quickly excite you with the possibilities inherent in Active Server Pages development.

For the Programmer New to Microsoft and the Web

If you have a programming background but have never worked directly with Visual Basic or TCP/IP-based network protocols such as HTTP, you have probably felt a little overwhelmed with the challenge of getting started. Maybe you have played with HTML and have been surprised by how quickly you have learned it, or maybe you have yet to even try it. Don't despair; with Active Server Pages and, as a direct result VBScript, the programming languages have finally evolved to a point where any person with a programming background can quickly get started.

Not to oversimplify: You have some work to do. You need to build a working understanding of HTML, a good knowledge of Visual Basic, and preferably some overview feel for the client/server model of the Web browser and the Web server. All of this and more will be delivered in the pages of this book.

This book provides a hands-on approach to making the transition to Web-based application development. Although we provide some help in getting your Web server set up, if you have not set up a Web server before, you might want to consider working with an Internet Service Provider (ISP) who supports Active Server Pages.

ON THE WEB

For more information finding an Internet Consultants and Web Presence Providers, see

http://www.yahoo.com/Business_and_Economy/Companies/Internet_Services/

How This Book Is Organized

In our effort to address the different needs and skill levels of programmers, we have organized this book in two primary ways. First, by providing a case study-based theme with comprehensive Web site backup material, this book can act as a complete jump-start for a programmer trying to get up to speed in Web-based development. Second, within the case study theme, each section and chapter has been designed as a module-based guide, organized to provide readers with the capability to drill into one topic as a stand-alone guide in one particular aspect of the set of technologies discussed.

Specific parts of this book sequentially address the skills necessary to build a Web-based application:

- **Part I:** Working overview of the technologies detailed in the book.
- **Part II:** Study of Visual Basic Script and its application, from the basic variable typing issues, to the specific capabilities enabled in a Web-based development model.
- **Part III:** Step-by-step exploration of the Active Server object and component model and how to apply it. We address not only the methods and properties of the objects, but also the challenges they help developers overcome, from maintaining user state to accessing a database.
- **Part IV:** Specific exploration of Web-focused database programming, using both hands-on examples and a conceptual overview of where database programming on the net is headed.
- **Appendixes:** Finally, a case study that ties together all the technologies discussed into the process of building a comprehensive database-driven Web application. Dealing with aspects of the site in a modular format, the appendixes target areas ranging from managing a membership community to constructing a flexible administrative component for a site.

The module-based nature of the book allows you to delve deeply into what you need to know. Whether you want a quick study on conditional processing or a look at how to validate credit cards over the net, you can use the implementation-oriented book to leverage Active Server Pages.

As the last, and perhaps most valuable resource provided by this book, we have provided an evolving Web site, **http://www.quecorp.com/asp**, which contains the source code, documents, and additional reference material that you might normally find on a CD. Rather than lock in the additional materials provided with this book on a CD, we have chosen to focus entirely on a Web site to provide resources in this rapidly evolving development area.

In addition to the source code and other reference documentation provided, the Web site will identify additional resources available on the Internet, related to Active Server Pages.

A Final Note

As we built Web-based applications for businesses, we have often reflected that the continuing improvement of development tools and porting of more mature development languages to the Web environment continue to make application development easier and easier.

Most people stop before they get started because at first glance developing Web-based applications seems like such a fundamentally different environment. However, as we have trained programmers to implement Web-based applications based on leveraging HTML and CGI tools, we continually felt that a time would come when these technologies would become easily accessible to the general programming community. Well, that time is now, and the development tool that will bring the development community onto the Web is Active Server Pages.

We have waited with great excitement for the standards and tools to evolve to the point where commercial software vendors and general service providers would begin to rapidly provide Web software. And so it is with great excitement and pride that we offer this book to you in the hope that it will be a valuable guide in your efforts to becoming an active contributor in the emerging Inter/intranet application revolution.

Conventions Used in This Book

Que has over a decade of experience developing and publishing the most successful computer books available. With that experience, we've learned what special features help readers the most. Look for these special features throughout the book to enhance your learning experience.

Several type and font conventions are used in this book to help making reading it easier:

- *Italic type* is used to emphasize the author's points and to introduce new terms.
- Screen messages, code listings, and command samples appear in `monospace typeface`.
- URLs, newsgroups, Internet addresses, and anything you are asked to type appears in **boldface**.

 TIP Tips present short advice on a quick or often overlooked procedure. These include shortcuts that can save you time.

N O T E Notes provide additional information that may help you avoid problems, or offer advice that relates to the topic. ■

CAUTION

Cautions warn you about potential problems that a procedure may cause, unexpected results, and mistakes to avoid.

▶ **See** these cross-references for more information on a particular topic.

Sidebar

Longer discussions not integral to the flow of the chapter are set aside as sidebars. Look for these sidebars to find out even more information.

Setting the Stage for Active Server Development

## CHAPTER 1

Understanding Internet/Intranet Development

The hardware of the Internet

First, look at the plumbing that enables your software to operate. One important Internet hardware feature affects how you use all of your Internet applications.

The software of the Internet

Learn about the software of the World Wide Web, as well as that of its poor relation, the OfficeWide Web.

The protocols of the Internet

Take a quick look under the hood of the Web (and anticipate a thorough treatment of Internet protocols in later chapters).

This chapter was written for a special group of people: those who had an unusually good sense of timing and waited until the advent of Active Server Pages (ASP) to get involved with Internet/intranet development.

The chapter surveys an important part of the ASP development environment: the *packet-switched network*. You will learn what this important technology is and how it works inside your office and around the world. The chapter also is a cursory treatment of Internet/intranet technology; details await you in later pages of the book (see the "From Here…" section at the end of this chapter for specific chapter references). ▪

Understanding the Hardware that Makes the Internet Possible

The Internet is like one vast computer. It is a collection of individual computers and local area networks (LANs). But it is also a collection of things called routers, and other kinds of switches, as well as all that copper and fiber that connects everything together.

Packet-Switched Networks

Begin your exploration of this world of hardware by looking at the problem its founding fathers (and mothers) were trying to solve.

A Network Born of a Nightmare   A great irony of the modern age is that the one thing that threatened the extinction of the human race motivated the development of the one thing that may liberate more people on this planet than any military campaign ever could.

The Internet was conceived in the halls of that most salubrious of spaces: the Pentagon. Specifically, the Advanced Research Projects Agency (ARPA) was responsible for the early design of the Net's ARPAnet. ARPA's primary design mission was to make a reliable communications network that would be robust in the event of nuclear attack. In the process of developing this technology, the military forged strong ties with large corporations and universities. As a result, responsibility for the continuing research shifted to the National Science Foundation. Under its aegis, the network became known as the Internet.

Internet/intranet

You may have noticed that *Internet* is always capitalized. This is because Internet is the name applied to only one thing—and yet, that thing doesn't really exist. What this means is that there is no one place you go to when you visit the Net; no one owns it, and no one can really control it. (Very Zen, don't you think? At once everything and nothing.)

You also may have come across the term *intranet* and noticed that it is never capitalized. You can probably guess the reason: because intranets, unlike the Internet, are legion; they are all over the place. And every single one of them is owned and controlled by someone.

In this book, you will see the term *Web* used interchangeably for both the World Wide Web and the OfficeWide Web. When this book discusses the Internet, *Web* refers to the World Wide Web; when it discusses intranets, Web refers to the OfficeWide Web.

A Small Target   Computers consist of an incredibly large number of electronic switches. Operating systems and computer software really have only one job: Turn one or more of those switches on and off at exactly the right moment. The Internet itself is one great computer, one huge collection of switches. This is meant in a deeper way than Scott McNealy of Sun Microsystems intended when he said, "The network is the computer." We think Scott was referring to the network *as* a computer. We are referring, instead, to the switches that make up the Internet, the switches that stitch the computers all together into an inter-network of computers. Scott was emphasizing the whole; we are highlighting the "little wholes" that make up Scott's whole.

The reason this is important is fairly obvious. If you take out a single computer or section of the network, you leave the rest unfazed. It works.

So, on the Internet, every computer basically knows about every other computer. The key to making this work is the presence of something called the Domain Name System (DNS). You will learn details of this innovation in a moment; for now, just be aware that maintaining databases of names and addresses is important, not only for your e-mail address book, but also to the function of the Internet. The DNS is the Internet's cerebral cortex.

N O T E Ironically, the Net's distributed functionality is similar to the one the brain uses to store memory and the one investors use to diversify risk. It all boils down to chance: Spread the risk around, and if anything goes wrong, you can control the damage. This was the lesson lost on the designer of the Titanic. ▪

E-Mail   If it makes sense to use lots of computers and connect them together so that information can flow from one point to another, the same logic should work with the message itself.

For example, take an average, everyday e-mail message. You sit at your PC and type in what appears to be one thing, but when you press the Send/Receive button on your e-mail client, something happens: Your message gets broken up into little pieces. Each of these pieces has two addresses: the address of the transmitting computer and the address of the receiving computer. When the message gets to its destination, it needs to be reassembled in the proper order and presented intact to the reader.

Fractaled Flickers

Those of you interested in technically arcane matters might want to look at Internet/intranet hardware and software through the eyes of the *chaologist*—someone who studies the mathematics of chaos theory and the related mathematics of fractals.

Essentially, all fractals look the same, regardless of the level of detail you choose. For the Internet, the highest level of detail is the telecommunications infrastructure—the network of switches that carries the signal from your computer to mine. Another level of detail is the hardware of every computer, router, and bridge that make up the moving parts of the Internet. (Guess what, the hardware looks the same for each.) You look at the way the information itself is structured and see that the family resemblance is still there.

Someone should take the time to see if there's something important lurking in this apparent fractal pattern. Chaotic systems pop up in the darndest places.

An Unexpected Windfall   There is one especially useful implication to all this packet business. Did you know that you can send an e-mail message, navigate to a Web site, and download a 52-megabyte file from the Microsoft FTP site, all at exactly the same time?

Remember that any single thing (a "single" e-mail message) to you is a multiplicity of things to your computer (dozens of 512-byte "packets" of data). Because everything gets broken up when sent and then reassembled when received, there's plenty of room to stuff thousands of packets onto your *dialup connection* (defined in the section entitled, "Connecting Your Network to an Internet Service Provider"). Let your modem and the Internet, with all its hard-working *protocols* (defined in the last section of this chapter), do their thing. Sit back, relax, and peel a few hours off of your connect time.

Routers and Gateways

Remember that the Internet is a global network of networks. In this section, you get a peek at the hardware that makes this possible. You also will see how you can use some of this same technology inside your own office.

To give you some idea of how all this hardware is connected, take a look at Figure 1.1.

FIG. 1.1
An overview of the hardware that makes the Internet possible.

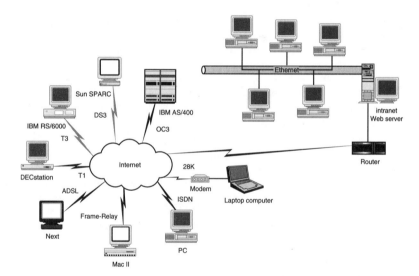

Routers: The *Sine Qua Non* of the Internet *Routers* are pieces of hardware (though routers can be software added to a server) that are similar to personal computers on your network. The main difference is that routers have no need to interact with humans, so they have no keyboard or monitor. They do have an address, just like the nodes on the LAN and the hosts on the Internet. The router's job is to receive packets addressed to it, look at the whole destination address stored in the packet, and then forward the packet to another computer (if it recognizes the address).

Routers each contain special tables that inform them of the addresses of all networks connected to them. The Internet is defined as all of the addresses stored in all of the router tables of all the routers on the Internet. Routers are organized hierarchically, in layers. If a router cannot route a packet to the networks it knows about, it merely passes off the packet to a router at a higher level in the hierarchy. This process continues until the packet finds its destination.

A router is the key piece of technology that you either must own yourself or must be part of a group that owns one; for example, your ISP owns a router, and your server address (or your LAN addresses) are stored in its router table. Without routers, we would have no Internet.

Gateways to the Web   The term *gateway* can be confusing, but because gateways play a pivotal role in how packets move around a packet-switched network, it's important to take a moment to understand what they are and how they work.

Generally speaking, a gateway is anything that passes packets. As you might guess, a router can be (and often is) referred to as a gateway. *Application gateways* convert data into a format that some kind of application can use. Perhaps the most common application gateways are *e-mail gateways.* When you send an e-mail message formatted for the Simple Mail Transfer Protocol (SMTP) to someone on AOL (America Online), your message must pass through an e-mail gateway. If you've ever tried to send an e-mail attachment to an AOL address, you know that there are some things the gateway ignores (like that attachment, much to your chagrin).

A third kind of gateway is a *protocol gateway. Protocols* are rules by which things get done. When you access a file on a Novell file server, for example, you use the IPX/SPX protocol. When you access something on the Web, you use TCP/IP. Protocol gateways, such as Microsoft's Catapult server, translate packets from and to formats used by the different protocols. These gateways act like those people you see whispering in the president's ear during photo ops at Summit meetings.

N O T E   When you are setting up your first intranet under Windows 95 or Windows NT, you need to pay attention to the Gateway setting in the Network Properties dialog box. This is especially important when your PC is also connected to the Internet through a *dialup* account with an ISP. ■

Getting Connected

If all this talk about what the Internet is leaves you wondering how you can be a part of the action, then this section is for you.

Wiring Your Own Computers   The simplest way to connect computers is on a local area network, using some kind of networking technology and topology. Ethernet is a common networking technology, and when it is installed using twisted-pair wire, the most common topology is the *star* (see Figure 1.2). Networking protocols are the third component of inter-networking computers (you will learn more about the defining protocol of the Internet in the last section of this chapter, "It's All a Matter of Protocol").

FIG. 1.2
The Star topology of
Ethernet requires all
computers to connect to
a single hub.

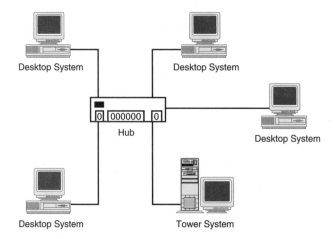

Desktop System

Desktop System

Desktop System

Hub

Desktop System

Tower System

T I P   When you wire an office for an Ethernet LAN, try to install Category 5 twisted-pair wire. Wire of this
quality supports the 100-megabyte-per-second (M/sec), so-called *Fast Ethernet*.

With Ethernet's star topology, the LAN wires that are leaving all the PCs converge on one
piece of hardware known as a *hub*. Depending on your needs and budget, you can buy inexpensive hubs that connect eight computers together. If your network gets bigger than eight computers, you can add another hub and "daisy-chain" the hubs together. Insert the ends of a short
piece of twisted-pair wire into a connector on each hub, and you double the size of your LAN.
Keep adding hubs in this way as your needs demand.

N O T E   If you're like me and you occasionally need to make a temporary network out of two PCs,
you can't just connect their Ethernet cards with a single piece of ordinary twisted-pair wire
(but you can connect two computers with terminated coax cable if your network interface card has that
type of connector on it). You need a special kind of wire that is available at electronics parts stores. ■

Each network adapter card in a computer has a unique address called its Media Access Control
(MAC) *address.* You can't change the MAC address; it's part of the network interface card
(NIC) that you installed on the bus of your PC. There are addresses that you can control, however. Under Windows 95, you can easily assign a network address of your choosing to your
computer. You'll learn how to do this in the section entitled, "Names and Numbers."

As you will see throughout this book, the single greatest advantage of the LAN over the Internet is bandwidth. *Bandwidth* is a term inherited from electronics engineers and has come to
mean "carrying capacity."

The Several Meanings of Bandwidth

Bandwidth, it turns out, is one of those buzzwords that catch on far beyond the domain of discourse
that brought them to light. Today, *bandwidth* is used ubiquitously to describe the carrying capacity of

anything. Our personal favorites are *human bandwidth* and *financial bandwidth.* One that we use— and that, to our knowledge, no one else uses—is *intellectual bandwidth.* Human and intellectual bandwidth obviously are related. The former refers to the number and the skill level of those responsible for creating and maintaining an Internet presence; the latter is much more specific and measures how quickly the skill-level of the human bandwidth can grow in any single individual. Intellectual bandwidth is a measure of intelligence and imagination; human bandwidth is a measure of sweat.

Oh, yes, and financial bandwidth is a measure of the size of a budget allocated to Web development. It also can refer to a Web site's ability to raise revenues or decrease costs.

Packets move across a LAN at a maximum of 10 million bits per second (bps) for Ethernet, and 100 million bps for Fast Ethernet. Contrast that with one of the biggest pipes on the Internet, the fabled T1, which moves bits at the sedentary rate of 1.544 million bps, and you can see how far technology has to go before the Internet performs as well as the LAN that we all take for granted.

Connecting Your Network to an Internet Service Provider   Whether you have a single PC at home or a large LAN at the office, you still need to make a connection with the Internet at large. Internet Service Providers are companies that act as a bridge between you and the large telecommunications infrastructure that this country (and the world) has been building for the last 100 years.

When you select an ISP, you join a *tributary* of the Internet. Certain objectives dictate the amount of bandwidth that you need. If you want only occasional access to the Internet, you can use a low-bandwidth connection. If you are going to serve up data on the Internet, you need more bandwidth. If your demands are great enough—and you have sufficient financial band- width—you need to access the biggest available data pipe.

Connecting to the Internet through an ISP can be as simple as something called a *shell account* or as complex as a *virtual server environment* (VSE). If the only thing you want to do is access the World Wide Web, you need purchase only a *dialup account.* Of course, there's nothing stopping you from obtaining all three.

TIP   I have two ISPs. One provides a shell account and a dialup account. The other ISP provides my VSE. At $18/month (for the first service provider), having two access points to the Internet is cheap insurance when one of those ISPs goes down.

You need a shell account to use Internet technologies like telnet (one of the book's authors uses telnet all the time to do things like check on due dates of books and CDs he's checked out of the Multnomah County Library or check a title at the Portland State University Library). We also use it to log onto the server where our many Web sites reside, so we can do things like change file permissions on our CGI scripts or modify our crontab (UNIX program that lets us do repetitive things with the operating system, like run our access log analysis program).

Dialup accounts are modem connections that connect your PC to the modem bank at your ISP. Equipment at the ISP's end of the line then connects you to a LAN that, in turn, is connected to a router that is connected to the Internet. See Figure 1.3 for a typical configuration.

FIG. 1.3
Here's an example of how all this equipment is connected.

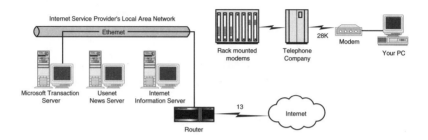

 TIP If you are using a modem to connect to your ISP, you may be able to use some extra copper in your existing phone lines. In many twisted-pair lines, there are two unused stands of copper that can be used to transmit and receive modem signals. If you use them, you don't have to string an extra line of twisted-pair wire just to connect your modem to the phone company. Consult your local telephone maintenance company.

Currently, all the Web sites for which we are responsible are hosted by our ISP. This means that many other people share the Web server with us to publish on the Internet. There are many advantages to this strategy, the single greatest being cost-effectiveness. The greatest disadvantage is the lack of flexibility: The Web server runs under the UNIX operating system, so we can't use the Microsoft Internet Information Server (IIS).

An attractive alternative to a VSE is to "co-locate" a server that you own on your ISP's LAN. That way, you get all of the bandwidth advantages of the VSE, but you also can exploit the incredible power of IIS 3.0. (By the time this book reaches bookshelves, that's what we'll be doing.)

The Virtue of Being Direct   Starting your Internet career in one of the more limited ways just discussed doesn't mean that you can't move up to the majors. It's your call. Your ISP leases bandwidth directly from the phone company, and so can you. All you need is money and skill. Connecting directly using ISDN (integrated service digital network) technology or T1 means that the 52M beta of Visual InterDev will download in one minute instead of four hours, but unless you need all of that bandwidth all of the time, you'd better find a way to sell the excess.

As you will see in the Epilogue, "Looking to a Future with Active Server Pages," choosing IIS 3.0 may, itself, open up additional revenue streams that are unavailable to you when using other server platforms.

The Client and Server

It's time to turn from the plumbing of the Internet and learn about the two most fundamental kinds of software that run on the it, the client and server. In Chapter 3, "Understanding Client/ Server on the Internet," you'll see more details about the history and current impact of client/ server programming on the Web. We introduce the concepts here, so you can see clearly the fundamental difference between these two dimensions, client and server, of Web programming.

> **N O T E** Clients and servers come in many varieties. Within the Internet, the big three are e-mail, file transfer protocol (FTP), and the Web. Outside the Net, client/server database management systems (DBMS) are the most common. In this section, we focus on the Web server and client. ▪

Web Servers: The Center of 1,000 Universes

Whether on an intranet or on the Internet, Web servers are a key repository of human knowledge. Indeed, there is a movement afoot that attempts to store every byte of every server that was ever brought on-line. The logic is compelling, even if the goal seems daunting: Never before has so much human knowledge been so available. Besides being easily accessed, Web servers have another ability that nothing in history, other than books, has had: They serve both text and graphics with equal ease. And, like CDs, they have little trouble with audio and video files. What sets the Web apart from all technologies that came before is that it can do it all, and at a zero marginal cost of production!

Originally, Web servers were designed to work with static files (granted, audio and video stretch the definition of *static* just a bit). With the advent of HTML forms, communication between server and client wasn't strictly a one-way street. Web servers could input more than a simple request for an object like an HTML page. This two-way communication channel, in and of itself, revolutionized the way that business, especially marketing, was done. No longer did the corporation have all the power. The Web is not a broadcast medium, however. On a Web server, you can only make your message available; interested parties must come to your server before that message is conveyed.

Today, there are two things happening that will be as revolutionary to the Web as the Web was to human knowledge: Processing is shifting from the server to the client, and much more powerful processing power is being invested in the server. In both cases, we are more fully exploiting the power of both sides of the Internet.

At its essential core, a Web server is a file server. You ask it for a file, and it gives the file to you. Web servers are more powerful than traditional file servers (for example, a single file may contain dozens of embedded files, such as graphics or audio files); but they are less powerful than the other kind of server common in business, the *database server.* A database server can manipulate data from many sources and execute complex logic on the data before returning a recordset to the client. If a Web server needs to do any processing (such as analyzing the contents of a server log file or processing an HTML form), it has to pass such work to other programs (such as a database server) with which it communicates using the Common Gateway Interface (CGI). The Web server then returns the results of that remote processing to the Web client.

With the advent of Active Server Pages, the Web server itself becomes much more powerful. You will see what this means in Chapter 4, "Introducing Active Server Pages;" for now, it is important for you to realize that a whole new world opens up for the Web developer who uses Active Server Pages. With ASP, you can do almost anything that you can do with desktop client/server applications, and there are many things you can do *only* with ASP.

Web Clients

The genius of the Web client is that it can communicate with a Web server that is running on any hardware and operating system platform in the world.

Programmers worked for decades to obtain the holy grail of computing. They called it *interoperability,* and they worked ceaselessly to reach it. They organized trade shows and working groups to find a common ground upon which computers of every stripe could communicate, but alas, they never really succeeded.

Then an engineer at the CERN laboratory in Switzerland, Tim Berners-Lee came up with a way that information stored on CERN computers could be linked together and stored on any machine that had a special program that Berners-Lee called a *Web server.* This server sent simple ASCII text back to his other invention, the Web client (actually, because the resulting text was read-only, Berners-Lee referred to this program as a Web *browser*), and this turned out to be the crux move. All computers universally recognize ASCII, by definition. The reason that ASCII is not revolutionary itself is that it is so simple, and programmers use complex programming languages to do their bidding. But when you embed special characters in the midst of this simple text, everything changes.

What browsers lack in processing power, they dwarf with their capability to parse (breaking a long complex string into smaller, interrelated parts) text files. The special codes that the Web client strips out of the surrounding ASCII text is called the HyperText Markup Language (HTML). The genius of HTML code is that it's simple enough that both humans and computers can read it easily. What processing needs to be done by the client can be done because the processing is so well defined. A common data entry form, for example, must simply display a box and permit the entry of data; a button labeled Submit must gather up all the data contained in the form and send it to the Web server indicated in the HTML source code.

The result of this simple program, this Web client, is real interoperability, and the world will never be the same. Think about it: Microsoft is one of the largest, most powerful companies in the world. Its annual sales exceed the gross national product of most of the countries on the planet. The abilities of its thousands of programmers is legendary, and today, virtually every product that they publish is now built on the simple model of HTML. Not even the operating system has escaped, as you will see when you install the next version of Windows.

Apparently, though, good enough is never good enough. The irony of the Web client is that its elegant simplicity leaves a vast majority of the processing power of the desktop computer totally unused. At the same time, the constraining resource of the entire Internet is bandwidth, and relying on calls across the network to the server to do even the simplest task (including processing the form enabled with HTML/1.0) compounded the problem.

What was needed next was *client-side processing.* First to fill this need was a new programming language, Java. Java worked much like the Web. In the same way that Berners-Lee's Web at CERN worked as long as the servers all had their version of the Web server software running, Web clients could process Java applets if they had something called a Java *virtual machine* installed on their local hard drive. A virtual machine (VM) is a piece of code that can translate the byte-code produced by the Java compiler into the machine code of the computer the Java applet runs on. Oh, and the compiler is software that converts the source code you write into the files that the software needs, and machine code consists of 1s and 0s and isn't readable at all by humans.

Microsoft took another approach. For many years, the company worked on something it called *Object Linking and Embedding* (OLE). By the time the Web was revolutionizing computing, OLE was evolving into something called the Component Object Model (COM).

▶ **See** "The Component Object Model" for more information about COM, **p. 88**

The COM specification is rich and complex. It was created for desktop Windows applications and was overkill for the more modest requirements of the Internet. As a result, Microsoft streamlined the specification and published it as ActiveX.

Since its inception in the late 1980s, Visual Basic has spawned a vigorous after-market in extensions to the language that was called the VBX, the OCX, and now the ActiveX component. These custom controls could extend the power of HTML just as easily as it did the Visual Basic programming language. Now, overnight, Web pages could exploit things like spreadsheets, data-bound controls, and anything else that those clever Visual Basic programmers conceived. The only catch: Your Web client had to support ActiveX and VBScript (the diminutive relative of Visual Basic, optimized for use on the Internet).

Most of the rest of this book was written to teach you how to fully exploit the client-side power of the ActiveX controls and the protean power of the Active Server. In this section, we tried to convey some of the wonder that lies before you. When the printing press was invented, nothing like it had come before; no one ever had experienced or recorded the consequences of such a singular innovation. We who have witnessed the arrival of the Web know something of its power. While we don't know how much more profound it will be than the printing press, most of us agree that the Web will be more profound, indeed.

Part
I

Ch
1

It's All a Matter of Protocol

This chapter closes with an introduction to the third dimension of data processing on the Internet: protocols. Protocols tie hardware and software together, as well as help forge cooperation between the people who use them. By definition, protocols are generally accepted standards of processing information. If the developer of a Web client wants to ensure the widest possible audience for his or her product, that product will adhere to published protocols. If the protocol is inadequate for the needs of users, the developer can offer the features anyway and then lobby the standards bodies to extend the protocol. Protocols are never static, so this kind of lobbying, while sometimes looking like coercion, is natural and necessary if software is going to continue to empower its users.

The Internet Engineering Task Force (IETF) is the primary standards body for the HTTP protocol. If you are interested in reading more about this group, point your Web client to:

http://www.ietf.cnri.reston.va.us/

In this section, we talk about the defining protocol for the Internet, the TCP/IP protocol suite. This collection of protocols helps hardware communicate reliably with each other and keeps different software programs on the same wavelength.

Hardware that Shakes Hands

As the name suggests, the two main protocols in the TCP/IP suite are the TCP (Transfer Control Protocol) and the IP (Internet Protocol). TCP is responsible for making sure that a message moves from one computer to another, delivering messages to some application program. IP manages packets, or, more precisely, the sending and receiving addresses of packets.

Names and Numbers   As mentioned earlier, all software is in the business of turning switches on or off at just the right time. Ultimately, every piece of software knows where to go in the vast expanse of electronic circuits that make up the modern computer, as well as to stop electrons or let them flow. Each of those junctions in a computer's memory is an address. The more addresses a computer has, the "smarter" it is; that's why a Pentium computer is so much faster than an 8088 computer. (The former's address space is 32 bits, and the latter's is 8— that's not 4 times bigger, that's 2^{24} times bigger!)

The Power of Polynomials

One way to measure the value of the Internet is to measure the number of connections that can be made among its nodes. This will be especially true when massively parallel computing becomes commonplace, but it begins to realize its potential today, as more people deploy more computing resources on the Internet. You will get a real sense of this new power in Chapter 5, "Understanding Objects and Components," and Chapter 14, "Constructing Your Own Server Components."

In the same way that a Pentium is much more powerful than the relative size of its address space, the power of the Internet is much greater than the sum of its nodes. The power curve of the microprocessor is exponential; for example, it derives from taking base 2 to different exponents. To be precise, exponential growth usually is expressed in terms of the base *e*, also known as the *natural logarithm*. Microprocessor power is more accurately described as geometrical.

The Internet's power, on the other hand, is a function of the size of the base, not the exponent. Specifically, the growth rate (or imputed power rate) of the Internet is expressed polynomially; namely, $(n^2-n)/2$. An interesting property of this kind of growth is that as the number of nodes (n) increases, the rate of growth increases (getting closer to half the square of a number).

This is both good and bad news for the Internet. Prophets like George Gilder maintain that it is this intrinsic power of polynomial growth that will fuel the economics of the future Internet. And then there are prophets of doom like Bob Metcalfe, the father of Ethernet, who lament that the inherent complexity of such an infrastructure will be its downfall.

If Metcalfe is correct, the Internet may turn out to be much like some of us: The seeds of our destruction are sown in our success.

The point in the sidebar, "The Power of Polynomials," is that all computers are driven by addresses. Typing **oara.org** may be easy for you, but it means diddly to a computer. Computers want numbers.

When one of the book's authors installed Active Server Pages on his PC at home, the setup program gave his computer a name: **michael.oara.org**. When you install the software on your PC, its setup program may give you a similar name (or it may not). If your ASP setup program follows the same format that it did on the author's machine (and providing that no one else at your organization uses your name in his or her address), then that simple name is sufficient to uniquely identify your computer among the 120 million machines currently running on this planet. We think that's remarkable.

The computer's not impressed, though. By itself, **michael.oara.org** is worthless. On the other hand, 204.87.185.2 is more like it! With that, you can get somewhere—literally. All you need to do now is find a way to map the human-friendly name to the microprocessor-friendly address.

N O T E   In the Epilogue, "Looking to a Future with Active Server Pages," we introduce the idea of a virtual database server. To hide the fact that the server may not belong to you, you can access it by using its IP address instead of its domain name. Hiding such information is only an issue of appearance, a holdover from the days when it was embarrassing to have a Web site in someone else's subdirectory. If keeping up appearances is important to you, then this is an example of one time when you might prefer to identify an Internet resource the way your computer does. ▪

This is the function of name resolution. Before we begin, we want to define two terms: *networks* and *hosts*. Networks are collections of host computers. The IP is designed to accommodate the unique addresses of 3.7 billion host computers; however, computers—like programmers—would rather not work any harder than necessary. For this reason, the Internet Protocol uses router tables (which in turn use network addresses, not host addresses) to move packets around.

N O T E   Recall from the section "Routers and Gateways" that routers are responsible for routing packets to individual host computers. ▧

Once a packet reaches a router, the router must have a way to figure out what to do next. It does this by looking at the network address in the packet. It will look up this network address and do one of two things: route the packet to the next "hop" in the link or notice that the network address is one that the router tables say can be delivered directly. In the latter case, the router then sends the packet to the correct host.

How? There is a second component of the IP address that the router uses: the host address. But this is an Internet address, so how does the router know exactly which PC to send the packet to? It uses something called the Address Resolution Protocol to map an Internet address to a link layer address; for example, a unique Ethernet address for the NIC installed on the PC to which the packet is destined.

This process may sound hopelessly abstract, but luckily, almost all of it is transparent to users. One thing that you must do is to assign IP addresses properly. You do this from the Network Properties dialog box (right-click the Network icon on the Windows 95 or Windows NT 4.0 desktop, and then select Properties at the bottom of the menu). Select the TCP/IP item and double-click it to display its property sheet. It should display the IP Address tab, by default. See Figure 1.4 for an idea of what this looks like.

FIG. 1.4

Here's what the Network Properties dialog box looks like.

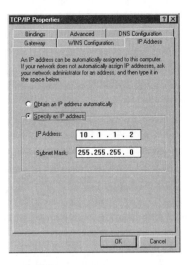

If you're on a LAN that is not directly connected to the Internet, then get an IP address from your network administrator, or, if you are the designated administrator, enter a unique address like **10.1.1.2** (adding 1 to the last dotted number as you add machines to your network). Then enter a subnet mask that looks like **255.255.255.0**. This number should be on all machines that are on the same workgroup. This number is one that tells the network software that all the machines are "related" to each other (the mathematics of this numbering scheme is beyond the scope of this book).

N O T E   If you also are using a *dialup network* (DUN) connection, you will have specified similar properties when you configured a dialup networking connection. These two settings don't conflict, so you can have your DUN get its IP address assigned automatically, and you can have your PC on your LAN have its own IP address and subnet mask. ▪

If your computer has dialog boxes that look like Figure 1.5, then you, too, can have an intranet and an Internet connection on the same PC. The Web server on your intranet will also have its own IP address (we use **10.1.1.1**). The NT domain name given to that server also becomes its intranet domain name, used by intranet clients in all HTTP requests.

FIG. 1.5

This is what the DUN dialog box looks like.

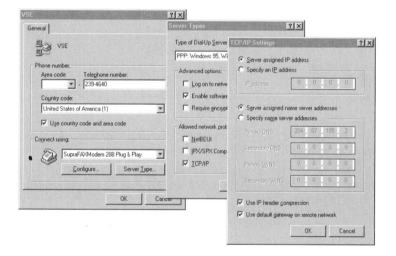

The NetScanTools application, by Northwest Performance Software, is a useful tool for experimenting and troubleshooting IP addresses. Download a shareware copy from:

http://www.eskimo.com/~nwps/nstover60.html

Transfer Control Protocol   The Transfer Control Protocol operates on the Internet in the same way that the transporter did on Star Trek. Remember that on a packet-switched network, messages are broken up into small pieces and thrown on the Internet where they migrate to a specific computer someplace else on the network and are reassembled in the proper order to appear intact at the other end.

That's how packets move from computer to computer on the network, but you also need to know how the messages are reliably reconstituted. In the process of learning, you will see that when transporting pictures, reliability is actually a disadvantage.

To understand the Transfer Control Protocol, you need to understand two key things:

- Its use of ports to which to deliver messages so that application programs (for example, Web clients such as Internet Explorer 3.0) can use the data delivered across the Internet

- Its use of acknowledgments to inform the sending side of the TCP/IP connection that a message segment was received

Ports   Whenever you enter an URL into your Web client, you are implicitly telling the Transfer Control Protocol to deliver the HTTP response to a special address, called a *port,* that the Web client is using to receive the requested data. The default value of this port for HTTP requests is port 80, though any port can be specified, if known. That is, if the Webmaster has a reason to have the server use port 8080 instead of port 80, the requesting URL must include that port in the request. For example:

```
HTTP://funnybusiness.com:8080/unusual_page.htm
```

Think of a port as a phone number. If you want someone to call you, you give him or her your phone number and, when they place their call, you know how to make a connection and exchange information. Your friends probably know your phone number, but what happens when you leave the office? If you don't tell the person you are trying to reach at what phone number you'll be, that person won't know how to contact you. Ports give the Transfer Control Protocol (and its less intelligent cousin, the User Datagram Protocol, or UDP) that same ability.

Polite Society   This ability to convey two-way communication is the second thing that the Transfer Control Protocol derives from its connection-oriented nature. This quirk in its personality makes it the black sheep of the Internet family. Remember that most of the Web is connectionless. However, TCP's mission in life is not just to make connections and then to forget about them; its job is to ensure that messages get from one application to another. IP has to worry only about a packet getting from one host computer to another.

Do you see the difference? It's like sending your mom a Mother's Day card rather than making a phone call to her on that special day. Once you mail the card, you can forget about your mother (shame on you); if you call, though, you have to keep your sentiment to yourself until she gets on the line. Application programs are like you and your mom (though you shouldn't start referring to her by version number).

The Transfer Control Protocol waits for the application to answer. Unlike human conversations, however, TCP starts a timer once it sends a request. If an acknowledgment doesn't arrive within a specified time, the protocol immediately resends the data.

When Reliability Isn't All that It's Cracked Up to Be

This handshaking between the sending computer and the receiving computer works extremely well to ensure reliability under normal circumstances, but there are cases when it can backfire. One such case is when streaming video is being sent, and another is when you are using a tunneling protocol to secure a trusted link across the (untrusted) Internet.

Microsoft's NetShow server uses UDP instead of TCP to avoid the latency issues surrounding the acknowledgment function of the Transfer Control Protocol. Because your eye probably won't miss a few bits of errant video data, NetShow doesn't need the extra reliability, and UDP serves its needs admirably.

Connecting two or more intranets, using something like the Point to Point Tunneling Protocol (PPTP) on low-bandwidth connections also can cause problems. If the *latency* (the delay between events) of the connection exceeds the timer's life in the TCP/IP transaction, then instead of sending data back and forth, the two host computers can get stuck in an endless loop of missed acknowledgments. If you want to use PPTP, you can't switch to using UDP; you must increase the bandwidth of your connection to shorten its latency.

Communicating with Software

Most of the information about the Internet protocols just covered will be useful to you when you first set up your network technology, as well as when you have to troubleshoot it. The rest of the time, those protocols do their work silently, and you can safely take them for granted.

There is one protocol, however, with which you will develop a much closer relationship: the HyperText Transport Protocol (HTTP). This is especially true for ASP developers, because Active Server Pages give you direct access to HTTP headers.

N O T E   Referring to the Web in terms of hypertext is anachronistic and betrays the early roots of the Web as a read-only medium. Because most Web content includes some form of graphic image and may utilize video as well, it would be more accurate to refer to Web content as *hypermedia.*

As you probably can see, the hypertext misnomer is related to another misnomer that you'll see in Internet literature: *Web browser.* A Web browser is a browser only if it merely displays information. When a Web client enables dynamic content and client-side interactivity, it is no longer a browser. ▓

Great Protocol   HTTP does three things uniquely well, the first two of which are discussed in this section (the third was earlier in this section.):

- ▓ It permits files to be linked semantically.
- ▓ It renders multimedia in a *thin client.*
- ▓ It works on all computers that support the TCP/IP suite.

Everything Connected...Take a Look!

Our favorite story about the Eastern mind brings light to the present discussion.

It seems there was a very left-brain financial analyst who decided to go to an acupuncturist for relief from a chronic headache that the analyst was feeling. After some time under the needle, the analyst looked at her therapist and said, "Why do you poke those needles everywhere except my head? It's my head that hurts, you know."

continues

continued

The gentle healer stopped his ministrations, looked into his patient's eyes, and simply said, "Human body all connected...take a look!"

The same connectedness applies to human knowledge as much as to human bodies. We have argued that knowledge lies not in facts, but in the relations *between* facts, in their links.

Remember the earlier comments about how fractal Internet hardware is? This concept holds true for the software, as well. Hyperlinks in HTML documents themselves contain information. For example, one of this book's authors has published extensive HTML pages on chaos theory in finance, based on the work of Edgar E. Peters. Peters's work has appeared in only two written forms: his original, yellow-pad manuscripts and the books he has written for John Wiley & Sons. The closest thing that Peters has to a hyperlink is a footnote, but even a footnote can go no further than informing you of the *identity* of related information; it cannot specify the *location* of that information, much less *display* it.

But hyperlinks can.

Semantic links are otherwise known as Universal Resource Locators (URLs). On the one hand, they are terms that you as an HTML author find important, so important that you let your reader digress into an in-depth discussion of the highlighted idea. On the other hand, an URL is a highly structured string of characters that can represent the exact location of related documents, images, or sounds on any computer anywhere in the world. (It blows the mind to think of what this means in the history of human development.)

One of the nicest features of the Web is that Web clients are so easygoing. That is, they work with equal facility among their own native HTTP files but can host many other protocols, as well; primarily, the file transfer protocol. To specify FTP file transfers, you begin the URL with **FTP://** instead of **HTTP://**.

N O T E   Most modern Web clients know that a majority of file requests will be for HTTP files. For that reason, you don't need to enter the protocol part of the URL when making a request of your Web client; the client software inserts it before sending the request to the Internet (and updates your user interface, too).

You already have seen how domain names are resolved into IP addresses, so you know that after the protocol definition in the URL, you can enter either the name or the IP address of the host computer that you are trying to reach.

The final piece of the URL is the object. At this point, you have two choices: Enter the name of the file or leave this part blank. Web servers are configured to accept a default file name of the Webmaster's choosing. On UNIX Web servers, this file name usually is **index.html**; on Windows NT Web servers, it usually is **default.htm**. Regardless of the name selected, the result always is the same: Everyone sees the Web site's so-called *home page*.

N O T E There is a special case regarding Active Server Pages about which you need to be aware. How can you have **default.htm** as the default name of the default page (for any given directory) and use .asp files instead?

The simplest solution is to use a **default.htm** file that automatically redirects the client to the .asp file. ▧

File Names Another decision that the Webmaster must make is how to structure the Web site. This choice often is constrained by the presence of Windows 3.1 clients. That is, this version of Windows can't read long file names (including files with four-letter extensions), unless they are accessed through HTTP.

N O T E As mentioned earlier, Web clients are smart enough to know that if you don't specify a protocol, they will insert the HTTP for you. The clue that the client gets from you is the forward slash/es (also called "whacks" because it's much easier to say "HTTP colon whack whack" than "HTTP colon forward slash, forward slash") in the file path.

You also can access files without invoking HTTP. If you enter backslashes in the path, the client assumes that you want to open a file locally and automatically inserts the **file://** prefix in the URL. If you call on a *local* (that is, on your hard drive or on a hard drive on the LAN) file with long file names or extensions, Windows 3.1 complains that the file name is invalid. Remember that you can work around this problem if you use the **HTTP://** syntax.

Be careful when you do this with an .asp file. The result will be exactly what you asked for: a display of the .asp source code. If you don't call on the Internet Information Server with the **HTTP://** prefix, the ISAPI filter never fires, and the .asp source code doesn't get interpreted. By the way, this unexpected result also occurs if you forget to set the execute permission on for the directory that contains your .asp file. ▧

This nuance of file systems notwithstanding, you have two basic choices when it comes to identifying files: Use a subdirectory to store related files or use long file names. We have never been fully satisfied with either option—each has compelling pros and repelling cons.

Long file names have the virtue of being easier (than a bunch of subdirectories) to upload from your development server to your production server. It's also a lot easier to get to a file when you want to edit it (you don't have to drill down into the directory structure). With the File Open dialog box visible, just start typing the file name until the file you want appears; hit the enter key, and you can open the file directly.

Using long file names has two drawbacks. In all cases, you give up the ability to have a default home page for each section of your Web site. There can be only one **index.html** or **default.htm** file (or whatever you decide to call the file) for each directory, and because there's only one directory using this strategy, you get only one home page. Another disadvantage becomes more serious as the number of files in your Web site increases. That is, you have to scroll down farther than you do when you group files into subdirectories.

Of course, there's nothing to keep you from using a hybrid strategy of both directories and long file names. This would be the logical alternative if your problem was a large site, meaning one whose size became inconvenient for you given the limitations noted.

Whatever strategy you choose, be consistent. If you decide to name your files with the HTML extension, do it for all your files. If one of your home pages is **index.html**, make all sub-directory home pages the same name.

> **CAUTION**
>
> Be really careful when you upload files with the same name in different directories; it's all too easy to send the home page for the first subdirectory up into the root directory of the production server.

As mentioned, the only policy that can be inconsistent is the one that uses both long file names and directories.

On the Client, Thin Is Beautiful   Remember the early days, the time when a Web client needed to be less than 1M? Now *that* was a thin client. Today, Netscape and Internet Explorer each require more than 10M, and there is absolutely no evidence that this trend will slow, much less reverse. Indeed, if Netscape is to be taken at its word, it intends to usurp the functionality of the operating system. Microsoft is no better; it wants to make the client invisible, part of the operating system itself. In either case, referring to a *thin client* is rapidly becoming yet another misnomer.

Still, there is one thing that remains steady: Using a Web client, you don't have to know anything about the underlying program that displays the contents of your Web site. All files are processed directly (or indirectly) through the client. The basic programming model of the Internet remains fairly intact—real processing still goes on at the server. This is especially true with database programming, and most especially true with Active Server Pages. As long as this Internet version of the client/server model remains, clients will remain, by definition, thin.

This is a good thing for you, because this book was written to help you do the best possible job of programming the server (and the client, where appropriate).

HTML   This book assumes that either you already know how to write HTML code or have other books and CDs to teach you. Because this chapter was designed to introduce you to the environmental issues of Web development, we close the chapter by emphasizing that the original goal of the Web has long been abandoned. The Web geniuses at the Fidelity group of mutual funds recently were quoted as observing that visitors to their site didn't want to read as much as they wanted to interact with the Web site. Have you noticed in your own explorations of the Web that you never seem to have the time to stop and read?

About a year ago, the raging controversy was this: Does good content keep them coming back, or is it the jazzy-looking graphics that make a Web site stand out amid the virtual noise? Even the graphics advocates quickly realized that in the then-present state of bandwidth scarcity, rich images were often counterproductive. In the worst case, people actually disabled the graphics in their clients.

So it does seem that people don't have the time to sit and read (unless they're like me and print off sites that they want to read later), and they don't even want to wait around for big graphics. If the people at Fidelity are right, users want to interact with their clients and servers. Presumably, they want a personalized experience, as well. That is, of all the stuff that's out there on the Web, users have a narrow interest, and they want their Internet technology to accommodate them and extend their reach in those interests.

When you're done with this book, it's our hope that you'll have begun to see how much of users' needs and preferences can be met with the intelligent deployment of Active Server Pages (and ActiveX controls). Never before has so much processing power been made available to so many people of so many different skill levels. Many of the limitations of VBScript can be overcome using custom server components that are operating on the server side. Access to databases will give people the capability to store their own information (such as the results of interacting with rich interactive Web sites), as well as to access other kinds of information.

And besides, the jury's still out on whether rich content is important or not. In spite of our impatience, there still are times when gathering facts is important. Indeed, we had pressing needs for information as we wrote parts of this book. It always took our breath away for a second or two when we went searching for something arcane and found it in milliseconds. This book is much better because we took the time to research and read. It's only a matter of time before others find similar experiences.

When that happens, we will have come full circle. The Web was created so that scientists could have easy access to one another's work (and, presumably, to read it), so that scientific progress could accelerate. For those knowledge workers, the issue was quality of life. Then the general public got the bug—but the perceived value of the Web was different for them than it had been for others. The Web's novelty wore off, and people started to realize that they could use this technology to give themselves something they'd never had before: nearly unlimited access to information. They also started publishing information of their own and building communities with others of like mind. The medium of exchange in this new community? Words, written or spoken.

From Here...

This chapter was the first of a series of chapters that set the stage for the core of this book: the development of Active Server Pages. In this chapter, we highlighted the most important parts of the environment that is called the Internet. You read about the basic infrastructure that enables bits to move around the planet at the speed of light. You looked under the hood of the Internet to see the protocols that define how these bits move about, and you saw the two primary kinds of software—the server and the client—that make the Web the vivid, exciting place that it is.

To find out about the other important environments that define your workspace as an Active Server Pages developer, see the following chapters:

■ Chapter 2, "Understanding Windows NT and Internet Information Server," moves you from the macro world of the Internet to the micro world of Windows NT and Internet Information Server.

■ Chapter 3, "Understanding Client/Server on the Internet," moves from the limited view of client/server programming as it is currently done on the Internet to a general view of client/server programming at the desktop. The hybrid of these two schools is the Active Server Pages methodology of client/server programming. It truly is the best of both worlds, enabling the advent of a whole new world of powerful programming technologies.

■ Chapter 4, "Introducing Active Server Pages," is the core chapter of this first section. It introduces you to the general features of ASP's revolutionary approach to Web development.

■ Chapter 5, "Understanding Objects and Components," shows you an extremely important dimension of Web development, using Active Server Pages. Most of the programming power out of the ASP box comes from base components that ship with Internet Information Server 3.0, but the true genius of ASP is that it permits unlimited extension of the server with custom components. With ASP, components don't require sophisticated programming skills, nor is an intimate understanding of a complicated and arcane application program interface (API) necessary. Minimal competence in Visual Basic is the only price of admission.

## CHAPTER 2

Understanding Windows NT and Internet Information Server

Assuming that, as a developer, you have a network administrator and NT specialist backing you up in the setup and configuration of all related software services, you can skip right over this whole chapter. If you want to have an understanding of all the pieces of the puzzle making this application work, however, spend a few minutes reviewing the components to facilitate application design and to speed troubleshooting problems. ■

The software required to start

Windows NT, Internet Information Server, and other software components play critical parts in bringing an Active Server application on-line.

Windows NT with TCP/IP

Active Server, as a part of Windows NT, relies on built-in services and applications for configuration and management; a good overview of the relevant components can speed the application development process.

Internet Information Server

Like Windows NT at large, the proper setup and configuration of an IIS system provides a starting point for developing and implementing an Active Server application.

Security setup

Active Server applications, like all Web-based applications, require understanding security issues. Windows NT and IIS security both play roles in the management of application security issues.

N O T E   While this book does not focus on hardware requirements, the hardware compatibility list
provided with NT 4.0 and the minimum requirements documented for the Internet
Information Server all apply to Active Server. The current Hardward Compatibility List or HCL, can be
found on your Windows NT Server CD but for the most current information visit Microsoft's Web site at
HTTP://www.microsoft.com/ntserver/. ■

Active Server Pages has become a bundled part of the Internet Information Server version 3.0
(IIS 3.0) and as a result is installed along with IIS 3.0 by default. However, while it is a noble
goal to have applications running perfectly right out-of-the-box, based on Plug and Play, the
Active Server Pages applications you develop rely on a series of technologies that must work
together to operate correctly. Because Active Server Pages relies on a series of different technologies, you need to take some time to understand the critical points at which these applications can break down. By understanding the possible points of failure, you will gain useful
insight, not only into troubleshooting the application, but also into how to best use these tools
in your application development efforts. This chapter explores the related technologies that
come together to enable the Active Server Pages you develop including:

- Windows NT 4.0 Server or Workstation
- The TCP/IP protocol
- A Web server that supports Active Server, such as IIS
- Optionally, ODBC and a database server such as Microsoft's SQL Server

This chapter provides an overview of all the tools necessary and available within Windows NT
4.0 to configure the security, database, networking, DCOM, and Web services potentially used
in your Active Server application.

Software Requirements

You only need to purchase one software product, Windows NT. Active Server applications
currently require Windows NT and a compatible Web server. Windows NT Workstation with
the Personal Web Server provided or Windows NT Server with the Internet Information
Server reflect the two alternative Web server and operating system platforms currently supported. The remainder of this book focuses on an implementation based on Windows NT
Server and Internet Information Server, though most of the topics covered apply equally, regardless of which implementation you choose.

CAUTION
If you run Windows NT Workstation with the Personal Web Server, the IIS configuration information will vary,
but the syntax and use of objects all apply.

Additional software referenced in examples throughout the book include databases and e-mail
servers. The databases referenced include Microsoft SQL Server and Microsoft Access and for
e-mail, Microsoft Exchange Server.

N O T E   All references to Windows NT or NT assume Windows NT Server 4.0. ■

Using Windows NT with TCP/IP

Although Windows NT, by default, installs almost all software necessary, certain components may not yet be installed depending upon the initial NT setup options selected by the user. The options required for use of Active Server include:

■ Internet Information Server

■ TCP/IP networking support

N O T E   Although networking protocols generally bind to a network adapter, TCP/IP can be loaded for testing on a stand-alone computer without a network adapter. ■

Testing TCP/IP Installation   To ensure proper installation of the TCP/IP protocol, from the Windows NT Server, or a computer with network access to the NT Server, perform either of the following tests:

■ Launch a Web browser and try to reference the computer with either the computer name, IP address assigned to the computer, or full DNS name assigned to the computer. If the computer returns a Web page of some kind, then the machine has TCP/IP installed.

■ Go to a command line on a Windows 95 or Windows NT machine and type **ping** *computer_name*, or alternatively exchange IP Address or DNS name for the computer name. If this returns a data with response time information rather than a time-out message, then TCP/IP has been properly installed.

N O T E   Ping refers to an Internet application standard like FTP or HTTP that, in the case of Ping, enables a computer to request another computer to reply with a simple string of information. Windows NT and Windows 95 come with a command line Ping utility, which is referenced in "Testing TCP/IP Installation." ■

N O T E   Depending on your network environment, you may not have a DNS name; or due to Firewall/Proxy Servers, you may not be able to use the IP Address; or you may not be able to directly reference the computer by NetBIOS computer name. If you think you are facing these problems, you should contact the network administrator responsible for your Firewall for instructions on how to reach your server computer. ■

Installing TCP/IP   This section provides only an overview of the TCP/IP installation instructions; for detailed instructions on installing TCP/IP, consult Windows NT Help files. If you want to attempt to add these services, log on as an administrator to the local machine, and from the Start Button, select Settings and then control panel to open the control panel (see Figure 2.1).

Part

I

Ch

2

For TCP/IP Services: Select the Network icon, and add the TCP/IP protocol; this step probably will prompt you to insert the Windows NT CD. In addition, this step requires additional information, including your DNS Server IP Address(es), your computer IP address, and your gateway IP Address (generally a Router device).

FIG. 2.1

Use the Windows NT Control Panel to install Network TCP/IP.

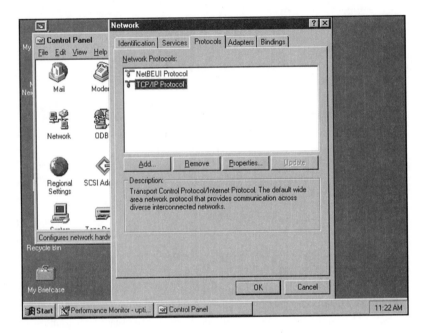

N O T E If you have a server on your network running the Dynamic Host Control Protocol (DHCP), you do not require a local IP and can allow the DHCP server to dynamically allocate it. ▪

Using Internet Information Server with Active Server Pages

Internet Information Server 3.0 should have properly installed both your Active Server Pages components and your Web server. In addition, it should have turned your Web server on and set it to automatically launch when Windows NT Server starts. The remainder of this chapter provides instructions for confirming that your Web server is operating properly.

Testing IIS Installation To ensure proper installation of the Internet Information Server (IIS), from the Windows NT Server, or a Windows NT Server with IIS installed:

▪ From the local machine's Start button, look under program groups for an Internet Information Server group. Launch the Internet Information Manager to confirm the server installation and check to ensure that it is running (see Figure 2.2).

FIG. 2.2

The Start Menu illustrates the program groups installed on the Windows NT Server, including the Internet Information Server program items.

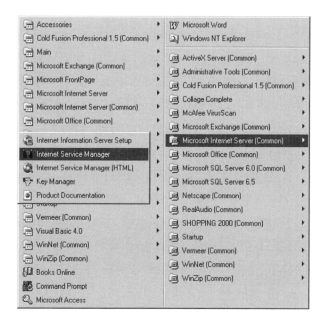

Part

I

Ch

2

■ From a remote Windows NT Server, launch the IIS Manager, and attempt to connect to the server by selecting the File, Connect to Server option and specifying the NetBIOS computer name (see Figure 2.3).

FIG. 2.3

Use the IIS Manager Connect To Server dialog box to browse, or type in the Web server to which you want to connect.

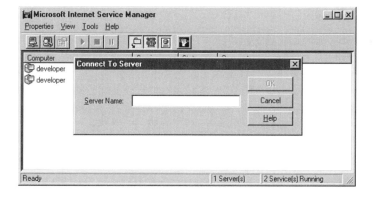

Installing IIS

> **CAUTION**
>
> This section provides only an overview; for detailed instructions on installing TCP/IP and IIS, consult the Windows NT Help files.

To add the missing services, log on as an administrator to the local machine and open the control panel.

For IIS Installation: Run the Windows NT add software icon from the control panel and add the Internet Information Server option (see Figure 2.4). This step will probably require the Windows NT CD and will launch a setup program to guide you through the installation.

FIG. 2.4
Use the Add Software icon in the Control Panel to add and remove registered programs.

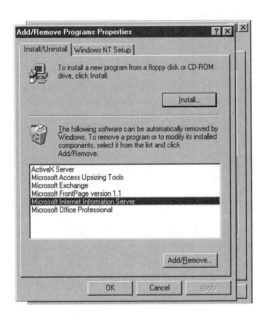

Database Services

For the examples in this book and for many applications, accessing a database becomes a driving component to a Web-based application. While the majority of Active Server syntax and objects have nothing to do with databases and simply can't use them, the ActiveX Data Object (ADO), which is discussed in Chapter 15, "Introducing ActiveX Data Objects," requires ODBC-compliant databases. The ADO Component, if used, requires an additional software component, the 32-bit ODBC Driver. While not natively installed with Windows NT, this software can be freely downloaded from **http://www.microsoft.com/** and probably already resides on your server computer. Because ODBC drivers are installed by default with most database programs, chances are that if you have Microsoft Access, Microsoft SQL Server, or some other ODBC-compliant database installed, you already have ODBC drivers installed.

> **CAUTION**
> Active Server's Connection Component requires the 32-bit version of ODBC.

To test if ODBC drivers are currently installed, open the control panel on the local machine, and look for the ODBC 32 icon as illustrated in Figure 2.5.

FIG. 2.5

Use the Control Panel to invoke the ODBC 32 icon if it is installed.

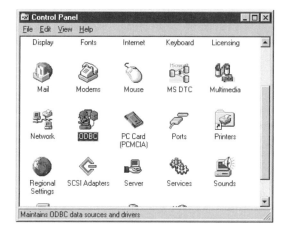

Understanding Windows NT

After working with Windows NT since the Beta release of 3.1 in August of 1993, we have developed an appreciation for the elegance, stability, security, and, unfortunately, the complexity of this powerful server product. Although administration has become greatly simplified by the developing GUI tools in version 4.0, understanding how Active Server relies on the built-in NT infrastructure and understanding some basic tools for controlling these built-in features greatly simplifies bringing your Active Server application on-line. The primary NT features that impact Active Server include:

- NT services model or the way NT manages background applications
- NT registry settings and editor, which control the configuration settings for the operating system and installed programs
- NT file and directory security model, which manages access permissions to the hard drive
- NT user and group manager, which controls the permissions and profile information about users' and groups' setup for the NT Server or Domain

Secure NT File System (NTFS)

Windows NT has four file systems (HPFS, NTFS, FAT, CDFS) that it supports, but only one, NTFS, supports the file and directory security that has enabled NT to boast C2 security clearance for the Federal Government applications. In practice, the CD file system and the High Performance file system can be ignored. You need to know if the hard drive upon which your application will reside runs FAT or NTFS. If your hard drive runs the standard file allocation table (FAT) used in most DOS-based systems, for all intents and purposes you have lost the ability to invoke security based on the file and directory-level permissions. If, on the other hand, your system runs NTFS—which this book recommends—you will have access to managing file and directory-level permissions.

TIP Among other tests, you can test the file system simply by opening Windows Explorer on the local machine and looking at the file system designation next to the drive letter, e.g., NTFS, FAT. You also can check the Admin Tools, Disk Manager to find the file system designation.

By running NTFS, the NT operating system can set properties on each file and directory on your hard drive. In operation, the Web server evaluates the permissions on every file requested by a Web browser, and if the permissions required exceed those allocated to the default user specified in the Web server, the Web server will force the browser to prompt the user for a username and password to authenticate. This authentication provides the primary means by which the IIS manages what files and directories can be used by users requesting files from the Web server. The permission options are detailed in Figure 2.6 and can be configured from the Windows Explorer on the local machine by selecting Properties and then the Security tab as illustrated in Figure 2.7.

FIG. 2.6
Use the Permissions window to set file and directory permissions for users and groups on the NT Server or Domain.

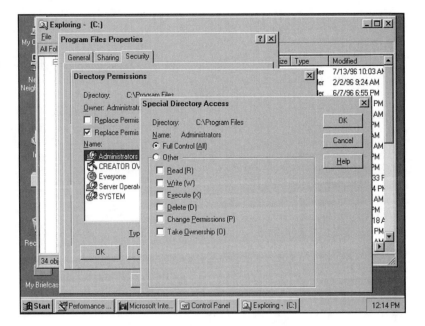

What Is a User?

A user is an individual or program whose transactions have received a Security Token containing the transaction's permissions, based on a user account's permissions. In more detail, an individual accessing an NT Server either goes through a logon process or uses the permissions of an already running program, which has logged on on behalf of the individual. During the logon, the NT Server has authenticated the individual or program, based on a user account to issue the transactions conducted by that individual or program a Security Token containing the transaction's permission level.

FIG. 2.7
Use the permissions
configuration to assign
users and groups with
the appropriate level of
permissions.

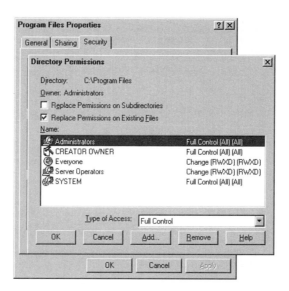

The NT standard file and directory permissions, and the methods for configuring them, drive the Active Server security model.

Using the User Manager

NT Server manages security permissions relating to file, directory, and access to programs through assigning permissions to users and groups. Even if you chose not to use the features of NTFS for securing files and directories, IIS still relies on the security tokens assigned by the operating system to users and groups as they access the NT Server for managing the security permissions of the Web server.

N O T E   When a Web browser accesses the NT Server, the Web browser does not always invoke the NT Server security. In the case of a standard, non-authenticated Web browser request, the Web server uses the security permissions of the user account set up as the anonymous user in the IIS configuration. ▨

The User Manager, as illustrated in Figure 2.8, operates both for a domain-level security list and for local machine security lists. If your server operates as part of a domain, the user accounts will be managed by the computer empowered as the domain server or Primary Domain Controller (PDC). Alternatively, your computer may operate independently, similar to peer-to-peer networks, where your computer maintains its own user and group accounts. Either way, these accounts drive the permissions checked as the IIS attempts to comply with requests from Web browsers.

FIG. 2.8
Use the User Manager to assign permissions to user and group accounts.

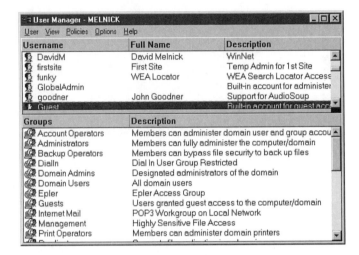

NOTE This summary look at security should be complemented by a review of the NT help files if you are responsible for managing user and group accounts. ■

Windows NT Services

Similarly to how UNIX runs daemons or how Windows or Mac machines run multiple applications, Windows NT runs *services*. Services reflect the running programs that the NT Server has available. An example of services includes the "Simple TCP/IP Service," which enables your computer to support communication over a network. For Active Server, you should expect to see at least the following services running:

■ Server
■ Simple TCP/IP Services
■ World Wide Web Services

To view the running services, select the Start button, followed by Settings and then Control Panel. When the Control Panel window appears, select the Services icon to view the active services, as illustrated in Figure 2.9. Other services of importance to your development that may be running include Microsoft SQL Server and the series of services associated with Exchange Server.

The importance of this area primarily results from a need to do some quick troubleshooting if something goes wrong or if you need to restart your Web server. This utility provides an authoritative method for ensuring that your programs are running.

TIP When the IIS Manager launches and shows a running or stopped status, it is the same thing as viewing the service in the control panel services. And restarting has the same effect regardless of whether you are in the control panel services or the IIS Manager.

FIG. 2.9

Use the control panel Services utility to start and stop services, as well as to set their behavior when Windows NT Server starts up.

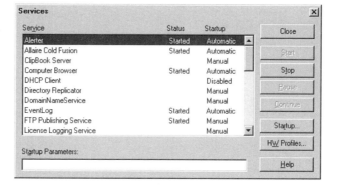

DCOM Registration and the Registry

Registration plays an important role in the NT world. Your overview understanding of NT's registry model will support your development efforts when utilizing Distributed Components (DCOM) and the Active Server model in general. COM and DCOM objects are discussed in detail in Chapter 5, "Understanding Objects and Components."

The NT registry provides NT with a hierarchical database of values that NT uses during the loading of various operating system components and programs. This environment replaces load variables that windows included in files such as the win.ini, sys.ini, autoexec.bat, and config.sys. The RegEdit program provides a graphical user interface for managing registry settings as illustrated in Figure 2.10

FIG. 2.10

Use the Registry Editor Program to review and, when necessary, to edit operating system and program configuration information.

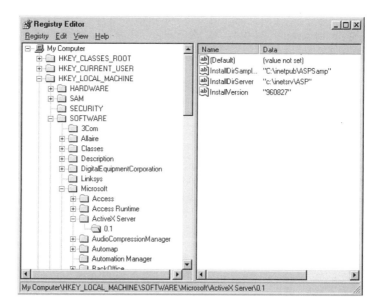

CAUTION

While viewing the registry is safe, changing registry settings incorrectly can cause your NT system to fail. Be cautious when attempting direct changes, and whenever possible, avoid directly tampering with the Registry.

The Registry stores settings related to, among other things, your IIS setup. The ISAPI filters and components all have their settings maintained in the Registry. Your primary use of the regedit.exe program is a read-only one. By default, NT does not even include the regedit.exe program as an icon in the program groups, precisely because they are difficult to understand settings maintained in the Registry by the operating system and installed software programs. Users attempting to manage these settings run the risk of damaging their NT installation.

All ISAPI and DCOM components that take the form of .dll files will be installed and registered as part of setup programs and will not require direct use of the registry. If a new DCOM object is made available and requires registration, a separate command line utility can be used to register it. To invoke a command, select the Start button and then Run. When prompted by a dialog box, type **command** and then press OK. The command prompt will start, which by default will look very similar to the DOS environment with the c:> prompt. With this command line utility, type the following line in at the c:> prompt:

```
Regsvr [/u][/s] dllname
```

where the u is for un-register and the s is for silent or with no display messages.

In addition to the standard Registry, NT provides a utility for managing the extended features of DCOM. This utility is not set up in the NT Admin tools group and may require review if you incur security problems invoking your components. For the review of this utility, run the DCOMCnfg.exe in the NT System32 directory. The configuration window illustrated in Figure 2.11 starts.

 The primary DCOM problem users run into results from a lack of access being assigned to the default user account defined in the IIS configuration. If you have these problems, check to ensure that the default user account in your IIS has permissions in the DCOM configuration utility shown in Figure 2.11

COM represents the evolution of what previously was OLE Automation Servers, and DCOM represents enhanced COM features. DCOM and COM vary only slightly for the purposes of this book. The COM standard provides the framework for building DLLs that will be used as components by the Active Server. DCOM provides a richer threading model and enhanced security for distributed processing, but because all calls are generated by IIS invoking DLLs existing on the local machine, understanding the subtleties of this model is not important for the purposes of this book.

N O T E For a more detailed treatment of COM and the enhancements provided by DCOM, try **http://www.microsoft.com/**. ▪

FIG. 2.11
Use the DCOM
Configuration
Properties areas to
assign security
permissions for
executing DCOM
objects.

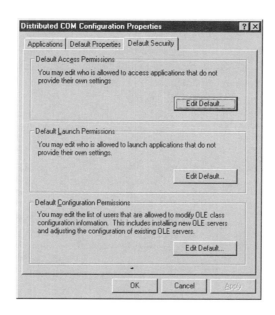

Part

Ch

2

Using the Internet Information Server

The Internet Information Server acts as the gateway for all incoming client requests. For requests of files ranging from HTML to graphics to video, the process follows conventional Web server methods, such as sending a requested file to the browser. Unlike conventional Web server methods, when an .asp file request comes to the Web server from the browser, it invokes the ISAPI filter or DLL component, which parses the requested .asp file for Active Server related code. As a result, the requester must have the authority to execute the ASP page and to conduct any of the actions that the code attempts to perform at the server. The Web server then returns what, you hope, resembles a standard HTML or other type of file.

For this process to perform successfully, you must have:

- Properly configured IIS-served directories
- NT user accounts
- DLL components
- NT security

The importance of understanding this process increases as your application performs more and more complex activities on the server. For example, to execute a script that counts to ten, you need to ensure execute permission only in the directory served for the default user. To write a file to the server hard drive, however, you need to have provided a default or other user with sufficient permissions to write a file to a location on your hard drive. Further still, to enable a user to request a page that accesses a SQL Server database, the user must have further permissions still in order to gain access to the SQL Server.

Web Server Directories

The IIS provides access or serves information from directories on your server's hard drives. All requests to the Web server attempt to get authentication for access to the information initially based on the user account setup in the IIS configuration. As illustrated in Figure 2.12, the default or anonymous logon in the IIS manager matches the user account setup with full control in the directory permissions window for the served directory. This ensures that the NT file system authorizes the user, not only to read, but also to execute files in the directory.

FIG. 2.12

Use the IIS Default User configuration to set the user account that the Web server will invoke for security access.

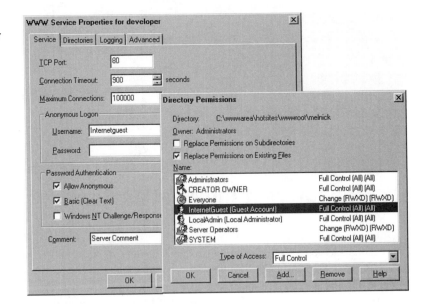

> **CAUTION**
>
> The file system permissions are invoked only for files running on NTFS drives as discussed in the previous section, "Secure NT File System (NTFS)."

In addition to the file system permissions, one prior level of basic security is invoked by the IIS before even attempting to request the file from the operating system. A basic read or execute permission is established on every directory served by the IIS. This level of permission is configured at the IIS level and can be configured through the IIS Manager, as illustrated in Figure 2.13.

FIG. 2.13

Use the Directory Properties dialog box to set Read/Execute permissions levels separate from the standard NT file system security.

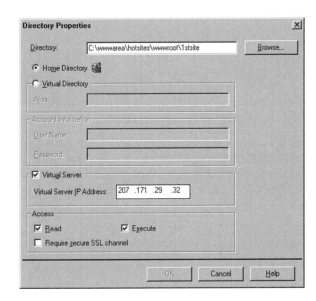

Managing User Accounts

User accounts provide the primary vehicle for managing security within an IIS application of any kind. Because the IIS completely integrates with the NT security model, understanding user and group permissions becomes critical to any application that utilizes more than just the anonymous logon. The key areas of concern relating to security include:

- Sufficient user authority for a task
- Proper security within the anonymous logon
- Enhanced security through NTFS file permissions

Establishing Enough Authority to Get Started   As illustrated in "Web Server Directories," the IIS configures a default account for accessing all pages requested. Many initial problems can result if you create .asp files that the default user can read but then secure components that the default user cannot invoke, thus forcing your code to generate an error. The default account must have execute permissions for any Active component that your pages will utilize, including the registered directory where the basic Active Server Pages file resides. Focus on securing your .asp files and directories, not your components. Additional areas of caution for security include accessing databases and trying to write files to a server hard drive.

The execute permissions for the Active Server default components should already be configured for the anonymous logon account, but if you have unexplained security problems, you may want to start in the IIS configuration area for debugging.

Managing Anonymous Logon   A comprehensive security implementation can be created without ever going to the User Manager. Before diving into the complex and powerful world of NT user and group accounts, make sure you have exhausted the simple and flexible alternatives. One method involves tracking users in a database and authenticating by lookup. This approach enables you to more easily manage users through database or file lookups. If this model does not provide sufficient control or security, however, many enhanced security options can be invoked to control access and use of your application.

Enhanced Security Options   For more sophisticated security, you can set up directories and .asp files where the logon permissions provided by the Web server's default user account are insufficient. When insufficient file system security is detected by the Web server, the browser will be prompted for a logon, which the Web server attempts to authenticate. Once authenticated, this user ID is passed with subsequent requests from the browser allowing the Web server to utilize the authority of the logged-in user.

> **CAUTION**
>
> Ensure that these new users have the execute permissions available to the anonymous account. The system setup process automatically provides permissions to the anonymous user account for execute permissions in directories in which key DLLs reside, but all users might not have these permissions by default.

Users and groups allow you to differentiate permissions at the .asp file level, providing file level control over what permissions a user has on the system. This mechanism enables you to take advantage of the comprehensive auditing and tracking features available in NT.

From Here...

From our brief overview of the setup, configuration, and maintenance of the Windows NT and IIS environment, we now turn to the specifics of building an Active Server application. Although many of the chapters rely on the proper configuration of your network and server, our focus will be on the application development model enabled by Active Server, not on network and operating system issues. If you are responsible for setting up the NT server and found this section to be inadequate, STOP and consult more authoritative support documents or our Web site for more details. At this point, if you have a properly set up NT server, you should turn to the design and development of the application itself.

For additional discussions of some of the topics covered in this chapter try:

- Chapter 5, "Understanding Objects and Components," provides a more detailed discussion of components and the Active Server object model.
- Chapter 13, "Interactivity Through Bundled Active Server Components," provides a more detailed discussion of components bundled with Active Server Pages.

- Chapter 15, "Introducing ActiveX Data Objects," provides a more detailed discussion of database programming and use of ODBC.
- Appendixes A-E provide a case study of an actual Active Server Pages site with comprehensive discussion on setup, monitoring, and performance issues associated with Web servers and Active Server Pages.

Part

I

Ch

2

Understanding Client/ Server on the Internet

Adecade ago, everyone was excited about a new technology architecture that was going to revolutionize the way business is conducted in corporate America. It would provide a new paradigm for information processing that would facilitate collaboration and information sharing across a vast number of systems and organizations. What was this new technology? Client/server computing.

Now the chorus sings again about the latest revolutionary technology, the World Wide Web. You learned in 8th grade Social Studies that history is bound to repeat itself, and those who do not learn from the mistakes of the past are doomed to repeat them. With this in mind, we are now poised on the edge of the next technological precipice. There have been numerous systems development failures using client/server architecture, but there also have been many successes. By understanding the strengths of the client/server architecure, you will be able to implement them in your Active Server Pages development.

There are two major keys to the successful implementation of any new technology—a solid understanding of the foundations of the technology and a framework for its implementation in your business. Throughout this book, you will learn about the tools and techniques to meet this new challenge (opportunity) head-on and how to leverage this experience in your own development. ■

Understanding client/server architecture

This provides a brief overview of the architecture and how it has evolved over the years.

Examining client/server on the Web

The client/server revolution of the early eighties was a boon to developers for a number of reasons. Looking at its implementation in the past enables you to leverage the inherent strengths of client/server in your ASP development.

Understanding static versus dynamic content creation

Scripting enables for a simple yet powerful method of adding dynamic content to your Web site.

Leveraging scripting in a distributed environment

The choices you make as you decide where to place functionality, on the client and on the server, will expand your application options.

Understanding the Client/Server Architecture

Do you remember the first time that you ever used a PC database? For many of you, it was dBase. dBase and those programs like it (Paradox, FoxPro, and Access) provide a quick and easy way to create two-tier client/server applications. In the traditional two-tier client/server environment, much of the processing is performed on the client workstation, using the memory space and processing power of the client to provide much of the functionality of the system. Field edits, local lookups, and access to peripheral devices (scanners, printer, and so on) are provided and managed by the client system.

In this two-tier architecture, the client has to be aware of where the data resides and what the physical data looks like. The data may reside on one or more database servers, on a mid-range machine, or on a mainframe. The formatting and displaying of the information is provided by the client application as well. The server(s) would routinely only provide access to the data. The ease and flexibility of these two-tier products to create new applications continue to be driving many smaller-scale business applications.

The three-tier, later to be called multi-tier, architecture grew out of this early experience with "distributed" applications. As the two-tier applications percolated from individual and departmental units to the enterprise, it was found that they do not scale very easily. And in our ever-changing business environment, scaleability and maintainability of a system are primary concerns. Another factor that contributes to the move from two-to multi-tier systems is the wide variety of clients within a larger organization. Most of us do not have the luxury of having all of our workstations running the same version of an operating system, much less the same OS. This drives a logical division of the application components, the database components, and the business rules that govern the processes the application supports.

In a multi-tier architecture, as shown in Figure 3.1, each of the major pieces of functionality is isolated. The presentation layer is independent of the business logic, which in turn, is separated from the data access layer. This model requires much more analysis and design on the front-end, but the dividends in reduced maintenance and greater flexibility pay off time and again.

Imagine a small company a few years back. They might produce a product or sell a service, or both. They are a company with a few hundred employees in one building. They need a new application to tie their accounting and manufacturing data together. It is created by a young go-getter from accounting (yes, accounting). He creates an elegant system in Microsoft Access 1.0 that supports 20 accounting users easily (they all have identical hardware and software). Now, move forward a few years: The company continues to grow, and they purchase a competitor in another part of the country. They have effectively doubled their size, and the need for information-sharing is greater than ever. The Access application is given to the new acquisitions accounting department, but alas, they all work on Macintosh computers. Now, the CIO is faced with a number of challenges and opportunities at this juncture. She could purchase new hardware and software for all computer users in her organization (yikes!), or she could invest in creating a new application that will serve both user groups. She decides on the latter.

FIG. 3.1
Multi-tier architecture
supports enterprise-
wide applications.

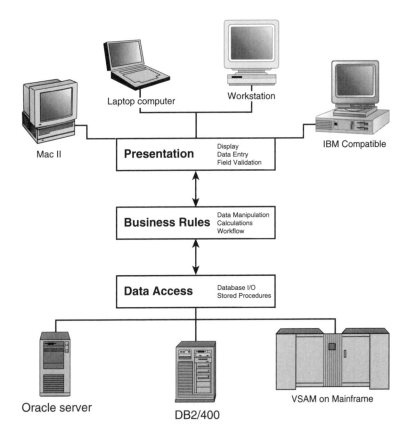

A number of questions come to mind as she decides which path to take:

- What model will allow her company to provide the information infrastructure that is needed to successfully run the business?

- How can she ensure that the application won't need to be rewritten after the next acquisition?

- How can she provide external clients access to parts of the system?

A few years ago, you might have suggested using a client/server cross-platform development toolkit or a 4GL/database combination, which supports multiple operating systems. Today, the answer will most likely be an intranet application. A multi-tier intranet solution provides all of the benefits of a cross-platform toolkit without precluding a 4GL/Database solution. If created in a thoughtful and analysis-driven atmosphere, the multi-tier intranet option provides the optimal solution. Designed correctly, the intranet application will provide them with the flexibility of the client/server model without the rigid conformance to one vendor's toolset or supported platform.

In her new model, the client application will be the browser that will support data entry, local field edits, and graphical display of the data. The entry to the database information will be the intranet Web server. The Web server will interact with a number of back-end data sources and business logic models through the use of prebuilt data access object. These objects will be created and managed through server-side scripting on the Web server. This scenario that has just been discussed can be implemented today with Active Server Pages, using the information, tools, and techniques outlined within this book.

Client and Server Roles on the Inter/Intranet

The same way that businesses have been effectively using multi-tier architectures on their LANS and WANS can now be taken advantage of on the Internet and intranet. The role of the client (aka browser) and the server, when designed correctly, can provide the best of the traditional client/server architecture with the control and management found in more centralized systems.

Developing a multi-tier client/server system involves three basic steps:

1. Selecting the Network Component
2. Designing the Application Architecture
3. Creating the User Interface

Take a look at each of these steps, and by the end of the following discussion, you will understand how to effectively use the C/S model in your Inter/intranet development.

The most important step, of course, is the first. Before undertaking any new development effort, you need to have a thorough understanding of the information your users require. From this, you can develop a firm, well-documented feature set. From these pieces of information, you can continue on and complete the functional specification for the new application.

> **CAUTION**
>
> It is always so tempting, with the advent of RAD (Rapid Application Development) tools, to write code first and to ask questions later. While this is a method that can be successful in small applications, it can lead to major problems when used in a more substantial systems development effort. Just remember, your users can have a system chosen from two of the following three attributes: fast, good, and cheap. The fast/cheap combination, however, has never been a good career choice.

You now have the idea, the specifications, and the will to continue. Now you can use the C/S model to complete your detail design and start development. But first, take a brief look at each of the steps (bet you're glad this isn't a 12-step process) and how the client and server component roles are defined.

The Network Component

In traditional C/S development, the choice of the communication protocol is the basis for the system. Choosing from the vast number of protocols and selecting appropriate standards is the first step. Specifying connectivity options and internal component specs (routers, bridges, and so on) is again a vital decision when creating a system.

In the Internet world, these choices are academic. You will utilize the existing TCP/IP network layer and the HTTP protocol for network transport and communication.

Designing the Application Architecture

Now you get to the heart of your application design decisions. Sadly, there are no quick and easy answers when you begin to choose the data stores that your application will interact with. What is important to remember is that the choices that you make now will affect the system over its entire useful life. Making the correct choices concerning databases, access methods, and languages will guarantee the success or failure of your final product.

A very helpful way to think about your application is to break it down into functions that you wish to perform. Most client/server applications are built around a transaction processing model. This allows you to break the functions into discrete transactions and handle them from beginning to end. In the Internet world, it is very helpful to think of Web pages as being a single transaction set. The unit of work that will be done by any one page, either a request for information or the authentication of actions on data sent, can be considered a separate transaction. Using this model, it is easy to map these document-based transactions against your data stores. The Active Server Pages environment, through server-side scripting and data access objects, enables you to leverage this model and to create multi-tier client/server Internet applications.

If your application will be using legacy data from a database back-end or host-based computer, you need to have a facility for accessing that data. The ASP environment provides a set of component objects that enable connectivity to a number of DBMS systems. Through the use of scripting on the server, you can also create instances of other OLE objects that can interact with mid-range or mainframe systems to add, retrieve, and update information.

Front-End Design

As you have already learned, one of the great benefits of the C/S architecture is its fundamental guidelines to provide a multi-platform client application. Never before has this been easier to achieve. With the advent of the WWW and the Internet browser, you can provide active content to users from a variety of platforms. While there has been a great movement toward standardization of HTML, there are many vendor-specific features found in browsers today. This means you have a couple of important choices to make, similar to the choices that you had to make when creating traditional multi-platform client applications. When developing with traditional cross-platform toolkits, you have a number of options.

Code to the lowest common denominator.   This involves selecting and implementing the features available on all of the client systems you wish to support. This is a good way to support everyone, but you'll have to leave out those features within each system that make them unique. For example, you might want to implement a container control for your OS/2 application, but there is no similar control available on the Mac. As a consequence, this falls out of the common denominator controls list.

Create a separate application for each client.   This option ensures that each client application takes full use of the features of the particular operating system. The big drawback of course is that you have multiple sets of client code to support. This might be achievable for the first version, but having to manage and carry through system changes to each code base can be a huge effort.

The majority of the client code is shared.   This last option is a good choice in most scenarios. The majority of the code is shared between applications. You can then use conditional compilation statements to include code which is specific for any one client system. This is even easier when using a browser as the client. Within an HTML document, if a browser does not support a particular tag block, it will ignore it.

What Is Client/Server Anyway?

As stated laboriously in the preceding sections, the client/server has been a buzzword for years now. Many definitions of this architecture exist, ranging from an Access application with a shared database to an all-encompassing transaction processing system across multiple platforms and databases. Throughout all of the permutations and combinations, some major themes remain consistent:

- **Requestor/Provider Relationship**

  The client and the server have well-defined roles, the client requesting a service and the server fulfilling the service request.

- **Message-Based**

  The communication between the client and server (or the client-middleware-server) is a well-defined set of rules (messages) that govern all communications—a set of transactions that the client sends to be processed.

- **Platform Independence**

  Due to the clearly defined roles and message-based communication, the server or service provider is responsible for fulfilling the request and returning the requested information (or completion code) to the client. The incoming transaction can be from a windows client, an OS/2 machine, or a Web browser.

- **Dynamic Routing**

  The client can send a transaction to a service provider and have the request fulfilled without having to be aware of the server that ultimately fulfills the request. The data or transaction might be satisfied by a database server, a mid-range data update, or a mainframe transaction.

Keeping Your Users Awake: The Challenge of Providing Dynamic Web Content

We remember when we first started surfing the Web. One of our first finds was a wonderful and informative site offering the latest and greatest in sporting equipment. They had a very well organized page with interesting sports trivia, updated scores during major sporting events, and a very broad selection of equipment and services. Over the next few months, We visited the site from time to time to see what was new and interesting in the world of sporting goods. What struck us was that the content did not seem to change over time. The advertisements were the same, the information provided about the products was the same, and much of the time, the 'updated' information was stale. Last summer, while looking for new wheels for roller blades, it was a surprise to find that the Christmas special was still running.

We surf the Web for a number of reasons: to find information, to view and purchase products, and to be kept informed. There is nothing worse than going to a fondly remembered site and being confronted with stale advertising or outdated information. The key to having a successful site is to provide up-to-date dynamic content.

Most of the information provided by current sites on the Internet consists of links between static informational pages. A cool animated GIF adds to the aesthetic appeal of a page, but the informational content and the way it is presented is the measure by which the site is ultimately judged.

To provide the most useful and entertaining content, you must be able to provide almost personal interaction with your users. You need to provide pre- and post-processing of information requests, as well as the ability to manage their interactions across your links. You must provide current (real-time) content and be able to exploit those capabilities that the user's browser exposes. One of the many components that is available in the Active Server Pages environment is an object through which you can determine the capabilities of the user's browser. This is just one of the many features you will be able to use to provide a unique and enjoyable experience for your users.

▶ **See** "Using the Browser Capabilities Component" for more information about the Browser Capability object, **p. 249**

A great, yet basic and simple example of something that really shows you how a page is changing with each hit is the hit counter. This capability, while easy to implement, will in itself show the user that the page is constantly changing. It is also very easy to have the date and time show up as a minor part of your pages. All of these little things (in addition, of course, to providing current information) help your Web site seem new and up-to-date each time it is visited.

As you head into the next several chapters, you will be given the tools and techniques to provide dynamic content in your Internet and intranet applications.

Part

I

Ch

3

The Keys to the Kingdom: Scripting

There are a variety of tools available today that enable you to create Internet applications. The best of the new breed of tools, called scripting languages, enable you to add value to your Web pages by providing client-based functionality. You can perform field edits and calculations, write to the client window, and employ a host of other functions without having to take another trip to the server for additional information.

What is so exiting about the newest scripting technology is that it is implemented, not only on the client, but now also on the server. With Active Server Pages, you can leverage your knowledge of scripting on the server. In addition to the basic control and flow that many scripting languages provide, you also can access objects from within your scripts that provide additional functionality and power. These objects, discussed in Part III, provide you with the capability to communicate with those multiple tiers of information in the client/server model.

Take a quick process check: You know about the C/S multi-tier architecture and how to effectively use it on the Internet and intranet. You have a good understanding of the type of content that you must provide, and you have learned about the scripting, which can tie all of the pieces together and make them work. The next step is to decide what functionality should go where.

Obviously, a great chunk of the processing ultimately resides on the server. All database access and access to other internal data sources will be provided from the server. The inter-page linking and responding to user requests will also be on the server. The decision as to what functionality to place in the browser client is the same as you discovered when reading about the challenge of supporting multiple operating systems in the traditional client/server environment:

■ **The lowest common denominator approach:**

This will provide the greatest guarantee that your active content can be viewed in its entirety on any browser.

■ **OS specific- (browser specific-) based functionality:**

By determining the capabilities of the browser as the information is requested, you can tailor the returned document to exploit the browsers capabilities.

■ **A combination of the two:**

Most sites that you visit today have a link to a text-only version of the document. This capability is important, not only to ensure that all users can get the information, but also to enable those users with less capable equipment to have a full and rich experience from your active content.

The scripting language you use on the client depends wholly on the capabilities of the browsers that request your pages. Java Script is supported in the Netscape Navigator family of browsers. VBScript and Java Script are supported in the Microsoft Internet Explorer browser. Given the remarkable changes to the browser software over the past year, you can expect that the two major scripting dialects will be supported across all major browsers in the near future.

VBScript and Java Script

When used within the confines of Internet Explorer, VBScript and Java Script are functionally equivalent. They both provide a rich, basic-like scripting language that is interpreted by the browser at run-time to provide client-side intelligence and an enhanced user experience. VBScript is a subset of the popular Visual Basic language. For the legions of Visual Basic developers, VBScript is a natural progression and tool for creating interactive Web pages. With the release of Active Server Pages, scripting has been taken to another level. Now you can use the same versatile scripting to add value to the server-side of the process as well as to the client side.

From Here...

Figuring out how to best employ scripting in an Internet environment can be a daunting task. You have learned how you can benefit from the experience of thousands of developers who have used the multi-tier architecture for creating enterprise-wide applications. You can create Internet applications with the same transaction-based, flexible, and client-neutral functionality that has been driving businesses for the past decade.

Here are some of the topics that are discussed in the coming chapters:

- Chapter 4, "Introducing Active Server Pages," provides more details about the ASP environment, the Active Server object model and how the framework provides an excellent tool for creating multi-tier Inter/intranet applications.
- Chapter 5, "Understanding Objects and Components," gives you an overview of how objects and components interact within the Active Server Pages environment.

Introducing Active Server Pages

Up to now, this book has covered information leading to the door of the book's heart. Behind that door lies the information you need to create your first Active Server Page and your first Active Server Pages application. You've been introduced to the essence of Internet/intranet design. You've also seen the role that Windows NT plays in this new design environment and the particular advantages that the design of the Windows NT operating system brings to the Web development table. In Chapter 3, "Understanding Client/Server on the Internet," we began our discussion of the basics of information architectures and gave you a feel for the historic roots of ASP development.

This chapter will introduce the players in the new game, the Active Server Pages development game. This chapter also serves as a wrap-up of the material covered thus far. The aim here is coherence—giving you a firm, conceptual foundation from which to build a solid understanding of the underlying technology of Active Server Pages. ■

Learn what an Active Platform is

You will see the abstract features of Microsoft's Active Platform, and you will learn about the Active Desktop and the Active Server, two symmetric programming models that will revolutionize the development of client/server programming for the Internet and for intranets of all sizes.

Get acquainted with the plumbing of Active Server Pages

Learn the implementation details of Active Server Pages and what it takes to make them work.

The inside of Active Server Pages

You've seen how ASP's abstract parts relate and what its infrastructure looks like; now see what the inside of an .asp file looks like.

Introducing the Active Platform

In November 1996, Microsoft formally introduced the Active Platform at the Site Builders Conference and the Professional Developers Conference. At those events, the audience saw a graphic, similar to the one in Figure 4.1, that outlined the major parts of Microsoft's vision of the future of Internet development. The two pillars of client-side and server-side scripting share a common tool set and are both based on consistent standards and protocols. It is a complete model and is presented in detail in the rest of this chapter.

FIG. 4.1
The Active Platform incorporates similar functions for the client and the server, exploiting their individual strengths.

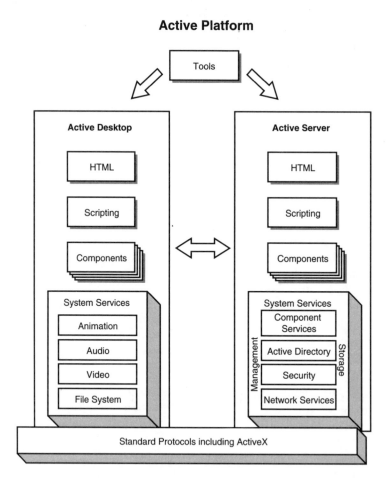

The Vision

The Active Platform is Microsoft's vision of the next generation of distributed computing. It exploits the best of the centralized programming models, as well as the best of decentralized programming. The Microsoft vision has profound implications for the Internet (not merely for industrial-strength client/server programming) and for the way that systems are developed and deployed. Microsoft's model creates applications that are *logically centralized* and *physically decentralized*. A *logically centralized* system can be administered from anywhere. Such a system is conceptually simple, and when properly tooled, is easy to manage. *Physically decentralized* systems can be more efficient, fault tolerant, powerful, and scaleable.

Two Profound Paradigm Shifts

There are two more key features to Microsoft's vision, and we return to them often in the pages to come. First, until the advent of the Active Server, programmers spent too much time worrying about infrastructure (e.g., programming Database Management System (DBMS) connections) and not enough time in their core competence (i.e., doing something useful with the recordsets fetched from the DBMS). By bringing the system services closer to the program and abstracting these services into server components, Active Server Pages promises productivity gains absolutely unrivaled in the history of computing.

The other feature of Microsoft's vision for Active Server Pages is in one of the company's key design goals for ActiveX Data Objects: *universal access, not universal storage*. This preference to know where everything is instead of collecting everything in one place is the natural extension of the overall mission of Active Server Pages—to keep things logically centralized and physically decentralized.

A Symmetric Programming Model

The most striking thing about Figure 4.1 is that both sides of the diagram are almost identical, evidently different only to the extent of system services. You may want to protest that "I thought you said this was client/server programming," but don't allow looks to deceive you. Under this apparent similarity are important differences. Let's start there.

Scripting As you shall clearly see in Part II, "Programming Active Server Pages with VBScript," client-side scripting and server-side scripting have different missions in life. Client-side scripts most often add improved user interface and data validation (when HTML forms are used). Server-side scripts, especially in Active Server Pages, are practically unlimited; but they are primarily used to capture business rules and access to data (the second and third tiers in 3-tier client/server programming).

The important thing to stress here, however, is that server-side can, if properly implemented, create client-side scripts. One of the most important questions in Internet development is the one that makes you choose between programming to the broadest audience and programming for the richest on-line experience. To the extent that you choose the former, server-side scripting is important for two reasons:

- Server-side scripts can sense the capabilities of requesting client programs.
- They can be as powerful as you, the designer, want, regardless of how thin the client is.

For example, the thinnest client on the Internet is the one that cannot render graphics of any kind. The ALT parameter of the IMG tag in HTML originally was intended to help such clients interpret important parts of the screen that they otherwise couldn't see, by describing the area in words instead of an image. With an Active Server Page, your application can sense when such a browser (for that's what these kinds of programs are—as opposed to Web client programs that have more processing power) is making a request of your Web site. You can then present such graphics-challenged browsers with whole paragraphs, not merely short expressions, to give them as much information as possible, given their inherent limitations.

In today's Internet, a major difference between Web clients brands is whether they recognize ActiveX controls or not. Again, the Active Server Page doesn't care one way or the other. If it senses the ability to interpret ActiveX controls, it presents them; otherwise, it includes static images (or text, if necessary).

Of far greater importance than these mundane issues is the fact that Active Server Pages promote a new level of processing power into the Web server. It is critical to remember that the Web server was never designed to be an application server. It was designed to deliver HTML. This remains its primary mission, even on the Active Platform, but with Active Server Pages, this design constraint ceases to be a constraint at all.

The scripts that are contained in Active Server Pages, especially those driven by Active Server components (discussed in the next section), bring virtually all the power of traditional client/server programming to the Web server. Indeed, to the extent that Active Server components are utilized, Active Server Pages can do things that even the most sophisticated client/server programs can't. That's a pretty strong statement. Let's see if we can back it up in the next section.

Components Components may be the single most important feature of Active Server Pages. Their importance to ASP is understandable when you step back and see how pervasively Microsoft has embraced components in virtually everything they create. Everything from the Internet Explorer to Windows NT 5.0 has been "componentized" by Microsoft engineers. Components give programmers many advantages, including lower development time and cost, added flexibility, easier maintenance, and most important, easier scalability.

For the ASP development community, on the server-side, server components are either intrinsic to the Active Server or they are user-defined. On the client-side, ActiveX controls provide functionality similar to server components.

N O T E Because the word "component" is a generic term meaning any kind of part, you will see the expression "server component" in this book when it refers to those special features of Active Server Pages, viz., server components. ▪

Active Server Components Active Server Components basically do two things. First, they directly expose operating system services to your Active Server Pages. Second, they encapsulate business rules in a way that is extremely easy to program. Perhaps even more important in the long run, Active Server Components are easy to create. That is, by using programming tools and environments optimized to work with the Active Platform, writing sophisticated server components is no longer the province of the advanced programmer.

There is a truism in programming that the best programmers are users. Active Server components will prove that not only to be true but important, as well. In the summer of 1996, it was estimated that the number of lines of Visual Basic code finally exceeded the number of lines of code written in COBOL, the perennial champ. Perhaps the biggest reason Visual Basic is so prolific is that users, not professional programmers, wrote these "extra" lines of code. Active Server component development will bring the same ease of programming to the Internet that Visual Basic brought to creating Windows programs.

To get a feel for what server components are and what they do, take a look at a few of those that ship with the Active Server.

The Browser Capabilities component is the component that permits an Active Server Page to determine what kind of browser or Web client program is making a request. It makes this determination by looking to the User Agent HTTP header and looking up the identified browser in the browscap.ini file. All of the listed features of the browser are exposed as properties of the Browser Capabilities component.

The Browser Capabilities component is a clever piece of code, but it doesn't have anything to do with the operating system. One component that does get closer to the OS is the TextStream component. This component relies on the FileSystem object, which, as the name suggests, accesses low-level file I/O. With this component, opening or creating text files in the directory system is simple and direct. Navigating through the files' contents is equally straightforward.

▶ **See** "Using the Browser Capabilities Component" for more information about the Browser Capabilities component, **p. 249**

▶ **See** "Textstream Objects" for more information about the TextStream component, **p. 262**

There is one Active Server Component that may keep you up nights, though. It's the Database Access component, and it exploits an operating system service of earthshaking importance: objects in the directory system. Actually, the earth won't shake until Windows NT 5.0 ships in 1997; at that time, ActiveX Data Objects (ADO) will be incorporated into the Windows NT Directory Services. That is, the directory system will be able to be managed like a database. Files become database objects with properties that will be exposed to ADO. You can already see what this will look like when you select the Properties menu option of a file on your Windows Desktop. By the way, these directory services aren't restricted to the Windows Explorer and the local file system; they reach out to every file system on the Internet!

We mentioned that a key design goal of the ADO team was to enable universal access to information—they do mean *universal*. To ADO, it won't matter if the data is a record in an ODBC database or a message stored in Exchange Server. It won't matter if the data is stored on your own hard drive or on one in the Smithsonian. ADO will find it and present it to your application (possession is no longer nine-tenths of the law). Again, this is the logical conclusion of the Web. The Web doesn't let you take possession of HTML; it just lets you see it. ADO doesn't let you possess the data, either; it just makes it available to your application.

Part
I

Ch
4

N O T E   When a connection is made to a data store with ADO, you can specify how long to wait for a connection to be made. If the connection isn't made in time, the attempt is abandoned, and the data provider returns a trappable error to ADO. This feature will not be supported by all data providers. ▪

Now, imagine programming when most of the work done by your applications is done with the aid of other peoples' server components. Whether you're using a server component to access an interactive feature in your Web site or you access network functionality in Windows NT 5.0, you will be able to do far more programming of the real task at hand. No more time wasted doing things that every other programmer in the world is doing at the same time you are.

Even if the objects exposed by Active Server components don't qualify as "true" objects in the minds of the purists, the kind of object-centric programming that will become commonplace in Active Server Pages development will have an impact great enough that most of us will forget about polymorphism and inheritance.

ActiveX Controls   ActiveX controls are used like server components, only on the client side. That is, you instantiate an ActiveX control in a client-side script with the OBJECT tag, and then you manipulate this control through its exposed properties and methods. Most ActiveX controls enhance the user interface of your Web applications, but some can simply return a value directly to your application. For example, you can write an ActiveX control that makes a complex calculation from given inputs. The control would receive the inputs through its properties, and the resulting calculation would be returned to the calling application through a separate property.

On the other hand, Active Server components never have a user interface. They are designed to render services to your server application for the purpose of producing standard HTML output. In other words, Active Server Pages are never used directly by people. Active Server Pages produce the HTML that users see, and that HTML may include ActiveX controls. So sensing browser capabilities or manipulating text files or providing HTML source code with a randomly selected image or filling the controls on an HTML form with data from a database are all examples of the usefulness of server components.

One of the most important things about the relationship between those two "pillars" of Figure 4.1, the Active Desktop and the Active Server, is that server components can be made from existing ActiveX controls. In fact, Microsoft encourages this approach for three reasons. First, you don't need to reinvent the wheel. Second, it's too easy to incorporate ActiveX controls into server components to not exploit this advantage. Finally—and this is especially important in the context of Java—ActiveX controls can give you direct access to the Windows graphical user interface. Indeed, more and more of Windows will be available to the ASP developer through this medium. Get used to taking advantage of it now. Dividends await the astute.

You may be tempted to suggest that Microsoft also wants you to use ActiveX controls for self-serving reasons, but this allegation carries less weight now that the Open Group is responsible for the standard.

N O T E   The Open Group, created in 1996 to act as the holding company for The Open Software Foundation (OSF) and X/Open Company Ltd., provides a worldwide forum for collaborative development and other open systems activities. ▨

ON THE WEB

http://www.microsoft.com/corpinfo/press/1996/oct96/stkhldpr.htm   See this Web site for further details of the transfer. More information on the Open Group is at **http://riwww.osf.org/**.

System Services

Writing a book about emerging technology is never easy. Writing this one was particularly challenging, because even the operating system was making profound changes under our feet. When the first readers open the pages of this book, Microsoft probably will have shipped the next generation of its Windows NT operating system, Windows NT 5.0. At the same time, Microsoft is developing and shipping servers meant to be integral parts of Windows NT—most of which cost nothing to add on. These servers are awesome achievements in data processing. Things like the Microsoft Transaction Server (MTS), the Message Queuing Server (MQS), and the Index Server all are vital parts of the extended Active Platform. A detailed discussion of each of these assets would require a separate book for each one.

The point to grasp here is that, as powerful and revolutionary as the Active Platform is, it will not fully empower you as a user, programmer, or developer until you bolt it into related technologies like those just mentioned. For example, if you become proficient at developing Active Server components and start to develop sophisticated, n-tier client/server apps using DCOM (Distributed Component Object Model) to widely deploy your components and Active Server Pages, you do not want to administer this far-flung empire without the managerial genius of the Microsoft Transaction Server. If you expect difficulties and delays in the actual day-to-day use of your application, and if you don't want the entire system to come down while you wait to sort out the inevitable traffic jams on the Internet, then you do not want to leave town without the Message Queuing Server.

A View of the Active Server Programming Model

Having outlined the abstract features of the Active Platform, we turn your attention to the Active Server programming model. How do you actually implement Active Server Pages?

As you can see in Figure 4.2, the processing environment of Active Server Pages is much richer than your run-of-the-mill Web site. Actually, the full richness of this environment is impossible to depict in a simple graphic, and we hope that you come to appreciate this truth as you work your way through this book. You can see from the figure that there's a lot going on with Active Server Pages.

Part

I

Ch

4

FIG. 4.2

The programming environment of the Active Server is both rich and accessible to all programming skill levels.

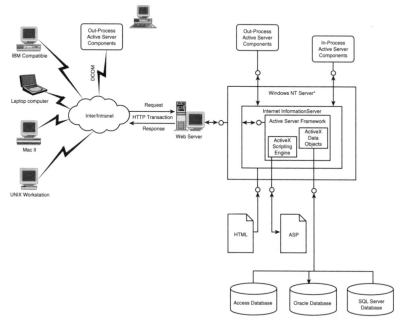

Finally—A Foolproof Answer to the Cross-Platform Problem

The first thing you notice about Figure 4.2 is that four different client platforms are represented. Four is arbitrary. ASP serves all clients, versions, and platforms because ASP produces nothing but HTML. The constraint is not in ASP but in HTML. If you want ASP to produce HTML that's rich in ActiveX controls, ASP will comply without complaint, but any clients that are not ActiveX-enabled will not work the way you expect. With ASP you can produce HTML code consistent with the capabilities of the client, from the most basic feature set to the most advanced.

The real power to bridge this "feature gap" using ASP comes when a user interface is not what's unique about your application. Business and science will be the two disciplines that most severely test the practical feasibility of the Web because computation drives most of the need for their data processing.Because computation is encapsulated in components, and because ASP is a componentized development and deployment environment, it will shine brightly, attracting the best programming talent in the world. Instead of having to write large complex applications, these programmers can write compact computationally intense programs. That is a fundamental paradigm shift of the first order.

This brings up the next most noticeable features of Figure 4.2: the out-process server and DCOM. What are they? The answer is in the next section.

Distributed Component Computing

As you may know, the entire vocabulary of OLE was supplanted recently with a new moniker, Component Object Model (COM). With the advent of Windows NT 4.0, COM evolved into the Distributed Component Object Model (DCOM). This specification was designed to permit developers to store their Active Server components (or access someone else's) anywhere on any network. For the purposes of Figure 4.2, you need to understand that part of your ASP application can be out there on the Internet; it doesn't have to be on your own Web server.

▶ **See** "Distributed Computing" for more information about DCOM, **p. 96**

▶ **See** "A COM Server" to understand the difference between in-process and out-process servers, **p. 92**

Currently, only out-process servers can be deployed with DCOM (the implication in the Microsoft literature is that one day, in-process DLL servers will run in another server's address space on a remote machine).

A Quick Overview of Server Types

If you look in your Windows directory you will see two predominant file types: .exe and .dll. The .exe file can be activated directly by the user; the .dll (which stands for Dynamic Link Library) file, on the other hand, can only be used by another program. This means that the .exe file runs in its own address space, and the .dll file runs in the address space of another .exe file. For example, the ASP.DLL (the Active Server Pages program) file runs in the address space of INETINFO.EXE (the Internet Information Server program).

Any program that runs in its own address space is called an out-process server, and any program running inside an out-process server is called an in-process server.

Part

I

Ch

4

At this point, you might be wondering, so what? Isn't the Internet just one big computer system where you can call any file on any server and have the results delivered to the client that addressed you with the request? What does DCOM give you that's unique?"

Fair enough, but let me warn you at the outset that the answer you read here will make much more sense once you've read Chapter 14, "Constructing Your Own Server Components." The simplest way to answer the question is to say that DCOM permits the ASP developer to create instances of objects from components that are not on the same machine, and to do it in the context of a single program, a single HTTP transaction.

To better understand this, again think about what would have to happen in a large, complex ASP application if you wanted to use the Internet instead of DCOM. To use the Internet to access other servers and their resources, you need a separate HTTP transaction. You can't nest HTTP transactions, because they're all self-contained units. When you call a server with an URL, you initiate an HTTP transaction with a request, and your client waits for the HTTP response. If your ASP application already has been called and is in the process of delivering the requested resource, it can't stop what it's doing, initiate another HTTP request, and then incorporate the response into the response that it then will make itself. Do you see the quandary?

With DCOM, none of this is a problem. You use the out-process Active Server component that you are accessing with DCOM *exactly as if it were on your own computer.* You instantiate it just like in-process DLL servers, and you manipulate it with its exposed methods and properties exactly as you do its lightweight cousin, the in-process server. Think of DCOM as an "Internet inside the Internet." Absolutely brilliant.

The Bridge from Desktop Apps to Client/Server Apps (and Beyond)

Active Server Pages have everything a programmer (or power user) needs to turn her old desktop applications into full-blown, three-tier client/server applications, almost overnight. Truly.

In the "Active Server Components" section, you saw that there's a lot of Visual Basic code out there. Porting the business rules contained in that code to VBScript is a slam dunk. Using Visual Basic 5.0 Control Creation Edition to turn those programs into real DLLs is now simple, accessing data through ActiveX Data Objects is an integral part of Active Server Pages, and using DCOM to distribute them around the world, if necessary, finishes the transformation.

And there's more in store. Porting legacy applications is one thing, but writing new code from scratch (still using the tried and true friend, Visual Basic) you now can create *asynchronous servers*—servers that take your requests, return a success code to the client, and then do time-consuming processing, updating the client program's user interface later, when everything's done.

For example, say that you are a financial advisor and you have a client who makes a request of one of these asynchronous servers. Your client wants to know his current position in the market but doesn't want to sell his stock unless his portfolio is in real need of rebalancing. He then launches Internet Explorer and calls a *portfolio server*, hosted by you, the financial advisor. Your server knows what assets your client holds, as well as where the last asset allocation model is stored. It retrieves the model and reruns it.

Your asynchronous server then makes a request of the *virtual operations center* (which collects the transaction and pricing data for all your clients, as well as those of several other financial advisors across the country) and updates your client's portfolio with the most current data.

> **N O T E** Hiding in the preceding story is a subtle but important advantage of ASP apps. They can hide the details about how you interact with the structure of a database system, yet they give your client all the access he needs to that data. The watchword here is *control*. No one has to know anything about your system, only what methods and properties are exposed by its mediating objects. ∎

While the transaction data is being collected, your asynchronous server makes another request of yet another asynchronous server that handles mutual fund analysis. It asks for the top ten mutual funds whose asset classes match those required by the asset allocation model that it passes along for reference. While it waits for the list of funds, your asynchronous server gets updated with the results of the latest transactions, and it sees that the market has been good to your client. Your portfolio server then re-balances your client's portfolio, lopsided in stocks, and makes another request of the mutual fund server for any new asset class it has selected as a result of optimizing the portfolio.

Your asynchronous server then places all this data and its recommendations for sells and buys in an e-mail message and sends the message to you, with an Urgent flag attached. You see the urgent message appear on your screen while reading your personal edition of one of the main investment e-zines (also driven by an Active Server Pages application). You review the results of processing, and, in the interest of prudence, make the necessary changes that the over-aggressive portfolio server suggested.

When the dust settles, your client gets an e-mail message notifying him that all processing has been completed and is ready for his review and approval. He sends an HTTP request to another Active Server Page, which displays the new information, and your client approves it for implementation.

Every piece of the previous programming scenario can be written today by a sufficiently skilled ASP developer. By the time you're done with this book, perhaps that developer will be you.

Seeing Where ASP and HTTP Fit Together

There really are three entities involved in an HTTP transaction: the Web client, the Web server, and the human being.

The Web client and Web server communicate using HTTP *headers*. These are collections of data that the client and server exchange with one another to ensure that, regardless of the contents of the body of the HTTP transaction, the entire transaction remains coherent and complete.

The data displayed to the human being is transmitted from the Web server to the Web client, and the Web client transfers the text and the interpreted HTML source code to the screen or printer, so the human can read it.

Active Server Pages permit the developer to affect all facets of the HTTP transaction. The ASP objects known as Request and Response interact with the HTTP body and headers, respectively. This feature gives the ASP developer almost unlimited flexibility in management of interaction on the Web.

For example, using these two objects lets the developer authenticate secure HTTP transactions and control the contents of the STATUS header, blocking access to requested content when such access would violate established security policy. Even complex authentication schemes can be implemented using new headers defined just for your ASP application.

The Active Server is implemented as an ISAPI filter running under IIS. Whenever a Web client makes an HTTP request of a Web server, the Active Server ISAPI filter gets a chance to intercept the request. If the request is for an .asp file, the Active Server takes over from IIS, parses the entire file from top to bottom, processes the server script(s), and returns an HTML output file to IIS. IIS then returns this data stream to the requesting Web client.

CAUTION

Be careful when you enter an URL for your .asp files. If you don't use the protocol prefix, **http://**, the browser interprets the request as a call to display a file. This command bypasses IIS, so the filter never gets its chance. As a result, under Windows NT, the contents of the file is displayed instead of the results of the .asp source code. Under Windows 95, if a file has been associated with the .asp extension—for example, an excellent ASP editor, such as HomeSite—then that program launches and opens your .asp file outside the Web client window.

Remember, because an .asp file needs to execute IIS, use HTTP in the URL.

Exploiting the Power of Windows NT Technology

The Active Server is running in the same address space as IIS, and IIS is running as a service under Windows NT, so both IIS and the Active Server inherit all the security features of the Windows NT operating system. Security comes through four access mechanisms: IP address, user account, virtual directory, and the NT File System (NTFS). User account access is granted by using one of two authentication methods: basic authentication and NT Challenge/ Response authentication. Virtual directories enable IIS to control access to specific directories (and all subdirectories) that were identified by a single name, an alias. Access Control Lists (ACLs), a product of the NTFS, permit you to specify access permission for individual users or groups.

N O T E　Use the Microsoft Internet Service Manager to specify IP address restrictions (from the Advanced tab) and to configure virtual directories (from the Directories tab). Specify ACLs in the Windows NT Explorer through the Security tab on Properties dialog box of the directory or file to which you want to restrict access. ▨

Because the Active Server is linked to IIS through the ISAPI filter mechanism, and because IIS runs as a service under NT, all your .asp files have direct access to these programming assets. This means that your ASP applications are highly scaleable: Their performance doesn't degrade as demands on them increase.

Because everything is running as a service under NT, there may be other services available to your ASP programs. Of these services you are most likely to use the other two perennial Internet severs, FTP and Gopher. Other important servers are the Microsoft Index Server, a Personalization Server, and a Proxy Server. Microsoft Exchange Server now has a Web interface as well, and the directory services provided by NT also are ready to be pressed into action.

Where's ActiveX in Active Server Pages?

You've seen that HTTP is what gets an Active Server Page running, but what makes it tick? In a word, ActiveX. But what kind of ActiveX?

If you did any advanced HTML programming before coming to Active Server Pages, you already may be familiar with ActiveX controls. ActiveX controls are slimmed-down OLE Automation servers. That is, Microsoft reduced the number of object interfaces required by OLE objects so that they would work more efficiently in the bandwidth-challenged world of today's Internet. ActiveX controls, therefore, work wherever OLE Automation servers worked in the past.

ActiveX controls usually have a user interface and some way to interact with it at runtime. Other ActiveX controls have no user interface, such as computation engines or text-formatting functions.

The Active Server can be extended using Active Server Components. You will learn all about Active Server Components in Chapter 14, "Constructing Your Own Server Components;" for now, you need to understand that Active Server Pages are *object-centric* programs. Most of the work done in an .asp file is done by some kind of object.

N O T E We use the term *object-centric* to distinguish the informal kind of object commonly encountered in computer programming from the formal objects encountered in full-blown object-oriented programming languages like C++, Java, Smalltalk, and Delphi. Most of the features of real objects are found in object-centric languages, but some of the most problematic—such as inheritance—are missing.

The most important feature of all objects is that they are self-contained programs that encapsulate data and source code. In ASP development, objects expose collections, methods, and properties by which work is requested and results are accessed.

The Active Server is a collection of objects, but it also can interface with any other programs written to the ActiveX specification. In the same way that ActiveX controls are OLE Automation servers on a diet, so Active Server components now are ActiveX controls with a reduced set of interfaces. Specifically, the only interfaces that an Active Server Component needs to support are `IUnknown`, `IClassFactory`, and `IDispatch`. The other feature recommended, though not required, for a program to be an Active Server component is a type library.

N O T E The ActiveX scripting engine with which the Active Server Engine interfaces is the same one with which the Web client interfaces. So, if you develop a scripting engine of your own, all you need to do is incorporate the ActiveX scripting interface into your own scripting engine, and your work will work on both the client and the server.

Because Active Server components are running on a controlled server and not on a user's desktop, they have full access to the server's file system and network resources. This makes them a natural alternative to client-side scripting technologies such as Java and the twin client-side scripting engines, VBScript and JavaScript.

An Active Server component can be instantiated in the `global.asa` file and stored as a `Session` property. This component can be accessed simultaneously by all sessions (assuming that it uses one of the multithreading models supported by the Active Server). Here, then, are the

Part
I

Ch
4

reasons why in-process Active Server components are so superior to the traditional CGI implementation of Web interactivity:

- The server doesn't do any context-switching.
- The Active Server component runs in the address space of the server.
- With Application scope, only one instance of the object exposed by the Active Server component is necessary to enable its use across all sessions of your ASP application.

Seeing Where ASP and HTML Fit Together

You've seen how Web clients access IIS (IIS is running as a service of Windows NT) and how IIS communicates with the Active Server (which is running in the address space of IIS). Now take a look at the last step in this process.

Basic HTML Output Although an .asp file contains text, HTML source code, and scripts, the only thing it produces is HTML. The Active Server is merely an HTML factory—it writes HTML code for you. This code actually might be written by you along with scripting logic that determines what, if anything, will be returned to the client. Or it might be an .asp file that generates HTML entirely on its own from source code stored in a database record.

CAUTION

When you call an ASP program that contains only .asp source code, which generates no HTML, your Web client complains because there is no data in the response body. Sometimes the program won't even run.

If the program does run, the error message that invariably appears includes an evident *non sequitur*: "The operation completed successfully." This means that the Active Server ran to completion, but the client wasn't happy with the result.

If you need to create what is basically an ASP utility (a function that does not deserve to be made into a full-fledged Active Server Component), find a way to return some HTML, even if it's merely a <BR>. Even better is a redirect to another .asp file.

 Many editors permit you to create a template .html or .asp file. If you have, at a minimum, the standard HEAD and BODY tags in your template, you will never run into the error noted above.

Data-Driven HTML Most HTML on the Internet always has been and still is static. Forms provide a basic level of interactivity, and ActiveX controls can give static HTML pages a dynamic appearance and enhance interactivity, but that depends on the client software supporting the ActiveX specification. Using Active Server Pages immediately does two things for you: It enables the highest form of interactivity on the Web—namely, secure commercial transactions —and it encourages the greatest amount of dynamic content. Whether that content changes because the Ad Rotator randomly selected another banner ad or because the structure of the HTML page was generated to suit the ActiveX control-enabled client program, it all was done automatically by your ASP application.

Part III, "Working with Active Server Objects and Components," and Part IV, "Database Management with Active Server Pages," are dedicated to showing you exactly how to move up to this level of Internet development.

Special Cases

With sufficient experience, you may find that there's nothing beyond your reach with ASP extending your grasp. This new power won't come without exacting a cost, however. To really improve your reach with Active Server Pages you will have to meet the following two challenges, at least.

- .asp files can populate client-side scripting objects with data that is accessed through ADO.
- They can be used to generate data inside the Microsoft Layout Control's .alx file.

To whet your appetite, we close this section with a brief introduction of the programming problems posed by the particular challenges of these two special cases.

Dynamic Client-Side Scripts   The first challenge presents itself when the server is called to create a dynamic client-side script. The most frequent occurrence of this almost certainly will be in filling out on-line forms. For example, say you have an HTML FORM with SELECT tags and TEXT fields in it. Further suppose that the specific variables displayed in these controls are stored in your database. The OnLoad event of your scripted page would normally populate the SELECT tag. With ASP, the server-side script would first fetch the SELECT options from the database, and it would then be able to write the client-side script that would run when the OnLoad event fired. The result is a dynamic SELECT tag.

▶ **See** "Modifying Client Scripts from the Server" for more information about modifying client-side scripts with server scripts, **p. 116**

HTML Layout Controls   Once you get past the more common dynamic HTML challenge, you will likely be confronted by the second challenge: using the ActiveX Layout Control in your .asp file. The trick is to give the file created in the ActiveX Control Pad an .asp extension, instead of the standard .alx value. There are other requirements that have to do with protecting the .asp delimiters embedded in the .alx/.asp file, but details dictate a prerequisite knowledge of .asp syntax that you won't learn until Chapter 11, "Building a Foundation of Interactivity with *Request* and *Response* Objects."

ON THE WEB

The program is free and can be downloaded from the Microsoft Web site at:

http://www.microsoft.com/workshop/author/cpad/cpad.htm.

Complete documentation for the Microsoft HTML Layout Control is at:

http://www.microsoft.com/workshop/author/layout/layout.htm.

The ActiveX Control Pad and the .alx file

Standard HTML is a structural language, not a page layout language like PostScript. HTML is only interested in specifying the components of a document, not for their relative positions on the page. Microsoft introduced what they called a 2-D control called the Microsoft HTML Layout Control. This control permits the HTML author to specify precise locations for controls. With this control you can also specify the layering of objects and their transparency. The results can look pretty spectacular.

These specifications, and any scripts that manipulate the controls contained within the Microsoft HTML Layout Control, are stored in a separate file that uses the .alx extension.

Creating an instance of the Microsoft HTML Layout Control is facilitated by the Microsoft ActiveX Control Pad program. This small application was designed to help identify and configure ActiveX controls and to create the ALX file.

At any rate, being able to use the sophistication of .alx files *and* .asp files—and in the same file—perhaps is the most impressive example of how ubiquitous .asp source code will be in your Web applications. Are you beginning to see how the advent of the Active Server Page is going to empower Web developers like nothing else in the history of the Internet?

Understanding the Structure of Active Server Pages

There is no structure, per se, in an .asp file that isn't already there in the structure of the HTML, Visual Basic, or JavaScript code. In this respect, .asp files are not really programs. Indeed, a single .asp file can implement any combination of supported scripting engines, using languages as diverse as Perl and Rexx to Visual Basic and JavaScript. ASP is an "ecumenical" programming environment.

HTML, All by Itself

It is acceptable, though not necessarily recommended, to rename your HTML files with the .asp extension and turn them all into Active Server Pages. That's all that's required to make an ASP application. If you only want to control more of the HTTP headers in your HTML files, then you may see minimal .asp source code in those renamed HTML files. But if you want to turbo-charge those sluggish old HTML files, or if you want to stop maintaining two versions of your Web site (one for the interactive-impaired), then read on.

HTML Mixed with .asp Source Code

Once you choose to add .asp source code to your HTML files, you have to make several more choices. If you are silent, the Active Server Engine makes a few of these choices on your behalf. The choices fall into two categories: to use scripting or not and, if so, what kind(s) of scripting.

For the purposes of this discussion, .asp source code consists of either *native ASP commands* or *scripting commands*. Native commands are those that access Active Server Engine objects and components. Scripting commands rely on a particular syntax, as well. This means that you have to tell the Active Server Engine which language to use to interpret the commands. If you are silent, the engine will use VBScript by default.

This choice is not trivial when you are using Active Server Pages to write client-side scripts. As soon as you opt for this feature in your Web site, you're back to square one: Are you writing to a captive audience such as an intranet, where all the client programs are the same brand and version? Even if all the browsers are the same brand and version, do they all support VBScript, or will you have to rely on the more ubiquitous JavaScript?

N O T E   As noted in the introduction to this section, you don't have to choose one scripting engine. Choose the ones that suit your needs. If you have a nifty Perl program that you'd like to use, use it. If most of your server-side scripting will be done in VBScript because that's the language in which you are most fluent, use it. And if you need a generic, client-side scripting engine, use JavaScript, while you're at it. ▦

Once you have made the preliminary choices, you must begin to contend with the challenge of separating the HTML source code from its ASP counterpart.

You have two basic choices here: Use code delimiters `<%...%>` or use the HTML `<SCRIPT>...</SCRIPT>` delimiters. When you are mixing scripting engines, you must use the `<SCRIPT>...</SCRIPT>` tags, because you have to identify the scripting engine to the Active Server. You identify the language with the LANGUAGE parameter (the comment delimiter is different for each scripting engine as well, and comments are an integral part of the `<SCRIPT>...</SCRIPT>` tag).

N O T E   Comments are necessary in client-side scripts because browsers that cannot interpret scripts need to ignore everything within the `<SCRIPT>...</SCRIPT>` tag. However, if you use a comment in the server-side version of a script, nothing will happen. In other words, do not use comment lines when defining server-side scripts. ▦

Part

I

Ch

4

.asp Source Code

As mentioned, you can write an .asp file with only .asp source code, but if you intend to have a client program call the file and there isn't a stitch of HTML in the output, your client is going to balk.

An important advantage of using scripting delimiters is that the .asp source code never is visible to the reader of the HTML that is sent by the Active Server Page. This is because the source code is processed entirely at the server. This invisible source code trick holds whether you use the `<%...%>` or the `<SCRIPT>...</SCRIPT>` options. However, to the extent you have client-side scripts in the HTML output, you are directly exposing your programming expertise to anyone who looks at the HTML source code.

Scripting Functions and Subroutines

For server-side scripting functions and subroutines to work, they must be delimited by the `<SCRIPT>...</SCRIPT>` tags, and the RUNAT parameter must be set to Server so that the client scripting engine doesn't get its hands on it. You cannot use the `<%...%>` delimiters to define a function because you cannot give names to .asp code blocks. Even if you could, there's no inherent way to get a code block to return a value, the required function of a function.

To use .asp files to generate client-side scripts, you need to mix the `<SCRIPT>...</SCRIPT>` tags with the .asp source code delimiters, `<%...%>`. That is, client-side scripts consist of `<SCRIPT>...</SCRIPT>` blocks. When those scripts need content generated by the server (namely, filling form controls with database contents, as mentioned earlier), you must tell the Active Server Engine which code is to be executed at the server and which is to be streamed to the client and executed there.

Sound complicated? It's not, really. Most of the secret is in the fact noted a couple of paragraphs ago: The Active Server Engine won't run a script unless the RUNAT parameter equals Server. Obviously, then, all other occurrences of scripts will run at the client, and the `<SCRIPT>...</SCRIPT>` commands are just plain old HTML, dutifully sent back to the client in the response body of the HTTP transaction.

There is no hard and fast rule for where to put your functions and subroutines. A common practice is to put them in the `<HEAD>` section of your HTML file. Short functions sometimes can be installed directly with the HTML command. You will have ample practice with all of these design alternatives when you get to Part II, "Programming Active Server Pages with VBScript."

Server-Side Includes

Server-Side Includes are powerful tools for programmer productivity. In a sense, they are the most basic kind of reusable code. Their primary purpose is to insert text file contents into .asp files. Server-Side Includes can contain other Server-Side Includes, so you can stuff an incredible amount of text into an .asp file with a single command.

▶ **See** "Using Server-Side Includes" for more information about Server-Side Includes and examples of how they are used, **p. 168**

Because Server-Side Includes are included in your .asp files before any of the files' ASP commands are executed, Server-Side Includes can't do anything fancy, such as looking up database records. They can, however, call other Server-Side Includes.

Server-Side Includes insert text in exactly the same place in your file as they are located. In other words, they replace themselves at runtime. This distinction can be important when the resulting text has a particular role to play and that role has a particular place in the file to play it. At other times, this is not so important. One of the most common uses for the Server-Side Include is when you need to refer to constants in your .asp source code. For example, the adovbs.inc file contains all the VBScript constants used by ActiveX Data Objects.

A final point about Server-Side Includes is that they really don't add any marginal overhead. In a UNIX shop, however, .html files are usually not opened before they are sent on to the client program. But to process a Server-Side Include, the server must open the .HTML file and the Server-Side Include file. It must then insert the text in the Server-Side Include into the .HTML file at the proper location Finally, it must close the .HTML file and send it on to the Web client.

Under the Active Server, the .asp file has to be opened anyway, so the extra effort of inserting the text is negligible. Anyway, this entire file I/O is processing in the address space of Windows NT, so even in the worst case, the overhead of processing .asp files in this way is nothing compared to the power you get in the bargain.

From Here...

In this chapter, you were introduced to the results of what can only be described as the most spectacular course correction ever attempted by an American corporation. In less than a year, Microsoft redeployed all of its resources to incorporate and exploit the revolution in data processing that is the Internet. If the definition of an *asset* is "anything that enables you to do something you couldn't do before," then the Internet is one of the most amazing assets ever to appear on this planet—look at what its mere presence did for Microsoft. But if the Internet is a consummate example of an asset, then the technologies that Microsoft has built and delivered can only be described as a mutual fund of technology. This mutual fund goes by the name of the Active Platform.

Perhaps the most remarkable Internet development asset in this mutual fund is the Active Server Page. Designed to be used by anyone who can deliver content to the Internet (and that's practically anyone who can type), it is typified by a single file that can be packed with an incredible amount of processing power. You can mix a virtually unlimited number of scripting languages into a single .asp file, each language used for the kind of work for which it's optimized. In that single file, you have immediate access to all the processing power of the Active Server Engine's internal objects and components. And if they don't do what you need, you can build your own Active Server Component. Once registered, your component is accessed and behaves exactly like those components that ship with the server. You can build those components in any language that conforms to the COM specification, from C++ to Java to Visual Basic 5.0. And you can store those components anywhere on the planet and use them as if they were on your desktop. With Active Server Pages, there are no separate files to compile (or even store). Everything can be contained in a single file extension, if you want.

Nothing even comes close to the breadth and depth of processing horsepower that you have at your fingertips when you have mastered the Active Server Framework.

From here, you will progress through the following chapters on the road to mastering the Active Server Page:

- Chapter 5, "Understanding Objects and Components," surveys the COM specification and examines what is required from that large standard to implement your own server components.

- Chapter 6, "Integrating VBScript into HTML," shows you the specifics of scripting basics including copious source code examples.

- Chapter 7, "Understanding Variable Typing, Naming, and Scoping," helps you get the most out of your VBScripts in terms of speed and ease of program maintenance.

- Chapter 8, "Working with Program Flow and Control Structures," shows you how to build complex VBScripts with conditional logic and program loops.

- Chapter 9, "Calling Procedures: Functions and Subroutines," will teach you how to structure VBScript code to make it reusable (and thereby save you development time later on), enable it to manage the inevitable errors that will crop up, and it will show you exactly how and when to use Server-Side Includes.

- Chapter 14, "Constructing Your Own Server Components," helps you pull together all you've learned. With this knowledge you will be able to join the front lines of the revolution in n-tier client/server programming that is about to sweep through the computer world.

Understanding Objects and Components

The people, places, and things with which you come in contact each and every day are the objects of your life. You have a transportation object (your car), a companion object (your spouse, children, or pet), and a number of other objects that you interact with throughout the day. This is not a suggestion that you are living a mechanical life, but rather that you can express the relationships between yourself and those things around you by thinking about the attributes that define those objects. It is this set of specific, meaningful attributes that lets you differentiate between the kitchen chair and the sofa. Both provide you a place to sit, but each has its own specific function within your life.

Abstracting the essence of real-world objects, events, and processes and then creating a road map or blueprint of that occurrence is the rationale behind object-oriented development. This chapter examines objects, their attributes, and their relationships to other objects. By understanding the pieces of the underlying technologies (OLE, ActiveX) and how each fits into the Active Server Pages environment, you will become a more proficient and educated developer. ■

Understanding Object-Oriented Development

You will see object and component used somewhat interchangeably within this chapter. When you hear component, you can think object, but with one main difference: The component is always packaged separately from the application, as a dynamic link library or as a COM or ActiveX object. This provides a number of benefits that will be examined in the section "The Component Object Model."

In the aftermath of the Second World War, the United States was the world's provider of choice for goods and services. Shortly after that time, a man named Dr. W. Edward Demming spoke of a new concept in manufacturing: total quality management (TQM). At the time, not many U.S. companies were interested in TQM. They already were the world's first and best supplier. So Dr. Demming took his message to the Japanese, who quickly took his teachings to heart. Now, some 50 years later, that country is beating most others in quality production at nearly every turn.

In the past ten years, the idea of total quality management was revived in the offices of corporate America. What corporations had once spurned, they now embraced. Out of this new focus on quality, a number of methods and techniques were developed to examine problem processes within an organization and ferret out the root causes. The next steps involved process redesign and, in many cases, process automation. The developer was given a process map that showed the new process to be automated, and more specifically, the way the data flowed through the process. Many developers then used this as a road map to develop the new application. The problem with the result was that it was a data-centric, not a process-centric, design.

For the developer, this road map was a godsend, giving him a step-by-step, data-driven guide to developing the system. Many systems continue to be developed in this manner today. There are, however, a number of issues that arise from this traditional, structured application-development methodology.

Working from a data-driven process map, the developer tends to focus on creating functions that let the data flow as it does in the map. This is a great way to implement the application, based on the process flows. In reality, however, most processes that are reengineered are changed again (*tweaked*) just before or shortly after implementation. So a step that was in the beginning of the process might be moved to the middle, and then a few weeks later, it might be moved to the end and then back to the beginning. Adapting the procedural, data-based application to these changes is a major effort, and in most cases, the application cannot adapt to the requested modifications.

The ability to rapidly change an application in a changing environment faces every developer. As a solution to this issue, many development shops have moved to object-oriented design and development. Traditional application development involves using a structured methodology, looking at top-down functional decomposition of the processes involved and their associated systems. When you use data flow diagrams and structure charts, the processes are identified, as is the data that moves through the processes.

Object-oriented development is a methodology that strives to decrease the complexity of a problem by breaking down the problem into discrete parts, which then manifest as objects. The objects within this problem domain are then discovered and abstracted to a level where the inherent complexity within the real-world object is removed. What you are left with is some number of objects that have a state (data members) and that provide services (methods) for other objects within the domain. The nice thing about encapsulating functionality within objects is that they are self-sustaining units. If a process step is changed within a flow, there is no need to change the object itself, just its place within the program.

As new requirements are added, new functionality can be easily added to the object. Even better, when a new application is required, existing objects can be used in the new development, either directly, through combination, or through inheritance, all of which you will learn about in this chapter. Even though there is no support for object-oriented development *per se* using VBScript, many of the lessons learned about the value of code reuse and encapsulation (data hiding) can be applied in your ASP development.

Understanding Classes and Objects

To you, the Active Server Pages developer, an *object* or *component* is a prebuilt piece of functionality that you can immediately integrate in your scripts. These include components such as database connectivity, interaction with a host environment, and a number of other functions that you cannot perform through scripting alone. By understanding the principles that drive the component implementation, you will be better able to leverage components' use in your development.

At its most basic level, an object is an instantiation of a class. A *class* is a blueprint for the creation of an object and the services that reside within it. The class describes the state of the object using data members (private) and provides services (member functions or methods) that are available to owners of the object (those that are public members) and to the object itself for internal use (non-public members: protected or private). The class also may be related to other classes through inheritance or composition.

Which came first, the object or the class? The question certainly falls into the chicken or the egg category. Who has the time or energy to try and figure that one out?

Abstractions

When you begin trying to identify objects within your problem domain, you are struck by the complexity of the world in which you live. *Abstractions* are a useful way of reducing your environment's complexity into manageable pieces. When you use abstraction, you pick out the most important elements or properties of an object that let you view the object from a higher place, a reduced complexity.

If you look at a piece of paper under a microscope at high magnification, you see millions of fibers, intertwining with no discernible pattern. As you lessen the magnification, the fibers begin to run together. Eventually, you are at 0× magnification (looking at the page on a table, perhaps), and the fibers within the paper are abstracted to such a level that they become insignificant. For understanding the use of paper in a printer or to write on, the microscopic level has been abstracted, so the piece of paper (object) can be understood and utilized. The more an object is abstracted, the smaller the number of intricate details involved. Of course, you can abstract something too much, to a point where you lose the essence of the object. As a developer, you will determine the level of abstraction that will enable you to integrate the object into your code.

As you abstract objects, you identify those attributes that are essential to understanding the object. After the attributes are identified, you can move into the services or member functions that operate to manipulate the object attributes that were abstracted.

Protecting Your Object's Data: Encapsulation

As your applications begin to interact with the objects in your Active Server Pages scripts, you will set properties and call methods of those objects. All your interactions with those objects take place when you access them through a well-defined set of functions, or a *public interface*. When you execute a method of an object, you don't need to know how the object will perform its duties; you just need the object to get the job done.

The idea of having a public interface and private implementation is one of the key OO (Object-oriented) concepts. You might have heard this concept referred to as *data hiding*; another name for this technique is *encapsulation*. In essence, all the implementation details, all the internal variables that are created and used, and all the internal support functions are encapsulated within the object. The only view into the object that you as a user of the object have is the public interface.

Encapsulation provides a number of benefits. First, you don't need to know how the requested service is implemented, only that the object performs the requested service. The second benefit is that the underlying implementation of the services that the object provides can change without the public interface changing. The client (calling procedure) often is totally unaware that the implementation of the function has changed at all, because it never has access to that part of the object.

Many people refer to this type of system as a *black box* interface, and this is a fair analogy. Imagine that you are creating a transaction program to interface with a legacy database system. You will define a set of transactions that the black box, or object, will accept, and then it will return the result set to your client application. Initially, the communication between the black box and the legacy system will be performed using LU6.2 communications. A few months later, the protocol changes to TCP/IP. Your client application is never aware of the protocol that the black box is implementing, and the change does not affect the client app at all, because the public interface (the transaction set) does not change. This is the benefit of encapsulation: The public interface remains constant, and the implementation can be changed without affecting the object's users.

Understanding Inheritance

The only thing you need to know to understand *inheritance* is how to use *kind of* in a sentence, as in "a bicycle is a *kind of* vehicle." The whole idea behind inheritance is that you create a class of a base type (say, vehicle) and then derive a new class from the base class (bicycle). The neat thing about inheritance is that all the functionality residing in the base class are available to the derived class. Those functions unique to the derived class are then implemented within the new class, called the *subclass*. There is also the opportunity to then derive a new class, say Huffy, from the bicycle class. The Huffy class will again have all the methods from each of the classes that it is derived from. This is called single inheritance, when a subclass is derived from only one base class.

In the preceding example, the vehicle base class has a number of functions that include things like starting, stopping, and turning. All the vehicles derived from the base class (bicycle, car, motorcycle, boat) have the methods of the base class, but their implementation is different. To turn right in the car class, the steering wheel is turned. On a bicycle, the handlebars are moved. I think you get the idea.

In another case, you can derive an object from more than one base class. This is called multiple inheritance. Say you are creating an object that will provide a visual interface for the abstraction of a document scanner; you can derive a `ScanView` class from a `ViewWindow` class and a `ScannerControl` class.

Polymorphism

You might be saying to yourself, so what? Why do I need the base class, when many of the functions in the subclasses are implemented differently anyway? Well, the answer is illuminating. *Polymorphism* lets you use a variable of a base class type to reference any of the classes derived from that base type. This means that you can have a procedure that accepts as a parameter an object variable declared as a vehicle. Then you can call the procedure passing any of the subclasses of vehicle that have been derived—boat, car, and so on. The great thing is that when you say `objectVar.TurnRight()` within the procedure, the *appropriate method within the subclass* is invoked. As you can see, this is unbelievably powerful.

Your application can be controlling any type of vehicle, turning left or right, starting, or stopping, regardless of the class of vehicle it is controlling. But just as important, each time you create a new abstraction of a vehicle, you don't need to start from scratch. All the basic functions already have been defined for you. Those methods that need additional implementation code are all that you have to add. Notice in the following code, Listing 5.1, that the procedure takes as a parameter, a pointer to a vehicle.

Part

I

Ch

5

Listing 5.1   DRIVE.C—A Sample of Using Polymorphism Within a Procedure

```
Bicycle bike;
Drive(&bike);

void Drive(Vehicle * veh)
```

continues

Listing 5.1   Continued

```
{
    veh->TurnRight(); // wil invoke the method TurnRight in
                     // the Bicycle class, not the vehicle class
}
```

When the method TurnRight is called from within the Drive procedure, the correct method, within the subclass, is called.

Here's another example. You are working for the zoo and are in the midst of creating an audio application that will reproduce the sounds of all the zoo's animals. You create a base class called Animal, with an associated member function Speak. Now, you derive each of your subclasses—goat, bird, and so on. Back in the application proper, the user selects an animal sound to hear. An instance of that animal subclass is created and passed as an Animal. Then, when the Speak method is called, the appropriate animal sound is played.

Comparing Static and Dynamic Binding

To enable implementation of polymorphism with your classes and objects, the object variable veh within the Drive function, in Listing 5.1, must be associated with the actual Bicycle object at runtime. In effect, the object is sent the "turn right" message and figures out how to implement it. This ability to assign the object type during the program's execution is called *dynamic binding* and is the method through which polymorphism is executed.

Static binding, on the other hand, is what happens when all object references are resolved at compile time. During static binding, the object associated with any object variable within the application is set by the object declaration. As you can see, dynamic binding is imminently more powerful—and required—within an OO environment.

Working with Composition

In the section "Understanding Inheritance," inheritance was expressed as a "kind of" relationship. Classes created through composition are expressed through a "part of" relationship. For example, a car is a type of vehicle, but a vehicle is not a part of a car. When you use composition to create a class, you are finding those classes that are a part of the class that you are building. An engine is a part of a car. Wheels are a part of a car. A windshield is a part of a car. You can create a car class composed of an engine, wheels, a windshield, and any other parts that are appropriate to the car class.

The car class will be derived from vehicle, but those other "parts" of the car class, the engine object, the wheel object, and so on, will become private member variables of the car class. Listing 5.2 shows a class definition for our hypothetical Auto class.

Listing 5.2   AUTO.HPP—Defining the Auto Class, Using Inheritance and Composition

```
Class Auto: public Vehicle  // inheritance from Vehicle class
{
   Public:
      Auto();
      ~Auto();
   Private:            // composition of objects within the class
      Engine engine;   // engine object as private member variable
      Wheels wheels;   // wheels object as private member variable
};
```

The Bottom Line: Object Reuse

Why all the fuss about object-oriented development? The most important feature that OO provides is the capability to create new applications from existing code without introducing new bugs. This is not to say that there will be no bugs within your implementation, just that there should be no bugs *within* these production-hardened objects that you are going to use.

This capability to reuse proven, production-ready code is one of the main forces driving the OO movement into corporate development. As the business environment continues to become more complex, developers need to be able to quickly represent that complexity within the systems they build. In addition, the rapid changes in the current business environment demand systems that can be modified easily, without having to recompile an entire application each time a change is made. If your system is developed using component objects, when the objects are enhanced, the client will not need to be changed.

Using OO in Active Server Pages Development

The object-oriented methods of inheritance, composition, and polymorphism are not implemented in VBScript within the ASP environment. Nevertheless, you can take the overriding principle of OO development to heart as you develop ASP applications. That principle is reuse of existing, production-ready code. You can create libraries of functions that you can include within your Active Server Pages applications. You will also be able to imbed the functionality of ASP component objects and other third-party components within the functions that reside in your library.

▶ **See** "Examining Procedures" for information about creating libraries of functions to include in your Active Server Pages applications, **p. 160**

Using Components

There are a number of prebuilt components that ship with Active Server Pages. If you had to reproduce the functionality of each of the components, either in native scripting or by creating your own components in Visual Basic or Visual C++, you would expend a considerable amount of time and money. The wonderful thing about components is that they give you innumerable choices for implementing solutions to a particular problem.

We've known (actually, still know) developers who have a particularly disturbing disorder. This disorder has been known by many names over the years, but we tend to refer to it as NBH Syndrome, for *not built here*. Anything that these developers did not create within their development shop is no good, no how. True, they have created some exciting applications over the years, but the time they take to create them could have been cut by at least half had they integrated other development groups' code into their own.

The same is true of components. It is easy to say, "Sure, I'll build it myself. How long could it take?" Many have fallen into this trap. One good example of a build/buy component decision that often comes to mind is the ubiquitous calendar control. This is a user interface component that lets you select a date from a calendar by clicking a calendar graphic. There are hundreds of applications that require this type of functionality. Although it is not an overwhelming project to design and build a calendar component, why should you bother? There are numerous calendar components available out there in the market. They have been tested and proven in production. Why waste time implementing an object that is available in the market? You have business process expertise. You understand the specific business logic that rules the process. Put your development time to the best use by implementing the business processes. Don't waste time reinventing the wheel. In the build versus buy decision, remember that a development project's success is determined by how well an application meets a business need, not by who built a particular component that is part of an application.

We'll hop off the soapbox now. We were getting a little lightheaded up there, anyway.

The Component Object Model

The history of the Component Object Model (COM) follows somewhat the history of Windows and the applications created for use on the system. In the early days of the Windows environment, the need for users to have the capability to share data across applications was paramount. The capability to copy and paste data between applications using the Clipboard metaphor was the first step. In the late eighties, Microsoft implemented the *dynamic data exchange* (DDE) protocol to provide this Clipboard functionality in a more dynamic implementation. The only problem was that this new dynamic implementation was quirky, slow, and somewhat unreliable.

By 1991, DDE effectively was replaced by a new technology called *object linking and embedding,* or OLE 1.0. The new OLE enabled applications to share data or to link objects, with the linked data remaining in the format of the application that created it. When you embedded or linked objects, they would show up within the client application. When the linked data needed to be edited, the object would be double-clicked by the user, and the application that created the base data would be started.

As nice as OLE 1.0 was, it still was a far cry from the easy application integration promised in Microsoft's "Information at Your Fingertips." From this point, Microsoft came to the conclusion that the only way to provide truly seamless object integration was to create little pieces of functionality that could be plugged from one application into another to provide specific services. From this was born the idea of *component objects,* objects that could provide services to other client applications. The Component Object Model (COM) specification came out of this desire to create a standard for component objects.

COM, as implemented with OLE 2.0 in 1993, became more than just a specification for component objects. COM supports a vast range of services that let components interact at many levels within the application environment. The same service that provides local processing can be invoked on a remote machine to provide similar services, all of which are transparent to the user.

Component Design Goals

As Microsoft moved from DDE to OLE 1.0 and finally to the component model specification, there were a number of design goals that guided the company in the development of COM and OLE. This set of functionality was derived partly from the history of creating monolithic, complex applications, but more so from the ongoing maintenance and inevitable changes that an evolving environment demands on any system.

To create a truly generic interface architecture, the model was created with the following goals in mind:

- **Generic access path.** For any components that reside on a system, there must be a method in place that provides the capability to find any available service through a unique identifier.

- **Transparent access.** In a distributed computing environment, the client must not be required to know specifically where a service resides. The access to the component and the services that it provides must be transparent to the user, whether the component is running locally on the same system in the same process, in a different process on the same machine, or on a system across the country.

- **Implementation independence.** The component services must be designed with a well-defined binary public interface that enables the use of a component by any compliant client, without regard to the actual implementation details or language that created the component.

- **Adaptability to change.** As implementations change or as new functionality is added, the component must continue to support existing public interfaces. This enables the component to be modified without a resultant change in the client application.

- **Advanced versioning capabilities.** The component object must be able to make known to the client program what compatible versions are available within the component to the client, so new versions of the component will not break older client applications.

Part

I

Ch

5

■ **Interoperability between service providers.**   The components themselves must provide standard binary interfaces to let them operate across vendors and operating systems. Without a standard across service providers, interoperability is impossible.

■ **Conformance to OO development.**   The component model must support key OO principles such as inheritance, composition, and polymorphism. The key objective is to provide enhanced object reuse to enable creation of dynamic, component-based applications—no more complex, monolithic designs.

All of the design goals in the preceding list boil down to providing developers with the tools to create dynamic, flexible applications that are quick to create and easy to maintain. As business processes continue to become more complex and require increasing levels of adaptability, the old monolithic development architecture is breaking under the weight of the changes. In traditional development, when one part of an implementation within a system changes, the entire application needs to be recompiled to ensure that all references to functions are correct. The need to provide dynamic changes, without new versions of applications having to be compiled, is another central goal of the component model.

To support larger applications and distributed data, client applications must be able to access appropriate services, wherever they reside, to fulfill user requests. Once again, if a service resides on another machine, across the hall, or across the continent, the client must not be aware of the difference.

As corporations move toward improving quality within their organizations, every process is being looked at and, where appropriate, redesigned. The requirement for new applications continues to outpace information systems' capability to keep up. By creating new applications from proven, existing components, new applications can be built more quickly and more reliably. As improvements are made to base components and rolled into production, each new application can immediately benefit from the new refinements, while existing applications will not break.

COM: The Component Solution

COM is an object-based model, a specification and implementation that defines the interface between objects within a system. An object that conforms to the COM specification is considered a *COM object*. COM is a service to connect a client application to an object and its associated services. When the connection is established, COM drops out of the picture. It provides a standard method of finding and *instantiating* (creating) objects, and for the communication between the client and the component.

Under COM, the method to bring client and object together is independent of any programming language that created the app or object, as well as from the app itself. It provides a *binary interoperability standard,* versus a language-based standard. COM helps ensure that applications and objects that are created by different providers, often writing in different languages, can interoperate. As long as the objects support the standard COM interfaces and methods for data exchange, the implementation details within the component itself are irrelevant to the client.

COM Interfaces

Client applications interact with components through a common collection of function calls named *interfaces*. An interface is a public agreement between a service provider and a service requester about how to communicate. The interface defines only the calling syntax and the expected return values for the member function. There is no definition or even hint about how the services actually are implemented by the service provider object. The interfaces available within an object are made known to COM through the IUnknown object, which then makes them available to other applications.

Here are some key points to help you understand what a COM interface is and is not:

- **The interface is not a class.** A class defines the public and private functions and data within the object, as well as the implementation of those functions. The interface is a description of the public view of the class but has no implementation details.

- **The interface will not change.** Each time an interface is defined for an object, it creates a new public interface for the object. There is no inherent versioning. As each new service is added, an additional interface is added as well, with its own unique identifier. In this way, all previous interfaces always are available to a client program.

- **The interface does not define the object.** An object is defined by its class. The interface is a means, at a binary level, of letting a client and the component communicate via COM's introduction services.

- **The client sees only the interface.** When a client instantiates a COM object, it is returned a pointer to that object through which it can invoke its services. The private data of the object, along with its implementation, is hidden totally from the client application.

All COM objects must implement a generic interface known as IUnknown. This is the base interface of a COM object; the client uses it to—among other things—control the lifetime of the object that is being instantiated. It is the first interface pointer returned to the client. To find out what additional interfaces are supported by the object, the QueryInterface method of IUnknown is called using the initial IUnknown pointer. QueryInterface is called with a requested interface and returns a pointer to the new interface if it is implemented within the object.

QueryInterface must be implemented in all COM objects to support adding additional functionality to objects, without breaking existing applications expecting the original object; in effect, not requiring the client application to be recompiled. Through use of the QueryInterface, objects can simultaneously support multiple interfaces.

In Figure 5.1, you can see an example of how the interfaces supported by an object can grow over time, as well as how new interfaces don't break existing applications. In the top pane, you can see that the first version of the client is connected to the component's interface A. Later, a second version of the client also uses interface A. In the second pane, when the component is modified to add a new interface, the new client takes advantage of the newer functionality. Notice that the original client still is fully functional and using the original interface of the object. Powerful stuff, huh?

FIG. 5.1

An object's interfaces never change; they just add new ones.

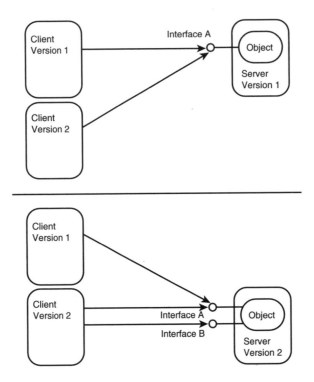

A New Versioning Scheme

Using a naming convention to ensure that all functions have unique names within an application is a perfectly viable solution to the name collision problem. Any name collisions within modules are caught by the compiler at runtime. In the object universe, where the object can live on a local computer or a remote host, the number of opportunities for getting the wrong object increase exponentially. To make sure that the correct object always is instantiated, COM uses globally unique identifiers (GUID).

Globally unique identifiers provide a method to ensure that each object residing on a system has a unique ID that identifies it. GUIDs are 128-bit integers generated by an algorithm that guarantees that they are unique at any given place and time in the world. The parameters to the function that determine the GUID are the machine's Internet address and the date and time that the function is called.

A COM Server

A COM Server is a piece of code that lets the COM service locator find and call upon it to enable the classes residing within the server to be instantiated. The servers can be implemented as a dynamic-link library (DLL) or as executables (.EXE).

The server must implement a *class factory* (IClassFactory) interface for each interface supported. The class factory is responsible for creating the object for the client. The general graphical syntax for expressing interfaces within servers is to portray an interface for an object as a socket or plug-in jack (a circle, sometimes shaded). The known interfaces are defined on the right or left side of the object, with the IUnknown interface coming out of the top of the server. Given this representation, Figure 5.2 shows the structure of a COM Server.

FIG. 5.2

A graphical illustration of the structure of a COM Server.

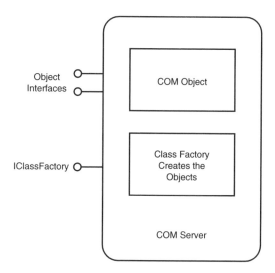

Server Types: In-Process and Out-of-Process

A server is implemented in relation to the context of the client using it. A server executes *in-process,* meaning within the address space of the client, or *out-of-process,* meaning in another process on the same or a different machine. These server types break into three conceptual types, as outlined here:

- **In-process server.** A server loaded into the address space of the client on the same machine. In the Windows environment, these are implemented as dynamic-link libraries. In other environments, the implementation will be different.

- **Local server.** An out-of-process server that executes its own process on the same machine as the client. The local server is implemented as an .EXE.

- **Remote server.** A server (of course, out-of-process) that executes on a machine other than the client. It can be implemented as a DLL or an .EXE.

During this discussion of COM Servers, think of them in terms of the objects they create instead of as the server itself. As far as the client knows, all of the objects are accessed through the function pointer to the object, whether in-process or out-of-process, on the same machine or a different one.

Because all function pointers are, by default, in the same process, all the COM objects accessed by the client are accessed in-process. If the object is in-process, the client connects directly to the object. If the client is on another machine, the client calling the object is a stub object created by COM; this, in turn, picks up a *remote procedure call* (RPC) from the "proxy" process on the client machine. The net result is that through COM, the client and the server believe they are dealing with in-process calls. This transparent access mechanism is illustrated in Figure 5.3.

FIG. 5.3

The client and server have location transparency within the COM model.

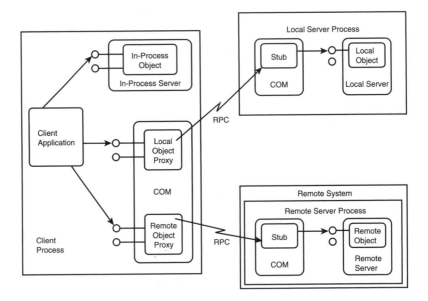

COM's Implementation of Inheritance

COM itself does not support the traditional method of inheritance and, for this reason, is considered by many object purists to be of little value. While working within the framework of object-oriented development, the inheritance mechanisms available under COM are *aggregation* and *containment/delegation*. Although they are not implementations of true inheritance based upon the definitions found in the earlier section "Understanding Inheritance," they do provide a framework for reaping some of the same reuse benefits.

In containment/delegation, there are two objects participating to fulfill a service request. One object, the outer object, becomes a client of the second object, the inner object. In effect, it passes the service call or reissues the method, from itself to the inner object to be fulfilled. The client of the outer object is not aware of this handoff, so encapsulation requirements are fulfilled in containment/delegation. The outer object, being a client of the inner object, accesses its services only through the COM interface, just like a normal client. The outer object *delegates* the fulfillment of the service to the inner object. So, although inheritance is not explicitly supported in COM, the capability to call the methods of the contained object provides similar functionality to calling the method of a base class from a subclassed object.

When using aggregation, the interfaces of the inner object are again exposed to the client application via IUnknown, but in this case, the client interacts directly with the inner object through an interface pointer to the inner object returned.

Controlling the Lifetime of COM Objects

There are two basic operations that all COM objects must support. The first, exposing and navigating between the interfaces provided by an object, was covered in the discussion on IUnknown and the QueryInterface member function in the earlier section "Com Interfaces." The second is a method to control an object's lifetime.

Speaking of an object's lifetime when that object is an in-process server is very different from discussing an object's lifetime in a heterogeneous, distributed environment. Because COM objects support multiple instances, there must be a way to ensure that all clients have completed their use of an object before it is destroyed. This is handled by using *reference counting* within the COM object.

During Active Server Pages development, you create objects and then release them when they are no longer needed. In C++ development, any memory that you dynamically allocate must be freed. If the memory associated with an object is not freed when all the object's users are done using it, you have what is called a *memory leak*. Now, if the memory taken up by the leak is only 1K per object, and you create one object a day, no big deal. But if you are in a transaction environment where you might perform thousands of transactions per hour, those leaks add up fast!

The same care that you take to free any objects that you create in ASP is also taken for objects within the environment by COM. Each COM object must implement the two IUnknown functions, AddRef and Release. These two functions are used to fulfill the reference-counting specification, as the mechanism to manage the object's life. Each time an object is instantiated, the reference count is incremented. It is decremented as clients implicitly call the release function. When the reference count eventually returns to zero, the Release function destroys the object.

Part

I

Ch

5

A Few Words About OLE

Over the years, many developers have been confused as OLE 1.0 came on the scene, followed by COM, and then OLE 2.0—which was totally different from OLE 1.0. There also has been much confusion over COM versus OLE—are they the same thing? Can one exist without the other?

OLE is a number of services and specifications that sit on top of the basic COM architecture and COM services. OLE version 2.0 is the first implementation of this extended COM specification.

As an Active Server Pages developer, you will be interested primarily in the custom services supported through the OLE specification. They include such services as OLE Documents, OLE Controls, OLE Automation, and drag-and-drop.

OLE acts as a facilitator for the integration of component objects into applications and into a system itself. OLE through COM provides an open, widely supported specification to enable developers to create component software. In the real world, the distinction between COM and OLE has become cloudy. Just remember that OLE is drawing on all of the basic object services that COM provides to standardize the next level within component development.

Distributed Computing

The movement away from monolithic computer architectures began with the coming of the first client/server revolution. There were a number of reasons why information technology managers were so enamored with the multi-tier architecture that client/server proposed. First, there was a logical division of work between the client, the business logic, and the database back end. The client would be responsible for data input and front-end validation, as well as the graphical user interface and display. The business logic tier would handle the process-specific validation and calculation and send and receive the appropriate data to/from the database server.

Breaking the application down into these logical pieces provided a number of benefits for the organization. First, as each tier was created, it could be tested independently. This made debugging much easier. Also, as the pieces were put together, the appropriate hardware could be selected for each tier. The capability to scale the application by splitting out processing across multiple machines also was a boon to rapidly growing enterprises.

As new applications were developed, the existing middle and back-end services often could be reused, again enhancing the speed at which new systems could be implemented. There were, however, a number of challenges faced in developing and managing these systems. The mechanisms for the tiers to interact (protocol, transaction format, and so on) often were proprietary and specific for a certain type of operating system. It was difficult—and often not worth the time and effort—to move pieces of functionality between the tiers when it made sense to do so.

For example, say that a key piece of data validation that is called hundreds of times per client session is bringing the application to its knees due to the network traffic getting to the remote tier. Ideally, you just pick up this validation functionality and place it closer to the clients, or even on the clients themselves. Sadly, in the current environment, this requires a recompilation of all the client code, as well as demands changes to the interface for the validation routines.

In an effort to leverage the multi-tier architecture that makes client/server computing so attractive, as well as to deal with the problems encountered during its use, Microsoft created the DCOM specification.

Distributed Objects: DCOM

To address the concerns and problems associated with traditional program development on the desktop, the COM specification was created. As you learned in the section "The Component Object Model," COM provides the architecture and mechanisms to create binary-compatible components that can be shared between applications. The goal of distributed computing in a component-based environment is to ensure that the components working on a local machine look the same to the client as on a remote machine. Distributed COM (DCOM) is built upon the foundations of COM, and just as OLE provides a new level of services for the desktop on top of COM, DCOM extends COM's component architecture across the enterprise.

One of DCOM's main goals is to provide to the enterprise the same reduction in complexity that COM and OLE provide in desktop development. For developers, this means not having to learn a new set of interfaces, because COM and DCOM share the same component model. The open, cross-platform support of COM and DCOM provides the mechanism to let objects reside anywhere within the enterprise, transparently accessible from the desktop or other component servers.

The location of the component providing the service must be transparent to the local machine. For example, consider the case of a client accessing a remote database. You can provide a service on the local machine that will connect to the remote database and then execute queries against that database. In this scenario, there are a number of things of which the client must be aware.

First, the client needs to know where the physical data resides. Second, the client needs a connection to the database. In most cases, this connection is permanent for the duration of the query session. This might not be a big concern when only one or two users are concurrently accessing the database, but when the application scales, hundreds or even thousands of connections can be a huge overhead burden on the database server. Finally, the client must "speak the language" of the connection that provides the link between client and database. The majority of a user's time on the client is spent performing local tasks, formatting the data, creating queries, or building charts. The actual time that the database connection is in use usually is very short, yet the server is carrying the overhead of that connection.

Take the example a step further and examine a typical corporate application. In a company that processes mortgages, there are applications with extensive calculations to perform risk analyses on potential customers. In a distributed application built upon component technology, the calculation engine is a component on a server. The component pulls a variety of information from legacy databases and then performs the calculations. As the business environment changes and new Federal laws are introduced, the calculations need to be modified. Due to its basis in COM, the DCOM calculation component is the only object that needs to be modified, leaving the data-entry and processing applications as they are. In working with the database, the DCOM object may maintain five or six concurrent connections to the database, or it might, in turn, connect to another DCOM object that handles all database interaction. In either case, as requests come in, the database service spins off a thread to handle the request on one of the available connections. In this way, hundreds of users can be supported with only a few concurrent connections to the database.

DCOM Architecture

DCOM is created as an extension to the Component Object Model. As stated, COM provides a specification and mechanism to let clients and objects connect to other objects. When COM objects run outside the process of the client, COM provides the interprocess communication

Part

I

Ch

5

methods between the objects in a transparent fashion. When the interprocess communication takes place across a network, DCOM steps in to replace the interprocess communication with a network protocol.

DCOM Benefits

There are a number of benefits gained from using DCOM that are inherited directly from COM and fall out when the two new technologies are used in concert. A few of the more impressive benefits are outlined next.

Component Reuse   The client and the server under COM believe that they are running in the same process. A COM object originally created to perform services on a client desktop can be moved easily to perform the same functions on a server. DCOM provides the transparent access between the objects running on different machines. This lets the objects live in relation to each other in the most appropriate place, and as that place changes over time, they can be moved quickly to other locations.

Language Neutrality   DCOM has effectively inherited all of the benefits of the binary compatibility specification of COM. As new COM objects are created in a variety of languages, they can be scaled immediately for distributed performance under DCOM.

Scalability   When the same system can support one or hundreds of users, it is said to be scalable. Scalability refers to the ability to scale, increase or decrease, the number of users on the system without affecting the application's performance.

Say that you have just created a new COM component-based application that includes a user interface, a business rules logic, a transaction manager, and a database services component. This is amazing for a number of reasons, the first of which is that you currently are unemployed. Second, all of the COM components are running on the same machine. Next week, you decide to start your own business in the garage, and your application is up and running. Business picks up, and you hire four people to use the new system to keep up with demand. To allow all the new workers to use the same database, you move the (now shared) database access component to another server (which happens to be where the database lives). You don't have to change the client application at all (location independence). A few months later, business takes off further, and you find that all your business logic—which is quite complex—takes forever to process on your client machines. You go out, purchase a nice SMP box, and move the logic component to that box. Once again, there is no need to recompile any code. You just change the DCOM configuration on the clients, and *voilá*! You are back in business.

This scenario could be followed by your meteoric rise and the phenomenal growth of your company (and the continued scaling of your application)—we think you get the idea. The point to remember is that you can take a component-based application that resides on one box and split it across multiple machines.

From Here...

You spent this chapter learning about object models, COM, and distributed computing. You now can use this information as you begin to develop applications in the Active Server Pages environment. All of Part III is devoted to examining and showing you how to use all of the components that ship with ASP. Here's what you can look forward to in the chapters on the ASP objects:

- Chapter 10, "Managing States and Events with *Application* and *Session* Objects," examines how these objects let you track and manipulate user sessions within your scripts.

- Chapter 12, "Enhancing Interactivity with *Cookies*, Headers, and the *Server* Object," teaches you how to use the Server Object. You begin the exciting process of dynamically creating instances of server components.

- Chapter 14, "Constructing Your Own Server Components," shows you how to build your own COM objects for integration into your ASP applications.

Part

I

Ch

5

Programming Active Server Pages with VBScript

Integrating VBScript into HTML

The history of the BASIC language is a good place to start when putting VBScript and Active Server Pages development into perspective. The Beginners All Purpose Symbolic Instruction Code, more commonly known as BASIC, was developed in 1964 at Dartmouth College by Kenney and Kurtz. It was initially designed to provide students with an easy to understand procedural language, which would be a stepping stone to more powerful languages like FORTRAN. In the intervening 30+ years, a great deal has happened to this introductory computer language. ∎

The Microsoft BASIC story

A brief look at the history of the BASIC language, and Microsoft's role in its development.

Understanding the Visual Basic family tree

We take a brief look at the Visual Basic Family of Tools.

Examining scripting and HTML

This is our first look at how scripting looks within an HTML file, and how the two integrate to create dynamic content.

Understanding client versus server scripting

Scripts can be executed at the client, on the server, or on both ends of the connection.

Looking at other scripting languages

VBScript, while the default scripting language of Active Server, is not the only option for ASP script development.

A Brief History of Microsoft's BASIC Languages

The language has grown and become more feature-rich over the years due mainly to its vast acceptance in the marketplace. To understand the evolution of the BASIC language and how it has become the default language of Active Server Pages scripting, we begin our story in 1975 when a young man named Bill Gates was attending Harvard. Attracted by an article about the forthcoming M.I.T.S. Altair computer, Paul Allen and Bill Gates developed a version of BASIC that would run on the Altair and was eventually licensed to M.I.T.S. for its Altair computer. When version 2.0 was released later that same year, it was available in two versions, a 4K and an 8K. Imagine the entire development system implemented in 4,096 bytes! Today, you would be hard-pressed to find a Microsoft Word template that is that small. Basic was the first product ever sold by Microsoft. Two years later, after porting their version of BASIC to other platforms (CP/M, for example) the exclusive license with M.I.T.S. for Microsoft Basic ended. In 1979, Microsoft released MS-Basic for the 8086, a 16-bit product.

Bill Gates won the opportunity to provide the operating system for the new IBM personal computer after IBM's courting of Digital Research Inc. to license its CP/M operating system failed. Microsoft licensed the SCP-DOS operating system and modified it to run on the IBM-PC. The MS-DOS operating system version 1.0, bundled with MS-BASIC was the engine driving the beginning of the personal computer revolution.

Over the years, Microsoft saw how attractive BASIC was and created a compiler for the language in the form of QuickBasic. QuickBasic reigned supreme until version 4.5, when it was replaced with PDS Basic (Professional Development System).

We had no idea in that spring of 1991 that many of our lives were going to change so dramatically. Visual Basic was announced at the Windows World '91 conference on May 20, 1991. The Visual Basic environment was to provide graphical application development and an integrated debugger and to create compiled executable windows programs, all using the BASIC language. Many Windows developers still remember the first time that they used Visual Basic version 1.0. After thrashing their way though learning the ins and outs of the C language and building Windows applications with Microsoft C and the SDK, they couldn't believe the power inherent in this innocuous little visual development package.

Visual Basic for Windows was followed by Visual Basic for DOS. When the DOS version came out, there were (and still are) many programmers with DOS machines in our companies. The DOS version of VB addressed the RAD methodology on the DOS platform. Even though the product never made it past version 1.0, it was a useful tool for creating graphical applications for the DOS environment.

By the time Visual Basic version 4.0 was released in 1995, countless numbers of programmers were hooked on the Visual Basic development environment. It's easy learning curve, intuitive interface, and bundled components, combined with incredible extensibility and its tightly integrated environment make it the logical choice for millions of developers each day.

The Visual Basic Family Tree

As you learned in the preceding section, getting from the M.I.T.S to Visual Basic for Windows took some time. In the last few years, the Visual Basic family has been very fruitful (and has multiplied). In the next several sections, you will take a look at the various incarnations of the Visual Basic language as it is available today and develop a greater appreciation for the differences and similarities in the VB family. The family portrait is found in Figure 6.1. More specifically, for all of you Visual Basic programmers out there (VB or VBA), we will take a good look at what VBScript leaves in, and more importantly, leaves out.

FIG. 6.1
Each member of the VB family has an important role to play.

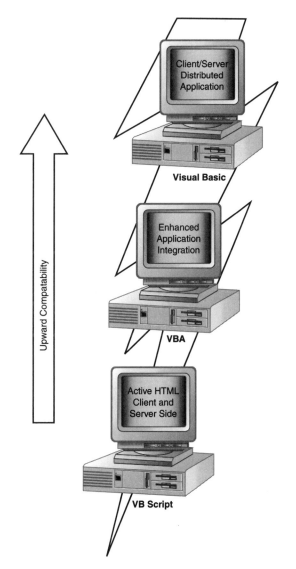

Visual Basic

The Visual Basic programming tool is a professional development environment suitable for developing multi-tier, enterprise level, client/server applications. Its inherent extensibility in the form of supporting OLE and ActiveX controls and its capability to integrate WIN32 API calls, as well as third-party DLLs provide a rich environment for creating applications.

Visual Basic is used by millions of programmers all over the world. It is used mainly for personal and corporate application development, but in the past few years, commercial applications that were developed in VB have been showing up in the market place.

The current version of VB is 4.0 and is available in three packages: standard, professional, and enterprise. The standard package is ideal for the computer hobbyist or student. It provides all of the base functionality without including (in the price or the package) a number of custom controls that are appropriate for larger-scale development. Moving up to the Professional addition provides additional custom controls, the capability to interact directly with databases (not requiring data-bound controls), and the capability to create remote automation servers. The professional and enterprise offerings differ only in their capability to provide remote data objects. The professional version is suitable for many corporate application development needs, while the enterprise edition also integrates Microsoft's Visual Source Safe, a source code management and team development tool.

In December, Microsoft made the Visual Basic Control Creation Edition available for download from its Web site **http://www.microsoft.com**. VB CCE is a new version of Visual Basic that provides a first look at some of the features that will show up in Visual Basic 5.0. The remarkable thing about VB CCE is that it can create ActiveX controls, which you can integrate into your Web applications on the client and server side.

As the Visual Basic product continues to mature, it will remain the tool of choice for millions of developers to create robust, scalable, multi-tier applications. With the introduction of Microsoft's Active Server framework and its middleware transaction processing product, code-named Viper, Visual Basic will come to the forefront as the tool for creating the client side of the next generation of corporate and commercial applications.

Visual Basic for Applications

Visual Basic for Applications, or VBA as it is more commonly known, is a powerful subset of the Visual Basic environment. Microsoft released, at the end 1996, VBA version 5.0. The company has integrated VBA across the entire Office 97 applications suite. It has also made it available to third-party developers for inclusion within their applications. At this year's Fall Comdex computer show, over 40 companies were showing their products with an integrated VBA programming engine. As of the printing of November's second week *ComputerWorld*, an additional 60 third-parties had signed up to integrate VBA into their products.

VBA is a shared development environment within the hosting application, including an integrated code editor and support for debugging. With its support for OLE automation, it is often used as an integrating tool to create custom applications from within Word, Excel, or Access.

Any application that exposes its objects as OLE or ActiveX controls can be used by VBA developers. Many of the familiar tools from the Visual Basic IDE also have made it into VBA 5.0. Features such as the code window, project explorer, properties window, and the object browser make the VBA environment very similar to its bigger sibling.

In the Office 97 products, as well as other products that host VBA 5.0, users will have access to Microsoft Forms, creating a development environment with the same forms metaphor as Visual Basic. Because all VBA 5.0 applications share the same forms environment, any form object created in one application can be used by any other application. This tight integration and code reusability make VBA the language of choice for embedded programming engines.

The wonderful thing about VBA is that you can learn the language from within one application or environment, and it is immediately transferable to (what will soon be) hundreds of other products. In addition, you can easily scale up to the complete Visual Basic environment or move down to create powerful Inter/intranet applications with VBScript and Active Server Pages. For anyone wanting to choose the best environment for learning to develop with VB within an application environment, VBA is an excellent choice.

Visual Basic Scripting Edition

The scripting edition of Visual Basic is a smaller subset of the Visual Basic for Applications language. It is intended for use in Inter/intranet application development and is currently supported in Microsoft Internet Explorer version 3.0 and above. It brings much of the power and flexibility of the Visual Basic language to the Internet and intranet. On the client side, there is the opportunity to interact with ActiveX controls to provide active and interesting content. On the server side, the scripting language is used and integrated within HTML to provide a new level of functionality and ease of use in Web site development.

For VB or VBA programmers, the transition to Active Server Pages development using VBScript from a traditional client/server environment will be less a challenge of learning the idiosyncrasies of a sister language than a challenge of changing to the new net development paradigm. Programming in any language consists of expressions, statements, and procedures. The trick is to figure out how the language integrates with the environment in which it will be implemented. In the case of VB or VBA, the environment is the Windows operating system.

VBScript, on the other hand, will be implemented on the client, using ActiveX controls, as well as on the server in ASP, integrating a variety of components to create dynamic pages. You will be dealing with, not only the scripting language, but also its integration into HTML code. At first, having your code in pieces throughout the HTML page will take some getting used to. But, just as it was a struggle to master the VB IDE, you will master VBScript and Active Server Pages development.

If you are coming to Active Server Pages development from a strictly HTML background, you also will have a learning curve to climb. If you have been developing Perl or REXX scripts, the language features of VBScript will not be that foreign to you. Also, you have been used to adding additional tags as the HTML standard emerges. You can treat VBScript and the associated implementation as just some additional tags to integrate. But, be sure to utilize the new components that ship with Active Server Pages. This powerful set of ASP components include such features as session and application management, and database connectivity. It would be very easy to use VBScript for some minor chores and revert back to the old CGI way of doing things for database access and other local processing tasks. Learning to use the VBScript language and its associated ASP components will be worth it. You don't have to rely on my word; just check out the hundreds of Active Server Pages sites that are already in production (including at Microsoft) even though as of this writing, the product is still in Beta!

▶ **See** "*Application* and *Session* Objects" for more information about Active Server Pages components, **p. 187**

Feature Set and Limitations in VBScript

I know that you are really looking forward now to a huge table filled with each and every difference between the lovable VB language syntax and VBScript. Well, we must apologize; we just couldn't bring ourselves to create that beast. What you are going to find in the next few pages is a list of some of the most important, or widely used functions that your typical Visual Basic developer might immediately miss. This is not going to be an exhaustive coverage. Just the facts Ma'am. If you must have the complete list, line by line, of the differences between VBA and VBScript, please refer to the VBScript documentation that ships with Active Server Pages.

Array Handling   Arrays are useful in hundreds of situations, and when you can have an array of objects, that number jumps again. Many times it is useful to change the base of an array variable for a specific implementation. For example, if we were to create an array representing the days in February, it would make sense to start the array at 1 and go to 28. This is not possible in VBScript. All arrays must have a lower bound of zero. The same is true of multidimensional arrays: all lower bounds begin at zero. This doesn't affect the performance at all; you just need to remember to get to element *n*, and always subtract 1. So, in VBScript, your February array index would go from 0 to 27.

Collections and Classes These are two of the most cherished features in the most recent release of Visual Basic. The addition of classes to the Visual Basic language enables us to get that much closer to fully supporting object-oriented development. You will not be able to create a user-defined collection within VBScript. You also will be unable to create a class. If you do want to add functionality within a class, create the class in Visual Basic and then create an OLE component. You can then create an instance of the class from within an Active Server Pages script using the `CreateObject` syntax. There are a number of collections that you will find within the Active Server Pages environment, and you will treat them as you would in Visual Basic: walking the collection, setting items, and so on; you just can't create your own.

Conversion   There are a number of conversion functions that are supported in VBScript. The most glaring omission is the `Format` command. This is the one command that will surely be missed the most. We understand that this is on the list for inclusion in the next release of VBScript.

Data Types   No intrinsic data types are found in VBScript. The only data type available is the `Variant`, which makes complete sense considering that VBScript is an OLE-implemented language. All passing of values between OLE objects is performed through `Variant` variables.

▶ **See** "Creating Your Server Component" for more information about creating your own components for use within VBScript, **p. 273**

▶ **See** "Understanding VBScript Data Types" for more information about data types and variants, **p. 122**

Dynamic Data Exchange   This venerable method of inter-process communication was the forerunner of OLE. I remember using DDE last year to interface with a software program controlling a PLC (programmable logic controller) to create a hydraulic pump testing system. Given the built-in support of OLE objects, DDE is not supported in any form in VBScript. This is a feature that could potentially, if included, violate the integrity of the client machine. Imagine a script that runs during startup and via DDE looks for the windows explorer, finds it, and then sends messages telling it to format your hard drive!

Dynamic Link Library Support   One of the features of Visual Basic that makes the product so extensible is the capability to declare and call functions within Dynamic Link Libraries (DLL). This feature provides you with the method to call any of the Win32 API functions and a host of other functions available in third party DLLs. Although many of the functions in DLLs are now available as OCX/ActiveX controls, there are many that you might have created over the years that you still wish to use. You have a few options: First, port the DLL to an ActiveX object. Next, if you don't have the source or are not wanting to change the DLL, you can wrap the DLL's functions within a VB class and then create an OLE Server for use in your ASP scripts.

Debugging Support   One of the nicest things about VB is its integrated development environment (IDE). You could debug your application line by line, changing variable values on-the-fly. There is no IDE for VBScript and Active Server Pages development (yet) and no support for the Debug.Print, End or Stop commands. Once again, you can build a simple component to provide the Debug.Print functionality very easily. On the client side, Microsoft just released in December the "Microsoft Script Debugger for Internet Explorer," which enables interactive debugging of scripts executing within Internet Explorer client. This free download is available from Microsoft at **http://www.microsoft.com/workshop/prog/scriptie**.

Error Handling   There is error handling available when developing ASP applications. The familiar On Error Resume Next command is still available, although branching on errors is not. You also have access to the Err object to retrieve error numbers and descriptions. When an error occurs in your .asp scripts, error messages are sent back as HTML to the client, and depending on their severity, can also be written to the IIS log and the NT Server log.

File Input/Output   All of the language features that enable access to local files (File I/O) on the system in which an application is running have been removed from VBScript to enhance the security of the language on the Inter/intranet. This prevents an errant VBScript program executing on a browser from damaging data on the client machine.

User-Defined Types   The last, and my favorite, feature of VB that is not included within VBScript is the capability to create user-defined types. There is no better construct for dealing with database and transaction-oriented data than the user-defined type. It will be sorely missed.

The Last Word   There are a number of features that are not yet or never will be available in VBScript. As the language is deployed and continues to mature, those features that are most requested and do not violate the security constraints will be added to the language. There are two main reasons why VBScript must be a smaller subset of VBA—security and size.

The VBScript code will be executing on the client and the server systems. If the VBScript code had access to the native file system on the computer that it was running, it could potentially wreak havoc with the data contained within. Imagine pulling up a new page and having your hard drive mysteriously formatted, or having key files destroyed. Just as we safeguard our computers with virus protection programs, Microsoft has safeguarded your browser by limiting the functionality of the VBScript language.

The second reason VBScript must be a subset is the "weight" of the language. This is a language designed for use over the Internet and intranet. If you end up shipping the OLE scripting engine over the net to fulfill a request, you want to ensure that the language is relatively small to minimize the transfer time.

Regardless of the real or perceived shortcomings within the VBScript language, there is nothing better or more powerful for creating and implementing dynamic content over the net, using Active Server Pages.

When executing code on the server, security is not as big an issue. Assume for the moment that any component you build will not damage the machine. With that said, any functionality that is missing in the VBScript language that you require can be easily added by creating an OLE component. Because VBScript can create an instance of any OLE or ActiveX component, it is easy to provide the native VB functionality to your server side VBScript Active Server Pages.

▶ **See** "Constructing Your Own Server Components" for more information about creating your own components, **p. 267**

Scripting and HTML

A script is composed of a series of commands that will be executed by the host environment, meaning that scripts will be executed on the client or on the server. Active Server Pages contain scripts that execute within the client browser as well as the server. Within a script, you can perform a variety of activities such as:

- Create a variable and assign a value to it.
- Perform operations upon variables.
- Group commands into callable blocks of code called procedures.
- Dynamically create client side scripts from the server.

The scripts within an ASP page are passed to a scripting engine within the client or server environment. A scripting engine is a Component Object Model (COM) object that is called to process the script. Within the scripting engine, the script is parsed, checked for syntax, and then interpreted. The resulting actions, deciphered by the interpreter, are then performed within the host environment. Because the scripting engine in the Active Server Pages environment is a COM object, you can add additional scripting engines to support multiple scripting languages. Support for VBScript and Java Script are bundled with Active Server Pages.

Script Delimiters

Within an HTML file, we use delimiters around tags to tell the client that we are requesting an HTML tag, not just text to be displayed. We also need delimiters to let the host environment know that there is scripting within the page. The scripting delimiters that wrap around our scripting are <% and %>. Text within the script delimiters will be processed within the host environment before the page is executed. Here are a few examples of how the script with delimiters looks within your ASP page:

```
<HTML>
<HEAD>
<TITLE>Scripting in HTML</TITLE>
</HEAD>
<BODY>
<P>We will now create a variable, assign a value to it and then <BR>
➥display the value of the variable within our page</P>
<% strName ="steve" %>
<P>We have created a script variable called strName and have<BR>
➥assigned a value to it. The value is <%=strName%> </P>
</BODY>
</HTML>
```

Notice that we can intersperse scripting commands almost anywhere in our .asp file. The script expression is evaluated, and the resulting value is inserted into the HTML file sent to the client. Within the first set of scripting delimiters, you create a variable strName and assign the value of steve to it, using the equal sign to perform the assignment. When we want to display the value of the variable on the client, we again use the equal sign to place the value into the HTML file =strName.

Scripting Statements

When you create variables or put single values inline in an .asp file, it is referred to as a *single expression*. Single expressions are bits and pieces of code that resolve to a value. Statements, on the other hand, are complete logical units that perform one type of action. An example of a statement can be shown using the If statement:

```
<%
If Time > #8:00:00AM# and Time < #5:00:00PM# Then
    strMessage= "Get Back to Work!"
Else
    strMessage = "You should be at home, resting."
End If
%>
<P> Sir or Madam, <%=strMessage%> </P>
```

Imagine the poor unsuspecting office worker who happens to pull up this page during the day from the corporate intranet. If the time is between 8:00 AM and 5:00 PM, he will get a

Part
II

Ch

6

Dilbert-style management command. Any other time, he will be reminded that there are much better places to be than at work. Now, I know that many of us are not fortunate enough to have a standard 8 to 5 job (and who really wants one anyway?), but it remains a good example of a scripting statement within HTML code.

▶ **See** "Variables 101: The Basics" for more information about Variables, **p. 122**

▶ **See** "Conditional Processing" for more information about statements and program flow, **142**

Scripting Blocks

Just as you enclose tables and forms in beginning and ending tags, you encode script blocks in beginning and ending tags as well. Using the `<SCRIPT>` and `</SCRIPT>` tags notifies the host environment to expect a block of scripting code within the tags. By using these tags, you can create procedures that can be called from anywhere within the page. A procedure is just a number of scripting commands that are grouped together to perform a specific function. If you try to define a procedure within script delimiters alone, you will generate syntax errors.

Now, combine the last two topics just discussed, scripting languages and procedures, and take a look at some scripting code in action. You are going to create two simple procedures, one in VBScript and one in Java Script that will be invoked within the same page. For now, don't worry too much about the scripting syntax; just try to get a feel for how the scripting is integrated into the ASP page. First, create the VBScript procedure:

```
<SCRIPT LANGAUGE=VBScript RUNAT=Server>
Sub vbwrite
    response.write("Hello from VBScript")
End Sub
</SCRIPT>
```

Now here is the Java Script procedure that will be invoked next:

```
<SCRIPT LANGAUGE=JavaScript RUNAT=Server>
Sub jwrite
    response.write("Hello from JavaScript")
End Sub
</SCRIPT>
```

Putting it all together with a little HTML results in:

```
<HTML><HEAD><TITLE>Mixing Scripts</TITLE></HEAD><BODY>
<P>First we have output from VBScript</P>
<% Call vbwrite %>
<P>Now from JScript</P>
<% Call jwrite %>
</BODY></HTML>
```

The VBScript and Java Script scripting languages are functionally equivalent and share much of the same syntax. If you start using other scripting languages like Perl or REXX, you will find that they are quite different in syntax than VBScript or Java Script, but retain the same programming constructs. But, if you are a crack Perl or REXX developer and want to make the transition to Active Server Pages development without learning a new language, you are in luck. Because the scripting engine is a COM object, which is called to process a file under ASP, you can integrate a Perl or REXX script processor into Active Server Pages.

Notice in the preceding example that we used an additional attribute of the <SCRIPT> tag, RUNAT. This attribute determines where the script is executed, and it is a nice transition into the next topics, the primary scripting language and client-side and server-side scripting.

Procedures are an ideal way to create logical units of functionality that can be called from within your Active Server Pages script. To reach the next level of functionality and to provide a medium for code reuse, ASP provides the capability to include code from another source file into an ASP script. This capability is called Server-Side Includes, and is a syntax used to insert the contents of one file into another.

This include capability is a familiar one to C and C++ developers who have been including header files since the day they began application development. Still, this simple feature adds an additional level of functionality to Active Server Pages. For example, if we had a great procedure in a file called grtproc.htm and wanted to add the procedure to our new file, we would use the Server-Side Include syntax as follows:

```
<!--#INCLUDE FILE="grtproc.htm"-->
```

Now you could call the great procedure in grtproc.htm in your new .asp file.

▶ **See** "Using Server-Side Includes" for more information about Server-Side Includes, **p. 168**

Changing the Primary Scripting Language

Embedding scripting within your ASP pages, using only the scripting delimiters, is referred to as primary scripting. The code in primary scripting is executed against the default scripting engine for the page. In Active Server Pages development, the default scripting engine is VBScript. You can select a different scripting language for a page or block of script within a page by setting the <SCRIPT> tag as follows:

```
<SCRIPT LANGUAGE=JavaScript>
```

This code line will notify the host that the script within the page uses Java Script syntax.

You can also mix multiple scripting languages within a page by changing the scripting language tags within the page itself:

```
<SCRIPT LANGUAGE=JavaScript>
...Java Script Code Here
</SCRIPT>
<SCRIPT LANGAUGE=VBScript>
...VBScript Code Here
</SCRIPT>
```

Client-Side Scripting

Client-side scripting refers to the scripts that are interpreted and executed in the client browser. When you are scripting for the client, you have access to the object model available

Part
II
Ch
6

within the browser. You will also create scripts to interact with user interface objects on the client.

There are a number of tools available to create client-side pages and their associated scripting. The ActiveX Control Pad is a good example of such tools. This Microsoft developed, freely available product enables you to design Web pages, adding ActiveX controls and standard HTML fields at design time. The program then generates the HTML code to create the page. After the page has been created, you can edit the file and add scripting to provide such client-side features as field validation, custom responses to user actions, and a host of other capabilities inherent in the client's browser. The ActiveX Control Pad can be found at **http://www.microsoft.com.**

As mentioned previously, the opportunity for field validation of data at the client is an important feature of client-side scripting. You can have the page validate the data *before* it is sent to the server. This ensures that you will not receive a message immediately back from the server requesting you to provide complete, or correct, information. In addition to providing validation errors more quickly to the user, this also can reduce network traffic. In the following example, you create a simple page that contains a field that you will validate.

```
<HTML>
<HEAD>
<TITLE>Scripting in HTML</TITLE>
</HEAD>
<BODY>
    Enter a Value <INPUT TYPE=INPUT NAME=TxtField SIZE=20>
    <INPUT TYPE=BUTTON VALUE="Submit" NAME="BtnSubmit">
```

You have now created an input field of name TxtField and have created a button to submit the page. You now create an event that executes when the BtnSubmit button is clicked.

```
<SCRIPT LANGUAGE=VBScript>
<!--
    Option Explicit
    Dim bValid

    Sub BtnSubmit_OnClick
        bValid = True
        Call CheckField(TxtField.Value, "Please enter a value in the field.")
        If bValid Then
            MsgBox "Thank you for filling in the field"
        End If
    End Sub
```

> **CAUTION**
>
> Although the default language of Active Server Pages is VBScript, in the Internet Explorer (IE), it is not. If you do not explicitly state LANGUAGE=VBScript, the default language in IE, JavaScript generates errors within your pages.

The first line is the script tag that you learned about in the section "Scripting Blocks."

This script tag lets Internet Explorer know that we are preparing to provide scripting instructions using the VBScript language. The next notable section is the procedure created to respond to the click on the BtnSubmit button. Notice the syntax OnClick makes perfect sense, and should be very familiar to you if you have any VB development experience, where the procedure would be named BtnSubmit_Click. This is the procedure that we want to execute when the button is clicked. The script then checks the field to see if it has a value in it. If so, the field information will be sent to the server. If not, the user sees a message to input an appropriate field value.

```
Sub CheckField(ByVal strFieldValue, ByVal strMessage)
      If strFieldValue = "" Then
         MsgBox strMessage, 0
         bValid = False
      End If
   End Sub
-->
</Script>
</BODY>
</HTML>
```

This last bit of code is the procedure that implements the field validation. Notice that we are only checking for any text entered in the field. We could have written a more involved procedure that could check for a range of values or convert the values to all upper- or lowercase. For now, don't worry too much about the syntax of VBScript (the rest of this section is devoted to that). You should just begin to get a feel for how the client scripting is integrated into the HTML code.

When you create a page with scripting and define procedures within script tags, the default RUNAT (where the script will execute) is the client. So, any scripting that you include within the scripting tags without specifying the RUNAT attribute will execute on the client.

Server-Side Scripting

Now we get to the meat and potatoes of our scripting discussion. Server-side scripting occurs when the scripts within the page are executed at the server, before the page is ever sent to the client browser, as shown in Figure 6.2. This is an incredibly important distinction. It means that the server is responsible for generating the HTML that is ultimately sent to the client. You do not have to worry about the client connecting to a database, reading from a file, querying an online service, or any of the thousands of other actions that take place on the server to fulfill the client request.

Active Server Pages provides server-side scripting for the Internet Information Server Web server. In addition to enabling custom scripting to be developed, you can also integrate almost any ActiveX component (that doesn't require a user interface, of course) into your server scripts. This opens the door wide and enables a level of functionality that was difficult, if not impossible, to achieve with traditional methods of server-side processing.

Part
II

Ch
6

FIG. 6.2
Active Server Pages
scripts execute on the
server before passing
the page to the client.

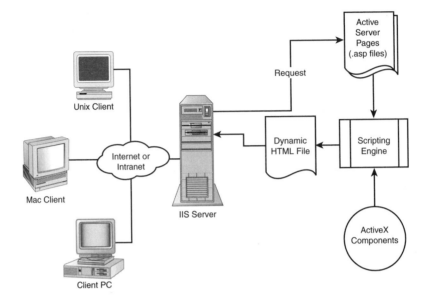

Server-side scripting blocks are executed at the server when the ASP interpreter finds the scripting tag with the RUNAT attribute set to SERVER. In code, it looks like this:

```
<LANGUAGE=VBScript RUNAT=SERVER>
```

When an Active Server Pages page is requested, the server will call ASP. The .asp file is read through from top to bottom. Any scripting that needs to execute on the server is performed, and then the dynamically created HTML page is sent back to the client.

Notice that the code in the CheckField subroutine creates a message box to respond to user input. If you were to mistakenly add the RUNAT=SERVER to the client code, the message box would never be shown on the client because at the server, there is no interface to show a message box upon. But, what you could do at the server is generate custom messages based upon the time of day, or based upon data in a database and pop those messages in the client browser when the validation takes place. You can do this by dynamically generating client-side scripts from the server.

Modifying Client Scripts from the Server

When we create Active Server Pages applications, we are normally interested in creating dynamic content for our clients to view. We do this by interacting with ActiveX components and databases and even legacy systems to provide dynamic, up-to-date information.

One of the more exciting aspects of this capability to create dynamic HTML content is the capability to create client-side scripting on-the-fly. In essence, we are dynamically creating scripting, based on server information and embedding it in the HTML page that we return to the client. These dynamically created scripts will then be executed on the client's browser.

The more you think about this capability, the more situations you will think of to use this powerful new functionality. You can create custom on_load events that are invoked when the page is loaded on to the client. You can also dynamically create scripts that respond to user events on the client.

Currently, there are a lot of pages out there full of VBScript and Java Script. The problem with them is that once they are created and posted to the net, you cannot do anything to change them without editing the source file. Now, using Active Server Pages, you can prepare scripting variables on the server side to be used by the client. For example, say that you want to create a VBScript array for use on the client with real-time information stored in a legacy system. Today, that would be problematic at best. Using server-side scripting, you can query the legacy system using a database access component and then populate the array before returning the page to the client. In another scenario, you could have custom client-side validation scripts generated by the server, based upon external values stored in a database.

When an Active Server Pages script is run, ASP processes any commands within a comment block with the scripting tags <% and %>, regardless of where they are within the script. In the following code, the server-side script will be executed within ASP, even though the script resides in a scripting block which has no RUNAT=SERVER parameter.

```
<SCRIPT LANGUAGE=VBScript>
<!--
    <% server side scripting commands %>
-->
</SCRIPT>
```

In the following example, the server script will create three VBScript subroutines which will subsequently execute on the client machine.

```
<HTML><HEAD><TITLE>Client Side Scripting From The Server</TITLE></HEAD>
<BODY>
<%
    tmeServerTime = Now
    For i = 1 to 3
%>
<SCRIPT LANGUAGE=VBScript>
<!--
    Sub Server_Time_<%=i%>()
        MsgBox "The time at the server is <%=tmeServerTime%>" _
               & " on pass <%=i%>"
    End Sub
    Server_Time_<%=i%>()
-->
</SCRIPT>
<%="Server side loop " & i & "<BR>"%>
<%
    Next
%>
</BODY>
</HTML>
```

Part
II

Ch
6

When you execute this code in your browser and look at the source, you will see three VBScript procedures named `Server_Time_1`, `Server_Time_2` and `Server_Time_3`. Each of these procedures was generated dynamically from the execution of the ASP script on the server. While this is a simplistic example, you should get a sense of the power of this ASP capability. "Thanks" to Dave Kaplin at Microsoft for the explanation of this powerful feature in a thread from the Denali list server.

The question you are probably wanting to ask is "Where do I put what?" meaning how do you decide what scripts should execute on the client and which on the server. The answer is that most of the client procedures will usually deal with data validation. All of the other procedures, accessing data, communicating with host systems, will take place within the server-side scripts. There is no hard and fast rule. Experience is the best teacher in this case.

> **CAUTION**
>
> Remember that all browsers do not support VBScript, or scripting at all. If you want to provide client-side scripting, be sure to interrogate the Browser Capability object to see which scripting language is supported. You can then return the appropriate client side scripts.

Java Script, REXX, and Other Scripting Languages

As discussed in the section "Changing the Primary Scripting Language," the default language of Active Server Pages is VBScript. Java Script is also supported by ASP "out-of-the-box." The OLE object model for scripting engines, which Active Server Pages supports, enables you to easily integrate other scripting languages and their associated engines into ASP.

The ability to host a variety of languages within the Active Server Pages environment is an incredibly powerful feature. If you are a developer with years of experience generating Perl scripts, there is no need to forgo all of that valuable knowledge. You can immediately become productive in ASP development. As you begin to learn VBScript or JScript you will be able to incorporate additional features such as dynamic client-side scripting.

REXX is one of the most widely used scripting/macro languages in existence today. It is available on platforms ranging from OS/2 to the AS/400 to the mainframe. There are even versions of REXX implemented today as visual languages. VisPro/REXX is one such example of a visual REXX environment. This OS/2 application provides an easy to use and incredibly powerful visual development metaphor, leveraging the REXX language. For more information about VisPro/REXX, point your browser to **http://www.vispro.com**.

For the countless REXX developers working in development today, the ability to plug a REXX scripting engine into Active Server Pages once again opens the gates wide to let the greatest number of people maximize their Inter/intranet development.

Selecting a Scripting Language for a Page

For those languages that follow the `Object.Method` syntax and use parentheses to enclose the procedure parameters, add the selected language using the LANGUAGE tag. The syntax of the LANGUAGE tag is:

```
<% @ LANGUAGE = ScriptingLanguage %>
```

Be sure to add this tag as the first line in your .asp file. If you want to change the default scripting language of all .asp pages, you will need to change the value of the `DefaultScriptLanguage` entry found in the NT registry to the new script type.

For languages that do not conform to the `Object.Method` syntax, you must add a registry key with the corresponding language name and value to the ASP\LanguageEngines registry entry. For more information on adding these types of scripting languages, see the "Using Scripting Languages" reference in the Active Server Pages documentation.

From Here...

In this chapter, you have had your first taste of the way in which scripting and HTML are integrated within an .asp file to create dynamic content within a Web page. You have looked at the Visual Basic family and discovered its humble roots. You have also received an introduction to the major ways in which scripting and HTML can be united to form a greater whole.

In the remainder of this section, there are a number of chapters that cover the nuts and bolts of VBScript development. We have chosen to focus on VBScript over Java Script because VBScript is the native language of Active Server Pages. Also, for those of you coming to ASP development without the benefit of having worked with Visual Basic or VBA, you will get a good foundation of the shared language syntax and constructs that enable you to easily and quickly use the VBA or VB tools.

Here is what you can look forward to in the rest of this section:

- Chapter 7, "Understanding Variable Typing, Naming, and Scoping," explains why variables are the building blocks of your applications. You will see all the ins and outs of variable usage in VBScript.

- Chapter 8, "Working with Program Flow and Control Structures," explores the constructs and control structures that provide conditional processing, looping, and testing of the variables and data that reside within your ASP applications.

- Chapter 9, "Calling Procedures: Functions and Subroutines," provides the foundation for logically grouping functions within your application. You will learn about subroutines and functions and be provided with a methodology to create efficient and reusable procedures.

Part

II

Ch

6

Understanding Variable Typing, Naming, and Scoping

Learning how variables work in your code

Variables can be used to store a variety of information for processing by your application.

Understanding data types and sub-types

Understanding variable data types and how they affect the information stored within a variable is important.

Declaring variables

How to declare variables, assign values to them, and use operators to interact with them is covered here.

Naming conventions

You must ensure that the code you produce is clearly understood and easy to maintain.

Arrays and array processing

There are several benefits of using arrays in program development.

Anyone who has taken algebra or geometry is already familiar with the concept of a variable. Do you remember Pythagorean's Theorem, which describes the relation of the hypotenuse to the other two sides of a right triangle? The equation is $c^2 = a^2 + b^2$, where a and b are the legs of the triangle and c is the hypotenuse. You substitute the length of the sides in the variables a and b and then calculate the value of the hypotenuse, c, from the formula $(a^2 + b^2)^{\parallel}$. When you assign values to a and b, you are assigning those values to variables that you then use to perform the operation to get the result. The same basic idea of assigning a value to a variable in geometry applies to variables in VBScript development as well. ■

Variables 101: The Basics

Active Server Pages programs, and specifically the VBScript embedded within them, are defined by commands and the data that those commands act on. Data is broken into variables and constants. When you declare or instantiate a variable, you are setting aside (reserving) a place in memory for a value that changes over the life of the variable. A constant declaration also reserves memory, but for a value that does not change during the life of the variable. The life of a variable is defined by its *scope* (more on scope later in the section "Examining the Lifetime of a Variable").

Variables have two characteristics that define their existence—a data type and a variable name. In the following sections, you examine each of these characteristics, leaving you with a complete understanding of the composition and use of variables.

Understanding VBScript Data Types

One of the challenges in developing applications in most programming languages is ensuring that the data types you select for your variables are of an appropriate size to hold the information that you want to store in them. Bad things happen when you try to assign a value that is larger than the variable can hold. The most likely outcome in that situation is that the program will abend abnormally when the variable assignment is hit. The worst case is that the program will continue to run, but it will calculate incorrectly.

In VBScript development, there is only one data type, the Variant. The Variant is a special all-purpose data type that acts somewhat like a chameleon, changing its outward appearance based upon how it is used. You can think of a Variant as a magic box that you can place any size object into. No matter what you put into the magic box, it will always appear to be a custom fit. If you place a thimble into it, it will look like a thimble case. If you put a piano into it, it will look like a piano crate.

Variants can contain a wide range of data such as numbers, dates, strings, and references to objects. A Variant will behave as the data type most appropriate to how it is used in any given context. If you assign a number to a Variant variable, the variable will behave as a number. When you assign a string (string being a group of characters like "String of Characters") to a Variant as shown in Listing 7.1, the variable behaves as a string variable, with actions appropriate to string operations. The Variant and its representation is a fluid assignment, changing as operations are performed upon it.

Listing 7.1 *I1.htm*—Declaring a Variable and Assigning a Value

```
<SCRIPT LANGUAGE="VBScript">
<!--
Dim aVariable                    'we have created a Variant variable
aVariable = "5"                  'now it looks like a string
aVariable = aVariable + 5        'now it looks like an integer with a value of 10
-->
</SCRIPT>
```

As you can see from the preceding code, the Variant is a powerful and complex data type. Because of its apparent simplicity, it is easy to assume that it can handle all manner of data, and more specifically, all operations performed upon it successfully. The reality is that when you have variables with different types of data within them interacting (evaluating together within an expression), you can end up with ambiguous or incorrect results if you don't have a firm understanding of the Variant data type and how it works.

Introducing Variant Sub-Types

A Variant can contain a number of different data types. When a value is placed into a Variant variable, the variable accepts the data and assumes an internal representation of that data, which is called a sub-type. You can put whatever you wish into a Variant, and most of the time, it will behave as you expect. Even though the Variant does most of the data-type conversion work for you, it is still important to understand each of the Variant sub-types, the values that they represent, and how they are used.

Boolean Sub-Type   A Variant with a Boolean sub-type can have only two values, true or false. we can't remember the first time we heard someone say that computers are just a bunch of zeroes and ones, but they continue to be correct today. The idea of a variable only having two possible values, 1 or 0, on or off, true or false is exactly what a Boolean sub-type represents (although in many languages the true condition evaluates to -1, we think you get the idea). The Boolean sub-type is extremely useful and is used for flags and settings. In the following example, `blnActiveMember` has a Boolean sub-type:

```
<SCRIPT LANGUAGE="VBScript">
<!--
if sngDuesPaid >= sngDuesDue then
    blnActiveMember = true
endif
-->
</SCRIPT>
```

Byte Sub-Type   The byte sub-type can contain a value from 0 to 255. This sub-type is the only safe way to access binary data on a byte-by-byte basis. Higher up in the Visual Basic family tree, you used to be able to operate on binary data by using a string data type. With the inclusion in Visual Basic 4 of support for the extended Unicode character set, however, the string data type is no longer one byte per character. A good example of the use of the byte sub-type is when you are reading from or writing to a binary data file.

Integer Sub-Type   This sub-type can store integer values in the range of -32,768 to 32,767. It is the sub-type that is used for counters and indexes.

Long Sub-Type   The Long sub-type contains a value in the range of -2,147,483,648 to 2,147,483,647. It has similar uses as the integer sub-type but can host a number of larger magnitudes.

Single Sub-Type   The Single sub-type contains a single-precision floating point number with a value in the range of 1.401298E-45 to 3.402823E38 for positive values and -3.402823E38 to -1.401298E-45 for negative values. If you want to assign a value to a Variant using exponential notation, it takes the form mmmEeee where mmm is the mantissa and eee is the exponent.

Part

II

Ch

7

Double Sub-Type   This sub-type contains a double-precision floating point number in the range of -1.79769313486232E308 to -4.94065645841247E-324 for negative values and 4.90465645841247E-324 to 1.79769313486232E308 for positive values. To assign a literal to a double, use the form mmmDeee where mmm is the mantissa and eee is the exponent. The D (in place of the E) causes the value to be treated as a double-precision number when converted from a string into a double during an arithmetic operation on the variable.

Currency Sub-Type   The currency sub-type is a special type that is used for monetary values. The valid range for currency sub-type values is -922,337,203,685,477.5808 to 922,337,203,685,477.5807.

Date and Time Sub-Type   The date/time sub-type is a most flexible data sub-type, which contains a date in the range of January 1, 100 to December 31, 9999. You can create a Variant of sub-type date in a number of ways. Here are just a few:

```
dtmCurrentDateTime = Now
```

will assign the current date and time from your system to the variable `dtmCurrentDateTime`. Notice the use of the system function Now. The Now function returns the current date and time based upon the system date and time.

```
dtmTheDate = #02/16/1993#
```

will assign the date 02-16-1993 to the variable `dtmTheDate`. If you want to assign a date to a variable using a string, enclose the date within # signs. The Variant date sub-type represents a date *and* a time. If you were to query the time from the `dtmTheDate` variable, you would get 12:00 AM.

> **N O T E**   Whenever you assign a date literal to a variable without specifying a time, the time defaults to 12:00:00 AM.

You also can create a date and time assignment for a variable using a string literal.

```
dtmTheDateTime = #02/16/1996 1:15:00 am#
```

The preceding line assigns the date and the time to the variable `dtmTheDateTime`.

String Sub-Type   The String sub-type contains a variable-length string that can be approximately 2 billion characters in length. It would certainly be a challenge to come up with a string to exhaust that maximum limit. The nice thing about the Variant in general, and the string sub-type in particular, is that it will only use as much memory as you need in any given context. It will not preallocate storage for 2 billion characters each time you assign a string to a variable.

Empty Sub-Type   This sub-type tells you that the variable has not yet been initialized. If you try to access its value, it will return 0 in a numeric context or an empty string " " in a string context.

Null Sub-Type   The Null sub-type occurs when a variable contains no valid data. This sub-type is only active when you explicitly assign a null to the Variant by an assignment or as the result of an operation on the variable.

Object Sub-Type This sub-type occurs when you have assigned a variable to hold a reference to an object that you have created.

▶ **See** "Managing States and Events with *Application* and *Session* Objects," for more information about the object sub-type and creating and using objects in your development, **p. 179**

Error Sub-Type The error sub-type contains a valid error number. You will examine the error sub-type and error handling in general in Chapter 9, "Calling Procedures: Functions and Sub-routines."

The Internal Structure of a Variant

Ok. This might fall into than "more than I want to know" category, but, it might be fun to take a quick look at the internal structure of the Variant data type to appreciate the complexity that we never have to deal with in Active Scripting.

The C structure is shown in Listing 7.2, which defines the Variant data type:

Listing 7.2   *variant.H*—The Header File for the *Variant Structure*

```
typedef struct tagVARIANT   {
        VARTYPE vt;
        unsigned short wReserved1;
        unsigned short wReserved2;
        unsigned short wReserved3;
        union {
                unsigned char     bVal;          /* VT_UI1                  */
                short             iVal;          /* VT_I2                   */
                long              lVal;          /* VT_I4                   */
                float             fltVal;        /* VT_R4                   */
                double            dblVal;        /* VT_R8                   */
                VARIANT_BOOL      bool;          /* VT_BOOL                 */
                SCODE             scode;         /* VT_ERROR                */
                CY                cyVal;         /* VT_CY                   */
                DATE              date;           /* VT_DATE                */
                BSTR              bstrVal;        /* VT_BSTR                */
                Iunknown          FAR* punkVal;  /* VT_UNKNOWN              */
                Idispatch         FAR* pdispVal;  /* VT_DISPATCH            */
                SAFEARRAY         FAR* parray;   /* VT_ARRAY¦*              */
                unsigned char     FAR *pbVal;    /* VT_BYREF¦VT_UI1         */
                short             FAR* piVal;    /* VT_BYREF¦VT_I2          */
                long              FAR* plVal;    /* VT_BYREF¦VT_I4          */
                float             FAR* pfltVal;  /* VT_BYREF¦VT_R4          */
                double            FAR* pdblVal;  /* VT_BYREF¦VT_R8          */
                VARIANT_BOOL      FAR* pbool;    /* VT_BYREF¦VT_BOOL        */
                SCODE             FAR* pscode;   /* VT_BYREF¦VT_ERROR       */
                CY                FAR* pcyVal;   /* VT_BYREF¦VT_CY          */
                DATE              FAR* pdate;    /* VT_BYREF¦VT_DATE        */
                BSTR              FAR* pbstrVal;  /* VT_BYREF¦VT_BSTR       */
                IUnknown FAR*     FAR* ppunkVal;  /* VT_BYREF¦VT_UNKNOWN   */
                IDispatch FAR*    FAR* ppdispVal;  /* VT_BYREF¦VT_DISPATCH */
                SAFEARRAY FAR*    FAR* parray;   /* VT_ARRAY¦*             */
```

Part
II

Ch
7

continues

Listing 7.2   Continued

```
          VARIANT      FAR* pvarVal;   /* VT_BYREF¦VT_VARIANT  */
          void         FAR* byref;     /* Generic ByRef        */
     };
};
```

The Variant is a structure with a type code and a variety of data members and pointers to the various sub-types of data that it can contain. What makes the Variant so prevalent in our development is that it is the data type for conversations with and between OLE objects. It is used to transmit parameters and return values from the OLE objects that we use in our Active Server Pages development. If you look at the top of the structure, you will see the vt variable of type VARTYPE. This is the variable type code, an enumerated type that contains the sub-type of the variable. When we call the VarType function, it returns the value in the vt variable of the structure, telling us the sub-type of the variable.

The data, depending on its type, is stored in the Variant structure, or within the structure, and has a pointer to where the data associated with the variable resides.

Determining Type and Type Conversions

The Variant gives us all the data types that we could possibly want without (usually) worrying about what sub-type the Variant actually is. When you do need to find out the sub-type of a variable, you have access to a function called VarType. This function will return the sub-type of the variable that we pass to it. The syntax of the command is

```
intVarType = VarType(variable_name)
```

where variable_name is any valid variable. This is especially useful when you are performing any type of arithmetic operations on variables. If you try to add a variable of string sub-type that cannot be resolved to a numeric value with a variable of a numeric sub-type, you will receive a data-type mismatch error. This error is generated because VBScript doesn't know how to add "This is a string" to 5 and come up with a value.

N O T E   Notice that in the VarType function, we have called the return value from the VarType function intVarType, telling you to expect an integer return type. Because the only data type that VBScript supports is the Variant, all functions return a Variant data type. The sub-type of the returned Variant from the VarType function, however, is of a sub-type integer. ■

There are a number of constants that will make the use of the VarType function shown in Listing 7.3 much easier. Instead of having to remember which integer value a particular sub-type correlates to, you can use these constants, outlined in Table 7.1, to check for the sub-type of a variable.

Listing 7.3   *i2.htm*—Constant Return Values from the *VarType* Function

```
<SCRIPT LANGUAGE="VBScript">
<!--
if (vbEmpty = VarType(aVariable)) then
   ...
else
   ...
end if
-->
</SCRIPT>
```

Table 7.1   VBScript Constants for the *VarType* Function Return Value

VBScript Constant	Value	Sub-Type	Description
vbEmpty	0	Empty	Uninitialized (default value)
vbNull	1	Null	Contains no valid data
vbInteger	2	Integer	Integer value
vbLong	3	Long	Long integer
vbSingle	4	Single	Single-precision floating-point number
vbDouble	5	Double	Double-precision floating-point number
vbCurrency	6	Currency	Currency
vbDate	7	Date	Date and Time value
vbString	8	String	String
vbObject	9	Object	OLE Automation object
vbError	10	Error	Error number
vbBoolean	11	Boolean	True or False
vbVariant	12	Variant	Used only for arrays of Variants
vbDataObject	13	Object	Non-OLE Automation object
vbByte	17	Byte	Byte data
vbArray	8192	Array	

Now, to avoid these messy implicit conversion issues (when you let VBScript decide how best to convert your variables between types), there is an entire host of conversion functions for converting between the numerous sub-types discussed previously.

Part
II

Ch
7

Because a Variant variable can represent a wide variety of data types, in many cases you will utilize conversion functions to ensure that the format of the variable data is appropriate for its use in a given context. The conversion functions available for your use are outlined in Table 7.2.

Table 7.2 VBScript

Function Name	Converts to Sub-Type	Usage Notes
CBool	Boolean	Passed-in value must resolve to a numeric.
CByte	Byte	
CCur	Currency	
CDate	Date	Use IsDate() function to ensure that conversion is valid.
CDbl	Double	
CInt	Integer	
CLng	Long	
CSng	Single	
CStr	String	Uninitialized values will return " ".

Conversions are handy to have around when you are performing operations that can lead to uncertain results. As an example, consider the case in which you have two variables that you want to add. To ensure that the sub-type of the resulting operation is, for instance, a single, you can convert each variable to type single.

```
<SCRIPT LANGUAGE="VBScript">
<!--
Dim valOne, valTwo, valResult
valOne = 1
valTwo = 2.1
valResult = CSng(valOne) + CSng(valTwo)
-->
</SCRIPT>
```

Declarations, Assignments, Operators, and Scope

A variable declaration tells the compiler (script processor) that you are reserving space for a variable to use in your application. You can create variables throughout your program within these system-enforced guidelines:

- Maximum 127 variables per procedure (arrays count as a single variable).
- Maximum 127 "script-level" variables per script.

The differences between declaring variables within a procedure and within a module will be discussed in the section "Examining the Lifetime of a Variable" found later in this chapter.

You declare a variable in your source code with the Dim statement. This *dimensions, or reserves space*, for the variable for use within the scope of the declaration. You also can implicitly declare a variable in your source code.

Implicit Variable Declaration

A variable that is declared implicitly is not dimensioned before its first use in your code. The script processor automatically creates a variable of the same name as the one that you have used. For example:

```
<SCRIPT LANGUAGE="VBScript">
<!--
Function leadingZeros(intNumber, intSize)
    j = intSize - len(aNumber)
    tempStr = string(j, "0")
    leadingZeros = tempStr & aNumber
End Function
-->
</SCRIPT>
```

VBScript will create the variables j and tempStr, and they can be accessed after their initial implicit declaration just as if you had explicitly declared them at the beginning of your function. Although this is a quick and easy way to declare variables, this can lead to numerous problems such as acting on an uninitialized variable or mistyping a variable in the body of your function, which will run, but will lead to erroneous results. Check out the code that follows.

```
<SCRIPT LANGUAGE="VBScript">
<!--
Function leadingZeros(intNumber, intSize)
    j = intSize - len(aNumber)
    tempStr = String(j, "0")
    leadingZeros = tmpStr & CStr(intNumber)
End Function
-->
</SCRIPT>
```

At first glance, the code looks fine. Notice, however, that on the last line of the function, tempStr was mistyped as tmpStr. As a result, the function returns the same number that was passed in, without those sought-after leading zeroes. The tmpStr variable would be created, but would be uninitialized and the leadingZeros function would then return the concatenation of " " and the intNumber passed in, which is, of course, intNumber. Not a great way to start off your coding day!

Part

II

Ch

7

Explicit Variable Declaration

To avoid the problems discussed previously with implicit variable declarations, be sure to include the `Option Explicit` command at the beginning of your source code. This will ensure that any variables used in the body of your source code have been explicitly declared by using the `Dim VarName` declaration. Notice that in the following code, the misspelling would generate a run-time error.

```
<SCRIPT LANGUAGE="VBScript">
<!--
Function leadingZeros(intNumber, intSize)
    Dim j, tempStr
    j = intSize - len(aNumber)
    tempStr = string(j, "0")
    leadingZeros = tmpStr & CStr(intNumber)
End Function
-->
</SCRIPT>
```

Examining the Lifetime of a Variable

The length of time that a variable exists, or can be utilized in your code, is defined as the variable's lifetime. The lifetime of a variable is determined by the position in your script that the variable is declared. Variables declared within a function or subroutine will be visible only (able to be operated upon) within that routine. By declaring a variable this way, you create a *procedure-level* variable with a *local scope*. When the program returns from the procedure, those procedure-level variables are said to have gone out of scope. Their values have been lost, and they cannot be operated on by any other function. Many times, it is helpful to have variables that can be used in all of the procedures within your script. When you declare variables outside of a procedure, they are visible to all the procedures in your script. These declarations create *script-level* variables. Table 7.3 provides a summary of variable scope.

> **CAUTION**
>
> All local variables will go out of scope (no longer able to access) when their procedure block ends. If you do not use the `Option Explicit` command, you can mistakenly try to access a local variable beyond its scope and end up creating a new implicitly declared variable of the same name in a different scope.

Table 7.3 The Lifetime of Variables Determined by Their Scope

Declared	Level	Scope	Lifetime
Within Procedure	Procedure-level	Local scope	Declaration to end of procedure
Outside Procedure	Script-level	Script-level scope	Declaration to end of script

After you have decided on the functions that you need to implement in your scripts, it is a fairly easy exercise to determine the scope of the variables that you need to declare. Procedure-level variables are great for temporary use within a function or subroutine for indexes, interim results, and any other case in which you will never need to reference the value of these variables outside of the procedure. Script-level variables are used for those variables that must be available throughout the life of the script. The memory allocated for procedure-level variables is released when they go out of scope. Script-level variables are not released until the completion of the script. As a general rule, use as few script-level variables as possible, although until VBScript allows the use of passing arguments by reference instead of by value, you will be using at least a few script-level variables.

▶ **See** "Calling Procedures: Functions and Subroutines," for more information about procedures, passing arguments and `ByVal` versus `ByRef`, **p. 159**

 T I P   Script-level variables should be declared at the top of your script to ensure that they are visible to all operations and functions within the script.

Using Variable Assignments and Operators

A variable is only as useful as the information that it contains. To put a value into a variable, you *assign* one to it by using the equal sign. For example:

```
intConnections = 4
```

assigns the value 4 to the `intConnections` variable. The variable is always on the left side of the equal sign. On the right side of the equal sign, you will place a value or an expression, which is just something (a literal, function, variable, calculation, and so on) that evaluates to a value. Here are a few additional assignment examples:

```
intCurrentState = 10              'intCurrentState has value of 10
intNewState = 20                  'IntNewState has value of 20
intOldState = intCurrentState     'intOldState has value of 10
intNewDate = CalcDate(Now)        'dteNewDate has the return value
                                  'from the CalcDate function
intCurrentState = intNewState     'intCurrentState has value 20
```

There is one special kind of assignment that is used when assigning a variable to an object. When you create an object within your script by using the assignment operator, you are setting a reference to the object in the variable. You will use the `Set` keyword to perform this task. The syntax for the `Set` assignment statement is shown here:

```
Set objectvar = {objectexpression ¦ Nothing}
```

The object expression can be the expression used to create the object or a variable which references an existing object. When you assign nothing to an object variable, the memory associated with the object is released if no other reference to the object is still active. In the following example, the variable `objBrowserCap` will be set to a reference to the Browser Capabilities object being created.

```
Set objBrowserCap = Server.CreateObject("MSWC.BrowserType")
```

 Part
 II

Ch

7

To release the memory associated with the object referenced by the `objBrowserCap` variable, you would set it to nothing.

```
Set objBrowserCap = Nothing
```

Introducing Operators

In Active Server Pages scripting, like most other programming languages, you have the ability to evaluate mathematical expressions by combining numeric data, by using operators. There are a number of different types of operators in the environment. Arithmetic, logical, comparison, and concatenation operations can all be performed within your scripts. A list of operators available within VBScript is found in Table 7.4.

Operations within an expression are performed like they are in algebra, following the mathematical principles of precedence. You can override the precedence by containing parts of the expression within parentheses. When you have an expression with multiple operator types, the operators are evaluated based upon the following hierarchy: arithmetic operators are evaluated first; comparison operators are evaluated next; and logical operators are evaluated last. Within any given expression group (within parentheses), operators of the same type are performed from left to right.

Table 7.4 Scripting Operators

Operator Type	Symbol	Description	Example
Arithmetic	*	Multiplication	2 * 2 = 4
	/	Division	4 / 2 = 2
	\	Integer Division	5 \ 2 = 2
	+	Addition	2 + 2 = 4
	-	Subtraction	4 - 2 = 2
	Mod	Modulus (remainder)	5 Mod 2 = 1
	^	Exponential	2 ^ 3 = 8
Comparison	=	Equal to	4 = 4 is true
	<>	Not equal to	4 <> 4 is false
	<	Less than	4 < 3 is false
	>	Greater than	4 > 3 is true
	<=	Less than or equal to	4 <= 3 is false
	>=	Greater than or equal to	4 >= 3 is true
	Is	Object Comparison	objOne Is objTwo
Logical	And	Conjunction	If a and b are true, then true

Operator Type	Symbol	Description	Example
	Not	Negation	If not a and a is false, then true
	Or	Disjunction	If a or b is true, then true
	Eqv	Equivalence	If a and b are both true or both false, then true
	Imp	Implication	If a true and b false, false, else true or Null
	Xor	Exclusion	If a true and b false or b true and a false, true
Concatenation	&	Concatenates values	"Mr." & "Smith" = "Mr. Smith"

In Table 7.4, there are two special operators that you should take note of. The first is the concatenation operator, &. This operator is used to concatenate two strings.

```
<SCRIPT LANGUAGE="VBScript">
<!--
strCaption = "My Name Is: "
strName = "Donny Brook"
strOutput = strCaption & strName
-->
</SCRIPT>
```

The resulting strOutput variable contains the string My Name Is: Donny Brook.

CAUTION

You can use the + operator to concatenate string variables as well, and this works fine when both are of sub-type string. If both sub-types are numeric, the values will be added. When one of the sub-types is numeric and the other is a string, the string will be evaluated to a numeric type (implicit conversion) and then added to the other numeric variable. If the string cannot be converted to a numeric value, a run-time error will occur. For safe concatenation, always use the & operator.

The second special operator is the Is operator. This operator will determine whether two object variables point to the same object, as in:

```
blnResult = objOne Is objTwo
```

If the two object variables point to the same object, blnResult will be true; otherwise, it will be false. The Is operator will become extremely useful as we get into the Active Server Pages objects and components discussions in Part III.

Implementing Variable Naming Conventions

What's in a name? Well, that depends. Application development will always be equal parts of art and science, and the process of selecting names for variables is no different. The names that you assign to variables do not affect the performance of the application in any way, but incorrect use of variable naming can lead to numerous problems. For example, we know several C developers who take pride in the terseness of their code. The more functions they can put on a line and the more inconsistent their use of naming rules, the better. Naming variables a, b, or c works extremely well in Euclidean geometry, but in your application source code, variable naming patterns can be directly correlated to the maintainability and readability of your code. We shudder to think of the countless hours we've spent working our way through poorly named and documented code, trying to understand what the variables represent and how they are used in the program.

 T I P When in doubt, use the most descriptive name possible for your variables. The next person to maintain your code will thank you for it. Use LoanNumber instead of lnbr, try CustomerAccount instead of actno. When you have only two or three variables in any scope, you have less reason to be so prolific, but as your scripts increase in size and complexity, these little hints that your variable names provide will be of immeasurable value.

There are naming rules that limit you to a certain extent as you begin to create names for the variables in your application.

All variable names:

- Must begin with an alphabetic character
- Cannot contain an embedded period
- Must be unique within the same scope
- Must be fewer than 256 characters

Now that the system-enforced rules are out of the way, you can move on to the variable naming conventions. Naming conventions are guidelines that are enforced only by the developer, but when used consistently across your source code, they will ensure that the programmers that follow you will have extra hints concerning the use of variables in your program. In C language Windows development, the naming convention that is most often used is called Hungarian notation. This is a C language naming convention credited to the Microsoft programmer Charles Simonyi, in which you can determine a variable's type simply by looking at its prefix. The same idea has been implemented for the naming conventions used in VBScript development. In the brief code snippets listed previously in the chapter, you might have noticed some strange-looking prefixes ahead of the variable names. These VBScript prefixes, found in Table 7.5, give you hints as to what sub-type to expect within the Variant variable.

Table 7.5   VBScript Preferred Variable Naming Conventions

Sub-Type	Variable Prefix	An Example
Boolean	bln	ActiveAccount
Byte	byt	ImageData
Date/Time	dtm	ClientBirthday
Double	dbl	MaxDelay
Error	err	AccountCreation
Integer	int	PassCounter
Long	lng	RateOf Travel
Object	obj	Database
Single	sng	AvgSpeed
String	str	LastName

The use of naming conventions in your development is entirely voluntary and is in no way enforced by the compiler or script processor. There is no system or server constraint that will require you to follow any particular naming convention. Professional developers utilize naming conventions in code because it enhances the quality and maintainability of their systems.

Your company has likely already implemented standard naming conventions for in-house development. If there are none, it is prudent to follow the vendor's naming conventions as that is most often what will be implemented in other development shops.

Constant Naming Conventions

As you read at the beginning of the chapter, data is broken down into variables and constants. VBScript provides the Const declaration to ensure that a constant variable is not assigned a value during script execution. To define a variable as a constant, you use the Const keyword, along with an assignment when declaring the variable. Also, when declaring constants, use all uppercase letters, separating words with underscores. This is another standard naming convention as shown in the following constant declaration:

```
Const MAX_ITERATIONS = 10
```

Now when you use the constants in your code, there is no mistaking their intent or their use. This will also help to ensure that Joe Programmer, who now maintains your code, will not mistakenly try to change one of your constant variables. If Joe does attempt to assign a value to a Const variable within the script, an illegal assignment run-time error will be generated.

Part

II

Ch

7

Scope Naming Prefixes

The last piece of the naming convention puzzle concerns the variable name's hint as to the scope in which it exists. For procedure-level variables, no prefix is recommended. For those variables that are script-level, add an s to the beginning of the variable name.

```
Dim sblnAccountActiveFlag    'Active Accounts have this flag set to true
```

Now, just by seeing the variable name, we know that this is a script-level variable that holds a variable of sub-type Boolean, and from the variable name, that the variable is a flag that shows the status of an account.

Commenting Your Code

We have been talking a lot about naming conventions, variable prefixes, and the use of descriptive names for variables to give you and other developers hints as to what you are trying to accomplish in your application. To take this to the next level, you will want to add comments to your code along the way as well. When you have to pick up code that you wrote five or six months ago to add functionality or (not that this will happen to you) to fix a bug, you will thank yourself for commenting your code. As Steve McConnel notes in *Code Complete*, commenting code correctly can enhance its readability and maintainability, but comments implemented poorly can actually hurt one's understanding of the code.

There are a few main rules that you can use as a guide for commenting your code.

- Any variables of significance, especially script-level variables, should be commented when they are declared.
- Do not comment code that is self-documenting. For example: `intCounter ' this is a counter.`
- Add comments to the beginning of the script, stating its purpose.
- Comment all functions and subroutines as to what they do.

A good template for commenting functions and subroutines follows.

```
'****************************************************
' Description: A brief description of the purpose of
'              the procedure
' Arguments  : A listing of each argument and what it
'              is used for
' Returns    : what, if anything, does the proc return
' Modified   : The date the procedure was last modified,
'              the developer who did it, and what was
'              changed.
'****************************************************
```

Comments within the code itself should be placed to enhance the understanding of the code. As you add blocks of functionality, you should add comments that help to explain the flow. For example:

```
<SCRIPT LANGUAGE="VBScript">
<!--
Dim objDBConnection, objRSCustomerList
```

```
Dim strQuery

'Create the database object and open the database
Set objDBConnection = Server.CreateObject("ADO.Connection")
objDBConnection .Open "UserDatabase"

'Select Customers that reside in CA
strQuery = "Select Name, Address from Customer where State= 'CA'
set objCustomerList = objDBConnection.Execute(strQuery)
-->
</SCRIPT>
```

Each major functional step should have an associated comment. As you nest and indent the code within loops, the comments should also be indented. A good rule of thumb for indenting code is to use three spaces for each logical nesting.

```
<SCRIPT LANGUAGE="VBScript">
<!--
if (blnActiveLoan) then
    'Update customer Information
else
    'Send negative acknowledgment
end if
-->
</SCRIPT>
```

Understanding Arrays and Array Processing

Many times, you will find yourself dealing with a number of related items that you want to perform the same or similar actions upon. Using unique variable names for these related items is quite easy when you are only dealing with three or four distinct data items. When you want to relate tens or hundreds of items together and perform operations on them, however, you need a special type of variable construct: the array. With an array, you can access a group of related data items by using the same name, and any particular data member by using a unique index. This makes processing the items within the array very efficient, as you can loop through the array data using an index value.

All elements of an array in VBScript have the same data type, the Variant. The added benefit of having Variant arrays is that you can have multiple sub-types across members of the array. You can declare two types of arrays: fixed-length and dynamic.

Fixed-Length Arrays

A fixed-length array is an array in which the number of members will not change over the lifetime of the array variable. To create a fixed-length array, you specify the number of elements that you want to have in the declaration of the array variable. For example, the declaration:

```
Dim dblCharges(10)
```

creates an array of 11 items with index numbers from 0 to 10.

Part
II

Ch
7

N O T E All VBScript arrays use zero-based indexes. Currently, VBScript does not permit you to change the base of indexes as you can in Visual Basic and Access. Also, it does not recognize explicit lower bounds. ■

To assign a value to a member of the array, you include the subscript on the left side of the assignment operator:

```
dblCharges(0) = 100.50
dblCharges(1) = 125.25
```

Assume that in the previous examples you have assigned each of the array elements a value. Determining the total of all the values in the array is simply a process of looping through the index and adding the values together as follows:

```
<SCRIPT LANGUAGE="VBScript">
<!--
Dim i, dblTotalCharges
For i = 0 to 10
    dblTotalCharges = dblTotalCharges + dblCharges(i)
Next
-->
</SCRIPT>
```

You can also create arrays with more than one dimension. In a two-dimensional array, you can think of the first array index as the row in a spreadsheet and the second as the column. To declare a two-dimensional array, just include a second index value on the declaration statement.

```
Dim intMultiArray(9,9)
```

This will create a two-dimensional array of 10 by 10 elements. You access the members of the multidimensional array just as you would a single-dimensional array.

```
Dim intMultiArray(1 to 9, 1 to 9)
intMultiArray(4,5) = 15
```

You also can easily loop through all of the elements in a multidimensional array just as we did for the single-dimensional array. By using the previously declared array, the loop looks like:

```
<SCRIPT LANGUAGE="VBScript">
<!--
Dim j, k, intTotal
for j = 0 to 9
   for k = 0 to 9
      intTotal = intTotal + intMultiArray(j, k)
   next k
next j
-->
</SCRIPT>
```

Dynamic Arrays

There are many situations in which you will not know how many array items you will ultimately require for a given process. You could declare a huge array and hope that you will not exceed its upper bound. This will surely work in most cases, but it is horribly inefficient, as well as quite inelegant. A better option would be to create a dynamic array.

A dynamic array can be resized over its lifetime. You can create single- and multi-dimensional dynamic arrays. To create a dynamic array, you omit the index number from the array declaration.

```
Dim dynArray()
```

You also can use the ReDim statement to declare a procedure-level dynamic array.

```
ReDim dynArray(25)
```

This will create a dynamic array variable with 26 initial elements.

To change the size of a declared dynamic array variable, you use the ReDim statement again, this time including the index for the number of items you want in the array. To increase the size of the array, you call the ReDim function again and again. If you want to keep the current contents of the array intact when you change the size of the array, use the keyword Preserve on the ReDim statement.

```
Dim dynArray()             'the dynamic array is declared
ReDim dynArray(15)         'set the array size to 16
ReDim Preserve dynArray(20)  'reset the size to 21, preserving the contents
```

CAUTION

If you ReDim Preserve an array to a smaller size than it currently is, you will lose the data beyond the new index size.

Also, if you ReDim a multidimensional array, you can change only the last dimension; otherwise, you will generate a run-time error.

And finally, the ReDim statement is allowed only within a procedure. It will generate a run-time error if used at any other level.

From Here...

You now know what a variable is, how to declare one, and how to use the operators provided by VBScript to create expressions. You also should have a good idea how to create meaningful, descriptive variable names as well as how to document your scripts. In the next few chapters, you round out your base skills to gain the tools to begin creating Active Server scripts right away.

Part
II

Ch
7

In the coming chapters, you will leverage your understanding of variable typing, naming, and scoping with:

- Chapter 8, "Working with Program Flow and Control Structures," discusses the language constructs to provide logical scripts.
- Chapter 9, "Calling Procedures: Functions and Subroutines," explores how to encapsulate functionality in code blocks to increase code efficiency and reuse. This chapter also covers error handling and the Err object.

Working with Program Flow and Control Structures

Understanding program flow

Based upon user input and responses from external data sources, you need to take different actions within your code.

Exploring program looping

When you need to perform the same operation(s) many times, you loop.

You have spent a good bit of time up until this point hearing about variables, operators, and arrays. You have all the ingredients to start creating Active Server Pages applications, but you have yet to begin mixing them together.

In this chapter, you will be introduced to the constructs that make the variables and data interact. Sure, it's a good thing to declare a bunch of variables and operators, but without conditional processing and looping, the program will execute from left to right and top to bottom, with ability to perform different functions based upon data passed in. As you will see, it is the conditional processing and looping that provide your programs with "flow." ■

Conditional Processing

You encounter conditional processing every day of your life. As a child, you are taught that there are consequences to your actions. The line, "if you hit your brother, you will be sent to your room," is a perfect example of a conditional process. The parent has defined a condition to test for (hitting) and an outcome based upon whether the condition has been satisfied (did you hit your brother?). This same idea of setting a condition and testing its outcome carries over into the control structures that you create for your Active Server Pages scripts.

The idea of conditional processing has an apt metaphor in the traditional flowchart. In a flowchart, you have process boxes and decision boxes. The process boxes are analogous to code blocks, and the decision boxes are analogous to If statements.

Examining the *If* Statement

The If statement provides for conditional processing based on the outcome of an expression (or value) meeting a condition. Just like in the preceding example, you use the If statement to evaluate a condition, and based upon whether the condition is met, your code will perform some action; for example, some block of code will be executed. The following is the template for the If statement:

```
If (condition) Then
    executable code block
End If
```

In the condition of the If statement, you will usually encounter one of the comparison operators discussed in Chapter 7, "Understanding Variable Typing, Naming, and Scoping." You can use any expression that evaluates to a numeric value as the conditional expression. If the expression evaluates to zero, the condition is considered to be not met (False). If the condition evaluates to any other numeric value, it is considered met (True), and the code within the If...End If block will be executed. Take a moment and walk through the following examples, which illustrate this point.

A user on your site has pulled up your guestbook page. You want him to fill in a few informational fields so you can provide him with updated information about changes to your site. Form fields on your guestbook page might include first and last name, address, and the type of computer he is using. The task you want to accomplish when you begin to process the page is to retrieve the information and then add the new user to your database. To see if he has entered his name, you check the length of the last name entry. If the length is greater than zero, the last name has been entered, and you assign the first and last name to a variable that will be inserted into your database.

```
If Len(strLastName) > 0 Then
    strName = strLastName & ", " & strFirstName
    InsertDatabaseRecord(strName)
End If
```

N O T E   Notice in the preceding example how the statements that are used to describe the desired functionality directly translated into the condition of the `If` statement. If the length of the last name (`Len(strLastName)`) is greater than (`>`) zero (`0`), then assign the full name to the `strName` variable and insert the record into the database (`InsertDatabaseRecord(strName)`). ■

If the length of the `strLastName` variable is greater than zero, you want to concatenate it with a comma, a space, and the first name and then assign it to the variable `strName`. In the preceding section, you learned that a condition, when resolved to a numeric value, is considered `True` if it has any value other than zero. Knowing this, you can rewrite the `If` statement condition without the greater-than comparison operator.

```
If Len(strLastName) Then
    strName = strLastName & ", " & strFirstName
    InsertDatabaseRecord(strName)
End If
```

The two examples are equivalent because when the length of the `strLastName` is greater than zero, there is a value in it (sure, it might just be embedded blanks, but we'll take care of that case in a moment). Because the `Len` function returns the number of characters in a variable, and the `If` condition will be `True` any time the condition expression evaluates to a number not equal to zero, the condition will be met in both cases if `strLastName` contains a group of characters (or even one character).

T I P   When processing the length of string sub-type variables, it is recommended to remove the blank spaces before and after the string data. You can accomplish this by using the `TRIM` function. This will ensure that you don't mistakenly operate on a large character string of embedded blanks.

Be sure not to confuse an empty string with a variable that has not been initialized. Using the `IsEmpty` function, which returns a Boolean sub-type, is not the same as testing the length of a string variable by using the `Len` function, unless the variable has not, in fact, been initialized. Consider the following code:

```
Dim strOne
If IsEmpty(strOne)Then    'Condition is True
End If
If Len(strOne) Then       'Condition is False
End If
strOne = ""               'assign an empty string to variable
If IsEmpty(strOne)Then    'Condition is False
End If
If Len(strOne) Then       'Condition is still False
End If
```

Before the `strOne` variable is initialized, the `IsEmpty` function will return `True` because there has not been a value assigned to `strOne` yet. The `Len(strOne)` function returns 0 or `False`, because the default value of a Variant variable, which has not been initialized, when used in a string context, returns `""`. After the `strOne` variable is initialized, even with an empty string, the `IsEmpty` function returns `False`.

You can have as many statements as you want within an `If...End If block`. If you are only going to execute one statement should the condition be met, you can put the code all on the same line and omit the `End If`.

```
If Len(Trim(strLastName)) Then strName=Trim(strLastName) & ", " &
➥Trim(strFirstName)
```

This is really useful in streamlining your code when the code itself tends to document the action you are going to perform.

 TIP Remember the variable naming conventions that you learned about in Chapter 7 "Understanding Variable Typing, Naming, and Scoping?" Notice that by identifying the string sub-type within the variable name (str), and the descriptive use of `LastName` and `FirstName` within the variable name, the code is self-documenting.

Adding the *Else*   In this next scenario, you are creating an Active Server Pages script that processes automobile insurance applications. You have created a form and have asked your user for a variety of information. Specifically, you zero-in on one particular piece of information that you will be processing, previous-claim information. Company policy dictates that you not accept an application from an individual who has had an insurance claim within the past three years. The makings of a great conditional statement are underway!

The insurance rates you will be quoting to your applicant are based on a number of factors, but, as per your acceptance guidelines, if there has been a claim within the last three years, your applicant will not be able to apply for the insurance plan. You will want to test for this condition, and if the criteria are met (no claim within the last three years), process the application. Otherwise, you will want to generate a letter to the applicant advising her of the decision based upon her claims history.

The `Else` case of the `If` construct provides the "otherwise" processing for this scenario. Take a look at the template for the `If...Then...Else` construct and then move on to our sample insurance case code.

```
If condition Then
    code to execute
Else
    code to execute
End If
```

If the condition evaluates to `True`, the first block of code between the `Then` and `Else` will be executed, otherwise, the second block of code between the `Else` and `End If` will be executed. The code for the insurance example might look something like the following:

```
If blnClaimLastThreeYears Then
    ProcessRejection
Else
    ProcessNewApplication
Endif
```

The Boolean variable `blnClaimLastThreeYears` holds the answer to the question: "Have you had an insurance claim within the last three years?" You could write the condition as `blnClaimLastThreeYears = True`, but this would be redundant. When a variable has a Boolean sub-type, there is no need for a comparison operator in the condition. The variable itself evaluates to `True` or `False`. As mentioned at the top of the chapter, conditional statements can be easily derived directly from a flowchart, as the insurance scenario is illustrated in Figure 8.1.

Part II

Ch 8

FIG. 8.1
Notice how easily *If, Then, Else* constructs flow from the flowchart.

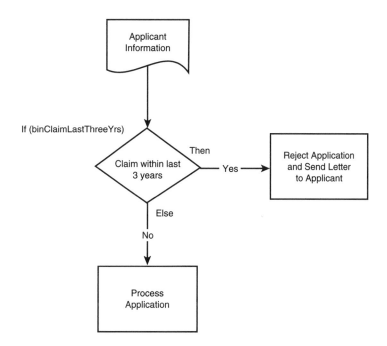

Using Logical Operators   You will encounter many cases as you continue to develop your applications in which you will want to evaluate multiple criteria in the condition of an `If` statement. Using logical operators is the key to evaluating multiple criteria in a condition. Through the use of truth tables, as outlined in Table 9.1, you can see what the results of evaluating a logical condition will be.

Table 8.1   The *AND* Truth Table

First Condition	Second Condition	Outcome
True	True	True
True	False	False
False	False	False
False	False	False

In the earlier example in which you were processing a guest page, you were testing the length of a `LastName` variable and then appending the `FirstName` to put the whole name into a variable for insertion into a database. In that example, you assumed that if the `LastName` were entered, so was the `FirstName`. Now, I don't need to tell you what happens when you assume…. If the `FirstName` were not entered, or were left blank, the previous sample code would continue to process. Now you'll update the code to ensure that both the first and last names are entered.

```
If Len(Trim(strLastName)) AND Len(Trim(strFirstName)) Then
    strName = Trim(strLastName) & ", " & Trim(strFirstName)
    InsertDatabaseRecord(strName)
Else
    ReturnInvalidNameError
End If
```

The logical `AND` operator is used to ensure both names have at least one character in them. If either variable evaluates to an empty string, you will return an error code to the client.

In other cases, you would want the condition to be satisfied if either one of the variables had a character in it. In that case, you would use the logical `OR`. The truth table for the logical `OR` operator is found in Table 9.2.

Table 8.2   The *OR* Truth Table

First Condition	Second Condition	Outcome
True	True	True
True	False	True
False	True	True
False	False	False

In the following example, the script determines the region of the guestbook user by evaluating the state passed in from the client.

```
If strState = "CA" OR strState = "AZ" Then
    strRegion = "Pacific"
End If
```

Within the code, you are accepting California or Arizona to meet the condition of a Pacific-region state. This is certainly not the best way to determine a region from a state, but it gets the logical `OR` point across. A match on either of the states will cause the condition to be met, and the code block within will be executed.

You can also use the negation logical operator to good effect in your `If` statement conditions. Sometimes, it just makes the code more readable to use the `NOT` operator. Table 9.3 shows the truth table for the logical `NOT`.

Table 8.3 The *Not* Truth Table

First Condition	Second Condition	Outcome
Not	True	False
Not	False	True

Now, you can take a look at a few additional examples to illustrate the outcomes of using AND, and then combining these logical operators within conditional statements:

```
If blnActiveAccount AND intYears >= 5 Then
    ProcessNomination
End If
```

In the preceding example, you are using the logical AND to determine whether to process the nomination of a hypothetical member of some group. When creating conditional statements, it is usually written exactly as it sounds. For example, you will process a nomination if the member is active *and* has been with you for at least 5 years. You can see the logical AND within the declaration. Use of the logical OR will follow along the same lines. The following code illustrates this type of declaration: If the account holder is the primary or secondary borrower on the note, release the account information, otherwise, notify them of the restrictions on disclosure.

```
If (strRequestor = "primaryBorrower" OR
    strRequestor = "secondaryBorrower") Then
    ReleaseLoanData
Else
    ReturnDisclosureNotification
End If
```

You can create very complex logical conditions for use with the If statement by combining multiple logical operators in the condition.

```
If (intDays > 5 AND lngMiles < 1000) OR (blnActive AND NOT blnDeceased) Then
    ProcessReimbursement
Endif
```

The expression in the preceding If statement is evaluated just like any other compound expression: Each expression is evaluated within the parentheses groups, and then logically OR'd (in this example) together. Ultimately, the condition evaluates to zero (False) or any other numeric value (True).

Implementing Nested *If* Statements   Nested If statements provide you with an added level of functionality when developing applications that require multiple levels of conditional testing. The nesting refers to the embedding of conditional If blocks within other If blocks. As you traverse through the nested levels, the inner If condition is evaluated only if the outer condition is met. The template for nested If statements looks like this:

```
If condition Then        'Top level
    If condition Then     '1st Nested Level
        If condition Then '2nd Nested  level
        End If
    End If
End If
```

The template can be expanded to include up to 8 levels of nesting. Each nested level can also include the Else case, which can in turn contain its own nesting.

One of the most useful things that you will use nested If processing for is data validation. Within your Active Server Pages applications, you want to ensure that all user-entered data coming in to your script is valid before processing it. Using nested If statements provides you with another great tool to use when performing data validation. To begin the discussion, our nesting scenario concentrates on validating the Date sub-type variable.

Dates are a major source of input data that are used in most business queries. Management needs to know what the value of the key indicators of your business are, but they must be evaluated within a specific context to have meaning: their value today, month to date, or year to date. Your users will want to see data for a given date range. They also might request a summary of information from a given date to the present date. The use of dates in your business applications are so prevalent, that it is worthwhile to discuss them now in a data-validation context.

When accepting input from a user, you want to ensure that any calculations you perform using a date passed to you is, in fact, a valid date. This will ensure that you can provide accurate information back to the client.

There are a few different levels of validation that you will want to perform for a given date value. At the lowest level, you want to ensure that the date variable contains valid data. This means the input data string will resolve to a date value. A variable with an invalid date might contain something like XXNNMYYZZZZ. Try to get a date value out of that string! The next level of "valid-ness" would be based on the context in which you will be using the date value. For a given context, you might restrict the date, based on a date range of the data available. Any date outside this range would be considered invalid in this context. A valid date might also be restricted to be greater than today's date or some other range that you create to define a "valid date" for your particular context.

To check these multiple levels of validity, you use nested If statements. At each of the nested levels, you will perform a date validation step. If the condition specified is met and the date is validated, you will proceed to the next level of nesting and the next level of date validation. Just remember that as you increase the number of levels, you increase the likelihood of errors within the nested block. The following code shows you date validation using nested If statements.

```
If IsDate(dteInput) Then
    If DateValue(dteInput) < Date Then
        ReturnDateRangeError
    Else
        ProcessDataRequest
```

```
    Endif
Else
    ReturnInvalidDate
End If
```

The first line of code ensures the variable dteInput contains a value that can be resolved to a date. The IsDate function resolves an expression to a date value. If the expression passed to the function can be resolved, it returns True. If the value cannot be resolved to a date, the function will return False. The wonderful thing about the IsDate function is that it will not generate a run-time error regardless of what you pass into it.

If the first condition is met, IsDate(dteInput) you now move on to the "next level" of nesting, verifying the validity of the date value in our context. The second test ensures that the now "verified" dteInput date is greater than the current date. The Date function returns the current system date. The DateValue function returns a date representation of the expression passed into it. If this second level of date verification passes, the request will be processed.

 TIP Whenever you are performing operations that use dates, like the DateValue function in the previous example, you always want to test to ensure the expression or variable can be resolved to a date by using the IsDate function. If you pass an expression to the DateValue function that cannot be resolved to a date, the code will generate a run-time error. You will always want to code to avoid possible run-time errors. That is called defensive programming, and it is one of the differences between a mediocre and a professional developer.

Nesting If statements are ideal when you want to test conditions against different variables at different levels. If you are setting up conditions for the same variable at each of the nesting levels, you are setting up a nested tandem If.

Tandem *If* Statements   When you want to take an action based upon the value of a variable, you use the If statement. You set up a condition that, if it evaluates to True, processes a block of code. There are many times that you will find yourself writing multiple If statements to check for a finite range of values within a *single* variable or expression.

In the next example, we are going to generate a custom response based upon the prefix of our user's name. It has a limited set of values (Ms, Dr, and so on) that you will test for. If one value is met, you can be sure that none of the other If conditions will be met because you are testing the same variable again and again.

```
If strNamePrefix = "Mr." Then
    code here...
End If
If strNamePrefix = "Ms." Then
    code here...
End If
If strNamePrefix = "Dr." Then
    code here...
End If
```

The type of code section just shown is referred to as tandem If statements. The statements work together to take an action based on the various types of data that the strNamePrefix variable will hold. Notice that each of the conditions in the preceding code are mutually exclusive. There are no duplicate conditions. This ensures that only one prefix response will be sent back to your user. The problem with this type of code is that without using a flag in each If block, you will be hard-pressed to provide a default value for the case where none of the conditions are met. You can provide a default value by combining the tandem If with the nested If...Then...Else...If code blocks.

```
If strNamePrefix = "Mr." Then
    code here...
Else
    If strNamePrefix = "Ms." Then
        code here...
    Else
        If strNamePrefix = "Dr." Then
            code here...
        Else
            default action here
        End If
    End If
End If
```

The nesting allows you to have a default action when none of the explicit conditions are met. As the number of possible values that strNamePrefix can hold increases, the level of nesting increases as well.

There is one last format for nesting of the If statement that provides the same functionality that you see in the last example. It just pushes the Else and If together to look more like this:

```
If strNamePrefix = "Mr." Then
    code here...
ElseIf strNamePrefix = "Ms." Then
    code here...
ElseIf strNamePrefix = "Dr." Then
    code here...
Else
    default action here
End If
```

This new format eliminates the need to explicitly close each If block with an End If. While greatly improving the look of the nested code, deep nesting in general can get ugly very, very quickly. We have had to work with programs over the years that have come to be known as "Nested If From Hell" programs. These programs (actually written in C, but we're sure there are some out there in VB and other higher level languages) have an If at the top of the module and an End If (or closing brace) at the bottom. In between, there are levels upon levels of nested Ifs. The complexity of the code is in direct proportion to its level of nesting. The more nesting levels, the greater complexity within the code. To avoid the temptation of the nested Ifs in these situations, the Select Case statement provides the same functionality in a much easier to understand and user friendly format.

Using the *Select* Statement

As you saw in the preceding section, the tandem `If` provides you with a framework for taking actions based upon a set number of known outcomes for a variable or an expression. The same functionality is found within the `Select Case` statement but in a much more elegant form. Here is the template for the `Select Case` statement:

```
Select Case testexpression
    [Case expressionlist-n
        [statements-n]] . . .
    [Case Else expressionlist-n
        [elsestatements-n]]
End Select
```

The first line sets up the condition or case that will be tested. The body of the `Select Case` statement contains the cases that you want to test for. Each of the `Case expressionlist`(s) have values that, when equal to the test expression, are considered met.

The test expression is any valid VBScript expression. It is evaluated and then compared to the values in the expression list in the `Case` statements under the `Select`. If the test expression value matches one of these expression list items, the code within that `Case` statement will be executed. If the test expression does not match any of the items in any of the `Case` statements, the code block under the `Case Else` statement is executed. The `Case Else` block is also referred to as the default case.

You must have at least one `Case` statement in the body of a `Select` statement. The `Case Else` statement is not required, although in most cases you will want to specify a default action. If there is no default action and none of the `Case` expression lists are met, the entire `Select` statement is bypassed. Look at the tandem `If` example from the previous section as constructed with the `Select Case` statement:

```
Select Case strPrefixName
    Case "Mr."
    Case "Mrs."
    Case "Dr."
    Case Else
End Select
```

The `Select` is a much better construct to use for this type of processing. It is easier to read and easier to implement. And you don't have to worry about having mismatched `If...End If` pairs in a huge nested mess. Now, there are situations where nested `If`s are the best solution to a programming challenge. With a little forethought, you can ensure that you use the right conditional process for each situation.

The `Select Case` statement is very flexible with regard to what you can put in the expression list. Often, you will need to have a range of values in the expression list. Take, for example, the case of determining benefits status for an employee, based upon the time employed.

```
Select Case intYearsEmployed
    Case 0 to 1
        strMessage = "Benefits will be available on the first anniversary with the
company"
```

```
      Case 1 to 4
         strMessage = "Your pension will be fully vested after year 5."
      Case 5 to 9
         strMessage = "You are now elligible for 3 weeks of vacation"
      Case Else
         strMessage = "You have been here a long time!"
   End Select
```

The level of benefits that an employee is eligible for is determined by her continuity of service, or how long she has been with the company. Using the Select Case construct, it is very easy to construct custom messages based upon an employee's years of service. Any time you want to take actions based upon a range of values for a variable, the Select Case is the construct to use.

In addition to specifying a range in the expression list, you can have multiple values within the expression list to provide additional options for hitting the case (matching the test condition). You can mix and match ranges and values to get the desired effect.

```
Select Case intLuckyNumbers
   Case 1 to 3, 7
   Case 4 to 6
   Case 9, 11
   Case 8, 12
   Case Else
End Select
```

One of the most useful places to use a Select Case statement is in processing error codes and returning custom messages to your user based upon the error code encountered at the back-end service.

```
Select Case sqlError
   Case 1024 'Insert Failed, Row Already Exists
      strCustomMsg = "Can not insert your record into the database.  " & _
                                 "The record already exists"
   Case 2001 'Insert Failed, Invalid Row Data
      strCustomMsg = "Insert failed.  There was invalid input data"
   Case Else
      strCustomMsg = "Sql Error processing insert: " & sqlError
End Select
```

As you get into Chapter 9, "Calling Procedures: Functions and Subroutines," you will be constructing functions that make full use of the Select Case construct's many useful features.

Understanding Looping

Looping is one of the most powerful processing constructs available. Programming loops provide your programs with the capability to execute the same block of code over and over again, until a predefined condition is met.

To understand looping, you need only take a look at any number of activities that you perform throughout the year. Take a moment to try to remember the last time that you planted a tree (or a bush, anything that you had to dig a hole to plant). Based on the type of plant and its size, you determine the size of the hole that you need to dig. You pick up your shovel and begin. You put the shovel in the dirt, kick it down, and throw the dirt to the side. Are you done yet? No? You start to dig again, and after each shovelful of dirt, you determine whether the hole is large enough. If not, you continue to dig. If it is, you plant your tree and go on to some other essential task, like cutting the grass or napping. The workflow of this planting process is shown in Figure 8.2.

FIG. 8.2

Examples of looping are found everywhere.

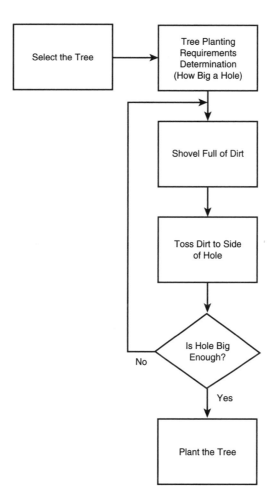

This outdoor planting exercise is a perfect example of how a loop works. You know you have to meet some predetermined criteria (a hole of a certain size). You have a block of work to perform (dig a shovelful of dirt each time) that will ultimately fulfill the requirement, but you are not sure how many times you will have to perform the work until the criteria is met. Then, you go ahead and perform the block of work until the condition is met. As you will see, constructing loops programmatically is implementing that same repetitive functionality in your code.

Do Loops

The Do Loop construct is one of the looping methods with which you can perform multiple executions of a block of code within your Active Server Pages scripts. The template for the Do loop is:

```
Do [{While ¦ Until} condition]
    [statements]
    [Exit Do]
    [statements]
Loop
```

Notice that the test to see if the condition is met is performed before the code within the loop is ever executed. In this case, the statements within the loop will be executed 0, 1, or more times. There are, however, a number of situations in which you want to ensure the code within the loop is executed at least once. To add this functionality, we move the test for the condition to the "bottom" of the loop, and now have the second form of the Do loop.

```
Do
    [statements]
    [Exit Do]
    [statements]
Loop [{While ¦ Until} condition]
```

In this form of the Do loop, the loop will be executed at least one time. This is an important distinction. Where you place the condition determines if and when the code within the loop is executed.

Don't let the While/Until confuse you. They are just two ways of expressing the same functionality. Which one you use will be determined by which "sounds" better. Because you usually code from pseudo code that was generated from business requirements, you select the one that expresses the condition best.

```
Do While intValue < 4
```

is functionally equivalent to

```
Do Until intValue > 3
```

The form of the Do loop (testing at the top or bottom) that you choose will be determined solely on whether you want to ensure the loop executes at least one time. Other than where the condition is tested, at the top or bottom of the loop, the two forms are functionally equivalent.

As your script merrily goes on its way executing the code within the loop, there will surely come a time in which you want to immediately exit from the loop. If you find this out at the bottom of the loop, you could just put a condition killer (a value that satisfies the condition, exiting the loop) into the variable that you are checking. This is not the best solution, and no solution at all if you are somewhere in the middle of the loop when you determine that you need to exit. To exit the loop at any time within the loop code block (before meeting the condition that causes the loop to end), use the Exit Do statement. This immediately causes the processing within the loop to stop.

You can also nest Do loops. The Exit Do statement will transfer control to the loop that is one level above the current nested loop. If the loop is not nested, or if you are in the top-most nested loop, the Exit Do statement returns control to the first statement immediately after the loop. Take a look at an example of nesting loops and the Exit Do statement.

```
Dim intCounter1, intCounter2

intCounter1 = 0
Do While intCounter1 < 10
   intCounter2 = 0
   Do
      intCounter2 = intCounter2 + 1
      If intCounter2 = intCounter1 * 2 Then
         Exit Do
      End If
   Loop While intCounter2 < 10
   intCounter1 = intCounter1 + 1
Loop
```

In the preceding example, the value of intCounter2 gets up to nine only five times. Notice the Exit Do in the nested loop will exit the inner loop but will not exit the outer one. After the outer loop is completed, intCounter1 will have a value of 10.

You will find there are situations when you want to start processing in a loop and never exit. The loop will not end until an error condition is raised or some internal flag is set to exit the loop. To set up this type of loop, you use True as the condition of the statement.

```
Do While True
   GetUserInput
   If blnError Then
      Exit Do
   End If
Loop
```

In the preceding example, the code continues to execute until the blnError flag is set to True. This "endless loop," as it is more commonly known, is not a favorable occurrence in most cases. If you did not explicitly intend for the loop to execute forever, and it does, you have a problem that needs to be addressed.

While...Wend

The While construct is a construct that is much like the Do...Loop construct. Its template follows:

```
While condition
    [statements]
Wend
```

This is functionally equivalent to the first form of the Do loop that was discussed previously. The major difference is the absence of an Exit While statement to leave the loop before the condition is met. The option of using Until in the condition is also lacking.

In the next example, you want to find out how many occurrences of the word "the" are in a text area passed back to us from a form. You can use the `While...Wend` construct to facilitate this activity.

```
Dim strTextArea, strSearch, intPosition, intOccurrences
intPosition = 1
intOccurrences = 0
strSearch = "the"
While InStr(intPosition, strTextArea, strSearch)
    intOccurrences = intOccurrences + 1
    IntPosition = InStr(intPosition, strTextArea, strSearch) + 1
Wend
```

You are using the `InStr` function, which returns the position of one string within another as your condition. A `While` condition is evaluated just like the condition of an `If` statement. If the expression evaluates to a numeric value, any value other than 0, the condition will be considered met or `True`. The `InStr` function returns 0 if the search string is not found. The `intPosition` is the position from within the target string to start the search. The `While` works well in this case because you do not need to exit the loop until the entire string is searched, nor will you have to execute the loop at least once. Either the condition is met (an occurrence found) or not.

In general practice, it is better to use the `Do...Loop` construct than the `While...Wend`. The `Do` loop is much more flexible and provides a number of additional features that are not available in the `While...Wend` loop. You will encounter this construct if you are converting from older code or adapting older VB code to be used by your Active Server Pages scripts.

For...Next Loops

The `For...Next` loop provides much of the functionality of the `Do` loop but with an important difference: You know before you enter the loop how many times you want to execute the code within the loop. The `For...Next` loop template is shown as follows:

```
For counter = start To end [Step step]
    [statements]
    [Exit For]
    [statements]
Next
```

The counter is initialized to the value in start and then incremented by step each time through the loop. If not ended prematurely, the loop will stop executing when the counter is greater than the end value. The counter is incremented at the bottom of the loop. The `For` loop also has an easy exit-the-loop statement, `Exit For`, which will break out of the loop regardless of the status of the condition, just like the `Exit Do` in the `Do` loop.

The power inherent in the `For Next` loop construct is demonstrated by creating a function to perform the calculation of a factorial. Factorials are mathematical calculations that multiply a value by each integer value less than the number you are computing the factorial for. For example, the factorial for !4 would be 24 (4 * 3 * 2 * 1). I know this is a bit premature, but you will now see a function to compute the factorial of a number, just a quick taste of what to expect in Chapter 9, "Calling Procedures: Functions and Subroutines."

```
Function ComputeFactorial(n)
   dim intCounter, intFactorial
   intFactorial = CInt(n)
   For intCounter = CInt(n) - 1 To 1 step -1
      intFactorial = intCounter * intFactorial
   Next
   ComputeFactorial = intFactorial
End Function
```

The `ComputeFactorial` function calculates the factorial of the number passed in. We know ahead of time that we want to loop for $n-1$ times to calculate the factorial. When the step is not explicitly stated, it defaults to 1. You can also have a negative value as the step value to decrement a counter over a given range. We could have written this code using a `Do` loop, or even a `While` loop, but the `For` loop is the best construct to use when you know the number of iterations you will be executing in advance.

One of the things that you will be using the `For` loop for is array processing. You can loop through the members of an array in no time using the `For` loop. Say that you have an array of names that define a set of active members of some group. You are now going to verify that a new user coming in to your site is a member of this list. You are going to fill an array of all the valid members from a database.

```
Dim memberArr(10), intIterator
...Code to load memberArr from database or flat file...
blnMember = False
For intIterator = 0 to Ubound(memberArr)
   If strUser = memberArr(intIterator) Then
      blnMember = True
      Exit For   'We have verified the user, exit the loop
   End If
Next
```

In reality, you would likely just query the database each time to verify the new user. It is possible that you could maintain a small list of users in a flat file and read that into an array to verify users, as well. Anyway, you use the `For` loop to walk the array from 0 to its upper bound. You then use a conditional `If` statement to see if the username that was passed in matches any of the names in the array. If they do, you set the member flag to `True` and immediately exit the loop using the `Exit For` statement.

From Here...

You have looked at a number of programming constructs that enable you to make decisions and perform operations on your data. Without the capability to process conditional statements or to perform looping in your code, you would be reduced to code each revolution of the loop individually. How would you like to spin through a 100-item array and have to create a new line of code for each array element!

You are headed toward the end of Part II. Here is how you will be integrating what you have learned so far:

▓ Chapter 9, "Calling Procedures: Functions and Subroutines," integrates the power of conditional processing and looping into reusable code blocks called procedures. You learn how to design, create, and test procedures, integrating all of the things you have learned up to this point about data, variables, and program flow.

Calling Procedures: Functions and Subroutines

Over the past few years, countless articles and books have been written and discussions held centering on code reuse. The latest development in code reuse— although it has been around now for quite some time— is object-oriented development. The basic concept involves encapsulating key pieces of functionality in different objects. Then, when you are ready to create your application, you have an inventory of prebuilt functional objects to choose from. The many benefits of code reuse can be reaped in almost any development environment (although many developers would like you to believe that it is only attainable via SmallTalk or C++). In this chapter, we will discuss crafting procedures to maximize code reuse in your Active Server Pages development. ∎

Partitioning your application

Partitioning involves the process of breaking down your application into smaller logical pieces to create a framework for encapsulating key functionality into procedures.

Creating VBScript procedures

This involves understanding the process and syntax of creating functions and subroutines for use in your scripts.

Tips and techniques for procedure design

We provide a blueprint to follow when you begin to build your procedures.

Handling errors

Proactive handling of errors ensures that your clients have a pleasant experience at your site.

Using Server-Side Includes

The use of Server-Side Includes provides a mechanism to add prebuilt functions to your script from external files.

Examining Procedures

As you begin to develop your Active Server applications, you will find that they consist of a number of interrelated pages; each page is a logical division of work, expressed by the functions you embed within that page relative to those pages that it is linked to. Within any specific page, you can also divide the functionality into discrete pieces by using procedures. A procedure is a logically related group of statements that can be *executed* by a single statement. Creating procedures enables you to encapsulate specific actions and calculations within a callable routine. As an example, in the following code snippet, the CreateNewUserID function is called. The function creates a new user in the database and returns the new ID as a string sub-type variant.

```
strNewID = CreateNewUserID()
```

For the moment, we will defer talking about the cases in which the ID was not created successfully. Instead, focus on the fact that with one line of code, you have executed a procedure that performs a logical unit of work (creating the ID). The implementation of the CreateNewUserID function could conceivably be fifty or sixty lines long. There are a number of reasons why it makes sense to logically divide up your page into statements of related functionality through the use of procedures. In the previous example, imagine that you need to create a number of new user IDs within a script. If you did not encapsulate the functionality within a procedure, you would have to copy/paste the fifty lines of code in each place within the script that you needed to create a new ID. In addition to the extra code that must be put in and parsed, if you were to change a line of code within the CreateNewUserID routine, you would have to change that line in each place that you copied the code to.

This need to find each statement to be changed also introduces another point of possible failure and inconsistency into your code. This is one of the main benefits of procedures. When you make a change within a procedure, all of the scripts that reference it will automatically benefit from the revised code. There is no chance of forgetting a place (each of those copy/paste steps) where the code needs to be changed. You will run into enough of those problematic situations in the first few months without any extra help!

In the preceding example, we mention that you might be calling the CreateNewUserID function a number of times within the same page. A more likely situation is one in which you want to use the routine in a number of *different* pages. Again, you don't want to resort to the copy/paste routine. You will want to utilize a functionality called Server-Side Includes, which allow you to share procedures, and any file for that matter, between multiple scripts. More on Server-Side Includes will be found later in this chapter in the section "Using Server-Side Includes."

You can use any combination of variables, arrays, and control statements found in Chapter 7, "Understanding Variable Typing, Naming, and Scoping" and Chapter 8, "Working with Program Flow and Control Structures," within the body of the procedures that you create. You can also integrate calls to the objects that are delivered with the Active Server Pages product, as well as any third-party objects that you acquire. This provides you with a powerful set of building blocks to begin crafting your procedure library. And in effect, what you will want to do is just that: Begin to create a library of procedures that you can use over and over again in your ASP development. This is a major source of code reuse that will make future applications much easier to develop.

There are two types of procedures within the VBScript environment, *subroutines* and *functions*. They both provide a method to logically group a related set of statements. There are, however, some subtle differences between the two, noted in the next two sections.

Subroutines

A subroutine is a block of code that you can invoke from anywhere within your script. The template for a subroutine procedure looks like this:

```
Sub procedure-name(argument list)
    statements to execute
    [Exit Sub]
    statements to execute
End Sub
```

The argument list contains the values that are passed into the subroutine, which can be referenced in the body of the procedure. In the Visual Basic environment, argument values are passed either By Reference (ByRef) or By Value (ByVal). Passing a variable ByRef enables the subroutine to alter the value of the passed-in argument. Passing a variable ByVal passes only the value of the variable into the subroutine. The variable cannot be changed within the Sub procedure. The current version of VBScript only supports passing arguments ByVal. Be sure to check the documentation as each new release is made available. We bet that you will be able to add the ByRef option to your VBScript repertoire shortly.

The Exit Sub statement found within the subroutine template is an optional statement that works just like the Exit Do or Exit For statements within a loop. When an Exit Sub statement is encountered, the subroutine is exited immediately. The Exit Sub statement is usually found with an If statement, as in: If a condition exists (an error, or other), leave the subroutine immediately.

 T I P Because VBScript only allows passing arguments by value, use script level scope variables if you need a variable to be visible in all procedures within a page.

There are two ways to call or invoke a subroutine. The first is to call the routine by typing the subroutine name followed by a list of arguments separated by commas. The second way is to use the Call statement in front of the subroutine name. If the Call statement is used, the parameters passed to the subroutine must be enclosed within parentheses.

The following examples show how a simple subroutine that writes a greeting to the HTML stream can be invoked, using either of the two subroutine calling syntax:

```
Greeting server.request(UserName)
```

or

```
    Call Greeting(server.request(UserName))
Sub Greeting(strUserName)
    response.write(strUserName)
    response.write(", welcome to our page!")
End Sub
```

Functions

A function is very similiar to a subroutine with two important differences. First, when calling a function, you must use parentheses around the argument list. If there are no arguments for the function, you must still include parentheses, although they will contain nothing: `FunctionName()`. The second difference is that a function will return a value to the calling procedure or statement. The template for the function procedure follows:

```
Function name [(arglist)]
    statements to execute
    [name = expression]
    [Exit Function]
    statements to execute
End Function
```

You will set the return value of the function by assigning a value to the function name within the body of the procedure. If you do not explicitly assign a return value to the function name, it will return zero. Until the `ByRef` argument passing option is added to VBScript, you will likely find yourself creating more functions than subroutines because you will not be able to change the value of the arguments passed to a subroutine.

The following example illustrates a common function, returning a description of an error, based on an error number passed in.

```
Function ErrorMessage(intErrorCode)
    Select Case intErrorCode
        Case 1024:
            ErrorMessage = "Insert record failed due to key violation"
        Case 1100:
            ErrorMessage = "Update failed.  Key not found"
        Case 1220:
            ErrorMessage = "Invalid Key for Update"
        Case Else:
            ErrorMessage = "Uncategorized Error: " & intErrorcode
    End Select
End Function
```

In reality, this function might include a hundred different error messages. The key thing to remember is that the return value for the function is set by assigning a value to the function name. Also, notice that this type of function is an ideal one to add to your function library. Error numbers and their associated error messages can be standardized across your site allowing one function to be used for all cases in which you need to return an error message to the client.

Error Handling Within Procedures

I have often heard it said that an ounce of prevention is worth a pound of cure. I was never sure what the cure was, but I'd sure prefer to expend the ounce up front, than to worry about the pound later. When a script that is processing encounters an error (an un-trapped error), the client browser receives an error message from ASP that can include the .asp file name, the line number of the error, a short description when appropriate, and other error information. Now, this is valuable information for you to use when debugging the application, but it is NOT the kind of impression that you want to leave visitors to your Web site with.

There are two main things that you can do to reduce the possibility of one of your pages blowing up in production. The first is to test, test, and test again. There is no substitute for testing your application, ensuring that the links are available and that calculations performed are accurate. We will talk more about testing in the section "Creating Reusable Procedures" later in this chapter.

The next activity that you need to perform is to embed error-handling logic within your procedures. Within the Visual Basic environment, there is a fairly robust mechanism for handling errors, even raising your own errors within the framework. The ability to raise custom errors and to trap them intelligently is a key component of integrating custom objects into your script development. In VBScript, your options are a bit more limited. Even though you have limited tools available to trap errors, with a little work, you can catch the majority of them.

The first (and only) construct that enables you to instruct the script processor to take an action when an error occurs is the `On Error Resume Next` statement. The syntax of the statement is:

```
On Error Resume Next
```

When ASP encounters an error executing a statement, the `On Error Resume Next` statement causes the script to jump to the statement immediately following the statement in error. You can think of it as *resuming* after an error at the `Next` statement. Using the `On Error` statement in tandem with the `Err` object enables you to respond to the majority of errors you will encounter in your Active Server Pages development. The `On Error` statement has scope, as well. You can set the scope at the script or procedure level, just as you set variable scope. Generally, you will want to implement error handling within your procedures (where most of your script code will live anyway).

Working with the *Err* Object

Information about errors that are encountered as your scripts execute is stored within the `Err` object, which is an intrinsic part of the VBScript language. It has properties that are set when errors occur, and methods that can be performed. The properties of the `Err` object are outlined in Table 9.1.

Part
II

Ch
9

Table 9.1 *Err* **Object Properties**

Property	Description	Example
Number	The error number for the most recent error	11
Description	A string containing a description of the error	Division by 0
Source	A string containing the source of the error	`Project.Class`

When an error is raised within a Visual Basic class module, the source property is in the format `Project.Class`, where project is the Visual Basic project file and class is the class name of the method that was executing when the error was raised.

▶ **See** "Handling Errors Within Your Classes" for more information about Visual Basic classes and raising errors from within class modules, **p. 272**

There are two methods associated with the `Err` object. The first, `Err.Clear`, is called with no parameters and clears any information residing in the properties of the `Err` object. The second method, `Err.Raise`, raises a run-time error. The template for the `Err.Raise` method is:

```
Err.Raise(number, source, description, helpfile, helpcontext)
```

The only required parameter is the number, which is the number returned from the `Err.Number` property. The source and description are string parameters, the uses of which are described in Table 9.1. In Active Server Pages VBScript development, you will not use the `helpfile` or `helpcontext` variables.

CAUTION

If you call the `Err.Raise` method and do not include all of the parameters, any values that were in the `Err` object will remain. To ensure that you do not inadvertently leave erroneous information in the object, call `Err.Clear` before you call `Err.Raise`.

Error Handling in Action

One of the best places to use error handling within your programming development is at the procedure level. Because procedures are logical units of work, it makes sense to have error handling that is specific to each procedure. In the following example, we have embedded error handling within our procedure to ensure that an error is appropriately trapped.

Do you remember imaginary numbers? Now there was a class of numbers that we could relate to. Their only use in high school was in taking the square root of a negative number. In the VBScript world, there is no support for imaginary numbers (only imaginary features), and if you tried to calculate the square root of a negative number, you would generate a run-time error, which, in this case is exactly what we are going to do.

```
<%
    dim intRC
```

```
    intRC = SquareRoot(-4)
    If (intRc < 0) Then
        response.write("Error calculating the square root")
    Else
        response.write(intRc)
    End If
%>

<SCRIPT LANGUAGE="VBScript" RUNAT=SERVER>
    Function SquareRoot(varNumber)
        On Error Resume Next
        SquareRoot = Sqr(varNumber)
        if Err.Number > 0 Then
            Err.Clear
            SquareRoot = -1
        End If
    End Function
</SCRIPT>
```

Part
II

Ch
9

To set up the scenario, the SquareRoot (Sqr) function is called, passing in a negative value as the argument. The first line within the function is the On Error statement. When an error is encountered, the On Error statement lets the execution pass to the next line. If you do not check the Err object for an error condition, and you have the On Error statement, your function can return invalid or incorrect information from your procedure if an error is encountered. The way to handle this is to add checks of the Err object in strategic places (those most likely to generate an error). You could, potentially, check the Err object after each statement is executed, but that would be inefficient. The key is to place the Err object check at critical points within the procedure. Because you will be creating procedures that perform one logical function, it should be easy to select the appropriate places to add Err object checks.

Back to our SquareRoot example code: If the number passed into the function generates a run-time error within the Sqr function, the function sets the return value to -1. This value notifies the calling statement that an error has occurred within the procedure. Notice that we are actually introducing another level of error handling into the script. We are handling the run-time error within the procedure, and then responding to an error condition (return value of -1) within the script proper. In most cases, you will be checking the value of a return code from a function to verify that the function has completed successfully and then code for appropriate action based upon the outcome.

Creating Reusable Procedures

Coding in VBScript is not a traditional object-oriented reuse exercise, but by creating useful procedures, combined with the Server-Side Include capability of ASP and Internet Information Server, you can ensure that you will be reusing your code just like the Object-Oriented developers (well, not just like, but close). For those of you who are Visual Basic developers, many of the functions (and those subroutines that don't change the passed in arguments) can be moved directly into your VBScript library.

To create a library of reusable procedures, you need some guidelines and a method to create them. The first bridge that must be crossed, of course, is to create the reusable procedures.

To be reusable, procedures must provide a level of functionality that is generic enough to be used in a variety of situations. These types of procedures include formatting code, header and footer code, advertisement code, database query code, and others that have wide applicability across applications.

The first step in creating world-class procedures is to define the requirements of the routine. This just requires some thinking to determine the exact functionality that the procedure will provide. For example, suppose you want to create a generic procedure to validate credit cards. There are a number of questions that come immediately to mind:

- What type of credit cards will be processed?
- How many digits are required for each type?
- Which back-end service will provide the authorizations?
- How often will the procedure be invoked?
- Are there turnaround time requirements?

You need to address every question that you come up with regarding the procedures functionality before you write a single line of code.

Once you have settled on the functions that the procedure will provide, the next step is defining the arguments that the procedure will accept, and optionally, the return value that the procedure will provide. Again, there are a number of questions relating to the arguments or parameters that the procedure will accept and to the return values:

- What parameters will be passed in?
- Are all the parameters required for the process?
- Are there any range restrictions on the parameters?
- Will the procedure return a value? If so, a number or a string?
- How will your procedure notify the calling statement of errors in the return value?
- If the procedure provides a return value, how will it be formatted?

You have answered all of the argument and return value questions (again, no coding yet). Now you are ready to begin examining the interfaces (if any) that your procedure will interact with. Interfaces include such things as database access, mini or mainframe connectivity, transaction processor access, and so on.

With all of the answers to the questions posed above in-hand, you can begin thinking about any algorithms that will be implemented locally within your procedure. Do you need to perform any calculations outside of the interfaces? Are there any complex looping or array handling requirements? Again, these are questions that you need to answer before you begin to code the procedure.

Coding the Procedure

The next step is to create the procedure skeleton. This includes the `Sub` or `Function` block, as well as selecting the name for the procedure. Just as you learned about the naming conventions for variables, there are naming conventions for procedure names as well. The naming conventions are more common sense and less rote, however, than those for variables. The best guide is to think of a name that, even if you had never seen the code, would give you a clear idea of what function(s) the procedure performs. For example, use `InsertNewDatabaseRecord` instead of `addrec`, or `AuthorizeCreditTransaction` instead of `authtran`.

Part

II

Ch

9

Now that you have gathered the necessary information about functionality and decided upon a name, you can begin to code the procedure. When you are developing a complicated procedure, it is often wise to code the entire procedure in pseudo code, and then implement it in VBScript. Using pseudo code will do two things for you. First, it enables you to write out the logic of the procedure in near-English and helps you to ensure that all of the functionality that was specified in your design is in the procedure. Second, the pseudo code becomes the documentation for each step within the procedure. You just add the comment delimiter in front of each line of pseudo code and violà, your code is fully commented!

Basically, pseudo code is the use of English phrases to illustrate the functions that your code will carry out. An example of this follows:

```
Function AuthorizeCreditTransaction(strAccountNumber, dblAmount)
    Verify that the account number is valid
    If the account number is invalid
        return invalid account
    Connect to the Credit Authorization Service
    Send the Authorization Transaction
    Receive the Authorization
    Return the Authorization to the calling procedure
End Function
```

Notice that we have not included a single line of VBScript in this psuedo code, but we have mapped out the entire procedure.

Now it's time to integrate the answers to each of the questions that you asked earlier. If there were range restrictions on the arguments passed in, add them now. For example, you might implement a mod 10 check digit routine on the account number before it is sent for authorization. A mod 10 check digit is an algorithm used to verify that an account number is valid within a vendor's range. This provides a local level of account verification before the transaction is sent to the authorization process. You also might ensure that the amount passed in is greater than zero. These would, of course, show up in your pseudo code as well. The mod 10 check digit also might be a function in and of itself that would be called from your `AuthorizeCredit Transaction` function.

Now, you can go back and add the scripting to complete each line of the pseudo-coded procedure. As you add the functional code, you will also introduce error handling code where appropriate, as discussed in the preceding section "Error Handling With in Procedures." When you have completed the procedure, it is time to test it.

Checking the Routine

As Vidal Sasson once said, "The only place where success comes before work is in the dictionary." This is true in creating successful procedures as well. You have surely spent a considerable amount of time already crafting the procedure, but your job is not yet done. Even though you have carefully coded the procedure and introduced error-handling code in appropriate places, there is no substitute for rigorous testing to ensure that the procedure functions in all circumstances in your production environment. There are a number of fine texts available that can guide you through this rigorous testing process. Presented below is an outline of some of the specific test methods to get you started:

Unit Testing   Unit testing involves testing your procedure against the outcome criteria that you determined in the questioning phase in a stand-alone environment. This ensures that all of the interfaces and internal procedure logic are working correctly without worrying about external factors affecting the procedures performance. Things to test during this phase include passing in valid and invalid arguments, making services unavailable to test the robustness of your error handling code, and processing the function to completion to check the return value, if any.

Integration Testing   After the unit tests have been completed successfully, you move into integration testing. This involves including the procedure into an application and again testing the scenarios outlined during the questioning phase. This enables you to determine any potential problems in integrating the procedure with other code. This would be a place that you could find (if for some reason you forgot the `Option Explicit` declaration) a common variable in your procedure that was not dimensioned, and was subsequently overwritten by a script-level variable within the integrated script.

Deployment   It is now time to deploy your procedure into production. If you have followed the testing steps above, you will end up with a logically sound, error free, and tested procedure that you can add to your growing procedure library. Now that you have all of these powerful generic procedures, you can maximize their use by including them into your pages. As it happens, we are now ready to discuss how to perform this feat, using Server-Side Includes.

Using Server-Side Includes

If you have ever done development in C or C++, you can think of Server-Side Includes as being somewhat analogous to the `#include` directive. In the C language, the `#include` directive enables you to insert the contents of one file into another file at compile time. Development in C and C++ would be impossible if you could not `#include` files in-line.

Server-Side Includes (SSI) perform a function similar to the `#include` directive. In its most basic form, SSI includes the contents of one file into an HTML stream before that file is sent to the client. The included file can be a text file, an .HTML file, an .asp file, a graphic file, or almost any other file existing on the server.

Imagine this scenario: You have a Web site composed of hundreds of linked pages for your company. You want to provide a standard look and feel across all of your pages, so you can project a single image to any point on your site where a client may be browsing. On most Web pages there are standard headers and footers with links or graphics or some other unifying display that is consistent across the site. But, the information in these headers and footers changes throughout the month (or even day). If you had to go to each page and change the information within the .HTML or .asp file, you would need to hire a team of Internet savvy Kelly Temps just to keep you up-to-date. Or, you could use Server-Side Includes and only have to change one or two Include files. Any changes made to the included files would then ripple through your entire site the next time a page was requested.

Scenario number two: You have yet to reach this part of the chapter. You were so excited when you learned about procedures, you stopped at that point and spent the next week or so developing procedures. Now it is a week later and you have a number of generic, well-thought-out, tested procedures that you are going to use in your Web pages. A few years ago, before the wizards that we find in most development environments these days were even a thought, the best way to start a new program was to find an old one that did something similar and then use the highly efficient CPC system (copy, paste, code) to complete your task. Although Server-Side Includes are not analogous to code wizards, they will let you avoid the CPC syndrome when you want to include pre-existing procedures into your Active Server Pages applications.

Server-Side Includes: How To

Before we begin, you must be aware that we are going to be discussing two types of Server-Side Includes. The first is provided by Internet Information Server (IIS). The Includes that are provided by ASP when processing .asp files are currently limited to including external files. As you continue through this section, the IIS versus ASP nature of the discussion will be clearly marked.

A couple of steps are involved in using SSI to enhance the functionality of your Web applications. The first step is to decide what file(s) you want to include. The second step is to add the Server-Side Include statement into the target .stm or .asp file. An .stm file is the same as an .HTML file, but causes the file to be pre-processed by the SSINC.DLL (Server-Side Include dynamic link library) which actually handles the Include functions for those non .asp files.

Server-Side Includes are through the use of pre-processing directives. These directives have the following syntax:

```
<!--#<PREPROCESSING_DIRECTIVE>-->
```

You will be examining a number of these directives, but first, you will move on to those that will be used most often in your development programming.

N O T E The default extension for the files that will be processed for Server-Side Includes by IIS is .stm. To change the default extension, edit the registry entry for the Server-Side Includes extension. ▒

Including Files   The following discussion on including files is applicable to both IIS and ASP. There are two ways that you can specify a Server-Side Include file to include within a target file.

The only difference in the two methods is where the Server-Side Include file is in relation to the target file. The first is the virtual file include method:

```
<!--#INCLUDE VIRTUAL = "inclfile.txt"-->
```

This will insert the file `inclfile.txt` into the HTML stream at the point that the Server-Side Include is found in the page. The file name is found in a directory, relative to the path for the base directory of the Internet Information Server (IIS). If you accepted the defaults when installing IIS, the base directory will be **\WINNT\SYSTEM32\INETSRV**, so the `inclfile.txt` will be located in that directory. You can also specify a path for a virtual Include. The path will be in relation to the base directory of IIS as well. For example, to include the following file:

```
\WINNT\SYSTEM32\INETSRV\INCLUDES\HEADER.TXT
```

You would use the following Include statement:

```
<!--#INCLUDE VIRTUAL="/INCLUDES/HEADER.TXT"-->
```

Notice that the directory delimiters (slashes) are in the opposite direction to what most of you are familiar with (unless you have worked in the UNIX or AS400 environments lately). They are used in that fashion because the Server-Side Include specification was developed in the UNIX environment. Even though the standard uses the forward slash, the backward slash will work equally well for Server-Side Includes.

The second method to include a file is with the `FILE` Include directive, which looks like this:

```
<!--#INCLUDE FILE = "inclfile.txt"-->
```

Using the `FILE` Include directive, the include file is located in relation to the location of the current target document. So, if you want to include a file in the same directory as the target file, leave off any directory path information. If you want to include a file that is under the target document—for example, a directory called scripts—then you would use the following statement:

```
<!--#INCLUDE FILE = "\scripts\inclfile.txt"-->
```

You might be wondering why there are two methods of doing what appears to be the same thing. Well, the real reason that you are given these options is to increase the flexibility of your Web development. There are generally two classes of files that you want to include. The first class is application-specific files, like the custom header and footer that were mentioned previously under "Using Server-Side Includes." These might be in a sub-directory stored beneath the location of the corporate Web pages default directory. In the next case, you will want to include, in many applications, all of those functional and thoroughly tested procedures that you have already developed. The two file Include methods give you the flexibility to easily process Server-Side Includes in both situations.

An Included file can have another Include directive within it. This is useful when you want to include a number of common procedures found in multiple files. In the first Include file, you will include directives including the common procedures. Then, in the target file, you would only need to include the first file containing the other Include directives, instead of an Include reference for each and every common procedure file. Just be careful not to include a reference to a file within that file. This will create an endless Include loop, NOT a good thing!

File Information Includes   In addition to including files into your document, you can also include a number of items (file size, last mod date) about a particular file into your HTML stream. The file information Includes are not currently supported within the ASP environment. To include the size of a file, you would use the following directive:

```
<!--#FSIZE [VIRTUAL][FILE]="inclfile.txt"-->
```

You can use either a virtual path or a relative path when using the FSIZE directive. The size of the file inclfile.txt, in kilobytes, will be included in the file. This is a particularly handy directive when specifying a file for download. You can include the file name and the file size, so your client will have an idea of how long a download might take. The number returned, using the FSIZE directive will be comma delimited in the thousands position. A 1 megabyte file will be returned as 1,024.

You can also obtain the date that a file was last modified to include in your HTML stream by using the FLASTMOD directive:

```
<!--#FLASTMOD [VIRTUAL][FILE]="inclfile.txt"-->
```

This directive also can be used with files that are referenced using a virtual or a relative path. By default, the date that is returned by using the FLASTMOD directive is in the format Weekday MonthName DayNumber YearNumber. The format of this date, as well as the default size returned by FSIZE (kilobytes) can be changed by using the configuration directive option of SSI.

Configuring Server-Side Includes   There are a number of options that you can specify to override the default behavior of the data returned from an SSI call. The format used when setting a configuration option is:

```
<!--#CONFIG OPTION ="optionstring"-->
```

The option string is relevant to the configuration option that you are setting. If you think about it, this is a powerful feature. You can change the format of the information returned from the include without having to provide any formatting for it in your scripts.

Setting the Format of the FLASTMOD Directive   As stated previously, by default, the FLASTMOD directive returns the last modified date of a file in the format Weekday MonthName DayNumber YearNumber (Tuesday, December 10 1996). By using the CONFIG directive with the TIMEFMT option, you have the opportunity to specify the information returned by the FLASTMOD directive.

```
<!--#CONFIG TIMEFMT ="date/time format string"-->
```

To specify a new date or time format, you create a format mask using the options specified in Table 9.2. The locale reference found in the table is referring to that on the server where the Include is taking place.

**Table 9.2 Parameters for Specifying Date and Time Formats for the
FLASTMOD Directive; Examples based on a date/time of February 23, 1996
at 11:01:55 PM**

Parameter	Description	Example
%m	Month as a decimal number	02
%b	Abbreviated month name	Feb
%B	Full month name	February
%d	Day of the month	23
%j	Day of the year	54
%y	Year without century	96
%Y	Year with century	1996
%w	Weekday as an integer	5 (0 is Sunday)
%a	Abbreviated weekday name	Fri
%A	Weekday name	Friday
%U	Week of the year, Sunday first day	8
%W	Week of the year, Monday first day	8
%I	Hour in 12 hr format	12
%H	Hour in 24 hr format	23
%M	Minute as an integer	01
%S	Second as an integer	55
%P	AM/PM indicator for current locale	PM
%x	Date representation for current locale	2/23/96
%c	Date/time representation for current locale	2/23/96 11:01:55PM
%X	Time representation for the current locale	11:01:55PM
%z	Time zone abbreviation or blank	CST
%Z	Time zone, or blank if unknown	Central Standard Time
%%	Percent sign in mask	%M%%%S

If you have ever used the Format function within Visual Basic or VBA, you will be very comfortable using the #Config formatting masks.

Here are a couple of examples of formatting a date and time, using different masks. For the purpose of these examples, assume that the last modified date/time on the file that you are going to use the #FLASTMOD directive on was February 6, 1991 at 11:05:09 PM.

```
<!--#CONFIG TIMEFMT ="%I:%M %P"-->
```

formats the time as 11:05 PM. You can include seconds in the time as follows:

```
<!--#CONFIG TIMEFMT ="%I:%M:%S %P"-->
```

To format the date as shown in the preceding paragraph, you would use the following date mask:

```
<!--#CONFIG TIMEFMT ="%B %dth, %Y"-->
```

The configuration of the TIMEFMT remains in effect until the directive is called again within the page, or until a new page is loaded.

Setting Default File Size Increments for the FSIZE Directive   As mentioned in the section about the FSIZE directive, the default number returned is in kilobytes. If you want to specify the file size in bytes, generate the following directive:

```
<!--#CONFIG ABBREV ="bytes"-->
```

This ensures that the file size returned to the HTML stream by the FSIZE directive will be in bytes, not in the default kilobytes. The number returned in bytes will be comma delimited in the thousands position as well.

Setting SSI Error Messages   When a Server-Side Include fails for any reason, by default, a detailed message is returned that contains information explaining why the Include failed. In many cases, you do not want this information returned to the client. To prevent this from happening, set the ERRMSG configuration option.

```
<!--#CONFIG ERRMSG ="Server Encountered an SSI Error."-->
```

Once this configuration option is set, the message set within the CONFIG directive will be the one returned to the client when an SSI error is encountered.

The Echo Directive   There are a number of "server" variables that are associated with any given request for the retrieval of a page. The Echo directive is not available in the ASP environment, but all of these server variables can be accessed within ASP by querying the Server object, discussed in Chapter 12, "Enhancing Interactivity with *Cookies*, Headers, and the *Server* Object." Some of these variables are available to you for inclusion into the HTML stream that you return to your client, using SSI. The syntax of the Echo directive is:

```
<!--ECHO VAR ="VariableName"-->
```

Depending on your requirements, you can use one or more or even all of the available variables. The most useful choices are shown in Table 9.3. For a complete list of all the variables available using the Echo directive, see your SSI documentation.

Part
II

Ch
9

Table 9.3 *ECHO* **Directive Server-Side Include Variables**

Variable Name	Description
LAST_MODIFIED	The date the document was last modified
PATH_INFO	Additional information about the document path, returned with a virtual path name
PATH_TRANSLATED	PATH_INFO with the virtual path mapped to the directory path
QUERY_STRING	The information passed to the script following the ? in the URL
DATE_GMT	The current system date in Greenwich Mean Time
DATE_LOCAL	The current system date in the local time zone
GATEWAY_INTERFACE	The current CGI revision level that is supported by the host server
HTTP_[header name]	All of the HTTP header information that will appear in a comma separated list
HTTP_ACCEPT	The MIME types that the browser can accept
HTTP_ACCEPT_LANGUAGE	The languages that the browser can accept
HTTP_USER_AGENT	The name of the browser software running on the client
HTTP_REFERER	The URL of the page that referred the client to the document on your site
HTTP_UA_PIXELS	The resolution of the client browser display
HTTP_UA_COLOR	The color palette of the browser display
HTTP_UA_OS	The operating system of the client browser

An example of including some of the server-side variables follows:

```
<HTML><HEAD><TITLE>#ECHO VAR Samples </TITLE></HEAD><BODY>
<P>Here are some examples of using the echo function<BR></P>
The Local Date    :<!--#ECHO VAR="DATE_LOCAL"--><BR>
The Remote Host   : <!--#ECHO VAR="REMOTE_HOST"--><BR>
All HTTP Header Information: <!--#ECHO VAR="ALL_HTTP"-->
</BODY></HTML>
```

The output from running this script will produce output like the following on the client:

```
Here are some examples of using the echo function
The Local Date  :Thursday December 26 1996
The Remote Host : 3.1.1.1
All HTTP Header Information: HTTP_ACCEPT:image/gif, image/x-xbitmap, image/jpeg,
image/pjpeg, */* HTTP_ACCEPT_LANGUAGE:en HTTP_CONNECTION:Keep-Alive
HTTP_HOST:selfanba HTTP_UA_PIXELS:1024x768 HTTP_UA_COLOR:color8
```

```
HTTP_UA_OS:Windows NT HTTP_UA_CPU:x86 HTTP_USER_AGENT:Mozilla/2.0 (compatible;
MSIE 3.01; Windows NT)
```

Executing Commands Using Server-Side Includes

The last directive that is currently supported only under IIS is the EXEC directive. Using this directive, you can execute a CGI script, a shell command, or an ISAPI application (all ISAPI apps are packaged as DLL's). After the command, app, and so forth has executed, the output is inserted into the HTML stream. If there is any HTTP header information in the returned data stream, only URL redirection information is recognized, and the message is replaced by the text This document has moved to 'new addr'.

Part

II

Ch

9

The format of the EXEC directive follows the preprocessor directive format and looks like this:

```
<!--#EXEC [CGI][CMD][ISA] ="Command/App/Script/ToExecute"-->
```

The CGI Option   Each of the options have slightly different meanings as they are implemented. The first, CGI, notifies the SSI processor that a CGI script (in its virtual path, if specified) is found in quotes after the equal sign. The CGI script can be formatted just as if you were calling it from your browser, with a ? and any parameters that need to be passed to the script delimited by +.

The capability to invoke CGI scripts in-line, using SSI is a powerful tool. Remember when you read about the benefits of including files within your pages? These same benefits accrue to using CGI scripting in-line. With a combination of these two methods, you can maximize code reuse while at the same time, minimize maintenance. A call to execute a CGI command in a cgi-bin subdirectory beneath the document directory looks like this:

```
<!--#EXEC CGI ="/cgibin/querytme.exe?1week+2days"-->
```

This executes the querytme.exe CGI script, passing in 1week and 2days as parameters. The output of the script is inserted into the HTML stream immediately after the EXEC directive.

A Commanding Option: CMD   When the CMD option is specified on the directive line, the CommandToExecute is the shell program to run. You can specify command line parameters, using the CMD option as well. You can specify a full path for the command, or you can let the server walk the path (those directories included in the PATH environment variable) to find the file. If the file is not found, an error message is returned as the text of the call. In this example, we are going to call the command cmdtest.exe and pass it a few parameters:

```
<!--#EXEC CMD ="/utils/cmdtest.exe?10024"-->
```

Including an ISAPI Application   When Microsoft released the ISAPI specification, it created an entirely new market for Internet development tools. With the ISAPI functions now residing within the Microsoft Foundation Classes, it is a quick and painless exercise to create Internet server applications using Visual C++ and IIS. This new API has also created another third-party boon for developers. What once would have been coded in CGI can now, in many cases, be purchased as an ISAPI application. These applications can be leveraged in the Active Server Pages environment as well. ISAPI applications are more efficient and perform better than CGI applications because they run in the same process space as IIS.

When you want to process an ISAPI application using SSI, you can also provide parameters, much like you did when using the CGI option. The syntax to call an ISAPI application named `isapitst.dll` with two parameters, an amount and a term, looks like this:

```
<!--#EXEC ISA ="/apps/isapitst?100.25+30"-->
```

From Here...

This chapter covers procedures: what they are, how to create them, how to ensure that they are error free, and finally, how to reuse them in your ASP development. Now that you have a firm grounding in procedure creation, it is time to move into some of the more advanced features of ASP application development: integrating your VBScript with the objects provided by ASP. Each chapter in Part III discusses a unique component that shows you how to integrate these incredible pieces of functionality to create dynamic ASP pages.

- Chapter 10, "Managing States and Events with *Application* and *Session* Objects," introduces you to the first objects available within ASP. You will learn how to interact at an application level and with each individual's user session.

- Chapter 11, "Building a Foundation of Interactivity with *Request* and *Response* Objects," shows you how to interact with forms through the *Request* Object and how to provide dynamic HTML to your users through the *Response* Object.

Working with Active Server Objects and Components

## CHAPTER 10

Managing States and Events with *Application* and *Session* Objects

Managing users as they navigate through an application represents a common and easily handled challenge in the traditional client/server application development world. In the Web world, in contrast, Internet application developers find managing this challenge or, in essence, maintaining a user's state, to be one of the greatest challenges to building a comprehensive Internet-based application. Because HTTP transactions between a browser and a Web server are independent with no persistence or connection state being maintained, even tracking a user as she moves from one page request to another can be a difficult task.

For managing a user from her first page request, Active Server incorporated a model based on *Cookies* to generate a unique ID for users' browsers. On the first page request, the session OnStart event fires. This event sets the scope of several properties for the life of this unique browser's session. At the same time, the event defines a Timeout property to manage the session length. The Timeout property measures inactivity from the Cookied browser. This chapter explores in detail the capability to track users, but goes way beyond that capability, in exploring the valuable set of functionality extended to programmers through the Session and Application Objects. ■

The problem of tracking user sessions

In most Web applications, tracking users and their activities from page to page requires a large portion of the overall programming effort.

Setting up an application

Active Server Pages utilizes directory structures and the global.asa file for managing applications.

Understanding *Application* and *Session* Objects

First, an overview of the Application and Session Objects' scoping, events, and properties.

***Application* Object, events, and properties**

The Application Object provides a mechanism to track sessions and store variables and objects for application-wide use.

***Session* Object, practical applications**

Use the Session Object to manage a user's flow from page to page, track user input, and cache information.

N O T E Cookies are a feature of HTML 2.0 that enable an HTML author to write a variable or named piece of information to the client browser. If the browser supports HTML 2.0 or greater, this information is then saved as a file by the client browser program on the user's hard drive, and the browser automatically sends that information with any browser request to that domain. The Cookie has a duration property as well. ▦

Active Server Pages Solves the Problem of Managing User Sessions

In the typical Visual Basic client/server development environment, the Visual Basic program operates as the client, capturing any user input and responding to events such as a mouse movement. These user inputs, ranging from a mouse movement to the pressing of a keyboard button, leave the programmer with absolute control in managing the user's choices and experience. The Web world of development has some important distinctions that frame the entire development model.

Because Active Server Pages operates completely at the server, from VBScript execution to storing of variables, the normal Visual Basic model does not apply. The VBScript source code and the objects it invokes and references, only come into play when a user connects to the server by processing a form page or selecting an URL. In short, Active Server Pages is only invoked when a user moves from one page to another. At this point when a browser requests a page, the HTTP request or transaction sends only the simple HTTP transaction, including the page requested along with form or URL fields and some general browser-related information like Cookies.

N O T E For a more detailed description, reference information on the HTTP transaction standard. ▦

The simple HTTP record layout passed between Web server and Web browser creates a challenge for managing an application. One of the key challenges becomes tracking users as they move between pages. This includes maintaining, in an easily accessible way, some unique tracking ID, as well as any information that must be displayed or manipulated such as a shopping basket of selected products in an order processing system. Several standard workarounds have emerged for dealing with this challenge, and Active Server Pages builds on the best of these approaches.

Tracking User Sessions: The Web Challenge

A key challenge of Web programming is tracking each user from one page to the next and making information from their previous pages available on subsequent pages. This challenge can be met by using several basic approaches. But without Active Server Pages, the problem requires complex functions for generating unique IDs and difficult workarounds for keeping track of information or in other words, maintaining variables scoping during a user's working session.

The challenge of tracking a user's session requires generating a unique ID and then ensuring that on every subsequent page that ID and any added user information continues to be available. Two basic techniques prior to Active Server Pages for accomplishing this include:

- Utilizing the Cookie feature of browsers
- Creating hidden fields/URL variables on a page

If you use the second technique, you must ensure that the hidden field or URL variable gets passed to all subsequent pages and created as a new hidden field or URL variable on those pages. This is done to always keep the variable alive as a hidden form field or URL variable.

An enhanced approach to moving hidden fields around involves maintaining a variable's scope by using a database or text file on the server to store this information based on the unique ID. Constant retrieval every time a new page gets requested, and passing the unique ID from page to page as hidden fields and URL variables requires careful planning because all possible page selections and flow must be carefully considered to ensure that unique IDs are not lost.

Generating Unique IDs for Tracking Users   The step of creating a unique ID and saving it as a variable requires more effort than you would expect at first glance. After generating and saving a unique ID, the ID must be carefully managed for it to be available to all subsequent pages during the user's session. Approaches to generating unique IDs generally result from some combination of date and time, user input, and IP addresses or, by using a database to generate a unique ID such as a counter field in Microsoft Access. Unfortunately, all of these approaches require careful planning.

Take the approach of setting up a Microsoft Access table with a counter field and using the counter fields as the unique IDs for users entering the Web page. The first step becomes inserting a new record when the user first hits the page. However, since the insert of a new record will not return the counter field, a query must be done to retrieve that ID field. This is one example of the difficulties. You can't just request the last ordinal record because, of course, within a second or so of the insert command, a second user might have requested the same page and inserted a subsequent record. As a result, you must actually take some value such as date/time and insert that value as well so that you can retrieve the counter value. Even with this approach, you run the risk of having two transactions with same date/time values, down to the second. To further complicate things, you must have the date/time field available as a form field in the HTML document to pass it as a parameter.

Managing User IDs and Scoping with *Cookie*/Form/URL Variables   Regardless of how you generate your unique ID, the immediate challenge that follows becomes keeping that ID alive or always in scope from one page to the next. Without the Active Server Pages Session Object, one approach involves ensuring that every HTML page passes the ID as either an URL variable or a Form field depending on whether the page request results from a hyperlink or Forms processing. This would take the form illustrated in Listing 10.1

N O T E   The empty string tests in Listing 10.1 determine if the variable exists because Active Server script returns an empty string when you attempt to reference an HTML field that does not exist.

Part
III

Ch
10

Listing 10.1 HIDDEN_VARIABLES.ASP—Scoping Hidden Variables from Page to Page

```
<%
'check if parameters are from a form or URL
'----------------------------------------
IF NOT request.form("router") = "" then
    'Parameters are Form Based
    '----------------------
    IF NOT request.form("userid") = "" then
        userid = request.form("userid")
    ELSE
        userid = 0 'New User
    END IF

    'Scope Router Variable for page processing
    '-------------------
    router = request.form("router")


    '--------------------------------
ELSEIF NOT Request.QueryString("router") = ""

    'Parameters are URL Based/Hyperlink
    '------------------------------
    IF NOT request.QueryString("userid") = "" then
        userid = request.QueryString("userid")
    ELSE
        userid = 0 'New Users
    END IF

    'Scope Router Variable for page processing
    '------------------------------
    router = request.QueryString("router")


ELSE
        'Variables not correctly passed, an error has occurred
        'set error routing flag
        '------------------------------------

        router = 0 'Error Routing for Lost Variables

'close IF, all variables set at this point
'----------------------
END IF
%>
```

Cookies drive another approach to managing user IDs from page to page. In a Cookies-based model, no hidden information must be moved from page to page because the Cookie provides a variable that the server writes to the browser and the browser stores locally by domain name. As a result, whenever the browser requests a page from a site within the domain name, such as **http://www.melnick.com**, the browser will pass the Cookie variable along with the rest of the request to the Web server.

Listing 10.2 shows how a Cookie evaluation would simplify the process of scoping user IDs and routing variables as compared to managing the process from page to page. A point here much more important than the complexity of the code comes from the problem that users might not necessarily move in a linear process through your Web pages. Users might bookmark and jump directly to a page or type an alternative URL directly into a browser, or click the Refresh button or the Back button. All of these maneuvers create uncertainty or more errors in the Listing 10.1 approach to managing users. Unlike the approach with hidden variables being kept alive, with Cookies, the variables are passed regardless of which page the user starts from. Your code loses its dependence on any order of page processing.

CAUTION

Cookies have received a lot of attention in recent months, and browsers including Microsoft's IE 3.0 currently enabled features to limit and potentially disable the use of Cookies.

CAUTION

In both Netscape 3.0 and IE 3.0, a flag can be set by the user that forces the browser to prompt the user every time a site attempts to write a Cookie. This prompt provides the user with the option of rejecting the Cookie. In addition, third-party programs are currently available to effectively disable Cookies as well. In practice, Cookies have become so prevalent that setting the prompt becomes quite annoying and as a result will probably not be actively used by any but the most vigilant and fearful users.

Listing 10.2   COOKIES_VARIABLES.ASP—*Cookies* and User IDs

```
<%
'check if cookie variables are available
'- - - - - - - - - - - - - - - - - - - - - - - - - - - - - - - - - - - - - - -
IF request.cookie("router") = "" then

    'Cookie Not Yet Set
    '- - - - - - - - - - - - - - - - - -
    userid = 0 'New Account
    router = 0 'New Account
    '- - - - - - - - - - - - - - - - - -
    'route to new account area and set cookie
    '- - - - - - - - - - - - - - - - -
ELSE
    userid = request.cookie("userid")
    router = request.cookie("router")

'close IF all variables set at this point
'- - - - - - - - - - - - - - - - - - - - -
END IF
%>
```

Without the use of `Cookies`, or when `Cookie` use only tracks the user ID and not other supporting information, the process of passing the variables from page to page requires the use of both hidden fields and URL links that add variables into them. As illustrated in Listing 10.3, both Form and URL variables must be utilized, so the user can't move to another page without passing the variables you have assigned.

Listing 10.3   FORMURL_FIELDS.ASP—Scoping Variables Through HTML

```
<html><body>
<FORM ACTION="next.asp" METHOD="post">
<!------------------------------------------->
<!-- hidden fields are added to URL link -->
<!-- so the link passes values          -->
<!------------------------------------------->
<a href="profile_top.asp?userid=<%=userid%>&router=<%=router%>">Next Page </a>
<a href="profile_display.asp?userid=<%=userid%>&router=<%=router%>">Next Page
➡</a>
<!------------------------------------------->
<!-- hidden fields are stored for passing-->
<!-- in form submit action              -->
<!------------------------------------------->
<INPUT NAME="router" VALUE="<%=router%>" TYPE=HIDDEN>
<INPUT NAME="userid" VALUE="<%=userid%>" TYPE=HIDDEN>
<CENTER>
<INPUT TYPE=SUBMIT VALUE="Continue" NAME="btn">
</CENTER>
</FORM>
</body></html>
```

The methods discussed previously provide a framework for how most of the CGI-based programs currently operate with respect to variables, scoping, and user tracking. These techniques are based on a combination of HTML fields, `Cookies`, and unique ID generation. All these techniques become more stable and more insulated from the developer in the Active Server Pages `Session` and `Application` Objects.

Active Server Pages to the Rescue

Active Server Pages provides an object model, which insulates the developer from all of the challenges relating to tracking users and generating unique IDs. The `Session` and `Application` Objects, not only provide support in generating unique IDs and maintaining the scope of variables, but they also implement the beginning of an event-driven model for developers. Active Server Pages defines an application as an execute permission-enabled directory served by an Internet Information Server. As a subset of the application, a session results when a browser requests a page from an application directory. The session involves one unique browser, so as other browsers request pages from the same application directory, they invoke additional sessions.

The first user to request a page from a directory that makes up an application invokes both an `Application` and a `Session` Object. As subsequent users request pages, they invoke additional

Session Objects. The invoking of an Application Object kicks off theApplication OnStart event, which executes scripts stored in the global.asa file. In addition, you can append variables and objects to the Application Object as new properties. When a developer's .asp file adds a new Application property, the Web server memory space is used to store the variable for use by future .asp files invoked.

As a browser requests a page or file from the application directory, the Web server checks to see if that browser is involved in an active session. If not, the Web server returns the requested page to the browser and the Web server also writes a session ID value as a Cookie to the browser. By writing this Cookie, the Web server has provided a unique ID for tracking this user session or browser during the scope of the session. The Web server maintains this ID and also monitors the Timeout property set for this session. If the time-out expires, the Web server abandons all information associated with this session. In addition, at the same time that the Web server writes the Cookie, it processes the OnStart event, executing any scripts stored in the global.asa for the Session OnStart event. Similar to the Application Object, Session Objects can have additional properties appended, enabling the storing of variables and objects for use by .asp files processed during that browser's session.

Setting Up the Application

Developing an application primarily involves establishing a directory that is served by an Internet Information Server and has execute permissions. This directory location contains the source code for the application. The source code includes individual files that follow the naming convention "name.asp." Web browsers will request these files similarly to the way files ending in .htm or .html are requested. In addition to general ASP pages, each application can have a single file named "global.asa," which stores scripts for the OnStart and OnEnd events for applications and sessions.

> **CAUTION**
>
> Though not explicitly restated here, in order to use Active Server Pages, the directory containing the described files must reside on a Windows NT Server with Internet Information Server set up for your directory.

IIS Directory Defines Application

Building an Active Server application requires a planned use of the hierarchical and logical directory trees created when configuring the Internet Information Server. In general, a single-served directory forms the application. All source files, including files ending in .asa and .asp will reside in a single-served directory. For more complex applications, a series of directories might be appropriate. In Table 10.1, the Root directory contains all pages associated with non-registered users. This area might use Session Objects to do extensive tracking on the pages visited to try and build profiles on non-registered visitors. In the Root/Members directory, on the other hand, the purpose of the Session Object might be much more focused on the maintenance of logon status and member permissions. Finally, the Root/Secure/directory would maintain Session information on administrative privileges available and perhaps support the maintenance of a comprehensive audit trail.

Table 10.1   Sample Directory Structure

Directory	Description
/Root/	All visiting or non-logged on users request pages
/Root/Members/	Log on page and all subsequent pages that require a logged in user
/Root/Secure/	Administrative area for site administrators to manage member accounts and system settings

The key point to remember here is the scope of the Application and Session Objects. Within each of the different directories, the Application Objects and Session Objects are completely different, with different roles, different scopes, and no relationship between the objects in separate directories.

Understanding the "global.asa" Role in an Application

The global.asa file provides the Application and Session Objects with the script, if any, to be invoked on the OnStart and OnEnd events for Application and Session Objects. Scripts for the OnStart and OnEnd events exist within the script tags with the RunAt property set to Server. These script tags can contain functions that can add properties to the Session and Application Objects for use by subsequent .asp files within the scoped session or application.

The following provides a sample of how a global.asa file might be utilized. In the Application Object, the OnStart event adds properties to the Application Object to initialize a series of variables for maintaining information on how many members and visitors have come to the site since the application started. In contrast, the Session Object deals with a specific user starting a new session. The OnStart event for the Session Object increments application-wide information and initializes user-specific information. In addition, the Session Object OnStart event alters the default Timeout setting and sets the time-out to 30 minutes for this session, which means that after 30 minutes of no page requests the session will be abandoned. Finally, when the Timeout expires, and the Session Object OnEnd event is invoked, this event decrements application-wide tracking information.

ON THE WEB

http://www.quecorp.com/asp   The actual source code for the global.asa described can be found on the Web site for this book.

Managing Source Code or .asp and .asa Files

Source code must be contained in an .asp or .asa file. This requirement stems from the method the Internet Information Server uses to process Active Server Pages. When the Web server receives a request for a file, the Internet Information Server first checks the registered ISAPI filters. Active Server Pages rely on an ISAPI filter to catch .asp files prior to returning anything to the Web browser. These files are then processed by the ISAPI filter, which strips out all "<%%>" tags, compiles VB Script, and invokes any components called, while making Application and Session Objects available during the processing of all Active Server scripts. All of this occurs prior to the Web server returning the results to the Web browser.

> **N O T E** ISAPI filters can be viewed by opening the Registry and looking under the IIS related setting in the current control set. Review chapter 2, "Understanding Windows NT and Internet Information Server," for more information on the Registry. ■

T I P .asp and .asa files are just standard text files. This enables you to use any editor to manage your source code. Microsoft's Source Safe, originally designed for managing source code associated with C++ or VB project files, would be an effective tool for tracking version and checkout status on a multi-developer project and Internet Studio could provide script development support as an .asp file development tool.

Part

III

Ch

10

Any type of file can exist in an Active Server Application directory including HTM/HTML, graphic images, video, sound and .asp/.asa files. The important distinction here becomes that only .asp/.asa files invoke the filter that makes Session and Application Objects available during script processing.

The Internet Information Server also contains features such as Server-Side Include, which you may utilize to further enhance your application management capabilities. This capability enables you to insert .asp or other files into a requested .asp file prior to the Web server invoking the ISAPI filter we discussed. These Server-Side Includes will be processed prior to script execution. The Server-Side Include features extend your capability to store files in different directories while still maintaining a single application directory for purposes of Application and Session Object scoping.

> **CAUTION**
> Be careful using Server-Side Includes during development. The IIS keeps track of the last modification date/time of files, but the IIS caches frequently used files in memory. In other words, a direct page request causes the Web server to check if a cached file has been modified since its last execution. If it has been modified, the Web server recompiles the file. Unfortunately, Includes do not follow this checking process and as a result do not get recompiled. In these cases, the Web server must be restarted to flush cached .asp files.

Using *Application* and *Session* Objects

In leveraging Application and Session Objects for the development of your application, carefully consider what information and objects should be stored at the application and session level. A good example of the value of Session Objects is the storing of a user's logon status for security. However, with a misunderstanding of the Session Object's scoping, a major security hole could be created. The primary `Application` and `Session` Object methods, properties, and events include:

- ◼ `Abandon` method   Session
- ◼ `Timeout` property   Session
- ◼ `SessionID` property   Session
- ◼ `OnStart` event   Session/Application
- ◼ `OnEnd` event   Session/Application

Scope of *Application* and *Session* Objects

The most exciting feature of the `Application` and `Session` Objects involves the capability to scope the objects beyond a single page and more important, the capability to scope the `Session` Object to a single user. Specifically, users invoke the `Application` Object when they request a page from an application directory for the first time since the Web server last started. This `Application` Object lives on from that moment until all sessions time-out or the Web server restarts. In contrast to invoking the `Application` Object, users invoke the `Session` Object when they request a page from a browser that is not currently involved in an active session. The `Session` Object, unlike the `Application` Object, will time-out based upon a 20-minute default, or a custom `Timeout` property, which you can set at runtime.

> **CAUTION**
> Avoid the temptation to store everything at the session level. While at first the convenience of the `Session` Object can lead to caching everything about the user, remember that all this information must be maintained in the memory space of the Internet Information Server.

After a user invokes a `Session` Object, all the `Session`'s properties and methods become available at runtime every time that same user requests an .asp file. A user's session at the Web site now can be managed through the `Session` Object. As long as error trapping addresses the situation in which a user times-out, you now have complete control of a user's session and the capability to add properties to the `Session` Object. These properties can include anything from strings and status flags to database `RecordSet` Objects. The `Session` Object and its scope now create the first stable method for developers to manage a user's experience at a Web site, as a user moves from page to page or even from your site to another site and back to your site.

N O T E   The Internet Information Server (IIS) manages the `Session` Object by writing a `Cookie`, or long integer, to the client browser. If IIS restarts, the `Session` abandons, or if the browser prevents `Cookies`, the `Session` Object will attempt to re-initialize on every page request. ◼

The scope of the `Session` Object must be understood in the context of the Web. The Internet Information Server creates the `Session` Object by writing a `Cookie` to the client browser and maintaining the long integer key and related properties such as the `Timeout` property and last hit date/time in the Web server's memory.

Beginning of an Event Model

The event model available in the `Session` and `Application` Objects represents a beginning to bringing event-driven programming to the Web, but stops short of providing what you might be hoping for. Because the Active Server Pages process at the Web server and not the client, your source code can not respond to the range of events that the client handles, such as mouse movements and keyboard presses. Instead, your code is invoked when the user processes a form or clicks a hyperlink. These events generate a request to the Web server, which invokes your source code.

The `Application` and `Session` Objects provide two events each—the `OnStart` event and the `OnEnd` event. The client invokes these events when:

- `Application OnStart`: Invoked the first time users request an .asp file from an application directory since the IIS last started or the application timed-out.
- `Application OnEnd`: When all sessions time-out.
- `Session OnStart`: Invoked by users when their browser requests an ASP page from the application directory either for the first time, or after a previous session with the client browser has been abandoned.
- `Session OnEnd`: Invoked after a user's session time-out property value has exceeded the number of minutes allowed since the last page request, or the `Abandon` method has been invoked by your code.

When a user invokes an `Application` or `Session` event, you can execute functions on the Web server. All source code invoked by `Session` and `Application` events must be stored in the global.asa file within an application's directory. The format of this text file follows the model in Listing 10.4.

Part
III

Ch
10

Listing 10.4   GLOBAL.ASA—Sample App/Sess Event Code

```
<SCRIPT LANGUAGE=VBScript RUNAT=Server>
SUB Application_OnStart
END SUB
</SCRIPT>

<SCRIPT LANGUAGE=VBScript RUNAT=Server>
SUB Application_OnEnd
END SUB
</SCRIPT>

<SCRIPT LANGUAGE=VBScript RUNAT=Server>
SUB Session_OnStart
END SUB
</SCRIPT>

<SCRIPT LANGUAGE=VBScript RUNAT=Server>
SUB Session_OnEnd
END SUB
</SCRIPT>
```

The scope of variables used in the global.asa scripts does not extend to the page actually requested prior to the event. This means that to store a variable for use in the current requested page or subsequent pages, you must save the information to an `Application` or `Session` Object property. The properties of these objects provide the only means for enabling scripts in .asp file to use the information available in the scripts run during these events. As a result, these scripts become useful primarily for saving information directly to a database or file, or saving information to `Application` or `Session` Object properties for use during the scope of the application or session.

Taking some time to understand how to leverage these events provides big benefits in helping your program manage a range of issues from enhancing the users Web experience to tracking site statistics. Don't make the mistake of overlooking the value of these events.

 T I P   Session and Application events provide a key mechanism to manage user status control mechanisms such as logon security.

Methods: Locking, Stopping, and Abandoning

Like events, the methods currently available seem quite limited compared to the event-driven development environments you might currently use in non-Web based programs. However, this represents a powerful beginning for the Web programmer. The only methods currently available to `Session` and `Application` Objects include: `Application Lock` and `Unlock` methods and `Session Abandon` method.

The `Application Lock` and `Unlock` methods enable you to change values to the properties shared across the application without fear of creating conflict with multiple users potentially changing the same property values concurrently. This Locking control will seem intuitive to database developers working in multi-user environments, which share this same risk.

The `Abandon` method plays a valuable role for managing a session. While during development and testing it can be useful for flushing a working session to begin again, it also has a role in the final application. For example, if a user requires the capability to logon and then perhaps logon again as a different user, the `Abandon` method could be used to enable the previously stored logon information to be cleanly dumped for a new logon.

These methods provide important functionality in utilizing the `Application` and `Session` Objects, but for real functionality you must look to the properties provided and use the capability to add properties to the `Application` and `Session` Objects.

Using Built-In Properties or Building Your Own

At first glance, the list of properties currently available appears quite unimpressive. But the real secret lies behind the built-in properties in the capability to add properties dynamically. Still the two built-in `Session` properties play an important role in all application development and should not be overlooked. The available properties include: `Session SessionID` property and `Session Timeout` property.

The capability to add properties on-the-fly, provides the developer with an approach to maintaining persistence or state. By having a server-based Session Object to manage variables, a user's activities and input can be used during their entire session or visit to your Web application. The capability to build your own variables will be demonstrated later in this chapter and extensively in the case study provided in the appendixes of the book.

The *Application* Object: How Much Can It Do

The Application events and methods provide the infrastructure necessary to maintain application-wide information that can be leveraged for managing all users within an application. Uses range from tracking the number of users currently active to dynamically altering content provided to a particular user, based on the activity of other users at large. These features lay the foundation for building interactive communities and more. To understand the use of these events and methods, the following overviews the specific capabilities provided.

Using the *Application OnStart* Event

The Application OnStart event can be likened to the initial load event of an application. This is not the loading of a single client, but rather the load event of the multi-user Web-based application. As a result, one use would be to initialize a series of variables that you need to frequently access in your application. The following example in Listing 10.5 opens a database and assigns a recordset of system error messages to the Application Object. As a result of loading this object, now *any page* processed can reference the recordset during execution and can utilize the recordset to loop through and display a particular error, based on a given situation.

Listing 10.5   SAMP_EVENTS.ASP—Sample *Application OnStart* Event

```
<SCRIPT LANGUAGE=VBScript RUNAT=Server>
SUB Application_OnStart
REM Open ADO Connection to Database
  Set Conn = Server.CreateObject("ADODB.Connection")
  Conn.Open("DSNName")
  RS = Conn.Execute("SELECT * FROM TblSysMessages;")

REM Set Recordset to Application Object and Close ADO
  If rs.recordcount <> 0 then
    application.lock
    Set application.ObjErrMsg = RS
    application.unlock
  Else
    Rem Error Condition
  End If
  rs.close
  conn.close

END SUB
</SCRIPT>
```

N O T E   The loading of the database recordset involved the Server Object and the ADO database Connection Object, which is discussed in more detail in Part IV of this book. ■

Using the *Application OnEnd* Event

The Application OnEnd event can be likened to the close of active forms or an application, however it provides more than that because it manages the environment for not just a single-user system, but for the multi-user Web-based environment. As a result, one use would be to flush all temporary user accounts that might have been created during the course of the day. This type of activity was previously available only by using time stamps and scheduled batch programs, running as services in the background. Now, when all users time-out, a database cleanup (or any other type of cleanup) can take place. The following example runs a SQL statement to purge all partially completed orders taken by a Web-based order processing system.

```
<SCRIPT LANGUAGE=VBScript RUNAT=Server>
SUB Application_OnEnd
REM Open ADO Connection to Database
  Set Conn = Server.CreateObject("ADODB.Connection")
  Conn.Open("DSNName")
  RS = Conn.Execute("Delete * FROM Orders where complete_status=0;")
  conn.close

END SUB
</SCRIPT>
```

Application Locking Methods

Similar to database record and page locking, Application locking simply ensures that no other user has simultaneously attempted to update the Application Objects property. This locking feature only applies to the Application, and not the Session, Object and should be followed to avoid creating any conflict or lost data.The following section of code shows you a specific use of the Session OnStart event.

```
<SCRIPT LANGUAGE=VBScript RUNAT=Server>
SUB Session_OnStart
  application.lock
    application("counter") = application("counter") + 1
  application.unlock
END SUB
</SCRIPT>
```

Scoping Application-Wide Variables

Adding properties to the Application Object provides one of the key values of the Application Object model. Application properties added this way are similar to global constants and variables in Visual Basic.

Practical uses of the Application properties include the capability to cache information frequently used to conserve resources. Current Web development environments require either database/file lookups or the passing of information from one page to the next in hidden fields.

The first approach requires extensive resources as an application's load grows, and the latter approach becomes difficult as users hit the refresh and back buttons or bounce from page to page through direct typing of URLs.

With the `Application` Object, information can be saved to an `Application` Object property as the result of a single lookup. From then on, any user can access that information. For example, as a Web-based store opens its doors as a result of the first user request (`Application OnStart` Event), a store's opening greeting (including number of visitors, date/time, or current sale items) can be saved to an `Application` property as illustrated in the following code sample.

```
Application.lock
Application("dateinfo") = date
Application("timeinfo") = time
Application("visitors") = Application("visitors") + 1
Application.Unlock
```

As a result, all subsequent pages can display that information as part of a standard greeting as shown in the following code.

```
<HTML>
<BODY>
Welcome to our store, open for business since <%=Application("timeinfo")%> on
<%=Application("dateinfo")%> with <%Application("visitors")%> so far.
</BODY>
</HTML>
```

More important than cached activity information, resources can be conserved by limiting the number of times components must be brought in and out of memory on the server. If you run a database intensive site, as many of us do, you may start your application by placing statements in every page to load DLL's into memory.

```
Set Conn = Server.CreateObject("ADODB.Connection")
Conn.Open("DSNName")
RS = Conn.Execute(SQL)
conn.close
```

This process, not only loads the Connection Component DLL if it is not currently loaded, but also closes the object, enabling it be taken out of memory. For a frequently accessed site, it might make more sense to load the DLL when the application loads and leave it in memory for frequent use.

```
Set Conn = Server.CreateObject("ADODB.Connection")
Conn.Open("DSNName")
Application("conn") = Conn
```

By loading the `Conn` Object into the `Application Conn` property, it can now be referenced by all pages for use.

```
set db = Application("Conn")
  set rs = db.execute(sql)
```

Part
III

Ch
10

N O T E The preceding examples provide only a starting point for the range of uses the
Application Object can play in the ASP application model you develop. Take the time to
think through the activity and caching issues that relate to your application before implementing a
model for your use of the Application Object. ■

The *Session* Object: Your Key to User Management

The Session Object, more than the Application Object, drives your Web-based environment.
Look closely at how the deceptively small number of methods and events can completely
streamline your method for managing a user's experience as well as your system level tracking
and control of that user. The Session Object, like the Application Object, enables new properties to be defined on-the-fly. And more importantly, the Session Object properties, like those of
the Application Object, can be referenced on any page, anywhere, and any time during that
active session.

Understanding *Session* Events, Properties, and Methods

The SessionID provides, without a doubt, the prebuilt property to watch. This property provides the persistence in a user session you should be looking for, but the OnStart event, OnEnd
event, and the Abandon method also play a valuable role in managing your application. The
following sections document basic application of the prebuilt events and methods before a
more practical discussion of how to put these to work.

Session OnStart Event The Session OnStart event can be likened to the initial load event of
a form or application. It provides a mechanism to identify the first activity of new users and
enables the initialization of whatever user information your application requires for managing
the user session. At the OnStart event you might reference Application Object properties to
track the new user in the context of your multi-user environment, but you will also want to
bring into existence any user-specific information you need for managing that user's session.
The event kicks off the script setup in the global.asa for the Session OnStart event in the following form.

```
<SCRIPT LANGUAGE=VBScript RUNAT=Server>
SUB Session_OnStart
  Rem Load User Specific Information
  Session("NewUserStatus") = 0

  Rem Load Application level info
  Application.lock
    Application("usercount") = Application("usercount") + 1
  Application.unlock
END SUB
</SCRIPT>
```

N O T E Though we are discussing the use the global.asa in detail, don't lose site of the fact that you
don't need to event create any functions in the global.asa or even a global.asa file at all. ■

Session OnEnd Event   The `Session OnEnd` event can be likened to the close of active forms or an application. However, this event does not require user action. In fact most often, the `OnEnd` event will be triggered by user inaction or time-outs. This event most often provides a mechanism for cleanup or closing of open resources. The system will lose all session information after this event, so any session information that you want to save must be saved during this event.

This event can be invoked by the user if he hits a page that executes the `Abandon` method. The `Abandon` method, and the `Timeout` property provide the two mechanisms for terminating a session. An example of clean up that can be done at the end or termination of a session has been illustrated in the following sample of code.

> **CAUTION**
>
> A crash or stopping of the Web server also terminates events, because the Web server memory space is where all session and application information resides.

```
<SCRIPT LANGUAGE=VBScript RUNAT=Server>
SUB Application_OnEnd
REM Clean up user activity information
  Set Conn = Server.CreateObject("ADODB.Connection")
  Conn.Open("DSNName")
  SQL = "Delete * FROM UserActivity where sessionID = " & session.sessionid & ";"
  RS = Conn.Execute(SQL)
  conn.close

END SUB
</SCRIPT>
```

Using the *SessionID* Property   The Active Server creates the `SessionID` when a user first requests a page from an Active Server application. The `SessionID` gets written as a `Cookie` with a long integer value to the browser and provides the core mechanism the server uses to track session information stored in memory. You should not use the `SessionID` as a unique ID to track users across multiple sessions because the value's uniqueness is only guaranteed for the current application. This value gives your application the time it needs to generate an ID that can be used across multiple sessions and provides a unique ID for all sessions currently running. You can reference the `SessionID` on any page in the form

```
session.sessionID
```

This value provides a key mechanism for managing users as they move from page to page, and it relieves you from the responsibility of trying to uniquely track individual users during a multiple-page request session.

Session Timeout Property   The server stores the `Session Timeout` property as a long integer that represents minutes and defaults to 20. The server takes full responsibility for tracking this 20-minute period. `Timeout` is tracked from the last date/time a page request is received by the browser. The `Timeout` property can be altered at runtime where you may set it in the `Session OnStart` event or any subsequent page. In determining how you will manage this property, you should consider the rate of hits by a single user during a session. For sites with long intervals between page requests, such as pages that require research, long review, or large amounts of input, you might want to increase the Timeout where more rapid sessions might require a shorter Timeout. Changing this property takes the form:

```
session.timeout = 30
```

> **CAUTION**
>
> After the Timeout occurs, all session information is lost and the next page request will be treated as a new session.

Session Abandon Method   The Session Abandon method provides a vehicle for you to force a session to terminate. Uses include the situation in which your user community takes the time to log off or in which you implement a discrete site exit page that invokes the Abandon method. This method takes the form:

```
Session.abandon
```

 During development, a page with the Abandon method provides a useful mechanism for restarting sessions. Often in development, a lingering session can make testing difficult.

Managing a User Session

The Session Object provides a rich environment for managing user sessions. The following sections show you a few examples of how you can put this object to work for developing efficient applications. As described in the first part of this chapter, the challenge of managing a user session has historically required difficult, code-consuming techniques for generating unique IDs and then for keeping session-related information alive from page to page.

Generating a Unique ID to Manage Users   As illustrated in Listing 10.6, the SessionID property takes care of most of the first problem by generating a session ID to keep track of a user's session. However, during this process if you need to track users over a longer life than just one session, you still need to create an ID that guarantees uniqueness for your application. This process generally involves a database for storing this user and his related information. After you design a database to store user information, you can rely on the wealth of features in databases to generate a guaranteed unique ID. A simple example of generating a unique user ID involves leveraging the counter field of a Microsoft Access database. The following code example in Listing 10.6 uses the current date and the SessionID to insert a record and then queries the table to retrieve the counter value once the record has been created. As a final step, the example sets the new counter value to a new Session property for reference on subsequent pages.

N O T E   Certain variable status designations such as the `logonstatus` variable have been
subjectively assigned values for tracking that in no way reflect any pre-set or required
approach to the tracking process. ▪

Listing 10.6   SESSIONTRACKING.TXT—Managing the Tracking of Users with *Session* Variables

```
<%
  Set Conn = Session("conn")
Select Case session("logonstatus")

Case 1 ' Already Past finished this insert step
    msg = "<Center><h2><blink>Please Record your new Member ID:
    ➥" & session("memberid") & " </blink></h2></center>
    ➥<h3>Your Ideal Mate Profile has already been saved,
    ➥please complete the process and
    ➥relogon in edit mode to alter you profile </h3>"

Case 2 ' Proper Status for Insert of new account

    set rsInsert = Server.CreateObject("ADODB.Recordset")
    Conn.BeginTrans
    rsInsert.Open "Members", Conn, 3, 3

    ' ---------------------------------------
    'Insert Record Using AddNew Method of ADO
    ' ---------------------------------------
    rsInsert.AddNew
    rsInsert("SignOnID")      = session.sessionid
    rsInsert("AdmCreateDate") = Date()
    rsInsert.Update
    Conn.CommitTrans
    rsInsert.Close

    ' ---------------------------------------
    'Look up generated record by referencing SessionID/Current Date
    ' ---------------------------------------
    sql = "SELECT Members.SignOnID, Members.memberid, Members.AdmCreateDate FROM
    ➥Members WHERE (((Members.SignOnID)=" & session.sessionid & ") AND
    ➥((Members.AdmCreateDate)=Date())));"
    Set RS = Conn.Execute(sql)
    msg = "<h2><Center> Please Record your new Member ID:
    ➥" & rs("memberid") & " </center></h2>"

    ' ---------------------------------------
    ' Set Session Object with memberid value
    ' ---------------------------------------
    memval = rs("memberid")
    session("memberid") = memval
    session("logonstatus") = 3
    rs.close
End Select
%>
```

> **N O T E** Time and User IP address can be added to the record inserted into the database for
> greater certainty of uniqueness. ▪

Using the *Session* Object for Caching User Information   After the user has a unique ID, the
next use of the Session Object focuses on the capability to cache user information you would
have previously stored in a database or text file for constant lookup and editing. The process of
querying a file or database every time users hit a page just to make basic information about
their sessions or accounts available reflects the status quo for current Internet applications.
This includes the lookup of a shopping basket for a user shopping in a Web-based store or the
lookup of account information for personalizing a user page. While some developers attempt to
move that information from one form page processed to the next, this problem creates serious
challenges for application design.

A good example of a Session Object property would be storing a system message for display
on subsequent pages as well as trapping basic name and last time online-type information. Like
the Application Object, properties can range in complexity from integers and string values, to
RecordSet Objects. The following example provides for storing personal information and redirection following a successful logon.

```
<%
'------------------------------------------------
' Lookup User Info
'------------------------------------------------
  sql = "SELECT members.admonlinedate, Members.MemberID, members.pass,
➥Members.FName, Members.LName, Members.AdmExpDate, Members.AdmStatus FROM Members"
  sql = sql & "WHERE (((Members.MemberID)=" & request.form("memberid") & "));"
  set db = session("conn")
  set rs = db.execute(sql)


'------------------------------------------------
' Logon Fail
'------------------------------------------------
If rs.eof Then 'No Record Found Bad ID
  rs.close
  session("msg") = "<h3><center>No Member ID equaling <em>" &
request.form("memberid") & "</em> exists</center></h3>"
response.redirect "fail.asp"

Else
'------------------------------------------------
' Success Logon Approved, Load Session and Status
'------------------------------------------------
session("logonstatus") = 1
session("memberid") = rs("memberid")
session("AdmOnlineDate") = rs("AdmOnlineDate")
session("fname") = rs("fname") 'First Name

' Update User Database Record with Last Logon Date
sql = "UPDATE Members SET"
    sql = sql & " Members.AdmOnlineDate = #" & Date() & "#"
    sql = sql & " WHERE Members.MemberID=" & request.form("memberid") & ";"
```

```
          set rs2 = db.execute(sql)

rs.close
response.redirect "start.asp"

end if
%>
```

As illustrated in the previous code sample, the statement setting the `logonstatus` property equal to a value creates the `logonstatus` property as a new `Session` property. No special statements to dimension the property are required, and after this information gets loaded into the `Session` Object, it can be referenced on any page requested by the browser that is sending the matching `SessionID`. The process for referencing the properties only requires a single statement of the form:

```
session("propertyname")
```

Part

III

Ch

10

Session Objects for Security, Status, and Caching

For managing an application, the `Session` properties can play the role of tracking the user status and security information. Because `Session` properties exist at the server without any information passed to the browser except for the `SessionID`, session properties provide an effective method for managing logon and other statuses. An .asp file with no purpose other than the validation of a user's `logonstatus`, can be included using the Server-Side Include feature of IIS. This approach to user authentication provides an effective method for trapping any user attempting to request a page he or she doesn't have authority to view. This method relies on the `Session` properties alone and not on any NT- based security controls as illustrated in the following excerpt of code.

```
<%
Select Case session("logonstatus")

Case 0 'New Session No Status
      session("msg") = "<h3><center> Your are currently not logged in or
      ➥your logon has timed out </center></h3> Please logon to continue your session,
      ➥sorry for any inconvenience</h4>"
      Response.Redirect "logon.asp"

Case 1 'Authenticated User Properly Logged On

Case 2 'New Member in Sign Up Process first page

Case 3 'New Member in Sign Up Process Record Created

End Select
%>
```

The process of actually validating a user after she enters a user account and password further illustrates how to manage a site's security and user's status through the `Session` Object. The following example in Listing 10.7 builds on the previous code, which simply adds `Session` properties after a successful logon, and in this case evaluates all possible results of a user's attempt to log on. The following example relies heavily on the `Response` Object's `Redirect` feature to route the user, based on the results of the logon validation.

Listing 10.7 LOGONVALIDATE.TXT—Validating and Redirecting Users Requesting .asp Files

```
<Script Language=VBScript runat=server>
Function redirect()
  Session("msg") = session("msg") & " Please enter a valid Member ID
  ➥and Password, if you have forgotten your ID try our Search based on
  ➥First Name, Last Name and your password"
  Response.Redirect "logon.asp"
end function
</script>

<%
'--------------------------------
'--------------------------------
'Level 1 Basic Validation Testing
'--------------------------------
'--------------------------------

'Test for Already Logged In
'--------------------------------
if session("logonstatus") = 1 then 'Already Validated
  session("msg") = "<h3><center>You are already logged in</center></h3>"
  Response.Redirect "start.asp"


'Test for Entry of Member ID prior to Running Search
'--------------------------------
elseif request.form("memberid")="" then ' NO Member ID Entered
  session("msg") = "<h3><center>No Proper Member ID Entered</center></h3>"
  Redirect 'Call Function to Exit Back to Logon Screen

'Run Search
'----------------------------
else 'Run Database Lookup
  sql = "SELECT members.admonlinedate, Members.MemberID, members.pass,
  ➥Members.FName, Members.LName, Members.AdmExpDate, Members.AdmStatus FROM
  ➥Members "
  sql  = sql & "WHERE (((Members.MemberID)=" & request.form("memberid") & "));"
  set db = session("conn")
  set rs = db.execute(sql)
end if

'--------------------------
'--------------------------
'Level 2 Validation Testing
'--------------------------
'--------------------------
'Member ID Entered Now Run Search for Record
'-----------------------------------------
If rs.eof Then 'No Record Found Bad ID
  rs.close
```

```
    session("msg") = "<h3><center>No Member ID equaling <em>" &
➥request.form("memberid") & "</em> exists</center></h3>"
    Redirect 'Call Function to Exit Back to Logon Screen


'Customer Record Found Now Check Password
'----------------------------------------
elseif not request.form("password") = rs("pass") then
    rs.close
    session("msg") = "<h3><center>Member ID OK
➥but Bad Password Entered</center></h3>"
    Redirect 'Call Function to Exit Back to Logon Screen

'Password OK now Check Expiration and Status
'-------------------------------------------
elseif not rs("admstatus") = 1 and rs("admexpdate") > date then
    rs.close
    session("msg") = "<h3><center>Not Active or Expired Account</center></h3>"
    Redirect 'Call Function to Exit Back to Logon Screen



'----------------------------------
'----------------------------------
' Level 3. Success Logon Approved, Load Session and Status
'----------------------------------
'----------------------------------
Else

session("logonstatus") = 1
session("memberid") = rs("memberid")
session("AdmOnlineDate") = rs("AdmOnlineDate")
session("fname") = rs("fname")


' Update users last online date
sql = "UPDATE Members SET"
      sql = sql & " Members.AdmOnlineDate = #" & Date() & "#"
      sql = sql & " WHERE Members.MemberID=" & request.form("memberid") & ";"
      set rs2 = db.execute(sql)

end if
rs.close
response.redirect "start.asp"
%>
```

▶ **See** "The Rest of the *Response* Object" for more information about the redirect feature, **p. 231**

The preceding example in Listing 10.7 uses a script tag to create a callable function for redirecting the user in the event that they fail the logon process at any step. The user is forwarded to the start page with a logged-on status only in the event that she passes all checks including password, account number, currently active status, and valid expiration date.

Part

III

Ch

10

From Here...

The Session and Application Objects form the building blocks for good application design. By understanding the features that enable user and application management, you now move toward enabling the specific features of the Web-based application you intend to build. Based on an understanding of the VBScript syntax from earlier chapters, you now build upon the remaining Active Server objects including Server, Request, and Response, as well as exploring the specifics of components. These objects provide a complete understanding of the Active Server application development infrastructure, which is at your disposal.

From here, you will progress through the following chapters on the road to mastering the Active Server Page:

- Chapter 13, "Interactivity Through Bundled Active Server Components," provides a more detailed discussion of components bundled with Active Server Pages.

- Chapter 15, "Introducing ActiveX Data Objects," provides a more detailed discussion of database programming and the use of ODBC.

- Appendixes A-E, present a case study of an actual Active Server Pages site, with a comprehensive discussion on setup, monitoring, and performance issues associated with Web servers and Active Server Pages.

Building a Foundation of Interactivity with *Request* and *Response* Objects

The first new business asset the World Wide Web gave us, and the single most important thing about the Web that changes traditional business models, is *interactivity*.

There are many ways to make a Web site interactive. Forms are the most basic because they use static pages in an interactive, goal-directed manner. In Part III, "Working with ActiveX Server Objects and Components," and Part IV, "Database Management with Active Server Pages," you learn about the other kinds of dynamic content that are not only possible now, but are actually easy to implement.

You will see that this capability can be tapped at two levels: First, ActiveX controls provide dynamic content on static pages; second, Active Server Pages provide dynamic content with dynamic pages. In other words, ActiveX controls provide objects to insert on a page, whereas Active Server Pages provide objects to create pages on-the-fly. With all this power, the ASP developer can now reach the ultimate in interactivity: commercial transactions.

Take a look at the old-fashioned way of adding interactivity to Web sites

Before Active Server Pages, what did it take to deliver interactivity on the Web? Examine the classic case: the ubiquitous Guestbook implemented using the Common Gateway Interface and Perl scripting language.

Get a glimpse of the way it will be

Examine the two Active Server objects designed to liberate Web developers from the time-consuming and demanding requirements of CGI scripting.

Create an ASP version of the Guestbook

Use the Response and Request Objects to create a Guestbook in 33 lines of code (including comments).

In this chapter you lay a foundation for the next generation of basic interactivity. Even at this fundamental level, we feel strongly that with such a quantum leap in productivity and ease of use, ASP development will spawn an equally abrupt leap in the amount of "interactive variety" on the Web. ■

In the Beginning...

The beginning of interactivity on the Web is the Common Gateway Interface (CGI). In the UNIX world, CGI remains the predominant technology of interactivity. CGI is an open architecture; it can be implemented in almost innumerable ways. This open-mindedness comes with a price, however. CGI is difficult to write and maintain, especially for those unfamiliar with UNIX computing. It is processor-intensive: Each CGI call spawns another process for the server, increasing demands on processing resources. Database connectivity remains the most difficult and expensive aspect of CGI interactivity. All of these weaknesses are reasons that CGI has limited appeal to on-line business models.

Arguably the most popular means of implementing CGI is the Practical Extraction and Reporting Language (Perl). For all their shortcomings, these two technologies, CGI and Perl, are modern miracles. CGI worked with stateless servers, and Perl was a powerful language designed to work with text files. They were mutually reinforcing.

There was only one problem: Most Webmasters had little hope of exploiting this synergy, unless they hired a Perl programmer. We used to define a serious Webmaster as one who wasn't intimidated by the CGI/Perl alliance. To a serious Webmaster, interactivity was worth whatever cost it exacted, whether in cash to buy the Perl programs called scripts, or in the exertion necessary to learn a new programming language. This make or buy decision is really tough for most people who face the dilemma. The Web is a technology for all of us, not just the big corporations and the well-trained Information Technology staffs. How maddening it is to be within reach of the prize and yet frustrated by ignorance.

Imagine, for a moment, the number of people who have had a great Web idea but who couldn't implement it. There are at least a dozen things over the last year we would like to have hosted on our Web sites. Multiply this by millions. There is a pent-up supply of creativity behind this block to dynamic interactivity. Active Server Pages will set loose this creativity. It's "scripting for the rest of us." Just imagine what the Web is going to look like when all of those ideas are implemented. It's going to be marvelous.

A Little Story

When one of the authors brought his first commercial Web site, **investing.com**, on-line in June of 1995, there was one *de rigueur* interactive feature he had to include, the Guestbook. The author's boss said, "I just want a form that has three lines and a button. How tough can *that* be?" Three days later after scouring the Internet, changing the source code to work on the site, uploading it to the UNIX server, changing the file permissions, testing, debugging, and testing again, he finally had a working Guestbook. Three days. That's one day for each line on the form. The button's a bonus.

Perhaps the single most frustrating thing about working with the Internet is having to be almost equal parts programmer and businessman. Most people don't have time to make them equal parts. The only option is to write as little code as possible and to suffer the consequences.

This quandary leads to one other important point about this section, "In the Beginning..." : In the past, one could not take interactivity for granted. At the processor level, for example, interactivity is a subtle and sophisticated series of events. Looking at the technical details that follow will help you understand what is happening, and it should help you appreciate the luxury of relying on ASP objects to attend to these details on your behalf.

Before you begin to see, in detail, what this liberation force of Active Server Programming will bring, take a look at a typical (and justly famous) Guestbook written in Perl by Matt Wright, a very good Perl programmer; many of us owe him much for his ubiquitous gem. By the way, Matt's source code is seven pages long! We're not going to clog up this chapter by listing it all here, but we are going to abstract key code blocks from it. If you've never done this kind of programming before, consider yourself lucky.

ON THE WEB

http://www.quecorp.com/asp   The entire CGI/Perl Guestbook is included at the Web site. For our purposes, we are ignoring the e-mail component of the application, as well as, in the CGI version, the feedback form.

The ASP Guestbook components (that you examine shortly) are also included in their entirety at the Web site. The Access 97 database, which is used to store Guestbook entries, is also available to the reader there.

Part
III

Ch
11

OK, so what does it take to make a Guestbook work using CGI, and why is it so difficult?

CGI Input

The first step is to get information from the client to the server. The CGI/Perl technique parses the standard input from the POST method, used in the form found in guestbook.html. Standard input is UNIX-speak for the stream of data used by a program. This stream can be all of the characters entered from a keyboard up to and including the Enter keypress, or it can be the contents of a file that is redirected to a program.

The Guestbook gets its stream of data from the transmission received through the POST method, used by the form in addguest.html. Recall from Chapter 4, "Introducing Active Server Pages," that in the HTTP transaction between the client and the server, something like this stream of data is called the "request body" (a term used often throughout this book). In the case here, this stream is a collection of name/value pairs for each form variable on the Guestbook (for fields left blank, the name variable has no value—which is, itself, a value). Here's your first look at the CGI source code (it reads standard input into a memory buffer for the number of characters passed to the server from the client):

```
# Get the input
read(STDIN, $buffer, $ENV{'CONTENT_LENGTH'});
```

Next, in Listing 11.1, the program splits these name/value pairs and stores them in an array (another memory buffer that stores values in a row, rather like a stack of kitchen plates). It can tell the boundary between pairs because the & character is used to encode them.

Listing 11.1 GUESTBOOK.PL—An Associative Array of Form Variables and Their Values

```
# Split the name-value pairs
@pairs = split(/&/, $buffer);

foreach $pair (@pairs) {
    ($name, $value) = split(/=/, $pair);
```

Now, each row in the array called @pairs has a string that contains the data entered in the form. Each row might also contain other special characters if the form data itself contains spaces or non-alphanumeric characters like & or %. These non-alphanumeric characters are converted to their hexadecimal ASCII equivalents. A % sign is inserted before these hex numbers to identify them as encoded characters (if the form data itself included a % sign then that character must first be converted to *its* ASCII value of 25. So that this value is not misinterpreted as the numeric value 25, it too must be encoded as %25). Spaces are always encoded with the plus sign.

T I P If you ever find that you need to imitate the client (for example, when you set the value of Cookies or you need to append a query string to a URL), rely on the Server Object's URLEncode method to do the dirty work for you. You'll be seeing a lot of examples of this technique in Part III, "Working With Active Server Objects and Components."

When a Web client program makes a request of a Web server, the client passes everything from the type of client software making the request to the name/value pair of form variables filled in by the user on the client side of the transaction.

For example, when visitors to a Web site fill in the Guestbook form completely, they send the following variables to the Web server: realname, username, url, city, state, country, and comments. Each variable has a value, and the pair is sent to the Web server in a form like this:

realname=Michael+Corning.

The entire string of variable/value pairs is encoded with the ampersand character like this:

realname=Michael+Corning&username=mpc%40investing%2Ecom...

N O T E Note the hexadecimal value for @ and . are 40 and 2E respectively, and each is identified as an encoded character with the %. Actually, this is a rather clever scheme that is very efficient. I've heard it said that the best way to tell a true programmer is to look at her tax return. Real programmers file in hex. ▪

A Note from the Author

This highlights an important point as we move from the programmer's world to the business world: Because HTML is a formal specification, a generally accepted standard, all browsers are compelled to send form data to a Web server the same way. It follows that there need be only one program that's necessary to decode the environment variable in the server that contains that string of form data.

It does not follow, however, that there is only one way to produce this program. Programmers live to find new and more efficient ways to do things. It matters not how pedestrian the process is, even something as prosaic as a query string. That's not the point. It's a matter of aesthetics. It's a matter of quality.

And it's this perfectionism that's so engrained in the programmer's work ethic that has made the Internet what it is today rather than some leftover notes on a white board at the Advanced Research Program Agency in the Department of Defense. To programmers, the Internet is never good enough.

So, back in Listing 11.1, because each name/value pair is separated by an equal sign, the script puts everything to the left of the = in the name field and to the right of the = in the value field. Presto! A decoded query string.

Next, in Listing 11.2, any special non-alphanumeric characters must be identified and converted back to their original values.

Part
III

Ch
11

Listing 11.2 GUESTBOOK.PL—Decode Non-Alphanumeric Characters

```
# Un-Webify plus signs and %-encoding
    $value =~ tr/+/ /;
    $value =~ s/%([a-fA-F0-9][a-fA-F0-9])/pack("C", hex($1))/eg;
    $value =~ s/<!--(.|\n)*-->//g;

    if ($allow_html != 1) {
        $value =~ s/<([^>]|\n)*>//g;
    }

    $FORM{$name} = $value;
}
```

Keep in mind that all of this splitting and decoding of strings is going on behind the scenes during ASP processing. As you will see shortly, the QUERY_STRING is the same regardless of the technology driving the server. We will turn to a detailed discussion of the Request Object in the next section, but first take a look at what else is lurking in guestbook.pl.

CGI Output

After the Perl script has figured out exactly what the Guestbook was saying, the program in Listing 11.3 opens the Guestbook's data file. Once open, the data file moves any contents currently in the file into another array (the Perl script is written so that new entries can be inserted or appended to existing data, according to the user's preference). The data file is then immediately closed with the close statement.

Listing 11.3   GUESTBOOK.PL—Editing of the Guestbook Entries File

```
# Begin the Editing of the Guestbook File
open (FILE,"$guestbookreal");
@LINES=<FILE>;
close(FILE);
$SIZE=@LINES;

# Open Link File to Output
open (GUEST,">$guestbookreal");
```

N O T E   It's interesting to note that at this level of programming, and when file I/O is limited to text format, you have to make many design choices that are moot when you use more abstract technology such as database tables. The ASP alternative in the section "Guestbook Made Easy," uses databases to store guestbook entries, and we leave sorting issues to the database engine; we don't have to worry about it when we first store the entries in a file.

Remember, we're showing you all this so that you appreciate how much work Active Server Pages is saving you. ▪

Listing 11.4, then, writes the form data to the Guestbook data file.

Listing 11.4   GUESTBOOK.PL—Writing the Entries to the Guestbook Entries File

```
for ($i=0;$i<=$SIZE;$i++) {
   $_=$LINES[$i];
   if (/<!--begin-->/) {

      if ($entry_order eq '1') {
         print GUEST "<!--begin-->\n";
      }

      $FORM{'comments'} =~ s/\cM\n/<br>\n/g;

      print GUEST "<b>$FORM{'comments'}</b><br>\n";

      if ($FORM{'url'}) {
         print GUEST "<a href=\"$FORM{'url'}\">$FORM{'realname'}</a>";
      }
      else {
         print GUEST "$FORM{'realname'}";
      }

      if ( $FORM{'username'} ){
         if ($linkmail eq '1') {
            print GUEST " \&lt;<a href=\"mailto:$FORM{'username'}\">";
            print GUEST "$FORM{'username'}</a>\&gt;";
         }
         else {
            print GUEST " &lt;$FORM{'username'}&gt;";
```

```perl
        }
      }
print GUEST "<br>\n";

    if ( $FORM{'city'} ){
        print GUEST "$FORM{'city'},";
    }

    if ( $FORM{'state'} ){
        print GUEST " $FORM{'state'}";
    }

    if ( $FORM{'country'} ){
        print GUEST " $FORM{'country'}";
    }

    if ($separator eq '1') {
        print GUEST " - $date\n<hr>\n";
    }
    else {
        print GUEST " - $date<p>\n\n";
    }

    if ($entry_order eq '0') {
        print GUEST "<!--begin-->\n";
    }

  }
  else {
      print GUEST $_;
  }
}

close (GUEST);
```

Part
III

Ch
11

Examples of How Much Easier ASP is than CGI

Did you notice all of the embedded HTML code? Again, with Perl and CGI using text file data storage, you have to do everything at the beginning. That is, you store everything you will later need to display the contents of the data file. In one respect, you are not only storing data entered from the form, you are storing the *programming* necessary to display it later.

Again, with ASP, you don't have to be so meticulous. You can also be more flexible. For example, you might change your mind and not want to display comments entered in the Guestbook in bold type. With ASP, you change the tag once. With the data file, you have to change it many times and only in certain places (for example, around the comments but not around the name [if the name were also meant to be in bold type]).

Things are looking pretty good, aren't they? With ASP technology you are going to see a lot more interactivity and variety because more people will understand Active Server Pages than currently understand CGI, don't you think?

Ninety-two lines of code! As we said previously, the other five pages of the guestbook.pl script are dedicated to sending an e-mail message to the person who just submitted an entry into the Guestbook and to displaying the contents of the entry for confirmation.

Whew!

> **N O T E** Care must be taken when designing interactive systems, even something as simple as a guestbook. The problem arises when there is a mistake in data entry. Haven't you ever filled in a guestbook and submitted it to later regret it? You look at your entry and find an embarrassing misspelling. You accidentally enter the form twice. Something. Anything.
>
> Interactivity that is data-based is much more forgiving. Exploit that power and make the interactive experience more pleasant and less threatening for the visitor. In the short run, such thoughtfulness is a competitive advantage. ■

Interactive Liberation

In this section, we are going to introduce the basics of the `Request` and `Response` Objects. You will learn just enough about these remarkable assets to construct a simple guestbook, exactly like the one you just looked at. In Chapter 12, "Enhancing Interactivity with *Cookies*, Headers, and the *Server* Object," you will have fun with a really powerful feature of Active Server Pages: their capability to call themselves.

The *Request* Object

In Chapter 10, "Managing States and Events with *Application* and *Session* Objects," you caught your first glimpse of the `Request` Object in action. There we saw how its `Cookies` collection was used to give the developer control over ASP sessions. In this section you explore a detailed discussion of this object. You will be going into some of the inner workings of HTTP. If that is material that you have been able to avoid up to this date, refer to the notes and sidebars we provide to fill the gaps in your understanding.

The `Request` Object is the first intrinsic server object you need to fully understand. It is the connection between the Web client program and the Web server. Across this connection flows information from the following sources: the HTTP `QueryString`, form data in the HTTP `Request` body, HTTP `Cookies`, and predetermined `ServerVariables`. Because the `Request` Object accesses these collections in that order, so will we.

Calls to this `Server` Object take the following generalized form:

```
Request[.Collection]("variable")
```

As you can see, it is not necessary to specify which collection you are referring to when using the `Request` Object. It will search for the variable in all collections until it finds the first one, and it searches in the order given previously. If it finds no occurrence of the variable in any collection, `Request` returns empty.

If you do specify a collection, however, you ensure two things:

- **Optimized performance**: If you are passing large amounts of data, and the variable you want to reference is in the ServerVariables collection, you get it immediately instead of walking through all the collections looking for it.

- **Minimized errors**: If you happen to use the same variable name in two different collections, the Active Server will stop when it finds the first occurrence of the variable. If the variable you want is in another collection, there is an error. Avoid it by specifying the collection when you call the Request Object.

The *QueryString* Collection   The QueryString collection is the first one the Active Server searches. This is because query strings come from an HTTP GET method, and the GET method is the default request method in HTTP (makes sense because it's the original method appearing in HTTP/0.9 in 1991—the POST method didn't appear until HTTP/1.0 when HTML forms were introduced).

ON THE WEB

For more information about the GET method, see the very readable and historic documents of the early development of Web and the HTTP protocol at

http://www.w3.org/pub/WWW/Protocols/Classic.html

Part

III

Ch

11

Query strings are the text that follows a question mark in a URL (which, by the way, is the reason they are called "query [or "question"] strings"), and can be sent to a Web server two ways:

- From form variables passed to the server using URL encoding with the GET method (not the POST method).

- "Manually," either by entering the query string directly behind the URL, or by programming the string to be appended to it (a form isn't necessary).

The first method is, by far, the most common way to create the query string. The second method is used by the Active Server when the client doesn't support (or has disabled) Cookies, and when you want to pass a parameter to an .asp file but don't want the trouble of a form. Session properties could also be used to pass parameters to an .asp file (see Chapter 12), but using the manual form of setting query strings takes less overhead (see note at the end of Chapter 12).

▶ **See** "URLEncode" for more information about variables passed to the server using URL encoding, **p. 240**

A Look Under the Hood of HTTP   HTTP is a stateless protocol. This means that each request from a client requires a new connection to the server. In the strictest implementation of the protocol, this means that an HTML document with text and an image requires two separate transactions with the server: one to get the text and a second connection to retrieve the image.

If the browser is capable, an HTTP connection header can be sent to the server with the keyword "Keep-Alive" so that subsequent calls by the client to the server will use the same TCP network connection. Internet Explorer 3.0 supports this header and owes much of its improvement in performance to this HTTP enhancement.

In HTTP/1.0 there are three primary methods with which a Web client requests information from a Web server: GET, POST, and HEAD. We will focus here on the first two.

As we said, GET is the most often used request method used on the Web. Every hypertext link uses it implicitly. When an HTML form is used, however, the HTML author decides which method to use to implement the Form element's ACTION. With forms there are issues the author needs to face in order to choose wisely. For the ASP developer, knowledge of the difference between these two methods ensures that the use of the Request Object will not yield unexpected results. For example, if you use a POST method in your form, don't expect to find the variable/value pairs to appear in the Request.QueryString collection. This collection is populated only when the form uses the GET method.

The difference lies in the fact that the GET method is basically the *read* request of HTTP, and the POST method is the *write* method. That's why the GET method is still the default request method because most of the time you want to merely read the contents of an HTML file somewhere.

Sometimes, however, you only want to read something special, so you include a query string along with your read request. Relying on an appended string is one of the major weaknesses of the GET method. The problem is that the URL and the query string go into an environment variable on the server. Each system administrator sets aside a fixed amount of memory for all environment variables. Many DOS programmers faced the same challenge as well. Because the environment space is limited, so is the size of the query string. There is no specific size to this limit, but there is always *some* size.

The POST method, on the other hand, does not use a query string to communicate with the server. This frees it from the limitations of the old GET method and enables much more complex form data to be sent to a Web server. With the Post method, content is sent to the server separately from the request to read an URL. For this reason, the server variables CONTENT-TYPE and CONTENT-LENGTH are used by the POST method (and not by the GET method).

Because the POST method is the *write* request of HTTP, we should not leave it before we note one important attribute of this method: It can write persistent data to the server. In other words, it can (theoretically at this writing) upload files. In November 1995, a Request For Comment was published by researchers at Xerox PARC. Their recommended changes to the HTML Document Type Definition (viz., the formal specification of some aspect of HTML) were simple, and the results of implementing the changes profound. It is important to remember that the POST method can write data to the server, and the GET method can't.

Confused? Let's recap with Table 11.1.

Table 11.1 Who's Who in the *Request* Object?

Activity	GET	POST
Appends query string to requested URL?	Y	N
Limited in amount of data passed to requested URL?	Y	N
Typically used outside of HTML Forms?	Y	N
Sends form variables to the Request.QueryString collection?	Y	N
Uses the QUERY_STRING server variable?	Y	N
Sends data to requested URL in separate transaction with server?	N	Y
Uses CONTENT-TYPE and CONTENT-LENGTH server variables?	N	Y
Sends form parameters to the Request.Form collection?	N	Y
Can write data to the server?	N	Y

Every time you use a search engine you send a GET request to a server with a query string attached. For example, when you enter the following URL in your Web client

```
http://guide-p.infoseek.com/Titles?col=WW&sv=IS&_
➥lk=noframes&qt=HTTP+GET
```

you are telling the InfoSeek search engine to find all files in its database that have the words HTTP and GET. Everything after the ? is the query string and would appear in the QueryString collection of the Request Object. Note, this URL is one long string with no spaces (they've been URL encoded and will be converted back to spaces on the server).

NOTE Note there are actually four variables being passed to the server, though we are interested in the variables used to query the InfoSeek database. Note, too, that the qt variable has two values: HTTP and GET. As we will see in a moment, the Request Server Object creates something like a 3-D spreadsheet when it parses an HTTP query string like this, creating a collection of variables and their values and a separate collection for variables that have more than one value. ▪

Now that you have a better understanding of the differences and similarities of GET and POST methods, return to a focused discussion of the QueryString collection.

The full specification of this method includes the way you access variables with multiple values:

```
Request[.Collection]("variable")[(index)¦.Count]
```

The brackets indicate optional details. You must always specify the variable in the Request collections to be retrieved, and you can optionally specify the collection name and information about any "data sets" that might be coming in from the client.

TIP If, for some reason, your application needs to see the URL encoded query string being sent from the client, you can access this string by calling the `Request.QueryString` object without any parameters at all. The result is the single string of characters received by the Web server and stored in its `Request.ServerVariables` collection.

What is a "data set?" It is a collection of data with a common parent, and the parent, in turn, is a member of the `QueryString` collection. An example will make this clear.

Suppose there is a form that is filled out by a financial planner. Financial planners can have many different designations, and they might want to be identified with all of them. So they fill out a membership application form giving their names and addresses. At the bottom of the form is a multi-select list box. If one particularly ambitious planner wants to add yet another acronym to his name, he must select all those designations that currently define his competence.

As a result, the filled-out form is sent to the membership program on the Web server with all the usual personal identification fields along with this special field named "designations" that contains the following values: "CFP," "CPA," and "CFA."

The `Request.QueryString` collection would have an item for each of the form variables, including one for "designations." The "designations" item would have a collection of its own (sometimes referred to as a "data set") and would return the value three with the call:

```
Request.QueryString("designations").Count
```

You could enumerate this data set two ways: First, by simply executing the command

```
Request.QueryString("designations")
```

you would see this result: "CFP, CPA, and CFA" (note it is a single comma-delimited string).

Alternatively, you can walk through the data set with the following code block:

```
<% For I = 1 to Request.QueryString("designations").Count %>
   <BR><% =Request.QueryString("designations")(i) %><BR>
<% Next %>
```

The result is three separate text strings, one for each designation in the collection.

The Form Collection   As we said in the previous section, the POST method in HTTP/1.0 was designed to enable large amounts of data to be passed between client and server. In contrast, the GET method is limited to a fixed number of characters that it can append to the URI (limited by operating environment constraints on the server). This data is processed by the server as if it were STDIN data (such as data entered from a keyboard or redirected from a file). The data passed to the server with the POST method is usually formatted the same way as the GET method (viz., by URLEncoding), but it can also be formatted in a special way when necessary.

There is one other subtle difference in terminology between GET and POST. With the GET method, elements of the query string are referred to as *variables*, and with the POST method they are *parameters*. This distinction serves to reinforce the simplicity of GET and the open-ended sophistication of POST.

Fortunately for ASP developers, the way we handle Form and QueryString collections is virtually identical. The most important things to remember about these two collections and the methods that populate them are:

- Choose the method best suited for your purposes (GET for simple requests, POST for complex or data-intensive ones).

- Look for the results in the correct ServerVariables collection (GET uses the QUERY_STRING variable, POST uses the HTTP request body to convey its information and uses the ServerVariables CONTENT_LENGTH and CONTENT_TYPE to specify attributes of the incoming data stream).

- In your .asp code, explicitly specify the collection you want the Request Object to interrogate (given your understanding of the above nuances).

The *Response* Object

The Response Object is responsible for managing the interaction of the server with the client. The methods of this object include:

- AddHeader
- AppendToLog
- BinaryWrite
- Clear
- End
- Flush
- Redirect
- Write

All but the Write method are advanced features of this powerful Response Object. In this section, you will learn the two ways this function is performed in .asp files, and you will see examples of when one method is more convenient than the other. We will also make some stylistic suggestions aimed at making your .asp files easier to read and to debug.

As with our preliminary discussion of the Request Object, we introduce enough of these tools of the ASP trade to construct a simple Guestbook. In Chapter 12, "Enhancing Interactivity with *Cookie*s, Headers, and the *Server* Object," we will cover the salient features of the remaining collections, methods, and properties of the Response and Request Objects.

The *Write* Method   The most fundamental process of ASP development is writing to the HTML output stream destined for the client. Everything else that .asp files might (or might not) ultimately ends up at the Write method.

Response.Write has a simple syntax. It needs only a quoted text string or a function that returns a string.

T I P   You can put parentheses around the string or function, but you can save a keystroke if you skip the parentheses and insert a space between `Response.Write` and its parameter.

There are two ways of instructing the Active Server to output characters: explicitly with the `Response.Write` syntax, and implicitly with the .asp code delimiters. That is, anything appearing *outside* the <% (to mark the beginning of Active Server Pages source code) and %> (to mark its end) tags is implicitly written by the Active Server to the HTML file returned to the client.

CAUTION

Do not nest <%...%> tags. That is, after you use <% in your source code, don't use it again until you have first used the closing source code delimiter, %>. This is a trap that is particularly easy to fall into when you are using the special case of the <%...%> delimiters, viz., when you are writing the value of a variable or method to the output stream.

Specifically, whenever you need to output a value, surround the expression with the <%=...%> tags. But remember to first close off any open script with the %> tag. If you look closely at the following example (that would fail if you tried this at home), you will see that you are nesting tags.

```
<%
If True Then
        <%= varResult%>
Else
        Call MyProgram
End If
%>
```

In the extreme, you could write all your .asp files using `Response.Write` to send all HTML commands to the client. All the other characters in your .asp file, then, would be .asp source code, and every line would be wrapped in the <%...%> marker. Alternatively, all the HTML source code in your .asp file could be written as if it were merely an HTML file, and you would cordon off the ASP commands with judicious use of the <%...%> delimiters.

Good programmers are far too lazy to use this method, but Listing 11.5 works:

Listing 11.5   A Method for People Who Like to Type <% and %

```
<%Response.Write("<!-- Created with HomeSite v2.0 Final Beta  -->")%>
<%Response.Write("<!DOCTYPE HTML PUBLIC " & CHR(34) & "-//W3C//DTD
➥HTML 3.2//EN"& CHR(34) & ">")%>
<%Response.Write("<HTML>")%>
<%Response.Write("<HEAD>")%>
<%Response.Write("<TITLE>Registration Results</TITLE>")%>
<%Response.Write("</HEAD>")%>
<%Response.Write("<BODY>")%>
<%Response.Write("<FONT SIZE=+3>Thanks for writing! </FONT><P>")%>
<%Set objConn = Server.CreateObject("ADODB.Connection")%>
```

```
<%objConn.Open("guestbook")%>
<%Set objRst = Server.CreateObject("ADODB.Recordset")%>
<%Set objRst.ActiveConnection=objConn%>
<%objRst.LockType = 3%>
<%objRst.Source = "tblGuestbook"%>
<%objRst.CursorType = 3%>
<%objRst.Open%>
```

Choosing which syntax to use should be guided by the rules of syntax in the English language and the rules of good government: less is better. Use punctuation only when it is absolutely necessary or when it improves clarity; write the fewest laws possible to ensure order and civility. In ASP development use the fewest delimiters possible.

There are two reasons for this: laziness and program maintenance. Clearly, `<% %>` has fewer (though awkward) keystrokes, so it serves the laziness inherent in all good programmers; and fewer odd characters makes for more lucid logic (unnecessary delimiters are distracting to the human eye and virtually transparent to the server's eye). Lucid logic is easier to maintain (thereby further serving the programmer's natural laziness—do I belabor the point?).

There is one other reason for choosing implicit `Write` over the explicit, but we will have to wait a moment to see why.

Listing 11.6 is easier to type and easier to read:

Listing 11.6   GUESTBOOK.ASP—Opening the Guestbook Database

```
<!--#INCLUDE VIRTUAL="/ASPSAMP/SAMPLES/ADOVBS.INC"
<!-- This document was created with HomeSite v2.0 Final Beta  -->
<!DOCTYPE HTML PUBLIC "-//W3C//DTD HTML 3.2//EN">

<HTML>
<HEAD>
      <TITLE>Registration Results</TITLE>
</HEAD>

<BODY>
<FONT SIZE="+3">Thank you for registering!</FONT><P>
<%
Set objConn = Server.CreateObject("ADODB.Connection")
objConn.Open("guestbook")
Set objRst = Server.CreateObject("ADODB.Recordset")
Set objRst.ActiveConnection=objConn
objRst.LockType = adLockOptimistic
objRst.Source = "tblGuestbook"
objRst.CursorType = adOpenKeyset
objRst.Open
%>
```

Part
III

Ch
11

TIP As with URLEncoding, there is one special case when `Response.Write` will get confused: when the character string `%>` appears in the method's parameter. This happens, for example, when you use `Response.Write` to define an HTML `TABLE WIDTH` as a percentage of the screen. If you absolutely must use `Response.Write` in these circumstances, use the following modification: `%\>`.

There is also another time when `Response.Write` can be a hassle: when you have embedded quotes in the string. As a matter of fact, this is a perennial programming problem. Our favorite solution is to insert `CHR(34)` wherever an embedded quote appears.

ON THE WEB

http://www.quecorp.com/asp A small .asp file, respfix.asp, is included at this book's Web site to demonstrate each of these workarounds. By the way, the source code makes use of the `PLAINTEXT` tag to render .asp syntax directly, without processing the .asp command first. There is also a note about errors (that cannot be trapped) if you don't implement the workarounds properly.

TIP Because VBScript functions and subroutines can only be created using the `<SCRIPT>...</SCRIPT>` tags and not the `<%...%>` tags, if you need to return HTML from a VBScript procedure, `Response.Write` is exactly what you need because you can't use `<%=...%>`.

If most of your .asp file is .asp source code (e.g., it has lots of ADO programming in it as the following Guestbook does), then you will use `Response.Write` only when you need to include HTML source code and it is not convenient to insert the end of .asp source tag, `%>`. This is awkward to describe, but easy to see, so take a careful look at the ASP version of the Guestbook that follows. Note: There isn't a single use of `Response.Write` in it.

N O T E It's worth emphasizing a subtle point here that will be frustrating to you later if you overlook it now. You separate script from HTML with either the `<%...%>` .asp source code tags or the `<SCRIPT>...</SCRIPT>` VBScript tags. Use the latter when you are creating named script functions, and when you do, use the `Response.Write` method to send HTML back to the client. Pay close attention to the demos and templates scattered throughout this book, and you will quickly make this second nature, part of your growing ASP programming sensibility. ▨

Guestbook Made Easy

Now that you understand the basic operation and tradeoffs for using the `Request` Object and its `QueryString` and `Form` collections, take a look at how ASP can radically reduce the work required to deliver even the most basic kind of interactivity on the Web.

Standard HTML

Using ActiveX and exploiting the power of ADO (which we will dive into with gusto in Part IV, "Database Management with Active Server Pages"), our Active Server Program uses 33 lines of code instead of 92, and it gives us the feedback form to boot! And we don't know about you, but we can actually read the Active Server Program.

The first part of the .asp file, given in Listing 11.7, is simple HTML.

N O T E What is important to note here is that the following HTML code is part of the program that processes the form data but that this first block does something the Perl script did not: It provides the feedback form displayed after the client posts their entry.

Listing 11.7   GUESTBOOK.ASP—The Header of the Guestbook Feedback Form

```
<!--#INCLUDE VIRTUAL="/ASPSAMP/SAMPLES/ADOVBS.INC"
<!-- This document was created with HomeSite v2.0 -->
<!DOCTYPE HTML PUBLIC "-//W3C//DTD HTML 3.2//EN">

<HTML>
<HEAD>
      <TITLE>Registration Results</TITLE>
</HEAD>

<BODY>
<FONT SIZE="+3">Thank you for registering!</FONT><P>
```

A Quick Review

For those readers who are new to HTML, here's a brief detour into the header of an HTML file (only in this case it's an .asp file that will produce HTML output).

The first line is a Server-Side Include directive. This tells the Active Server to insert everything in the adovbs.inc file, viz., all VBScript constants, into the guestbook.asp file while it interprets the VBScript.

The second line is required to meet the specs on HTML/3.2, and it is inserted automatically by the ASP editor, HomeSite.

The HTML and BODY tags are closed with </HTML> and </BODY> tags at the end of the .asp file (see Listing 11.10). They tell the Web client that everything in between needs to be treated as HTML output. Within the HEAD section, nothing is printed to the Web client's display window. The text within the TITLE tags is printed in the border of the Web client's main window. The FONT tag increases the default font by 3 sizes.

ASP code

At this point we start writing .asp code. In the first block, Listing 11.8, we are making a connection with a database and a table. We need access to the table that permits us to append a new record and edit the contents of that record with the values passed to guestbook.asp from guestbook.html. We instruct the Active Server to open this table with a keyset cursor, using optimistic record locking, and we instruct it to complete the update of Guestbook entries with Listing 11.9.

▶ **See** "Learning About Locks" for more information on record locking, **p. 338**

N O T E Note how we have organized the .asp code in Listing 11.8 so that we only need one set of `<%...%>` tags. ■

Listing 11.8   GUESTBOOK.ASP—Opening the Connection to a Database and a Table Within that Opened Database

```
<%
Set objConn = Server.CreateObject("ADODB.Connection")
objConn.Open("guestbook")
Set objRst = Server.CreateObject("ADODB.Recordset")
Set objRst.ActiveConnection=objConn
objRst.LockType = adLockOptimistic
objRst.Source = "tblGuestbook"
objRst.CursorType = adOpenKeyset
' Alternatively you could move the values from the previous four
' lines of code onto the next line as properties of the Open method.
objRst.Open
```

N O T E Note the form variables have already been decoded using the `Request` Object. We don't need all the low level source code provided by the Perl script. See Listing 11.1 and Listing 11.2. ■

Listing 11.9   GUESTBOOK.ASP—Adding a New Entry

```
objRst.AddNew
objRst("realname") = Request.Form("realname")
objRst("username") = Request.Form("username")
objRst("url")      = Request.Form("url")
objRst("city")     = Request.Form("city")
objRst("state")    = Request.Form("state")
objRst("country")  = Request.Form("country")
objRst("comments") = Request.Form("comments")
objRst.Update
%>
```

N O T E If you're accustomed to doing database programming in Microsoft Access or Visual Basic, then you will find programming in ADO very easy. The only real difference between Listing 11.9 and Access or Visual Basic is the use of the `Response` Object and its `Write` method. ■

Note the ending `%>` tag. If you think about these tags as if they were, themselves, programming logic (e.g., similar to the `If...Then...Else` construct), then you can see that to forget the `%>`

would be like forgetting the End If in a regular code block. You're certainly welcome to surround all ASP commands with <%...%>, but why bother?

Back to HTML

Having updated the underlying table with the new Guestbook entry, we continue writing the HTML file to the client. If we add another dozen lines to this program we can also redisplay the contents of the form and include a button that permits reentry. Alternatively, we could rename the guestbook.htm file into guestbook.asp and have it call itself changing the original "Submit" button to an "Update" button. We'll show you how to do this in the next Chapter 12, "Enhancing Interactivity with *Cookie*s, Headers, and the *Server* Object."

Listing 11.10   GUESTBOOK.ASP—Finishing Touches

```
<HR>
<A HREF="guestbook.html">Return to Guestbook</A>
</BODY>
</HTML>
```

That's all there is to it. Remember our story at the beginning of this chapter? Well, if ASP was around back then, we would have been able to say to our boss, "Sure, boss; that's a slam dunk. We'll have a Guestbook for you before lunch."

More Power To You

We have just skimmed over the power and features of the Request and Response Server Objects, just enough to be able to construct a simple Guestbook. There's much more available to the Active Server Program developer, however.

As you continue reading this book, please keep in mind one very important idea somewhere near the front of your mind: Active Server Programming is going to enable those of us who are not professional programmers to do things not even they have been able to do before. We are going to see an explosion of creativity the depth and breadth of which will surprise everyone. Everyone but you. You're leading the way.

From Here...

In this chapter, we have built a new programming foundation for interactivity. You have seen what it used to take to get a simple Guestbook implemented on our Web sites, and you have tried your hand at doing it the ASP way. It really is amazing how much work we can get done with two ASP objects like Request and Response, isn't it?

We turn our attention next to a discussion of the rest of the features of the Request and Response Objects, and we will introduce the Server Object.

■ Chapter 12, "Enhancing Interactivity with *Cookies*, Headers, and the *Server* Object," gets you into the nitty-gritty details of Cookies, especially the Cookies collection of the Response Object.

■ In that same chapter, you will come to understand the nature of HTTP headers and you will see how many of the Response Object's methods are designed to help you exploit these sophisticated and subtle aspects of HTML programming.

■ We then introduce the Server Object and its very useful methods that can take a lot of the drudgery out of ASP development.

■ Finally, the chapter also looks at a very cool feature of Active Server Pages: their capability to call themselves. In order to work this magic you need to have mastered the Request Object, and you need to brush up on your Session Object, too.

Enhancing Interactivity with *Cookies*, Headers, and the *Server* Object

This chapter brings you up a level in your capability to create pages that interact with the reader of your Web site. You will learn how to make your .asp code more efficient and easier to manage; you will complete your survey of the Request and Response Objects; and you will get your first detailed look at the Server Object. All of this should help you bring more life and vitality to your work on the Web. ■

ASP files that talk to themselves

A fascinating feature of Active Server Pages is their capability to call themselves. Learn how to exploit this novel feature in this section.

The *Request* Object

This section completes your introduction to the *Request* Object. Learn all about Cookies and the ServerVariables Collection.

More on *Response* Objects

Cookies are found in both the Response and Request Objects. Learn the difference and how to use each.

The *Server* Object at your service

The Server Object completes this chapter. Learn how it can take over the most laborious and tedious tasks in your Internet development.

Enhancing Your Programming

In Chapter 11, "Building a Foundation of Interactivity with *Request* and *Response* Objects," you learned how form data moves between client and server. This is the Web's most basic kind of interactivity. In that chapter, you had one guestbook.asp file, and you called it once to update your Guestbook's data file. This chapter covers error trapping, and provides a fuller treatment of client feedback.

▶ **See** "CGI Input" for more information about form data, **p. 205**

In this chapter, then, you enhance your basic Guestbook application with those two additional features. To accomplish this goal, you need only remember what you already know about the Request Object and you will learn how to get a form to call itself. In Chapter 11, you had separate guestbook.html and guestbook.asp files. In this chapter, however, you only have one guestbook.asp file. As you will see, this "reflexive" feature of the Active Server Pages (ASP) might be its most useful feature (with the exception of ADO, which is treated in depth in Part IV, "Database Management with Active Server Pages").

Using Its Own Output—Program Recursion

Recursion is a simple programming technique. You need it when a program must reuse its own output. The biggest problem with the technique is that it consumes memory at an alarming rate, and when recursion goes awry, it will cause something called a "stack overflow." As a result, it is not commonly used.

By the way, you can visualize stack overflow if you've ever worked in a restaurant: Dinner plates are stored in spring-loaded cylinders. As you add plates, the stack gets higher, and as you take plates away, each plate in the stack moves up. If you stack plates too high, they can overflow onto the ground and make a loud crash. Now memory is as silent as light, but it, too, can get in a muddle if you try to push too many calls to the same program into a limited amount of memory. Each call to a recursive program is a plate.

When an .asp file calls itself, however, the program contained in that file is not using recursion; it only looks as if it is. It's safe, and it will be one of the most immediately important features of ASP development. The key to the technique is the astute use of the Request.Form method.

There are several design objectives the ASP developer needs to keep in mind:

Default values for form variables must cooperate with the contents of the Request.Form collection.

Overhead should be minimized by caching session resources like connections and recordsets.

ON THE WEB

http://www.quecorp.com/asp   The advanced Guestbook program, guestbookpro.asp, is included at the Web site. It uses the same Guestbook database as its less sophisticated cousin.

In this section, you look at how .asp files work when they call themselves. In the next section, you include the code that you need to minimize overhead.

The ASP Program Model   The reason Active Server Pages have so little trouble calling themselves is ironic: ASP programs run on a stateless server. That's right—the one thing that makes database programming challenging makes reflexive programming easy. When you think about it, it's easy to understand: When an .asp (or HTML) file requests the attention of the server, it is served and then forgotten. Subsequent HTTP requests for the same file are totally unaffected by anything requested before. Form variables get passed exactly the same way with .asp files as with HTML files. In a sense, every instance of an .asp file is different from every other; the only thing they share is a name. Except for the referrer data (which contains the name of the file making the request) that's passed in the HTTP request, the request is an HTTP request, not the request of your specific Active Server Pages.

The point of all this is that your focus is on the HTTP request, not the file making the request. Think of each call made by an .asp file as one being made to a different file. In each case, the called .asp file has access to the Request.Form collection sent in the HTTP request transaction.

Setting Default Values   When an .asp file loads, the form fields it contains can have one of three values: a default (for example, you could hard-wire a value in its VALUE property), the value in some named parameter of the Request.Form collection, and, finally, a null value.

For .asp files that call themselves, the simplest technique is to put the Request.Form command in the VALUE property of the form field. For example, your Advanced Guestbook can use the code block in Listing 14.1 as a prototype for all the other fields:

Listing 12.1   GUESTBOOKPRO.ASP—Use Default Unless a Previous Value Was Entered

```
<%
varRealName = Request.Form("realname")
If IsEmpty(varRealName) Then
      varRealName = "Katy Corning"
End If
%>
```

Part
III

Ch
12

The entry in the <FORM> block of the ASP program would look like this:

```
<INPUT TYPE="TEXT" NAME="realname" SIZE=70 VALUE="<%=varRealName%>">
```

From these examples, you can see that the VALUE property is set with a variable, and the variable is initialized with NULL when the form is first called (or the Refresh button is pushed). If the variable is empty, initialize it with the field's default value.

However, on subsequent calls, the guestbookpro.asp file sees some value (perhaps the original default value, perhaps some value entered by the user) in the Request.Form collection's "realname" parameter. In this case, the variable used to set the VALUE property of the field gets the value in the Form collection. It's actually deceptively simple, after you get the hang of it.

Take a closer look at form fields that don't have VALUE properties.

On the Advanced Guestbook, you have a check box that the users select if they want to be notified of announcements on the *Working with Active Server Pages* Web site. To set the check box's default value, you have to see if it was "on" in the previous instance of the Guestbook form.

```
<%
If Request.Form("chkNotifyMe")="on" Then
        varCHECKED = "CHECKED"
End If
%>
```

TIP The comparison is case-sensitive. One thing you can do to control case sensitivity is force the left side of the expression to a case of choice, usually uppercase, using the UCase() function, and then compare the result to the test value (in uppercase if that's your case of choice).

From your example, it would look like this:

```
If UCase(Request.Form("chkNotifyMe"))="ON" Then
```

Actually, this is a good habit to use, regardless. That way, you never have to wonder if something is case-sensitive or not, or whether case sensitivity in an application changes as programs upgrade.

Caching Tasks

If your .asp file that calls itself uses ActiveX Data Objects (ADO), then you also have to attend to caching tasks. In this case, the stateless nature of HTTP is not a blessing as it was in "The ASP Program Model" section, but it's not quite a curse either. You just have to be careful that, if your .asp file has gone to the trouble of making a connection to an ADO data provider, you don't make it do that again each time the .asp file is called. This concern extends to any recordsets that might also be opened during previous calls to your .asp file.

As noted in Chapter 10, "Managing States and Events with *Application* and *Session* Objects," you can create Session Objects that are identified with individual parties using your Web application. Each user has a unique system-generated ID attached to every place she goes in your application. In the same way, ADO Connection and RecordSet Objects can be identified uniquely.

In your Advanced Guestbook, you test for the existence of these objects in the manner of Listing 14.2:

> **Listing 12.2 GUESTBOOKPRO.ASP—Testing for Objects**
>
> ```
> <%If IsObject(Session("SessionConnection")) Then
>     ' Reuse the ADO Objects
>     Set objConn = Session("SessionConnection")
>     Set objRst  = Session("SessionRecordSet")%>
>
> <FONT COLOR="Green">
> Using the Cached Session Connection and RecordSet
> </FONT><P>
> ```

```
<% Else

    ' This is the first time this user has called the file.
    ' Create the ADO Objects necessary to update the Guestbook.
    Set objConn = Server.CreateObject("ADODB.Connection")
    objConn.Open("Guestbook")
    ' Initialize the Session property with the Connection Object
    Session("SessionConnection") = objConn

    Set objRst = Server.CreateObject("ADODB.Recordset")
    ' Initialize the Session property with the RecordSet Object
    Session("SessionRecordSet") = objRst %>

    <FONT COLOR="Yellow">
    Opening the Connection and RecordSet
    </FONT><P>

<% End If %>
```

Take a good look at the Advanced Guestbook application at the Web site. I think you'll be amazed at how much work is being done with one program.

You have now completed your survey of basic Web interactivity using Active Server Pages instead of CGI. Now it's time to look at the next level of interactivity that this new technology enables. In the rest of this chapter, you will see that you can not only enable a richer interactive environment for the user and the Web site, but also enhance the interactivity between the client program and the server. You will reach this higher level of interactivity between client and server because you will do so on their turf: HTTP transactions using `Request` and `Response` headers.

The Rest of the *Request* Object

Part
III

Ch
12

You have covered the simplest and most often used methods and collections of the `Request` and `Response` Objects. You now complete your survey of the fundamentals of interactivity by exploring the nooks and crannies of `Cookies`, server variables, buffers, headers, and other arcane features.

How to Get a Header in Life

On the Web, there are always three entities communicating with each other: the Web server, Web client, and the human. Clearly, the language, images, and perhaps sound displayed on the screen or sent through the computer's sound card are how both the server and client software communicate with the human.

But how do the server and client communicate with each other?

With headers. Headers come in all shapes and sizes. Well, actually they come in four varieties: `General`, `Request`, `Response`, and `Entity` headers. These collections of data tell the server

continues

continued

vital information such as the media type of the returned entity. Remember, HTML can be almost any kind of information, from text, images, and sound to binary files and BLOBS. For all of the transporting infrastructure to work properly, knowledge of what is being transported is vital.

Most of the material in this section refers in one way or another to message headers.

N O T E   The definitive word on HTTP/1.0 is found at **http://www.ics.uci.edu/pub/ietf/http/ rfc1945.html#Product**. Section 4.2 describes all the details of message headers. A careful reading of this document is almost prerequisite to the serious use of most of the following features of the Response Object. ▧

The *Cookies* Collection

Cookies are an odd name given to an important task in programming stateless environments like the Web. If you're interested in all the technical details of this technique, direct your browser to an Internet-Draft entitled "HTTP State Management Mechanism," which is the official word on Cookies. It can be read at **http://portal.research.bell-labs.com/~dmk/ cookie-2.31-2.33.txt**.

Cookies: A Basic Recipe   You first looked at Cookies in Chapter 10, "Managing States and Events with *Application* and *Session* Objects." There, you learned about its use by the Active Server as a way to identify individual users and to do what's known as "manage state." In that context, the Active Server did all the work. In this chapter, you look at reading and writing Cookies yourself. I'll wager that most readers have not used Cookies yet. Until I found the Cookies Collection, I hadn't either; I had no idea how. You will see that reading and writing them really couldn't be easier. In fact, of all the header-oriented methods in ASP development, working with Cookies is the most direct and will probably be the most popular.

As you might guess, in the context of the Request Object, Cookies are read. In the section entitled "The Rest of the *Response* Object," you will learn how to write them.

To properly understand the function of Cookies takes some concentration. It's not difficult to understand, just backward. Here's what I mean: Cookies are unusual in HTML because they are data written to the local client-storage media. Except, perhaps, ActiveX controls and Java applets, nothing else in HTML writes to disk. But the real function of Cookies is to *request data*. That is, Cookies are used by clients to make specific requests of a particular server (defined as the domain and/or the path to an HTML document or an ASP application).

Cookies get confusing because we tend to think of them in the context of writing, not reading. Writing by the server is a necessary evil because Web clients usually never write data themselves; they must rely on the server to do that.

So, Cookies are used to request things. Here's an excellent example of what I mean: When Microsoft first hosted the version of their Web site that could be configured to individual client preferences, they used Cookies. After the preferences were selected and stored on client computers, subsequent requests for the MSN home page looked just like previous ones. The Cookies enabled the client to make a special request of the MSN Web server to deliver a custom document. See? Cookies are important because of what they do *after* they are created.

So, what's in a Cookie? A name? Yes. But what if two different servers need the same name? As other sites enabled the client to customize the interface to the server, this became more likely. The solution is stored in Cookie *attributes*. The two most important attributes are *domain* and *path*. One or both of these data points serve to uniquely match the Cookie with its server. When the server wrote the Cookie, it could have included a path back to itself. Say your ASP application is found at **your_company.com/data/web**. Suppose further that you have another ASP application at **your_company.com/data/web/tutorial**. If both applications have a Cookie named "last_visited" and if the client sends both "last_visited" Cookies to the server, Request.Cookies("last_visited") will return the value of the Cookie stored at **your_company.com/data/web/tutorial**.

Fancy *Cookies*   Cookies can also have "dictionaries." It's true. Dictionary objects can be anything that stores a term and a value, like its namesake stores a term and a definition. When it comes to Cookies, think of the dictionary as a dictionary of synonyms. Look at an example.

Say you need to store a Cookie called "client". This Cookie can have two key names: "last_name" and "first_name". You access each with the following syntax:

```
Request.Cookies("client")("first_name")
Request.Cookies("client")("last_name")
```

A Request.Cookies call without specifying a key will return an URL Encoded string of the name/value pairs for all entries in the cookies dictionary.

```
strQuery = Request.Cookies
```

would assign the variable strQuery the string value of

```
LAST%5FNAME=Mansfield%2DCorning&FIRST%5FNAME=Katy
```

Part

III

Ch

12

ON THE WEB

http://www.quecorp/com/asp   There's a demo program, cookies_walk.asp, at the Web site that shows writing and reading cookies with data you enter.

Working with *Request.Cookies*   Unlike its twin, Response.Cookies, Request.Cookies can appear anywhere in the HTML BODY section. As you will see in the next section, Response.Cookies is an HTTP header transaction. This means it must be completed before the entity body in the HTTP transaction is begun. Remember, headers are the means by which client and server communicate; the entity body is the part of HTTP that the client and server use to communicate with human users.

As previously noted, the syntax is simple:

```
Request.Cookies("cookie-name")¦("key-name")
```

If you request an undefined Cookie or key, the Request Object returns a null value.

Because Cookies is a collection, you can move through the collection with Listing 14.3. Note that this works without further modification with any Cookies Collection.

Listing 12.3   COOKIES_WALK.ASP—Walking Through a *Cookies* Collection

```
<H1>It's a Cookies Walk</H1>
<HR>
<UL>
<%
For Each cookie In Request.Cookies %>
    <LI>Cookie: <B><% = cookie %></B> = <% = Request.Cookies(cookie) %>
    <UL>
    <% For Each key in Request.Cookies(cookie) %>
     <LI>Key: <B><% = key %></B> is <% = Request.Cookies(cookie)(key) %>
    <% Next%>
    </UL>
<%Next%>
</UL>
```

The *ServerVariables* Collection

This collection tells you everything the server knows about the client and itself. There are three groups of data in this collection.

- HTTP Request
- Server Environment
- Everything else

As with all collections, you can use the For Each...Next control structure to enumerate the collection.

ON THE WEB

http://www.quecorp.com/asp   A two-file demo is included at the Web site, demo_servervar.htm and demo_servervar.asp, to show how selecting the two Request Methods, GET and POST, affects the ServerVariables Collection.

The Cookies demo mentioned previously also calls the demo_servervar.asp file and shows the effect on the HTTP_COOKIE variable in the ServerVariables Collection.

The HTTP Request group of variables describes important parts of the HTTP request transaction with the server. Things like REQUEST_METHOD, CONTENT_LENGTH, and CONTENT_TYPE are included here. Other important data points are the REMOTE_ADDR and the REMOTE_HOST variables. These two data points give you some idea of the IP address of the requesting client, and this is often used in programs that send e-mail via Web forms. The addresses returned (when they are, and that doesn't happen with all Web clients) are not always reliable or useful. On-line services have the same host, but often use a unique identifier in the address for individual users. However, this same user will have a different IP address the next time he logs on to the service. Other times, no address resolution is provided by the client software, usually because the user is coming from behind a firewall (a computer that protects a trusted network from unwelcome intrusions by outside computers).

The Server group of data points report facts about the server, such as SCRIPT_NAME and SERVER_NAME; these facts might be important in an intranet setting where there are as many HTTP servers as there are clients (for example, every Windows 95 machine is running the "Personal Web Server" application). Another important fact is SERVER_SOFTWARE; this would be important if all servers on an intranet were not running the same version of IIS (for example, IIS 2.0 does not have all the power and speed of IIS 3.0, because the ActiveX Server Engine is an add-on to the former and an integral part of the NT operating system in the latter).

The final group of server variables have the form HTTP_<header_name>. Some of the most useful variables are contained here. You'll find the Cookies Collection here, as well as the HTTP_REFERRER variable. This variable tells you the URL used to engage the current HTTP request transaction (unless the URL was entered manually), so you can see from whence your visitors have come. Another interesting fact is the HTTP_USER_AGENT; this variable tells you what kind of client software is being used at the other end (which can be helpful when you want to present HTML code that is optimized for any given client).

The Rest of the *Response* Object

Now return to your old friend, the Response Object. You have already covered the most frequently used method for this object, the Response.Write method. The rest of this object contains properties and methods almost exclusively for the management of HTTP headers.

Begin with your favorite topic, Cookies.

Response.Cookies Collection

Think of writing Cookies in the same way you would write a Registry entry in Windows 95 or an .ini file entry in Windows 3.1. Actually, in ASP development, writing Cookies is much easier than it ever was in Windows. There are no special API functions to write (and maintain when you upgrade your Windows). Just read and write, and let the server do the work. This is the way programming was always meant to be, isn't it?

N O T E   The NAME field is the only required field for Cookies, and its value is URL encoded. When you get to the Server Object in the next chapter, you learn how to use this method to do the dirty work of encoding Cookies values. ▪

CAUTION

Always put your Response.Cookies calls before the <HEAD> section of your .asp files. These are header transactions (as are most of the rest of the Response Object's methods) and will fail if the server has already written the header of the HTTP response transaction to the client.

If you spy on the `Cookie` collection using the `Request.ServerVariables`("HTTP_COOKIES") variable, you see that this collection can get full quickly. One of the reasons for this is that each `Cookie` is "attached" to SessionIDs (which have their own `Cookie` in this collection, "ASPSESSIONID"). Fortunately, the server takes care of the details. If you set a "LAST_VISITED" `Cookie` to the current time, all you have to do is `Request.Cookies`("LAST_VISITED") and you have its value, regardless of what else lurks down there in the cookie jar.

As you learned in the discussion of the `Request.Cookies` method, `Cookies` can have "dictionaries" (sometimes called "data sets"). These are like fields in a database record, and they're called "keys" (what keys have to do with `Cookies` is anybody's guess). The syntax is simple:

```
Response.Cookies("NAME")("FIRST")="Michael"
Response.Cookies("NAME")("LAST")="Corning"
```

When a `Cookie` has keys it also reports TRUE when the "HasKeys" attribute is tested. The other attributes are `Domain`, `Path`, `Expires`, and `Secure`. `Domain` and `Path` provide information that uniquely identify `Cookies` with the same name when they were created by interacting with different Web servers. For example, many servers will write a `Cookie` called "last_visit" and the `Domain` and `Path` attributes permit each server to identify its own `Cookie` and not confuse it with the `Cookie` left by another server. The `Expires` attribute tells the server when it can safely ignore the `Cookies`' value, and the `Secure` attribute tells the server that the `Cookie` can be used in a secure transaction.

N O T E Cookie attributes can only be set, not read directly. This is because they are useful only to the server.

Response Properties

The properties of the `Response` Object control how the HTML output stream is to be processed. Properties such as `ContentType`, `Expires`, and `Status` all have counterparts in HEAD tags that you might have used before, but we think you will find using `Response` properties to be simpler.

The *Buffer* Property   This property is important if you use the other properties and methods of the `Response` Object extensively. It is important because it permits you to relax the constraint that you must finish manipulating the HTTP headers *before* you start sending the body of the HTML transaction to the client.

Remember, the HTTP headers are used between the client and the server and are invisible to the output of the HTTP transaction; in other words, none of the header data appears on the client program's screen. Usually, the client and server are intolerant of any interference on the part of the human readable component of the transaction unless the `Buffer` Property is set true.

When true, none of the output data is sent to the client until all the ASP scripts are complete, or until the `Response.Flush` or `Response.End` methods are called.

ON THE WEB

http://www.quecorp.com/asp   The `cookies.asp` file in the /lab/ directory uses `Response.Buffers=True` to permit the `Request.QueryString`("yesno") variable to be displayed before the BODY section begins further down in the script. The `cookies.asp` file in the /lab/test/ directory uses conventional programming style to effect the same result.

The *ContentType* Property   This property is used to instruct the client how to display the HTTP Response Body sent by the server. For .asp files, setting this to "text/plain" will render the actual HTML source code instead of interpreting it. If you look on the bottom of the /lab/ cookies.asp screen, you will see an option, "View Source Code." If you select this, you send a query string to the .asp file that instructs it to set the `Response.ContentType` property to "text/plain." You can see the same result if you select the other option, "ServerVariable Collection" and choose View Source from your client program.

N O T E   Notice that there are no <HTML><HEAD><BODY> tags used in demo_server.asp. If those tags are present, they override the `ContentType` property. ■

The *Expires* Property   This property tells the browser how many minutes it has to live from the last time it updated. The default value is 0, meaning that every time the page is visited, it is refreshed. The twin cookies.asp files are an interesting test of this property. Take a closer look.

The /lab/test/cookies.asp file calls the lab/cookies.asp file. Note carefully: The cookies.asp file in the child directory calls its counterpart in the parent /lab/ directory. The first time this parent `Cookie` is called, its `LAST_VISITED Cookie` is set to the current time. From that page, you select the "Set test `Cookie`" option and the child `Cookie` page fires updating its `LAST_VISITED` `Cookie` to the current time. *Note this time before you return to the parent `Cookie`.* Now, when you immediately select the "Set lab `Cookie`" link, you will note that the `LAST VISITED Cookie`'s value *did not change*. Why?

Because the page was cached. If you look at the top of the parent `Cookie` page, you will see that it tells you that nothing new will appear on that page for at least one minute. For that minute, the Web client retrieves the cached copy instead of refreshing the link.

OK, so switch back and forth, now, between these two pages. Note the time on both pages. As long as there is a difference of less than sixty seconds between the two pages, the parent `Cookie` will not be refreshed. But as soon as the child `Cookie` page has a time one minute or more later than the parent `Cookie` page, it will refresh with a new time.

Clearly, you need to download the demo files from the Web site and conduct this experiment for yourself.

The *ExpiresAbsolute* Property   The only difference between the `ExpiresAbsolute` and the `Expires` properties is that the former includes a data and time. Use the pound sign (#) to delimit this value. For example:

```
<% Response.ExpiresAbsolute=#December 21, 1997 1:00:00 AM# %>
```

Part

III

Ch

12

The time is converted to Greenwich Mean Time before the Expires HTTP header is sent. GMT is the time that all servers use to stay synchronized.

If you leave the time blank, midnight on the date given is assumed. If the date is blank, the time on the date the script is run is assumed.

The *Status* Property   The Status property forces the Server to send whatever response value you give it. The most visible example would be to put the following line of code at the top of your .asp file:

```
<% Response.Status="401 Unauthorized"
```

The result of a call to an .asp file with this line in it would be a username/password dialog to request authorized access to the page.

Response Methods

The methods of the Response Object covered as follows help you do odd jobs around the Web site. You probably won't have much occasion to use these methods, but you need to be aware of what they can do, should the need arise.

The *AddHeader* Method   This method is not for the fainthearted. If you looked at the demo_servervar.asp program, you noticed that the end of the collection contained a whole bunch of ServerVariables that started with the "HTTP_" prefix. These headers are generally accepted data points that some or all client programs can consistently interpret.

Some of the most commonly used headers are HTTP_REFERRER, HTTP_USER_AGENT, and, of course, HTTP_COOKIE. When a client program sees these headers from the server in response to a request it made, it knows what the server is trying to "say" to it. This is what I meant earlier about the "other" interactivity going on over the Web; i.e., the interactivity not between user and machine, but between Web client and Web server.

One of the header fields that is exchanged in this category is the WWW-Authenticate header. This header "exists" in the HTTP specification but can be "customized" to meet the specific requirements of authentication required by any given server. It is possible that some challenge-response processes would require more than one WWW-Authentication header. The AddHeader method was created to cover this contingency.

The *AppendToLog* Method   This method adds a string of no more than 80 characters to the IIS log file. You must have IIS configured to log server transactions. You can confirm (or enable) logging by running the Internet Information Services Manager and selecting the Logging tab from the services window you select (for example, WWW service). This dialog box will also tell you where the log file is located.

> **CAUTION**
> Because the IIS log file is comma delimited, you cannot append a string with embedded comments. You might find it necessary to URLEncode the string first, but you will have to decode the string later if you need to refer to it.

One example of using this method is appending the HTTP_USER_AGENT to the transaction. This way, you can find out which browsers are going to certain pages on your Web site.

The *BinaryWrite* Method   Binary files are not text files. They are usually required by custom applications running on the client's computer. This method enables the ActiveX Server Engine to send this kind of file to the client. This method can be used in a way similar to the way Server Components are used (see the next section, "Server Components," for a detailed discussion). That is, you can create a component that creates objects, and then you can instantiate objects in your .asp file as follows:

```
Set objImage = CreateObject(ImageComposer)
imgPortland = objImage.PhotoShoot
Response.BinaryWrite imgPortland
```

The *Clear* Method   The Clear method is used in conjunction with the Buffer method mentioned previously. This method, along with the End and Flush methods coming up next, is useful when there is a lot of ASP processing necessary before a final result is ready to send to the client. This will make for some very creative and resourceful ASP code.

For its part, the Clear method erases the content of the response body. Remember, that's the part of the HTTP transaction that the client displays on the screen; it is not the same thing as the information contained in the response header. If the ASP code finds an error in processing or data, or if it needs to start processing over for any other reason, the Clear method gives it a clean "sheet of music."

The syntax is simple:

```
Response.Clear
```

The *End* Method   The End method stops ASP processing in its tracks. It functions like the Stop command in Visual Basic. When the ActiveX Server Engine sees this method, it flushes the buffer (which assumes, of course, that the Response.Buffer = True method was executed in the first line of the .asp file). Any contents in the buffer (including the response body, if any) are sent to the client. To send nothing, use the Response.Clear method first. As with its cousins, the syntax for this method is direct:

```
Response.End
```

The *Flush* Method   This method will send the buffer to the client without stopping the processing. It, too, only operates without error if the Response.Buffer method has been set to true.

```
Response.Flush
```

The *Redirect* Method   This method is most commonly used when you want to send clients to another URL instead of sending them an HTML stream. This is commonly needed when a Web site is substantially altered or moved. When someone returns to your site from one of their Shortcuts, Bookmarks, or Favorites entries, the Redirect method can be waiting for them in the now defunct HTML page. When a client requests this page before it can stream the entity body of the document back, the server sees that the URL contains a Redirect header and

Part
III

Ch
12

consequently changes the location of the requested URL. This is done without the user knowing it, though they will see that the URL in the Location box is different than what they entered.

> **N O T E**   This is also a useful method when you want certain clients to see HTML optimized for them. You can do the same thing using client-side scripting, but this alternative suffers the single weakness of all other client-side scripting strategies: Not all clients script. ■

> **N O T E**   To avoid this kind of confusion, it might be better to have an explicit message in the body of the outdated HTML page that tells the client that the URL is different and to update their Shortcut, Bookmark, or Favorites entry. ■

The *Server* Object

The `Server` Object can be a real workhorse and time-saver. Its primary mission is like all programming utilities that have come before it: Do the same old thing, and do it well and quickly. In one (limited) respect, utilities have been the precursor to objects. They have always been reusable code that did a clearly defined "administrative" task. Batch updates, directory maintenance, you name it; if it qualified as drudgery work, a programmer sat down and composed a utility program to do it. On the desktop, macros have generally served this function with distinction.

In the new world, we have come full circle: The utility is now an object (not a fully polymorphic, inheritance-capable object) with its own property and methods. It might not have an impeccable object-oriented pedigree, but it will quickly earn the affection of all Webmasters who can now delegate such routine tasks as rotating ads to it.

To start off correctly, remember that the intrinsic methods of the `Server` Object have two general roles:

- ■ To do things humans find difficult, such as encode URL and HTML strings, and keep track of the physical and logical representation of file paths
- ■ To create objects that can do almost anything else
  - ▶ **See** "Instantiating an Object" to learn the details of CreateObject, **p. 269**

Server Property: *ScriptTimeout*

This is the only property for the `Server` Object. It is designed to give the ASP developer some control over the contingency of script-processing time. Note I said "script" processing. If a server script calls a server component (such as those discussed in Chapter 14), then the `ScriptTimeout` property will not control that component (the developer of the component is responsible for that). So, if there is a chance that something might take an inordinate amount of time (this is the Internet, after all, and we all know it is not the fastest thing alive) to complete, you can take steps to avoid being deadlocked as a result.

This property is read/writable. To read the value of this property, use the following expression:

```
<% =Server.ScriptTimeout %>
```

If you need to set the property, for example, to three minutes, do it like this:

```
<% Server.ScriptTimeout = 180 %>
```

The default value of this property is 90 seconds.

Managing HTML

HTML was meant to be read by a machine, not by people. In the spirit of maximum productivity that drives nearly all Microsoft product development and usability testing, the Active Server provides some great little text manipulation utilities.

CreateObject   There are five Server Components that ship with the Active Server: `AdRotator`, Browser Capabilities, Content Linking, `TextStream`, and the Database Access Component. (This last component exposes interfaces to three more objects—the `Connection`, `Command`, and `RecordSet` objects.) The `Server.CreateObject` method is how we create instances of all these components. To be more precise: Each of these components produces an object. Remember, an object contains both data (properties) and programs (methods). Once created, these component objects act on things they were designed to do. For example, the `TextStream` component produces an object that acts on text files. Most of what you do with text files—opening and closing, reading, and writing—qualifies as utilities, something done the same way over and over again.

Because you tackle these utilities in alphabetic order, the first one you examine is the `HTMLEncode` method.

HTMLEncode   `Server.HTMLEncode` is closely related to `Response.Write` and, in special cases, to the implicit write method (for example, text appearing outside ASP code tags). All of these methods `Write` to the outgoing HTML data stream. To sort all this out, first see what the `Server.HTMLEncode` method needs for input and what it does with that input after processing.

Simply put, `Server.HTMLEncode` wants to see exactly what you do. If you want to see the actual HTML source code on your client's window, you give that string of characters to `Server.HTMLEncode`. It's pretty smart. It knows which characters in the input string will cause confusion to the rendering engine in the client, so it replaces these problematical characters with something the client will properly render.

The most obvious culprit is the angle brackets; they're the characters that tell the client rendering engine that the following text is HTML source and that it should interpret the text as commands.

ON THE WEB

http://www.quecorp.com/asp   Take a look at the HTML_tips_traps.asp file at the Web site for examples and comparisons of these issues and methods.

Part
III
Ch
12

ASP development adds another problem, for the <> characters can confuse the server too, and it will be confused before the client will be. In fact, it's possible that the ActiveX Server Engine will make your original problem even more confusing for the client. Confused? Try this again, only differently:

On both the client-side and the server-side, the < and > tells the software that everything in between those characters is source code, not text. But when you actually want to print the angle bracket (say you want to display an actual HTML tag on the screen), how do you tell the software to print it instead of interpret it? That depends on which software you're worried about. Any text surrounded by angle brackets is interpreted. On the server any text surrounded by <% and %> is interpreted.

CAUTION

When trying to output HTML-Encoded text, mistakes can be hard to interpret because of the mess it can make of the resulting HTML data stream. Other times context plays a role so that the same non-alphanumeric characters can have different effects.

In the latter category, my favorite is sending %> to the HTML data stream. Sometimes, the Active Server chokes when it hits what it thinks is the end of ASP code without first having encountered <%, the beginning tag for ASP code. Yet, if you refresh the errant .asp file, it seems no longer to be confused.

The safest approach is to experiment with the various techniques, find the one that gives the most consistent results, and stick with it. For example, you have already seen that sending %> can be trouble. Mitigating the potential threat by using `Server.HTMLEncode` is a good idea, but remember to include the escape character. The syntax is

`<%=Server.HTMLEncode("%\>")%>`

N O T E `Server.HTMLEncode` needs the = before it in order to send the encoded stream to the client. This is because the output of `Server.HTMLEncode` can be used in ways other than writing to the client (for example, its output can be the input to `Response.Write`).

`Response.Write` does not need the equal sign (output to the client is implicit; it's the only thing it knows how to do), but the equal sign won't get in its way, either. You might find it easier to always remember to put the = before methods whose output goes to the client (including `Response.Write`) than it is to remember which ones don't need it.

On the other hand, if others are going to see your source code, you might want to write it properly. Otherwise, it's like leaving too much space between your tie and your belt; to those who care about such minutiae, the appearance can be embarrassing. ▪

Generally speaking, using the `Server.HTMLEncode` method is safer than the `Response.Write` method. The reason: `Server.HTMLEncode` always replaces the angle brackets with their "entity names." *Entity names* are the special character strings that begin with the & and end with the semicolon. Examples include >, which always yields the ">" character; <, which yields the "<"; , which is a non-breaking space. `Response.Write` sends the literal character to the output stream, so it might backfire on you (but at least it will only be the client that gets confused).

ON THE WEB

http://www.quecorp.com/asp   There is a text file at the Web site that lists the most common entity names. But you shouldn't need to bother; `Server.HTMLEncode` makes the list almost obsolete (except for the one entity name `Server.HTMLEncode` can't capture, the perennial ` `).

T I P   When troubleshooting this kind of code, you can sometimes squeeze a little more troubleshooting data out of your Web client by looking at the HTML source code. The ActiveX Server Engine writes to the data stream up to the point of error, and sometimes it prints more data than is reported by the error alert.

MapPath   The `MapPath` method is necessary because of one thing: the definition of an ASP application; namely, all files stored in and under a virtual directory.

N O T E   If you come from a Novell network environment, you are already familiar with logical drives (indeed, in the old Dark ages Of Software [DOS] days, we had operating system commands like SUBST that also mapped directories to drive letters). ▪

IIS also uses this kind of technique to shorten the identity of a collection of files. This works great under HTTP with its object-centric orientation. The virtual directory is part of the URL for the Web site. But what happens when you need to do something to a file in that virtual directory, and you are not going to access it through a Web server?

For example, Chapter 13 discusses the Content Linking Component. This component needs access to a text file and will access it through the server's file system.

To access the file properly, the Content Linking Component must know where the file is. If the file is stored somewhere in the virtual directory, you can find it by using the `MapPath` method relative to the virtual directory. If the file is somewhere else, you need to take your bearings from the `ServerVariables` Collection's `PATH_INFO` variable. Here's how you do each thing:

Say that your application is called /web (that's its virtual directory) and that it is physically located in the c:/data/web directory. Recall that when you set up the virtual directory in the Internet Information Services Manager application, you specified this physical directory then. The `PATH_INFO` variable in the `ServerVariables` Collection keeps a record of this physical path. Therefore, when you invoke the `Server.MapPath` method using the `Request.ServerVariables("PATH_INFO")` syntax, you return the following string:

`c:\data\web`

If, in fact, the file you need to access is inside the virtual directory, you can specify its location relative to that directory. Here, the presence or absence of an initial slash character (forward or backward is recognized) controls whether or not the mapped path starts at the root of the virtual directory or relative to the current one.

If the parameter passed to the `MapPath` method begins with a slash, then `MapPath` begins at the top of the virtual directory. If no slash precedes the path passed to `MapPath`, then the result of the method is the fully qualified path to the file from the current directory.

▶ **See** "Content Is King" for more information about Content Linking Components, **p. 254**

Part
III

Ch
12

ON THE WEB

http://www.quecorp.com/asp   This is one of those topics that is so hard to describe, yet easy to demonstrate. We have included another or our famous demo applets at the Web site to show you not only what we've been talking about, but also how you might use it in your own applications.

URLEncode   You have already broached the topic of URLEncoding; you encountered it in the context of the `QueryString` passed in a `GET` request to the server. In this chapter, you have made your own query strings when you wanted to call an .asp file in a particular way (see the demo_cookies and demo_servervars .asp files for examples). You also noted that `Cookies` are URLEncoded (though you won't need to encode `Cookie` values since the `Response.Cookies` method does that for you).

The most common use for this method may just be in passing variable strings between ASP pages. To render a string according to the rules of URL encoding, simply send the string to the `Response.URLEncode` method like this:

```
<% http://lab/test.asp?Server.URLEncode("Katy Mansfield-Corning") %>
```

and you will send the correct string to the test.asp file that looks like this:

```
Katy+Mansfield%2DCorning
```

Managing Data with *CreateObject* (ADODB...)

We note the use of the `Server.CreateObject` method at the end of this chapter for the sake of consistency. Note the Server Component identifier used in the section heading. The "ADO" part of it stands for ActiveX Data Objects. The developers had to add the "DB" when they released Beta 2 because the underlying Server Component had been substantially improved. If you look in the Registry, you will see an entry in there identified by "ADODB." The ellipsis is there because there are three objects intrinsic to the ADODB component.

We will say a little more about this method in the next chapter when we introduce the Database Access Component and the ActiveX Data Objects, but this technology is so important that it deserves its own Part in the book, Part IV, "Database Management with Active Server Pages."

Before you leave this topic, note two things:

- Whenever you invoke this method in an .asp file, you must always use the `Server.CreateObject` syntax.
- Remember that you also can use ADO in programming environments other than ASP (Visual Basic, for example).

Outside of ASP, the `CreateObject` is handled as it usually is in that environment. Again, with VB, the syntax is simply `CreateObject`. As we said, there's plenty of time and space set aside for ADO in coming chapters.

From Here...

With this chapter, we leave the `Server` Object for the moment. Later in the book, we will need everything we've learned so far. In the following chapter, we conclude Part III with a discussion of a very important part of ASP development, Server Components.

Server Components permit something crucial to all modern programming development environments—extensibility. What the Integrated Development Environment (IDE) did for developers using Visual C++, Visual J++, Visual Basic 5.0, and the Visual InterDev, server components will do for users of applications written by Active Server Pages developers.

Perhaps put a better way, the advent of Server Components makes it possible to extend the functionality of the Active Server without interrupting what it already does so well. If the IDE was a boon to professional programmers, then Server Components will have the same impact on power users and Webmasters who do not hold themselves to a professional programming standard. It's an IDE for the rest of us.

- Chapter 13, "Interactivity Through Bundled Active Server Components," introduces HTML Components like the Ad Rotator, Browser Capabilities, Content Linking, and TextStream.The Database Access Component is also introduced but deserves, and gets, its own emphasis in Part IV.
- Chapter 14, "Constructing Your Own Server Components," shows you how to create your own components, including design-time components that help you create Active Server Pages.

Part
III

Ch
12

## CHAPTER 13

Interactivity Through Bundled Active Server Components

So far, it has been up to you to produce any interactivity in your Active Server Pages. You have seen the Active Server's intrinsic Objects (viz., Request, Response, Server, Application, and Session Objects—along with their collections, methods, and properties) that make doing this relatively easy. Having the horsepower of a well-equipped Web server means that you can deliver lots of custom features without being constrained by the Internet's current bandwidth limitations. But ASP development doesn't mean that *you* have to do all the work to make the best Web pages on the planet.

This chapter introduces you to a cadre of tools that want nothing more from life than to spare you the drudgery of the most mundane tasks of the Webmaster. This chapter explains Server Components; specifically, the Ad Rotator, Browser Capabilities, Content Linking, and the FileAccess Components. ■

Get an overview of Server Components

Find out where Server Components fit in the overall architecture of the Active Server.

See what makes the Ad Rotator Component tick

The Ad Rotator Component makes the most of precious advertising real estate on your Web page, and more.

Look under the hood of your visitor's browser capabilities

It's important that you understand the needs and limitations of the client software that visits your site.

Keep everything connected with content linking

The Content Linking Component helps you easily maintain a site map—an important aid to navigation for your Web site.

Learn the ins and outs of file I/O with TextStream Object of the FileAccess Component

Always useful, text files can be a bear to manipulate—unless you have this handy tool at your side.

Delegating Interactivity

Utility programs are a godsend to programmers. The utility functions provided by the Server Object (viz., CreateObject, HTMLEncode, MapPath, and URLEncode) are terrific at what they were designed to do. But their utility is limited.

This chapter begins to cross the bridge from predefined utility to virtually unlimited usefulness. You are introduced to five Server Components, each more powerful and flexible than its cousin in the Server Object's methods already examined.

One of these higher-level utilities, the File Access Component, permits you to do almost anything you want to a text file (contrast this capability with the Server.AppendToLog method, which adds only 80 characters and to only one file, the server log).

Table 13.1   The ASP Developer's ToolBox

Component	Enables You to
Ad Rotator	Randomly display hyperlinked images
Browser Capabilities	Optimize HTML for any browser
Content Linking	Create Web site table of contents
File Access	Manipulate text files

Chapter 14, "Constructing Your Own Server Components," introduces one other capability of the Active Server: Roll your own. That's right, the Server Components that ship with the Active Server are prototypes of what you can do yourself. We use Visual Basic (you can use many other programming tools) to show how to create a DLL and use it in your Active Server Pages. This extensibility of the Active Server means that it will live a long and prosperous life as a development environment.

Server Components are .dll files that run in the same address space as .asp files and IIS. They can be single-threaded or multithreaded, but the single-threaded programs will suffer the usual limitation of being able to be run by only one client at a time. DLLs created with Visual Basic 4.0 are single-threaded.

Server Components fall into two groups: HTML and database access. You could spend your whole ASP career working with only the HTML components discussed in this chapter and never touch a database. Indeed, that's how most Webmasters have spent their time; a vast majority of the content on the Web is static HTML (at least, static in the sense that it does not interface with a database).

Web development is more difficult and expensive and it is less flexible when the power of the modern database is excluded from the Webmaster's toolkit. With the advent of ASP, this no longer is necessary. All of Part IV, "Database Management with Active Server Pages," is devoted to covering this important innovation in great detail. In this chapter, you will focus on the HTML-based Server Components.

Ad Rotator Component Rotates Ads (and More)

Even in its earliest versions, a distinctive feature of HTML was its use of hyperlinked graphic images. Pictures, line art, virtually anything that could be painted on the screen could also be imbued with the power to transport the browser to another file. The HTML element that controlled this ability was the IMG tag.

```
<IMG SRC="test.gif" WIDTH=430 HEIGHT=180 BORDER=1 ALT="Any picture you want to
➡display">
```

The Ironic Component

Presenting the Server Components in alphabetical order, we come first to the Ad Rotator Component—and think it's ironic that we talk first of this tool. Advertising was one of the earliest forms of revenue for Web sites, but a vast majority of advertising revenue goes to a mere handful of Web sites. Clearly, volume controls the flow of advertising revenue, and only a handful of Web sites generate the volume necessary to justify the overhead of an advertising business model. What can the rest of us do to attract traffic? What can we do to keep visitors coming back?

Perhaps a richer, more interactive and personal experience is what the rest of us need to make adding ads to our business plans a feasible complement to our current strategy. Perhaps ASP gives everyone, even the smallest Web studios, the tools needed to reach a new level of excitement and loyalty in their readers. Time will tell. Meanwhile, let's see how these Server Components work.

The Ad Rotator Component yields the complete IMG tag of a graphic whose name and optional data are taken from a scheduling file. As the Ad Rotator's name suggests, this scheduling file may contain many images, each one assigned a relative frequency of display. In addition, the Ad Rotator Component can make the displayed image a hypertext link to another HTML page, perhaps the home page of the advertiser. Figure 13.1 shows the generic parts of the Ad Rotator Component and how everything works together. Table 13.2 maps the figure elements with the files used in Listing 13.1.

Table 13.2   Cross-Referencing Figure 13.1 and Listing 13.1

Figure 13.1 Element	Listing 13.1 Filename
.asp File	adrot.asp
Rotation Schedule File	adrot.txt
Advertiser's Home Page	adrot2.asp
Ad Rotator Component	MSWC.AdRotator
Redirect Client	adredir.asp

Part
III

Ch

13

FIG. 13.1

This displays all of the moving parts of the Ad Rotator Server Component.

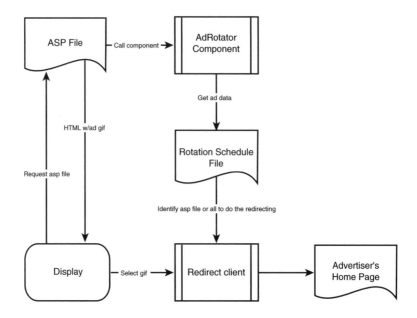

N O T E At the end of this section, after specifying details of the scheduling file and related programs, we suggest a novel use of the Ad Rotator Component. Perhaps our suggestion will inspire you to an equally novel offering on your own Web site that helps you compete with the big guys. ▨

Ad Rotator Component Properties

The Ad Rotator Component has three properties listed and described in Table 13.3. Each property can be modified at runtime to make the behavior of the Ad Rotator dynamic. You also could use the TextStream object of the File Access Component to modify the Schedule file on-the-fly, but that's tricky and much more difficult than using the exposed properties of the Ad Rotator Component.

Table 13.3   Ad Rotator Properties

Property	Use
Border	Change the width of a border surrounding your image. Set this property to 0 for an invisible border. Border width is measured in pixels.
Clickable	This Boolean property dictates whether or not the image is hyperlinked. If true, then when you click the image you will go to another page and image. False, and you only have a static image.

Property	Use
TargetFrame	This is the name of FRAME defined in the .asp or HTML file that defined the FRAMESET. This property serves the same function as the TARGET argument in the A HREF tag. Use it to display your image in the frame named with this property.

N O T E Setting the Border property to a negative number will yield a BORDER argument in the IMG tag of the resulting HTML file to 65535! Now that's a big border. It effectively makes your HTML page blank. The text is there—you just have to scroll way down and over to see it. ▪

Listing 13.1 is a typical example of how you set up an Ad Rotator Component. You only needed one <% and one %> marker to delimit the first four lines of .asp code in Listing 13.1.

The GetAdvertisement method looks to the single parameter it uses to identify the file that controls how the IMG tag will be written. In Listing 13.1, this file is adrot.txt, and it gives the Ad Rotator Component all the arguments it needs when it creates the IMG tag it passes to the Active Server. The Active Server then includes that IMG tag with all the rest of the HTML source code, if any, contained in the calling program (which in our case in Listing 13.1 is adrot.asp). The contents of adrot.txt are given in Listing 13.2.

Listing 13.1   adrot.asp—Setting the Default Values of the Ad Rotator Component

```
<%
Set objAd = Server.CreateObject("MSWC.AdRotator")
objAd.Border(1)
objAd.Clickable(FALSE)
objAd.TargetFrame(FrameAd)
%>

<%= objAd.GetAdvertisement("/lab/ar/adrot.txt") %>
```

N O T E Be sure to use the <%=...%> tag when calling the GetAdvertisement method; otherwise, if you forget the "=," you will not see an image in your .asp file. ▪

Keeping Track of Your Files

The path used by the GetAdvertisement method to find the Ad Rotator Schedule file is the alias of the virtual directory that holds your ASP application, assuming your application is in its root directory. This also is the same value used in the Schedule file itself to find the image file.

continues

Part

III

Ch

13

continued

Of course, these files can be anywhere; for example, the adredir.asp file can be in a utility directory of another ASP application that you created, and the file that is linked to the ad itself can be anywhere on the Internet.

If you're not sure what the alias is, run the IIS Manager applet, select the WWW service, and then point to the Directories tab. You'll find the value under the Aliases column.

The Schedule File   The adrot.txt file is the Schedule file, and it contains two sections of information separated by an asterisk (*). Listing 13.2 shows what a typical Schedule file looks like.

Listing 13.2   adrot.txt—The Data Used by Ad Rotator to Display an Image

```
Redirect /lab/ar/adredir.asp
width 349
height 235
border 0
*
/lab/apple.gif
/lab/ar/adrot2.asp
Click to go to adrot2.asp
30
/lab/pie.gif
/lab/ar/adrot3.asp
Click to go to adrot3.asp
70
```

The first section of Listing 13.2 contains optional data to control how file redirection will take place, and it controls the appearance of *all* the image files used by the Ad Rotator Component.

The second, third, and fourth lines in the adrot.txt file control are used by the Ad Rotator Component to specify the WIDTH, HEIGHT, and BORDER parameters of the IMG tag. If you don't specify values, the default values of WIDTH 440, HEIGHT 60, and BORDER 1 are used. These size defaults produce the traditional size of a banner ad, so if your image does not conform to that shape, be sure to specify the size; otherwise, you probably won't like how it looks.

 Some text editors will include the actual values for an image's WIDTH and HEIGHT parameters when you drag and drop the image into an .asp file. Most graphics editors also display the size of an image somewhere in their user interface, so you shouldn't have any problem coming up with the actual size of your image.

The second section of information contains URLs to the image file (a required data point) and to the hyperlinked HTML (or .asp) file. This section also includes the text for the .ALT parameter of the IMG tag that Ad Rotator Component will produce. The final attribute of this second section is a number between 0 and 4,294,967,295 (no, we didn't make that number up!). This number tells Ad Rotator Component the pro rata share of display impressions. For example, if the first image had 30 and the second had 70, the first one would display 30% of the time.

 T I P You can use the ALT text as a sort of ToolTip, instead of merely as text to display if the client does not support or has disabled graphics. This way, when the mouse is over the image, the reader can get a clue about what will happen when the image is selected. Choose this text wisely to complement the other visual clue, the URL that usually will display somewhere on the client's status bar.

The Ad Rotator Component with a Twist

Up to now, we have limited the context of this section to what the designers of the Ad Rotator Component had in mind—advertising—but now we suggest another use for the tool. Keep in mind that this is just an example, but we hope it fires your imagination and helps you find even more clever ways of using this and other ASP utilities.

Normally, when a reader selects an image presented by the Ad Rotator Component, that reader goes to the advertiser's Web site. But there's nothing to stop the reader from going to another Ad Rotator .asp file on your site.

 ON THE WEB

http://www.quecorp.com/asp   On this book's Web site, you will find a demo of a trivia game that we concocted from the pieces of the Ad Rotator Component.

In that demo, each image is not an ad but a trivia question. Clicking it sends you to the answer and then to another question. Note that most of the adrotX.txt files have more than one question in them. This gives you a little more variety with no additional work.

The system works because each file redirect goes to another adrotX.asp file, and each of those files has its own adrotX.txt file. Each adrotX.txt file instructs the Ad Rotator Component of the location of the next question, and each question tells the Ad Rotator Component the location of the next answer.

There's nothing stopping you from locating these questions on other people's servers. In this way, you could create an Internet "scavenger hunt." This kind of entertainment might be welcomed by many road-weary Internauts, and cooperating with other Webmasters can help develop relationships that have additional value for everyone involved.

Another use of image files could be patterned after the popular PointCast Network model. Using .avi files or animated GIFs, you could add some splash to your advertising.

Using the Browser Capabilities Component

You have read often in this book that as an ASP developer you have to choose between writing code to serve the widest audience and writing code for the richest possible experience.

Part

III

Ch

13

By using the Browser Capabilities Component, it is possible to have a great deal of both. With this Component, you can return code optimized for each browser or Web client that visits your site.

This doesn't mean you have to maintain separate pages, e.g., one that has been optimized with ActiveX controls and another that runs straight HTML. You don't even have to worry that the browser doesn't support JavaScript or VBScript.

As you know, Active Server Pages are cached on the server and run in the server's memory space. The result is pure speed. If you cache the Browser Capabilities Component as an `Application` property, it is available to every browser that enters your Webspace—that's every one, regardless of age or the platform upon which they run. None of these browsers needs to be able to interpret (literally) a scripting language, and all of them can get HTML optimized for their ability.

Sure, you still can use a scripting language on old browsers; they will ignore the `SCRIPT` tag, and the scripting source code is commented out, so they won't even see that. But doing this has one limiting consequence: All browsers that can't interpret a scripting language are treated the same way, the way that the remaining HTML treats them. No other processing is possible. There's got to be a better way.

Two Components of the Browser Capabilities Component

The Browser Capabilities Component is composed of two components: the browscap.dll file and the browscap.ini file. The browscap.dll creates instances of an object known as the Browser Capabilities Component. This object exposes the methods and properties that you will learn about in this section.

The browscap.ini file is your baby. The hardest thing about using it is keeping up with the breakneck speed of Web client software development. You also have control over how many of the extant clients you want to include. You can tell the browscap.ini file which browsers you want to include and for which of their features you want to test.

The Browser Has Grown Up

Call us picky, but we find it increasingly difficult to refer to a Web client as a *browser*. It was appropriate even a year ago, when virtually all content on the Web was static, but the advent of Java, ActiveX controls, and client-side scripting has changed all that forever—and there's no turning back. The term *browser* is anachronistic.

Nevertheless, the Browser Capabilities Component uses the term, so we use it, too, but only when we have no choice. Whenever we say "*Web client*," we are referring to "*browser*."

We recall reading an article last summer that said it was an offense to both Microsoft and Netscape to use the term *browser*. That must have been urban legend, no?

Instantiating the Browser Capabilities Component

The syntax for using the Browser Capabilities Component couldn't be simpler:

```
<% Set objBC = Server.CreateObject("MSWC.BrowserType") %>
```

The `Server` Object has a method that creates objects inside the Active Server. This is why we call the Active Server extensible, because we can add to the number of objects it can use to run our Web sites. This fact has two important consequences:

- You create an instance of a component object by using the `Set` command (we always use the variable prefix `obj` to remind us that we are working with an object and need to instantiate it with `Set`).
- You operate on an object through its collections, methods, and properties.

The Browser Capabilities Component is a little unusual. The object created with the `Server.CreateObject` method has no intrinsic methods. It has no collections, either. Indeed, the only properties the Browser Capabilities Component has are the ones you define for it. That is, you list those attributes of browsers that you want to track. Those attributes are stored in the browscap.ini file, as you will see in the next section.

Maintaining the browscap.ini File

The browscap.ini file is stored in the c:\inetsrv\ASP\Cmpnts directory when IIS 3.0 is installed and in C:\Program Files\WEBSVR\SYSTEM\ASP\Cmpnts under Personal Web Server. The path in your PC may be slightly different (up to the "ASP" or the "WEBSERVER" parts). Like all .ini files, browscap.ini is a simple text file. You can add comment lines to it by using a semi-colon. This commonly is used to group classes of browsers in the .ini file.

Each entry in the browscap.ini file (we will refer to an entry as a *browser definition block*) has a minimum of two parts: the name of the browser as identified in the `HTTP_USER_AGENT` header and at least one property.

A single browscap.ini file can contain an unlimited number of browser definition blocks. Each block begins with an `HTTP_USER_AGENT` parameter. This parameter is always enclosed in square braces, [*HTTP_USER_AGENT*]. Normally, this parameter's value is the text stored in the `Request.ServerVariables("HTTP_USER_AGENT")` parameter. There is one exception to these rules, which you will see in the "Default Browser Definitions" section.

▶ **See** "*The ServerVariables* Collection" for more information about the `HTTP_USER_AGENT` header,
   p. 230

Listing 13.3 shows a typical browser definition block. This one is for the Internet Explorer (IE), version 3.01, running under Windows NT.

Part
III

Ch
13

Listing 13.3   BROWSCAP.INI—A Typical Entry in the browscap.ini File

```
[Mozilla/2.0 (compatible; MSIE 3.01; Windows NT)]
parent=IE 3.0
version=3.01
minorver=01
platform=Win95
```

The optional `parent` parameter is used in the Browser Capabilities Component to refer to another browser definition block of the browscap.ini file. Listing 13.4 shows another case of a browser definition block in the browscap.ini file.

Listing 13.4   BROWSCAP.HTM—The *parent* Definition of the Requesting Browser

```
[IE 3.0]
browser=IE
Version=3.0
majorver=#3
minorver=#0
frames=TRUE
tables=TRUE
cookies=TRUE
backgroundsounds=TRUE
vbscript=TRUE
javascript=TRUE
ActiveXControls=TRUE
Win16=False
beta=False
AK=False
SK=False
AOL=False
```

After it finds this block, the Browser Capabilities Component assigns all properties found in the `parent` section to the current browser identified in the HTTP request and stored in the `HTTP_USER_AGENT` variable in the `Request.ServerVariables` collection. IE 3.01 has its four unique properties, as well as all the 16 properties recorded for all IE 3.0 browsers.

Incidentally, if any of the standard properties appears in both browser definition blocks, the one in the literal browser definition block overrides the one in the `parent` browser definition block. In Listing 13.3, the Browser Capabilities Component will use both the `version` and `minorver` parameters in the `[Mozilla/2.0 (compatible; MSIE 3.01; Windows NT)]` browser definition block.

This capability to reference a block of common features makes maintenance of your browscap.ini file much easier. When a new browser version is introduced, you simply add a new browser definition block to your browscap.ini file, refer to the `parent` block, and then add the unique properties of the current version.

Remember that you decide which properties you are going to test for any given browser. This means that your .asp source code must explicitly test for each property.

N O T E If you refer to a property that is undefined for the browser being interrogated, the Browser Capabilities Component returns Unknown if the property has never been used in the browscap.ini; otherwise, it returns 0 (an implicit False). The parameter names are not case-sensitive. ▪

ON THE WEB

For more information about the HTTP_USER_AGENT header, see the HTTP/1.0 specification RFC 1945, Section 10.15. It is available at:

http://ds.internic.net/rfc/rfc1945.txt

N O T E The Browser Capabilities Component accepts wild cards (for example, *) in the HTTP_USER_AGENT parameter. The component first searches in the HTTP_USER_AGENT parameter for an exact match of all browser definition blocks (while ignoring the wild card). If the Browser Capabilities Component fails to find a match, it searches by using the wild card (see the following Tip). ▪

 T I P If there is a wild card in the HTTP_USER_AGENT parameter of more than one browser definition block in the browscap.ini field, the Browser Capabilities Component stops at the first block that it finds. So be sure to enter your browser definition blocks in the order that you expect to encounter them.

Default Browser Definitions

You also may have a default browser category, but you need to be careful here. If your .asp file is requested by a browser not identified in your browscap.ini file, then the Browser Capabilities Component looks for a [Default Browser Capability Settings] browser definition block, and it assigns the properties there to the undefined browser. If this undefined browser really has all of those properties, then everything works fine. If it doesn't, the reader at the other end may be in for a big surprise.

For example, you are fairly safe to assume that the TABLES property can be set to True for your default browser. However, old AOL browsers don't know how to work with tables, and, if a table is encountered on the Web, the old AOL browsers display text that is difficult to read.

Therefore, it is wise to err on the side of discretion. Either use a wild card to identify old browsers and set the most conservative properties for them, or make your default properties braindead, with everything set to False.

Part

III

Ch

13

Other Tips

One of the least pleasant aspects of the Browser Capabilities Component is maintaining the browscap.ini file. Microsoft is on record with a promise to keep an up-to-date version of the browscap.ini file available on its Internet Information Server Web site. Keep your eye peeled to:

http://microsoft.com/iis/

Perhaps the most important use of the Browser Capabilities Component is in divining which browsers support ActiveX controls.

We have written pages that seemed innocent enough, with only a few ActiveX controls installed, but they were enough to actually cause Netscape 2.0 to crash (and on a Power PC, the crash brings the entire computer to its knees!). Listing 13.5 is an example of code that would flag troublesome browsers.

Listing 13.5 bcactivex.asp—Testing for ActiveX-Enabled Browsers

```
<HTML>
<HEAD>
    <TITLE>ActiveX Enabled?</TITLE>
</HEAD>

<BODY>
<% Set obj  = Server.CreateObject("MSWC.BrowserType")%>

<% Set objBrowser = Server.CreateObject("MSWC.BrowserType")%>

...later in the program we insert an ActiveX control only if it
supported

<% If objBrowser.ActiveXControls = "True" Then %>
    <OBJECT ...>
    </OBJECT>
<% End If %>
</BODY>
</HTML>
```

Content Is King

The next component in this pantheon of ASP utilities is the Content Linking Component—a very cool tool. Try to remember the number of times that you wanted a page to have a link back to a specific page or were embarrassed to instruct the reader to "select the Back button on your browser." With the Content Linking Component, those days are over. Every page can know the name and URL of the page that comes before it and the page that will follow it. By using this tool, you can turn your Web site into a book. The Content Linking Component becomes your table of contents.

ON THE WEB

http://www.quecorp.com/asp   This is one of those Server Components that is much easier to demonstrate than to describe. You will find an intriguing ASP application that demonstrates how to use the Content Linking Component on this book's Web site.

Click the "Show Me How" link and select the "Content Linking Component" option.

Table 13.4 shows you the ingredients list for the Content Linking Component. It shows you how to instantiate the Content Linking Component.

Table 13.4   What You Need to Use the Content Linking Component

Item	Use
Table of contents file	Make a list of all the pages you have on your site, and put them in the order you would read them if your Web site were a book.
A Content Linking Component object	This is the object whose properties you access and methods you invoke to return selected lines from the table of contents file for use by the Active Server when it builds your HTML on-the-fly. By making hyperlinks in that HTML output based on the URL and file name supplied by the table of contents file, you can get specific hyperlinks between pages without having to code the links yourself.
Files to link to	These are, in fact, the files you already have on your Web site. Their URLs and page titles are stored in the table of contents file so that the Content Linking Component can make complete HTML anchor tags in the HTML output stream returned to the client by the Active Server.

Essentially, the Content Linking Component reads a text file that contains the linear listing of all the pages on your Web site. Again, if you were to read all the pages on your Web site as if the site were a book, how would you organize it? Use a word processor or spreadsheet and build a table of contents for your site. Save the file as a text file with a descriptive name. An example table of contents is given in Listing 13.6.

Listing 13.6   NEXTLINK.TXT—An Example Table of Contents for a Web Site

```
intro.asp      Introduction
list.asp       The Linking List File
methods.asp    Component Methods
sample.htm     Sample Code
```

Part
III

Ch
13

N O T E Separate the two columns in the table of contents file with a TAB. ◾

The object itself that manages the nextlink.txt file and sends the correct HTML anchor tag to the Active Server is given in Listing 13.7.

Listing 13.7 INTRO-F.ASP—The Master .asp File that Instantiates the Content Linking Component and Creates the *FRAMESET* to Display the HTML

```
<!DOCTYPE HTML PUBLIC "-//W3C//DTD HTML 3.2//EN">
<HTML>
<HEAD>
</HEAD>

<%
If Not IsObject(Session("objNextLink")) Then
        Session("varLinks")="/lab/cl/nextlink.txt"
        Set objNextLink = Server.CreateObject ("MSWC.NextLink")
        Set Session("objNextLink")= objNextLink
        Response.Write("<TITLE>Welcome!</TITLE>")
Else
        Response.Write("<TITLE>Cached</TITLE>")
End If
%>

<FRAMESET ROWS="100%" COLS="40%,*">
        <FRAME NAME="toc" SRC="toc.asp" SCROLLING="AUTO" MARGINWIDTH=30>
        <FRAME NAME="text" SRC="intro.asp" SCROLLING="AUTO">
        <NOFRAMES>
                <BODY>
                This demo is running under FRAMES enabled browsers.
                </BODY>
        </NOFRAMES>
</FRAMESET>

</HTML>
```

Put .asp Source Code Around the *FRAMESET* Tag

Strictly speaking, files that create a FRAMESET do not output HTML directly. FRAMESET files instruct the browser how to display the HTML included in all the files it uses in its FRAME tags' SRC argument. However, an .asp file that contains the FRAMESET tag does produce HTML output. In the case of Listing 13.7, the .asp file also caches the instance of the Content Linking Component on the Session Object. So don't be afraid to put real source code in FRAMESET files.

After you have these preliminaries out of the way, you can start using the Content Linking Component. To do this, you will need to understand what the eight methods of this component do, and they are summarized in Table 13.5. All methods used by the Content Linking

Component have at least one parameter: the relative or virtual path and the file name of the table of contents file such as the one shown in Listing 13.6.

Table 13.5 Content Linking Component Methods

Method	Use
GetListCount	This method returns the number of links stored in the table of contents file. Use this property when you want to be able to go from the first entry in the table of contents directly to the last entry. See Listing 13.8 for an example.
GetListIndex	This method retrieves the current index into the list of links. Use this method to determine if you are on the first entry in the table of contents so that you can go to the last item in the table when the user selects the "Previous Page" link in the HTML returned to the Web client by the Active Server.
GetNextDescription	This method increments the file pointer to the next line in the table of contents file and returns the text in the second column of the table of contents, the Web page title.
GetNextURL	This method acts on the table of contents file in the same way as the GetNextDescription method except it returns the first string in the table of contents, the URL.
GetNthDescription	This method ignores the current file pointer and instead retrieves the file indicated by the second parameter to this method, the index number. The return value is the Web page title of the file selected.
GetNthURL	This method is the same as the GetNthDescription except that it returns a file's URL.
GetPreviousDescription	Like the GetNextDescription, this method moves back in the table of contents file by one line to retrieve the previous Web page title.
GetPreviousURL	This method behaves like the GetPreviousDescription method but returns a file's URL.

N O T E When you create your table of contents file, do not include the prefix "HTTP:" or "//" or "\\" in the URLs for the files listed in the table of contents. These are absolute paths. You can use only relative or virtual paths. ▨

▶ **See** "The *Server* Object" for more information about virtual paths, **p. 236**

A basic implementation of the Content Linking Component is given in Listing 13.8. As the file name suggests, Listing 13.8 can be used in other .asp files by merely inserting a Server-Side Include directive at the bottom of the other files with the following line:

```
<!--#INCLUDE VIRTUAL="/lab/cl/footer.ASP"-->
```

Part

III

Ch

13

Listing 13.8 FOOTER.ASP—A Basic Implementation of the Most Useful Methods in the Content Linking Component

```
<CENTER>
<HR ALIGN="CENTER" SIZE="1" WIDTH="300" NOSHADE>
¦ <a href="
<% If (Session("objNextLink").GetListIndex (Session("varLinks")) > 1) Then %>
        <%= Session("objNextLink").GetPreviousURL (Session("varLinks"))  %>
<%Else%>
        <%= Session("objNextLink").GetNthURL (Session("varLinks"),
Session("objNextLink").GetListCount( varLinks )) %>
<%  End If  %>
">Previous Page</a> ¦¦ <a href="  <%= Session("objNextLink").GetNextURL
(Session("varLinks"))%> ">Next Page</a> ¦
</CENTER>
```

A Linear Tool in a Non-Linear Space

It's important to keep in mind that while the Content Linking Component treats a Web site as if it were a book to be read from beginning to end, hypertext makes this behavior a limiting assumption. That is, a richly interrelated Web site is anything but linear, and to assume that readers will follow the Content Linking Component's lead is a dubious practice.

On the other hand, hypertext's nonlinearity can be detracting. There are times when a reader needs to be guided—getting lost in hyperspace is common and unpleasant. The Content Linking Component offers you a powerful way to have your hypertext and guidance, too.

Still, think carefully about the problems of hypermedia communication when you incorporate this useful tool into your work.

 The Content Linking Component is the forerunner to the sitemap specification currently under review by the W3 Consortium and in the Beta version of IE 4.0. Much of the work that you do with this component will be useful when the sitemap initiative takes hold. The sitemap and the Content Linking Component can coexist, because each serves slightly different functions.

We have found the Content Linking Component extremely useful for Web sites that use what we call the "round-robin" aid to navigation. Following is an explanation of this simple—if not perfect—way to help your readers keep their bearings.

While readers still can get off the trail in a complex Web site, you can give them the ability to go to the next, previous, and upper (and sometimes lower) pages, given the current page they're on.

At the top of each page is a graphic. The simplest method has three black arrowheads; one each for left, right, and up, as shown in Figure 13.2. More sophisticated pages call for more sophisticated icons; our favorite is the one depicted in Figure 13.2. In any case, the trick is to apply the correct URL to the appropriate image or area of the imagemap.

FIG. 13.2
Content-linking icons suggest what to do by their appearance.

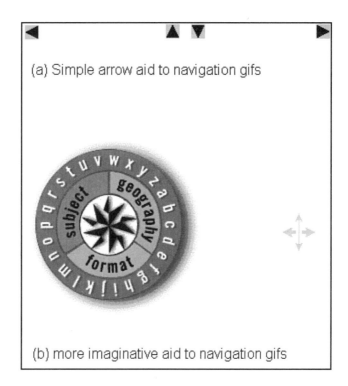

(a) Simple arrow aid to navigation gifs

(b) more imaginative aid to navigation gifs

Managing Text Files in Active Server Pages

The last utility you will learn about is the File Access Component. This Component gives you access to the file formats other than HTML and .asp. The most common file access needed is access to text files. The File Access Component uses two groups of objects as described in Table 13.6. The TextStream Objects turn text files into objects so that you can manipulate their contents by reading and changing their properties and invoking methods on their contents.

Table 13.6   Objects Used by the File Access Component

Object	Purpose
FileSystemObject	Instantiates TextStream Objects
TextStream Object	To instantiate an object for either reading or writing to a file system file

Each property listed in Table 13.7 describes the basic structure of all text files. Namely, all text files have a beginning and an end, and they all consist of rows and columns. The beginning of a file is defined by the Line property equals 1, and the end of the TextStream Object is defined

Part
III

Ch
13

when a special property, the AtEndOfStream property, is true. When you access these properties, you can monitor your position within the file as well as you could if you were using a mouse cursor on a visible file. All the properties of the TextStream object are read-only.

Table 13.7 *TextStream* **Object Properties**

Property	Use
AtEndOfLine	Enables you to read a line in a TextStream object one *character* at a time. Use it with the Read method. It can only be used on a TextStream object opened in read-only mode.
AtEndOfStream	Enables you to read a line in a TextStream object one *line* at a time. Use it with the ReadLine method. It can only be used on a TextStream object opened in read-only mode.
Column	This is an integer that tells you how far into a line the file pointer has moved. This property can be accessed for all TextStream object types and modes.
Line	This integer tells you how far down a TextStream object you are. When a file is initially opened, the Line property is set to 1.

The methods exposed by the TextStream object are in four logical groups, though they are listed in Table 13.8 in alphabetical order for your convenience. There are three reading methods, three writing methods, two skipping methods, and the Close method.

Table 13.8 **The Methods of the** *TextStream* **Object**

Method	Use
Close	Explicitly close a TextStream object. Once the TextStream object loses scope, such as when the user links to another Web page, the close method is automatically called.
Read	This method accepts one parameter, the number of characters, in order to get data out of the TextStream object. To read a single line one character at a time, use the AtEndOfLine property to end the program loop.
ReadAll	Moves the entire contents of a TextStream object into memory. For large files, this may not be the best use of memory.
ReadLine	This method moves the contents of each row of TextStream object into memory. To loop through a whole file, use the AtEndOfStream to sense when to close the loop.
Skip	Like the Read method, the Skip method moves the file pointer an indicated number of characters in a file.

Method	Use
SkipLine	Discards all the characters between the current position of the file pointer and the newline character at the end of a given number of rows in the TextStream object.
Write	A method that writes a string of characters (but *not* including the newline character) to the TextStream object. This method works only if the TextStream object were opened ForAppending.
WriteLine	Basically the same as the Write method, except the WriteLine method includes a newline character. If you invoke this method without a string parameter, then only a newline character is appended to the TextStream object.
WriteBlankLines	Basically the same as the WriteLine method without a parameter, the WriteBlankLines method requires a parameter indicating the number of newline characters to append to the TextStream object.

Syntax of Required Objects

If you forget to instantiate the objects required to manipulate the File Access Component, you get a runtime error saying Object Required. This usually means that you failed to use the Server.CreateObject method to create a working object. When you see this error, double-check your ASP source code; to work properly, it should look something like Listing 13.9.

Listing 13.9 DEMO.ASP—Required File Access Component Objects

```
<%
Set objFileSys = Server.CreateObject("Scripting.FileSystemObject")
Set objTextStreamIn = objFileSys.CreateTextFile(Server.MapPath("/lab") + "/ts/
➥demo.htm")
%>
```

How to Avoid Losing New Files

It's nearly always a good idea to liberally use the Server.MapPath method in File Access Component source code because with it you always know where your source code is.

If you don't use fully qualified paths, you never know where your newly created text file was created (other than that it was created in Windows' current directory). Now quick, without touching your keyboard, if your computer is running right now, tell us: What's your current directory?

See what we mean? You know where your file is; you just don't know its location.

The OpenTextFile method of the FileSystemObject has one required parameter—the file name—and three optional ones. The second parameter is the *I/O mode* and can take on two possible constant values: ForReading (the default) and ForAppending. The next parameter, create, is a Boolean value that's True when it's okay to create a file if the method attempts to open a nonextant file; otherwise, (by default) it's False. The last parameter, format, is used to specify something called a *tristate*: TristateTrue means that the file can be opened as Unicode; TristateFalse means that only ASCII files are supported; and TristateUseDefault uses the system default.

Unicode

In a nutshell, Unicode is an alternative to the ASCII character set. Contrary to popular opinion, the Internet is not solely the domain of America. International languages need some way to be displayed, and Unicode is the ticket.

In ASP development, Unicode can be problematic. Some software supports it, and others don't. Some operating systems support it (Windows NT), and others don't (Windows 95).

For more detailed information, take a look at an excellent Web page from Microsoft at:

http://www.microsoft.com/opentype/unicode/cscp.htm

The FileSystemObject's CreateTextFile method obviously is quite similar to the FileSystemObject's OpenTextFile method. The differences are the lack of a Tristate value and the fact that the Boolean value controls whether a new file overwrites an extant file with the same name. There is no need for the CreateTextFile method to distinguish between ForReading and ForAppending. Likewise, there is no Tristate value because you are creating the file and deciding which character set to use.

In spite of their differences, both the CreateTextFile and the OpenTextFile methods give you a TextStream Object or two (or as many as you want).

TextStream Objects

In Listing 13.10, you have three methods and two properties to work with: the AtEndOfStream and Line properties and the WriteLine, ReadLine, and Close methods.

Listing 13.10   DEMO.ASP—The File Access Component Demo

```
<FONT SIZE="+1"><STRONG>TextStream Object Demo</STRONG></FONT>
<P>
<%
' Create a single FileSystemObject and use that object to create
' as many TextStream objects as you need. This program needs two.
Set objFileSys = Server.CreateObject("Scripting.FileSystemObject")

' Without a fully qualified path, the output file could land almost
' anywhere; e.g., the c:\windows\system32\ directory (or whatever
' happens to be the last directory you ran a program in, viz., the
' Windows current directory).
varOutputFile=Server.MapPath("/lab") + "\ts\demo.htm"
' It's also helpful to output the result of the MapPath
```

```
%>
<%="Creating output file: " + varOutputFile + "<P>"%>
<%
Set objTsOut = objFileSys.CreateTextFile(varOutputFile,True)

' To demonstrate the consequences of not using MapPath,
' we'll create another output file. Good luck finding this one:
Set objTsOutThere = objFileSys.CreateTextFile("lostdemo.htm",True)
objTsOutThere.WriteLine("It's not pretty, but we were demonstrating
➥non-qualified paths, not formatted HTML...")

' It's generally best to use the MapPath method to create a fully
' qualified path to your target file too.
varInputFile=Server.MapPath("/lab") + "\cl\list.asp"

%>
<%="Reading input file: " + varInputFile + "<P>"%>
<%
Set objTsIn = objFileSys.OpenTextFile(varInputFile)

Do Until objTsIn.AtEndOfStream
    objTsOut.WriteLine(objTsIn.ReadLine)
    If objTsIn.Line=10 Then
        objTsOut.WriteLine("<PLAINTEXT>")
    ElseIf      objTsIn.Line=30 Then
        objTsOut.WriteLine("</PLAINTEXT>")
    End If
    objTsOutThere.WriteLine(objTsIn.ReadLine)
Loop
objTsIn.Close
objTsOut.Close
objTsOutThere.Close
%>

Examine the <A HREF="demo.htm"></A> file (you may need to Refresh).
<P>
See if you can find the file created without using the MapPath method.<BR>
  If it's <A HREF="lostdemo.htm">here</A>, you're lucky;
    ➥if it's not, try FileFind and use "lostdemo.htm" as the filename.
```

The two properties are straightforward. The AtEndOfStream property is False until the last byte is read from the input file. The Do Until command exploits this value. The Line property is helpful in this case, because you want to insert the <PLAINTEXT> tags at strategic points in the input file, list.asp. This property watches your progress through the file for you; when you hit the line that you need, you insert the tags.

The two methods also are self-evident. The WriteLine method does just what it says. Incidentally, this method belongs to the output file's TextStream object. Note that the only parameter that this method needs is a string. The string can be literal, a variable, or, as in this case, the output of the second method, ReadLine. The ReadLine method needs no parameters, but we find that we often forget to append the object reference to it; namely, the input file's TextStream object. In that case, the ReadLine method simply reads the current line (referenced by the Line property). The final method, Close, needs to be called by each of the objects in turn. (When the .asp file closes, the objects lose scope anyway, but using the Close method is better style.)

Some Suggested Uses of the File Access Component

The OpenTextFile method can access and report on the contents of files like server log files, application program .ini files, and miscellaneous text files of your own design. For example, you could have a "Tip of the Day" file that you could access with the File Access Component. You can also use low-level file access to get at data in legacy databases.

For example, our firm used a portfolio management program for twelve years before it was replaced with a Microsoft Access database. In order to continue to use the same reporting format our clients had become accustomed to, we had to incorporate the data from those old tables. The program was old enough that it did not include the usual format of comma-delimited ASCII text files we take for granted today. We had to write a low-level file access program that converted the text export files into a row and column format that Access needed to import the data. A similar procedure could have been used to access that data directly through a Web client if we needed to report on that legacy data in real-time by using an intranet system instead of a desktop database system.

Using the CreateTextFile method, on the other hand, enables you to create your own .ini files. Storing persistent data in this fashion is appropriate when using the Data Access Component is overkill. Storing session data in this way is more persistent than relying on storing the data on the Session Object. It is also more accessible than using the Cookies collection (that is, the data you store about a client is stored on the server, and in simple text, and not on the client). Indeed, the global.asa file in the Adventure Works sample application, which ships with Active Server Pages, opens a text file to see how many people have visited the site and updates the total when the application ends by storing the new total in the same visitors.txt file.

The main point is that text file access can be a very useful data storage and retrieval system, occupying a position between the Cookies collection and formal databases.

From Here...

This chapter showed you the Server Components that ship with Active Server Pages. You learned how to use the Ad Rotator Component to place hyperlinked images on your Web site. You learned how you could display one image randomly selected from a collection of images. The Ad Rotator, then, helps you keep your Web site fresh, and it helps you increase your revenue base of paying advertisers. You also saw how you might use the Ad Rotator Component in a novel way to link the Web sites of independent but related organizations and almost make a game out of surfing the Net.

Another Server Component you learned about in this chapter was the Browser Capabilities Component. You now know how this tool helps you identify each browser that visits your site. You now know how to identify the feature set of each browser so that you can return HTML optimized for each feature set. Browsers, for example, that can support VBScript or JavaScript can receive server-generated client-side scripts. Now you can sense when a browser can use ActiveX controls, and you can build HTML that includes those advanced user interface features without having to ask users to go to another ActiveX-enabled page themselves. In a sense, the Browser Capabilities Component enables you to create customized pages for each kind of browser on the planet and to accomplish this feat in far less time than it took to write standard HTML in the first place.

You also learned about the Content Linking Component. You learned how it can save hours of editing the URLs you add at the bottom of your Web pages that move the reader from one page to the next. You learned that all you have to do is maintain one text file that lists each page URL and title on your Web site. You learned how to instruct the Content Linking Component to navigate around this table of contents text file and to use the file information it finds on each row of that text file as ASP constructs your HTML on-the-fly.

Finally, you learned how to access text files by using the File Access Component. You learned how to display the contents of other files in your Web browser, and you saw other uses for text file access (e.g., accessing server logs and .ini files).

From here, you'll move to the high ground of interactivity: database programming. Here's what's coming in Part IV:

- Chapter 15, "Introducing ActiveX Data Objects," introduces you to the most recent incarnation of database connectivity from Microsoft: OLEDB and the ActiveX Data Objects (ADO) interface.

- Chapter 16, "Working with ADO's *Connection* and *Command* Objects," is the first in-depth chapter that will teach you how to get started managing data from a Web interface.

- Chapter 17, "Working with ADO's *RecordSet* Object," shows you how to create and manipulate RecordSet Objects, the workhorse of ADO. Learn how to add and delete, edit, and update database records from your Web client.

ON THE WEB

http://www.quecorp.com/asp   Look in the Chapter 13, "Interactivity Through Bundled Active Server Components," section of the Web site. By seeking, you'll find cool code that uses many of the tricks that we have sprinkled throughout the book. E-mail us and let us know what you discover.

Part

III

Ch

13

Constructing Your Own Server Components

Programming with class

Exposing the methods within your classes provides the functionality of your server component.

Understanding the OLE server

Learn how an OLE server will become your server component.

Creating the component

Get a step-by-step guide to server component construction in Visual Basic.

There are often times when you will want to use server-side functions that just cannot be accomplished through the use of a scripting language, either alone or in combination with the components that ship with Active Server Pages. When you hit this particular wall, you have a few options. First, you can check the market and try to find prebuilt components that satisfy your requirements. Second, you can contract with a third party to build a component for you. Last, and given the time and inclination, our favorite choice: You can build your own component.

When you create your own server components, you have the benefit of using a component built by someone who really understands your business. As you encapsulate line-of-business functions within your components, you can use them on your server and in your client applications or even give them to your clients for use on their systems (for a nominal fee, of course). This chapter focuses on creating server components using the Visual Basic programming language. If you already are familiar with VB, this will be a snap. If you are coming to VB a little later in the game, this chapter will provide you with the skills to begin creating components right away. ▪

Why Use Visual Basic for Component Creation?

There are a number of reasons why Visual Basic is an ideal tool for creating many of the server components that you will use. VB has grabbed the hearts and minds of millions of developers out here in the real world. As you already have learned, VBScript is a subset of Visual Basic. Everything you've learned about VBScript is immediately applicable to development in the VB environment, with a number of useful features not found in its younger sibling.

You will find (or already have found) hundreds of custom controls, such as ActiveX Components, that currently are available for use with Visual Basic. More controls seem to be available each day. The rub is that most of these components require an interface to use them in your development. VB provides a perfect way to wrap the functionality of these third-party components for use in your Active Server Pages development. In addition to the custom controls available in Visual Basic, you also have access to the Win32 API. You can access any number of functions on the system that are impossible to get to using scripting alone. You also can use most any DLL (dynamic-link library) to add additional functionality to the components that you create.

As stated previously, millions of developers have used Visual Basic for a number of years because of its ease of use and flexibility and the speed with which they can develop applications. If you were to hire a new Active Server Pages developer, it is likely that he or she would have VB skills. If not, those skills are just a class or two away.

Another advantage of developing your server components in VB is that there are so many resources available to help you. There are forums on CompuServe, AOL, and Prodigy. The Microsoft Web site provides a wealth of information about VB (a knowledge base, news groups), as well as links to other valuable sites. There are hundreds of quality sites out there dedicated to Visual Basic.

Of course, another benefit of developing your components in Visual Basic is that there are so many excellent sources of information available to help you in your own neighborhood. There are hundreds of texts at your local bookstore with *even more* information about creating objects in VB than you'll find in this chapter alone.

Finding A Touch of Class

Component creation is a process of building objects that you will instantiate in your Active Server Pages scripts. To create objects in Visual Basic, you need to define a blueprint to expose the functions within your object to other applications, in this case ASP. You will use classes to provide this blueprint, or definition and interface, for your objects.

Creating class modules in Visual Basic is the method through which you can develop reusable components. `Public` procedures within classes are the method through which you can expose functionality from within your class to other objects within your application and to other applications within the system. By creating your functionality within the class framework, you are able to harness the incredible power and ease of use in Visual Basic for your component needs.

Introducing Classes

As you begin to develop components, consider some of the following details of class development. A *class* is the description, or blueprint, of the object that will be created when the class is instantiated. You can follow some basic guidelines from general object-oriented development to ensure that your class will be a good component candidate.

The idea of *data-hiding* or encapsulation is a fundamental principle of object-oriented development. What this means in practice is that access to the data variables within your class should be performed only through member functions of the class. Effectively, you will be hiding the class data from the client program. This ensures that the client application will not unwittingly corrupt the `Private` object data. This also lets you change the `Private` members of your class "under the covers"—without changing the `Public` interface.

Think of your component in terms of properties and methods. The *properties* are a set of definitions that control attributes of your component. *Methods* are the actions that the component will take on your behalf. Look to the components that ship with Active Server Pages and Visual Basic and see how the properties and methods work together to provide the components functionality.

Always strive for limiting the functionality of a component to a basic set. Don't try to put the entire business in a single component. Try to view component creation as an exercise in creating building blocks. If the blocks are too big, you lose flexibility in the design. If they are too small, it will take forever to build the structure.

Understanding Object Lifetime: Class Creation and Destruction

When the client application instantiates your object (class), there is an opportunity to perform one-time initialization actions for your class. You do this in the `Class_Initialize` event of the class object. This is a handy place to initialize `Private` data members and perform any initial error checking, as well as any other functions that need to occur before any of the class methods (functions or subroutines) are invoked.

There is also an opportunity to perform actions immediately before the object is destroyed. This processing is performed in the `Class_Terminate` event of the class. You can destroy any memory that was allocated during the life of the class or perform any other required cleanup.

Instantiating an Object

After you have defined and coded the class, you can create an instance of the class in Visual Basic by initializing an object variable to that class type:

```
Dim TestClass as New ClassName
```

You also can instantiate a class object by using the `CreateObject` method within your script:

```
Dim TestClass
Set TestClass = Server.CreateObject("Component.ClassName")
```

Part

III

Ch

14

The variable `TestClass` now has a reference to the newly created object. Now you can invoke any of the methods of the newly created object by using the method name with the newly created object reference:

```
Avalue = TestClass.MethodName(Parm1, Parm2... ParmN)
```

When you are finished with the object, set the object variable to `Nothing` to ensure that all memory associated with the object will be released.

```
Set TestClass = Nothing
```

Understanding Class Methods

When we refer to the methods of a class, we are talking about the set of `Public` functions and subroutines that reside within the class. Methods are just a convenient way to talk about the procedures available to the user of a component. This is also an easy way to think of these functions, like the methods available to any of the other "objects" within Visual Basic: the form methods, the button methods, and all of the other intrinsic objects in VB that expose their functionality (methods) to you as a developer.

Any subroutine or function that you create in your class module will be visible to the client program if it is declared as `Public`.

```
Public Function CalculatePayment(LoanAmount, Term, InterestRate)
```

When you use the `Public` identifier in front of the function declaration, the `CalculatePayment` function is *visible* to any client that instantiates the class or to any variable that is assigned a reference to it. `Private` functions within a class are used to provide functions and services that the `Public` functions can use to fulfill client requests.

Using Property Procedures

In Visual Basic development, as well as HTML development, user interface objects have properties that you set to determine the look and actions of these elements. For example, to access the background color of a text box in the VB environment, you would access its `BackColor` property:

```
text1.BackColor = &H00FFFF00&
```

The use of properties is a simple and intuitive way to access the attributes of an object. You can provide the same functionality to access the properties of your components. This will be a familiar syntax to VB and Active Server Pages developers and will let you use the `<object>.<method>` notation with any component that you create. Using property procedures also will let you immediately validate the value of the property being set. If invalid data is passed in or a value out of range is provided, the component can respond immediately, instead of waiting for some point downstream in your code to notify the calling program of the error.

After you have determined what properties you want to provide for your class, you will set aside `Private` variables to hold these properties. You then need to provide the framework for accessing and updating these class properties.

The *Let* Procedure   The Let proedure enables your class users to set the value of a class property under the class's control. Take a quick look at a Let property procedure:

```
Public Property Let HostName(aHost)
    If Not Len(aHost) Then
        Err.Raise vbObjectError + CTRANSACT_ERR_HOSTLEN, "CTransact.Host", _
                "Set Host Name: Host Length Invalid"
    Else
        m_sHost = aHost
    End If
End Property
```

You certainly could declare the Private class variable m_sHost (declared as a string) as a Public variable and then let the user set the host name directly. If you did that, you wouldn't have the opportunity to ensure that the host name was valid. Within the Let procedure in the preceding code, in addition to testing for a zero-length string, you could also try to ping the host to ensure that it was a valid address or perform additional validations on the passed-in value. When using the Let procedure, you can provide the calling application with immediate feedback as to the status of the component property being set.

In addition to allowing for data validation when the property is set, you also can update other associated variables within your class. If there is another property, say the port to connect to, that is based upon the host that is entered, you can set the Port property when the host name is set. This again cannot be performed if you just declared the m_sHost variable as Public. Using the Let procedure can ensure that you don't get any component breaker values in the Private variables of your class. If, for example, a user were to put a NULL value into a variable, it could easily generate a run-time error in another method that references that variable. The rule continues to be "better safe than sorry."

The *Get* Procedure   The majority of your coding will set property values of the objects created within the script. Most of you could go the better part of a day without ever requesting the value of an object's property, but there are times when you need to check a property and determine its value. A good example would be the .text property of an entry field.

To provide the "getting" of a property within your class, you create a Property Get procedure. Using the preceding example, you would provide the HostName property procedure to your calling application with the following procedure:

```
Public Property Get HostName() As Variant
    HostName = m_sHost
End Property
```

Public **Procedures in Your Classes**

The Let and Get procedures are wonderful for creating properties within your class. Eventually though, you need your class to perform some function in order to become useful. To expose functionality to an external application from within your class, you declare a function or subroutine Public. This enables the application that created an instance of your class to access the procedure.

Part
III

Ch
14

Any procedure that is not directly used by the client application should be declared `Private`. This ensures that the client does not inadvertently call a function or subroutine that it should not. `Private` functions are used to perform internal activities for the component. As you will see in the component example, "Creating Your Server Component," the `Public` interface usually is the smallest part of the class code. The component interface is intentionally kept small and simple. If the implementation of the method changes (the `Private` functions), there is no need to change the external (`Public`) function declaration.

Handling Errors Within Your Classes

There are two ways you can handle errors within your classes. The first requires you to provide all methods as functions and return a completion code for all `Public` procedures. This requires a well-defined set of return codes and requires the client program to check for errors in-line after each call to the component returns.

A better way to handle error conditions within your class is to use the VB error-handling framework. If an error occurs within a class module, you will use the `Raise` method of the `Err` object to pass notification of the error to the calling program. The error percolates through the procedure levels to a place where an error handler has been registered within the calling program.

You notify the client application of an error by calling the `Raise` method of the `Err` object. The syntax for raising an error is shown here:

```
Err.Raise(Number, Source, Description, HelpFile, HelpContext)
```

The only required parameter is the `Number`. When you are creating server components, you usually should include the `Source` and the `Description` parameters as well. Say that you are trying to open a local file in a method in your new class. The file cannot be opened because the program cannot find the file on the disk. A run-time error that the component invoked in your code looks something like this:

```
Err.Raise vbObjectError + 55, "CFileMgr.ReadFile ", "Cannot find file specified"
```

The constant `vbObjectError` is a base number to add your component-specific error number to. This is the constant that is used when raising run-time errors within an OLE server.

▶ **See** "Error Handling Within Procedures" for more on error handling within your scripts, **p. 163**

OLE Servers—Exposing Your Class

Up to now, a number of pages in this chapter has been spent discussing the class module and how it provides the blueprint for your Active Server Pages when your component is invoked. This is well and good, but components live by more than class alone. You need to wrap the class in a suitable way so that you actually can create an instance of it. To do this, you create the class within an OLE server.

There are two types of OLE servers that you can create with Visual Basic. OLE servers can run either *out-of-process* or *in-process*. The distinction is basically evident in the server names.

An out-of-process server executes in a separate process from the client application that creates an instance of the server (component). An in-process server is packaged as a dynamic-link library and, when instantiated, shares the same process space with the application.

An in-process server has a number of inherent strengths that ensure that it is the type you will build when creating your server components. First, because the server will be running in the same process space as the calling application, the component will be faster, because there is no need to pass data across process boundaries. Second, because the server is packaged as a DLL, if it is already loaded in memory when a new instance is created, there is virtually no load time for the new object.

There are, however, a number of restrictions to keep in mind when creating in-process servers as components in Visual Basic:

■ **The servers are available only as 32-bit code.**

You must create the components using Visual Basic Professional or Enterprise Edition, version 4.0 or above. No 16-bit code support is provided.

■ **One `Public` class member is required.**

Because the visible functionality of your object is defined by the `Public` classes within your DLL, at least one class must be `Public`.

■ **No user interface allowed.**

Any user interface that you would embed into your class will not be visible to the browser requesting information from an Active Server Pages script and potentially could lock the server process requesting the service.

■ **No static or global variables are allowed.**

If you package multiple classes in your component, avoid the use of globals or statics in any shared modules. These will only complicate your coding and can lead to incorrect or corrupted memory across multiple instances of any given object.

Creating Your Server Component

It's time to begin creating your Active Server Pages component. It's useful to take a moment and discuss what it is, exactly, that your component will do for you. Many of you are working in heterogeneous environments, interacting with PCs, minis, mainframes, and, yes, even UNIX boxes. The component that you are going to build will provide access to a number of transactions living on a multiple host system.

Here's the scenario: Say that for a number of years, your hypothetical company has been processing TCP/IP requests from external vendors to authorize credit card transactions. You have a well-defined transaction header structure that is used to send a transaction through the system. You want to provide the same authorization transactions from your Web servers.

There are a number of commercial packages out there (even Microsoft's own Internet Control Pack) that provide generic TCP/IP communications. The problem with most of these packages

Part

III

Ch

14

is that they are set up to provide an event when a transaction (or any data, for that matter) is received back from a previous request. By design, they are *asynchronous,* meaning that the receipt of the response from the transaction occurs some time later. The program or thread execution will not *block* waiting on a response from the server. This is ideal for interactive client/server applications where you are doing other things while waiting for a response (or multiple responses). Due to the stateless nature of connections on the Internet, there is no facility to continue to process the script and then respond to this "transaction complete" event later.

So what you are going to build is a TCP/IP transaction class that lets you call a method that sends a transaction to your host system and waits for a response before returning from the procedure call. All formatting of the transaction takes place within the class, as well as all of the communications details. The only things that the script must provide are a host name and port to connect to, an account to validate, and an amount to authorize. We're sure you can think of a number of situations in which you would want to leverage TCP/IP transactions from your servers. This component can easily be modified to accept different header and transaction types. Out-of-the-box, it should give you a good sense of the steps involved in building your own server components.

First Steps

The first thing you need to do is ensure that you have a copy of the 32-bit version of Visual Basic, either the Professional or Enterprise Edition. Then open up a new project to begin creation of your transaction component.

It's that easy. Now you are ready to begin.

Slimming Down the Server

When you start a new project in Visual Basic, there are a number of custom controls and object references that get added to your project for free, or they seem so at the time. In fact, they are not free at all. If you open the file AUTO32LD.VBP (found in the directory where the VB32.EXE lives on your system) in Notepad, you see the default objects that are loaded each time you request a new project. To permanently change these defaults, you can edit this file to remove the object references.

Any component or reference that you do not use but do retain in your project when it is built, tags along for the ride, even though it never is invoked. This adds overhead to your application and swells the number of disks required to distribute your new component.

So now you will remove all the custom controls that you can from your newly created default project to reduce this overhead:

1. Select Tools, Custom Controls, or press Ctrl+T.
2. Select Tools, References.
3. After Form1 is selected, select File, Remove File from the main menu. This removes the form from the project.

The first step brings up a dialog box with all the controls available for your use, shown in Figure 14.1, as well as those currently active in your project. Those that are active will have the check box checked. Remove all the currently selected objects by removing the check in any checked box. Then click the OK button to save your changes.

FIG. 14.1
Lighten up the application by removing unused controls.

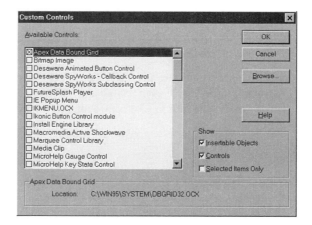

The second step brings up a dialog box with all the references available for your use, in addition to those currently in use for the project. If you are not going to be performing any database functions using the Jet database engine, remove the reference to the DAO library. This cuts your distribution down by over a meg. If there are any other references that you will not need, remove them as well by unchecking the checked boxes.

There are no user interface attributes in your server component, so remove the default form that loaded in your new project. To remove Form1, as outlined in step three, select the form from the project window. If the project window is not visible, press Ctrl+R to show it.

Main Street: The *Sub Main* Function

While all functionality that you will expose to your client application—in this case, an Active Server Pages script—is through the Public methods of a class, there still is component-level initialization that can take place when the component is created. Component-level initialization takes place in the Sub Main procedure of the component.

To add the Sub Main procedure to your new project, you need to add a code module. To do so, follow these steps:

1. Select Insert, Module from the main menu.
2. Press F4 to pull up the module properties.
3. Change the name Module1 to CTransact_Main.
4. Move back to the newly named CTransact_Main code window.
5. Type in **Sub Main**, and then press Enter.

Part
III

Ch
14

These steps add a new module to the project. The module defaults to Module1 in the project window. You are creating a component that will provide transaction processing for your server, and this component will be called CTransact, so you will call the module with Sub Main in it CTransact_Main.

You now have created an empty Sub Main procedure in the CTransact_Main module:

```
Sub Main()

End Sub
```

Because you will perform no component-level initialization in your transaction component, you can leave the Sub Main procedure empty. Even though no explicit initialization takes place, you must have a Sub Main procedure defined in your component, or you will receive an error when you try to instantiate the component.

The Project Dialog Box

Now is a good time to save your project. Before you do that, though, set up the project so that the compiler creates an OLE in-process server instead of a normal Windows executable program. The settings regarding the code generation are found on the Options dialog box. To get there, follow these steps:

1. Select Tools, Options from the main menu.
2. Select the Project tab on the dialog box.

N O T E The menu options for Visual Basic 4.0 specified in the steps defined within this chapter may change in version 5.0. ▪

As shown in Figure 14.2, you will notice a number of user-definable options for the project. The first thing you need to do is specify the Project Name. The Project Name will be the name you will use when specifying an object to create within your Active Server Pages script.

1. Enter the name **CTransact** in the Project Name field.

   The StartMode setting specifies whether you will build a normal Windows executable file or an OLE server. Of course, you want to build an OLE server.

2. Select the OLE Server radio button.

   The last field that you will edit on the project is the Application Description entry field. This will be the text that you will see when you browse the objects and components currently available on a system. You want to provide a short and concise description of your component.

3. Type **TCP/IP Transaction Black Box** in the Application Description field.

4. Before you leave, jump over to the Advanced tab and select the Use OLE DLL Restrictions check box. This ensures that, as you debug your application, the same restrictions placed on an in-process OLE server will apply to your component during debugging.

5. Click the OK button to save the project changes that you just made.

FIG. 14.2
The Project tab defines
your component
naming.

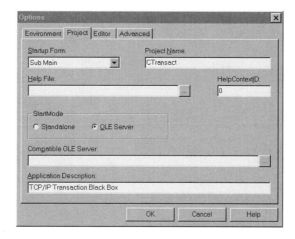

6. Select File, Save Project from the main menu.

   You will be prompted to save the CTransact_Main.bas module in the default directory. Accept the default directory or create a new directory from the Save As dialog box, and then save the module. When prompted for the project name to save, replace the Project1 name with CTransact.

Congratulations! You have just completed the first task in creating your component.

Creating Your Transaction Class

Now the real work begins. Up to now, you have been dealing with the administration of creating a server component, setting up the project, selecting project options, and creating a main procedure. Now you begin to develop the class data and methods that will perform the transactions that you have been working toward.

The first step is, of course, to create the class module. The class information will live in its own class code module, a file with a .cls extension. To create the class module, select Insert, Class Module from the main menu.

Now you've added a new class module to your project. If the class module is not currently selected, select the module from the project window by double-clicking the name Class1 or by selecting Class1 and then clicking the View Code button of the project window. Remember that if your project window is not visible, you can pop it up using Ctrl+R.

In the next few steps, you will rename your class, set it to be Public, and select the instancing options. With the class code window active, press the F4 key to bring up the class properties window. It will look like the one shown in Figure 14.3.

1. Change the name Class1 to **Transaction**.
2. Set the Public property to True.
3. Set the Instancing property to Creatable MultiUse.

Part

III

Ch

14

FIG. 14.3
Editing class properties is just like changing any VB object's properties.

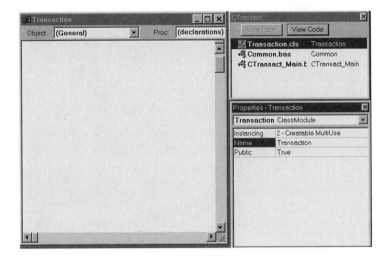

The first of the preceding steps, changing the name, is important, because the name of the class is referenced when you create an instance of your component. Just as you take care in naming your class methods, you need to make a good choice for the class name.

The Public property determines the visibility of the class outside your OLE server. If you were to leave the class private, no one could access any of the transaction functions that you will build into the class shortly.

The last property of your class that you set was the Instancing property. This property determines how the OLE server is managed when it is instantiated by a client application. You selected the Creatable MultiUse option, which enables the object, if already created, to be supplied by the existing object. If no object currently exists, one will be created. Contrast this to the Creatable Single Use option, where each CreateObject request causes a separate copy of the OLE server to be started. The Creatable MultiUse option uses memory more efficiently and is the primary choice for externally created components like the one you are building.

The *WinSock* Methods

To perform TCP/IP transactions, you will be using the Windows Sockets library calls in this section. One of the nice things about Visual Basic is that you can declare just about any dynamic-link library and use it in the VB environment. To use these WinSock functions within your component, you need to declare them to Visual Basic. This is done with the declare statements shown in Listing 14.1, in the general code of the Transaction class.

Listing 14.1 TRANSACTION.CLS—Declaring the *WinSock* Functions to Visual Basic

```
'Winsock calls in VB format, for 32 bit, WSOCK32.DLL
Private Declare Function bind Lib "wsock32.dll" (ByVal s As Long, _
```

```
                            addr As sockaddr_type, _
                            ByVal namelen As Long) As Long
Private Declare Function inet_addr Lib "wsock32.dll" (ByVal s _
                            As String) As Long
Private Declare Function gethostbyname Lib "wsock32.dll" _
                            (ByVal hostname As String) As Long
```

There are a number of other Win32 API functions that you will be using in your class. You can find all the declarations for these functions in the TRANSACTION.CLS module, in the declarations section.

There is also a number of helper procedures within the class that handle the dirty work of the TCP/IP communications. Generally, the flow for the transactions follows this path:

1. Connect to the host.
2. Send the transaction to the host.
3. Receive a response.
4. Check the return code of the response.
5. Pass the response back to the calling application.

Each of the preceding steps has a `Private` procedure that handles one part of the communications chore. Listing 14.2 shows the code for the `fn_Connect` function, which connects to the host system. All the helper procedures do one activity and return a Boolean value if the activity is completed successfully.

Listing 14.2   TRANSACTION.CLS—The *Connect* Function

```
Private Function fn_Connect(iSocket As Long, lAddress As Long, iPort As Integer)
➥As Boolean
   Dim sockaddr As sockaddr_type
   Dim rc As Integer

   sockaddr.sin_family = AF_INET
   sockaddr.sin_port = htons(iPort)
   sockaddr.sin_addr = lAddress
   sockaddr.sin_zero = " "

   rc = connect(iSocket, sockaddr, Len(sockaddr))
   If rc = SOCKET_ERROR Then
      Err.Raise vbObjectError + CTRANSACT_ERR_CONNECT,
               "Transaction.fn_InitSockets", fn_GetLastSockError()
      Exit Function
   End If

   fn_Connect = True
End Function
```

If the connection fails, an error is raised, passing back the error code as well as the text describing the reason for the connection failure. The `fn_GetLastSockError` function returns the error text for the most recent socket error, utilizing a call to the Windows Sockets extension function `WSAGetLastError()`. For additional information about the `WinSock` 1.1 specification, check out the Microsoft Web site at **http://www.microsoft.com**.

Private Class Variables

The first thing you need to do after setting up the declarations for `WinSock` and Win32 API functions is to create your `Private` class variables, as shown in Listing 14.3. They are dimensioned as `Private` so that your client does not have access to them, and cannot accidentally change one of their values at an inopportune time.

Listing 14.3 TRANSACTION.CLS—Declaring Class Variables *Private*

```
'Module Level Variable Declarations
Private msHost As String              ' Holds the host name
Private mlHost As Long                ' 32 bit host address
Private miPort As Integer             ' Host port to connect to
Private miConnectTimeout As Integer   ' connect timeout
Private miReceiveTimeout As Integer   ' receive timeout
Private msBuffer As String            ' buffer to hold transmitted data
Private mbInProcess As Boolean        ' in process flag
```

It is great that you have all these `Private` variables to use in your class, but you also need to get some pertinent information from the component user so you can send your transaction on to the correct host. In the section "Using Property Procedures," we talked about property procedures that enable your users to set properties within your component. Two properties that must be set for you to perform your transaction are the `Host` and `Port` properties. These will provide you with the name of the host to send the transaction to, as well as the port to which the host will be listening. The property procedure for the `Host` property is shown in Listing 14.4.

Listing 14.4 TRANSACTION.CLS—Property Procedures Enforce Data Hiding

```
Public Property Let Host(aHost As String)
   If Len(aHost) = 0 Then
     Err.Raise CTRANSACT_ERR_HOSTLEN, "Transaction.Host", "Set Host Name: Host
➥Length Invalid"
     Exit Property
   End If
   mlHost = fn_GetHostByName(aHost)
   If mlHost = 0 Then
     Err.Raise CTRANSACT_ERR_HOSTBYNAME, "Transaction.Host",
➥fn_GetLastSockError()
     Exit Property
   End If

   msHost = aHost
End Property
```

Notice in the code in Listing 14.4 that you are handling errors by raising run-time errors that your component user will catch in his or her code. If the Host length sent in by the application is zero, you will raise an error. Also, if the host name cannot be resolved to a physical address (the fn_GetHostByName function provides the name resolution services), an error is also raised. If you were setting properties just by allowing your component user access to a Public variable sHost, you would have to check for a valid host name each time you performed a transaction. By handling this check through the use of a property procedure, you can raise the error if needed immediately when the property is set.

The *Public Transact* Method

There is only one Public procedure in the CTransact class. This is the procedure that initiates the transaction and returns a completion code to the calling program. The function must be declared as Public so it will be visible from outside the component.

The first part of the method (or procedure) is the declaration. Parameters are passed to the method and a return code of type Long will be sent back when the transaction is completed.

```
Public Function Transact(transaction As Integer, Version As Integer, _
        inBuffer As String) As Long
```

There are a number of authorization transactions that can be processed by the back-end service. Also, to support new versions of transactions as time goes on, a version is passed in as a parameter as well. This is a handy way to enhance transactions while not having to change any of the clients currently using a previous version. The buffer that is passed in is the authorization string formatted by the Active Server Pages script.

The first part of the code, found in Listing 14.5, ensures that a valid Host property has been set, as well as a value for the Port property.

Listing 14.5   TRANSACTION.CLS—Verifying that Required Class Properties Have Been Set

```
If miPort = 0 Then
        Err.Raise CTRANSACT_ERR_PORTNOTSET, "CTransact.Transact", _
                "Port must be set prior to invoking Transaction method"
      Exit Function
   End If
   If mlHost = 0 Then
        Err.Raise CTRANSACT_ERR_HOSTNOTSET, "CTransact.Transact", _
                "Port must be set prior to invoking Transaction method"
      Exit Function
   End If
End If
```

You check for a valid host when the property is set, but you must also ensure that the property has been set before you begin the transaction. You could have added another Private variable as a flag, say blnHostSet, but it is just as easy to check the value of the miPort and mlHost variables. It also saves a bit of memory (the less module-level variables you use, the better).

Part
III

Ch
14

The interaction with the host system is through a standard header that is defined by the type TRAN_HDR. All of the transactions are performed using this header, and the return code from the transaction will be put in the ReturnCode member of the TRAN_HDR type. Ideally, you would send the structure in the transaction. In the C or C++ programming languages, you would just cast the structure variable as a char * or a void * and be done with it. In Visual Basic, you need to send the transaction as a string. To do this, we ended up creating a little C DLL to perform the conversion from a string to a type and back again.

ON THE WEB

http:www.quecorp.com/asp   At this book's Web site, you'll find the source code for VBUTIL.DLL and the project files to re-create it using Microsoft's Visual C++ product.

The next part of the code fills in the TRAN_HDR type, converts it to a structure, and prepares to send the transaction over the wire (see Listing 14.6).

Listing 14.6   TRANSACTION.CLS—Using the VBUTIL *CopyStructToString* Function to Simplify the String Conversion

```
hdr.PacketNumber = Format$(transaction, "00000000")
hdr.Version = Format$(Version, "0000")
hdr.ReturnCode = "9999"
hdr.OperatorNumber = ""
hdr.RecordLength = Len(hdr) + Len(inBuffer)

msg = Space$(Len(hdr))
rc = CopyStructToString(hdr, msg, Len(hdr))
```

Notice that you must pre-allocate the msg (which will host the string representation of the TRAN_HDR type) string by filling it with spaces equal to the size of the header into which you are going to copy it. If you forget to pre-allocate the msg string, you receive an error.

Now comes the heart of the communications functions. All the TCP/IP functions have been created for you as Private procedures in the class, and calling them within the Transact method is shown in Listing 14.7. As each function is called, the function returns codes that are checked after the call is made to ensure that you are still communicating with the host system.

Listing 14.7   TRANSACTION.CLS—The Bulk of the Communication Is Transparent to the *Transact* Method

```
socket = fn_OpenSocket()
   If socket = 0 Then
      Err.Raise CTRANSACT_ERR_OPENSOCKET, "CTransact.Transact",
➥fn_GetLastSockError()
```

```
      Exit Function
    End If

    If fn_Connect(socket, mlHost, miPort) Then
      If fn_SendData(socket, msg & inBuffer) Then
        msBuffer = fn_ReceiveData(socket, 60)
        If Len(msBuffer) Then
          rc = fn_CloseSocket(socket)
          rc = CopyStructToString(hdr, msBuffer, Len(hdr))
          retCode = hdr.ReturnCode
          ' remove rich header from data buffer
          msBuffer = Mid$(msBuffer, Len(hdr) + 1)
        Else
          Exit Function
        End If
      Else
        rc = fn_CloseSocket(socket)
        Err.Raise CTRANSACT_ERR_SEND, "CTransact.Transact",
➥fn_GetLastSockError()
      End If
    Else
      rc = fn_CloseSocket(socket)
    End If
```

There are a couple of return code type variables used in the Transact method. The first, retCode, holds the value of the returned code from the host transaction. This is a four-character string variable. The second, rc, is an integer that holds the transaction-specific return code that is sent back to the calling program. After you receive the return code (retCode) from the host, you interrogate it, as shown in Listing 14.8, to return the appropriate value to the calling application.

Listing 14.8   TRANSACTION.CLS—Formatting the Return Code for Your Calling Application

```
'Based upon the return code from the transaction, pass a value
  'to the calling app
  Select Case Left$(retCode, 2)
    Case "00"
      rc = TRANSACT_RC_SUCCESS
    Case "IL"
      rc = TRANSACT_RC_INVALID_ACCOUNT
    Case "IR"
      rc = TRANSACT_RC_INVALID_TRAN
    Case Else
      rc = TRANSACT_RC_SERVER_ERROR
  End Select

  Transact = rc
```

Part
III

Ch

14

Compiling the Component

The last step in building your transaction component is to generate the DLL. In the section "The Project Dialog Box," you set the project options to generate an OLE server. Now you just need to instruct the compiler to generate an OLE DLL:

1. Select File, Save Project from the main menu.
2. Select File, Make OLE DLL File.

That's it. You now have successfully built your first Active Server component. Of course, you can use this component with Visual Basic, Access, Excel, or any other application that supports OLE components. The new component was registered automatically for you on the system where it was initially created.

Using Your New Server Component

Now that you have built the component, you need to create the form and Active Server Pages script to invoke that component. If you are going to use the component on a machine other than the one you created it on, you need to register the component on that machine.

Registering Your New Object

When you create the OLE .dll file in the Visual Basic environment, the component is registered automatically on the machine where it is compiled. If you want to move the .dll and associated support files to another machine, you need to register the new control after you place it on the system. There are a couple of ways to do this. If you are going to distribute your component, you can create an installation program using the VB Setup Wizard or another third-party installation package. The control will be registered during the installation process.

You also can just move the files to the new machine and register the control using the REGSVR32.EXE program that ships with Visual Basic. You can find the registration application on the Visual Basic CD-ROM in the \TOOLS\PSS directory. Here's how to register the control using the REGSVR32 program:

1. Move the component DLL, and any supporting files (VB40032.DLL for example) to the new machine.
2. Copy the REGSVR32.EXE file to a directory that is in the path on the target system (for example: \WINDOWS\SYSTEM).
3. Switch to the directory where you copied the .dll file.
4. Type **REGSVR32 COMPONENT.DLL.**
5. When the component has been registered, you receive a "successfully registered" dialog box. Click OK to dismiss the dialog box.

Testing the Component

The easiest way to initially test your new component is to start another instance of Visual Basic, create a simple form, and create an instance of the component. Then you can set the properties and call the Transact method. This lets you fine-tune the component before you try to integrate it into your Active Server Pages scripts.

To test the component, start another instance of Visual Basic. Add a command button to the Form1 that's displayed at startup. Double-click the newly created command button to bring up the code window. Now type the following code found in Listing 14.9 into the code window to test your new component.

Listing 14.9   form1.frm—Test Script for the New Component

```
Private Sub Command1_Click()
    Dim tran As New Transaction
    On Error GoTo COMMAND_ERR

    tran.Host = "localhost"
    tran.Port = 7511
    rc = tran.Transact(1000, 0, "TEST TRAN")
    MsgBox rc
Exit_Sub:
    Exit Sub

COMMAND_ERR:
    MsgBox "Error: " & Err.Number & " " & Err.Description
    Resume Exit_Sub
End Sub
```

The only action left to take before testing your component is to add a reference to it in your new project:

1. Select Tools, References from the main menu.
2. Scroll down the list and check TCP/IP Transaction Black Box.

While testing, it's helpful to force errors to ensure that error handling within the component is functioning correctly. For example, you can comment out the line tran.Host = "localhost". This generates an error because, as you may remember from the HostName property procedure code found in the section "The Let Procedure," the host must be set prior to calling the Transact function.

▶ **See** "Checking the Routine" for more information about methods of testing, **p. 168**

The error will be raised in the component and caught in the calling app by this directive:

```
On Error GoTo COMMAND_ERR
```

Part

III

Ch

14

In your Active Server Pages development, you will not be popping up message boxes on your server, but at a minimum, you surely will want to log any communication errors for further study and return an appropriate response to your client.

Component Testing on the Net

To test the component on your server, you need to build a simple form that calls an Active Server script and passes the appropriate parameters to it (account number, authorization amount). Then you can create your transaction object, call the Transact method, and return the results to your client.

ON THE WEB

http:www.quecorp.com/asp   The HTML form code and the Active Server Pages script to process the authorization request can be found on this book's Web site. (The assumption is that you might not want to read through another bare-bones HTML forms lecture at this juncture.) All of the Visual Basic code for the component, as well as the CTRANSACT.DLL, are on the site. We also included the source code and DLL for the VBUTIL.DLL functions.

From Here...

We finished the section on working with Active Server Pages objects and components with this chapter on building your own components. You have walked through the steps to generate your own components in Visual Basic. You now have all the tools and knowledge to create an infinite variety of applications for your Internet/intranet site using custom components. In Part IV, you will focus on database management and providing active content with live links to your back-end database systems.

Here's what to look forward to in Part IV:

- Chapter 15, "Introducing ActiveX Data Objects," covers the data access objects that ship with Active Server Pages. They provide an intuitive method of accessing external data from your ASP applications."
- Chapter 17, "Working with ADD's *RecordSet* Object," continues the discussion of ActiveX Data Objects and dives deep into the properties and methods that these objects provide.

Database Management with Active Server Pages

## CHAPTER 15

Introducing ActiveX Data Objects

As you read in Chapter 3, "Understanding Client/Server on the Internet," computing originally started on large machines with dumb terminals. With the advent of the personal computer and powerful workstations, much of the processing migrated to the desktop. The introduction of the Web server shifted the balance of power back to a centralized programming model. Today, Java and ActiveX controls have, yet again, enabled the desktop to reassert itself.

In this book, you have seen how the Active Server has enabled a more balanced balance of power. That is, instead of these polarizing swings of focus from server to desktop and back again, the Active Server has shown its "diplomatic" side, enabling the ASP developer to decide the best combination of technologies that optimize processing load without sacrificing fault tolerance or scalability.

As important as this egalitarian trait of ASP is, everything done so far in the book is trivial when compared to the innovations in ActiveX that are covered in this part of the text. These innovations are called ActiveX Data Objects (ADO).

Where did ActiveX Data Objects come from?

Review the historic roots of ActiveX Data Objects, and see how they extend existing systems like Open DataBase Connectivity.

What's the underlying technology for ActiveX Data Objects, and how is it different from its predecessors?

Explore the exciting new software model that ActiveX Data Objects is based on. The prospects for this radically new approach to data management will take your breath away.

The Objects and Components

You get your first good look at the basic building blocks of ActiveX Data Objects.

An Object Model for ActiveX Data Objects

Introducing the methods and properties of ActiveX Data Objects.

Essential ActiveX Data Objects

See how the essential elements of an ActiveX Data Object program fit together and explore the interaction between object properties with a working .asp file.

The major theme of this chapter, then, is distributed, object-centric database management. Before getting into it, however, you should be aware of a few things. First, bandwidth is scarce on the Internet. Second, packet-switched networks are inherently latent (that is, they are subject to delays). ActiveX Data Objects are so revolutionary that they (and you, as an ASP developer) are slightly ahead of their time.

The apparent impediments of bandwidth and latency might actually be a blessing. Most of your ADO learning curve will probably occur on intranets—where bandwidth is measured in tens, if not hundreds, of megabits and where latency is practically zero. By the time we break the bandwidth bottleneck with Asynchronous Transfer Mode (ATM) switches (or, better, when George Gilder's vision of the "fibersphere," the all-fiber network, becomes reality), ASP/ADO development will be second nature to you. With those caveats in mind, get ready to take a deeper look into this radical new resource: ADO. ■

The Family Tree

Until Microsoft's acquisition of Fox Software in 1992, the database was conspicuously absent from Microsoft's desktop arsenal. Today, FoxPro (now matured into Visual FoxPro), Microsoft Access, and SQL Server round out a balanced database strategy. Each product is designed for a particular market. For example, Visual FoxPro uses an Indexed Sequential Access Method (ISAM) file format and is generally recognized as faster than Access but slower than SQL Server. As the other desktop application, Access uses a special file format that is accessed through the Jet Data Access Object (DAO) model. DAO gives the programmer direct access to the database structure, something not as easily done in Visual FoxPro. SQL Server, on the other hand, is a database server, not a desktop application. It is an industrial-strength application that is highly scalable. All three products use ODBC to share data with one another.

There is one other thing that these three products have in common, setting them apart from ADO: Their ability to be deployed in a distributed network is defined by the Remote Data Object (RDO) specification found in Visual Basic 4.0's Enterprise Edition. Specifically, they work in *connected* networks. The Internet, on the other hand, is a *connectionless* network—a packet-switched network.

In fact, Web servers are even more problematic for programmers, especially database programmers, because they are "stateless" as well as connectionless. They're called *stateless* servers because once they serve a client request, they forget that the client ever was served. The server does not keep track of anything going on with the client application. Web servers have short memories.

In the desktop world, when two applications communicate, they do so for a given period of time. For example, when an Access database is linked to external files, it tests for the presence of those files as soon as it is opened. As long as the Access database remains running, any interruption in the connection (for example, say that a Novell file server goes down) triggers an event in Access, and a warning flashes in the Access application that the connection has been broken. In SQL Server, the server is aware of the presence of a client application as long as that application is engaged in a transaction with the database server. The length of time of such a transaction is not necessarily as short as it is with a Web server.

A Web server knows about a client application only long enough to deliver a file, but an Active Server is different. While it, too, disconnects from the client as soon as a file is returned, it remains connected as long as necessary to do two things: first, process the database and produce a recordset; second, enable the application to make subsequent calls and still have access to previously returned data.

OLE DB

Before getting into the meat of ADO, take a closer look at the application program interface (API) on which ADO is built, OLE DB (OLE DB is Object Linking and Embedding applied to databases). ADO is the first Microsoft technology built on this exciting new initiative. If you thought that the Web spawned an avalanche of great software and business models on the Internet, just wait until developers hear about OLE DB! And, as an ADO programmer, you're leading the way!

First, it's best to set the context with a quick review of the interface, the Open Database Connectivity (ODBC) specification. ODBC is a desktop SQL-based specification whose API foundation is built on the C language. This means that it was designed for relational database systems, the kind with which you all are accustomed to working. ODBC is a real workhorse, enabling developers to build systems that integrate Jet databases, ISAM files in old FoxBase+ databases, and even SQL Server tables into one coherent user interface. ODBC is the lingua franca of all these relational dialects meaning it is the linguistic bridge connecting the disparate native languages of each database management system.

OLE DB, on the other hand, is a specification based on a C++ API, so it is object-oriented. OLE DB consists of *data consumers* and *data providers*. Consumers take data from OLE DB interfaces; providers expose OLE DB interfaces. ODBC now is a subset of OLE DB. Currently, Microsoft has developed an OLE DB data provider (code-named *Kagera*) that enables access to the old relational data. In fact, under some circumstances, OLE DB can access ODBC data faster than DAO or RDO. This is because DAO and RDO have to pass through the ODBC layer, and OLE DB connects directly to relational data sources. See Figure 15.1 for the subtle difference in the approach taken by ADO.

What's more, OLE DB can be used to extend the functionality of simple data providers. These more sophisticated and specialized objects are called *service providers*, and they can assemble everything needed by data consumers into a single table, regardless of data type (for example, ODBC, spreadsheets, e-mail messages, word processing documents, or file systems) or storage location (LAN, WAN, Internet, intranet). Service providers, therefore, are both consumers and providers. That is, a service provider could consume OLE DB interfaces and build a single table from that input; it then could expose OLE DB interfaces to a client application (such as an .asp file using ADO) for constructing its HTML output.

FIG. 15.1
OLE DB simplifies the connection of your program to database information.

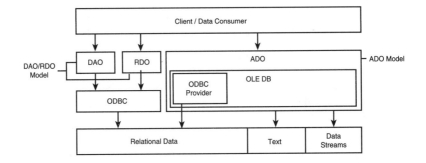

But OLE DB is, after all, a low-level specification. If you don't have time to learn a language lower down the food chain than Visual Basic, ActiveX is the answer. Specifically, ActiveX Data Objects use a language-neutral component technology to provide a high-level wrapper around the OLE DB API, which enables you to exploit all the power of OLE DB without resorting to low-level programming. On the one hand, this means that all Microsoft programming languages can use ADO to access data. On the other hand, ActiveX components (ADO is but one example) can themselves be built by using any language that complies with the Component Object Model. All of these rather subtle relationships are depicted in Figure 15.2.

FIG. 15.2
ActiveX is a language-neutral wrapper, giving the component developer free choice of the best breed of development environments.

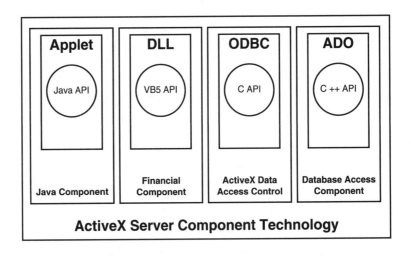

To recap: ADO works just like DAO and RDO, only more efficiently, especially in a stateless and connectionless environment like the Internet/intranet. ADO, an ActiveX component technology, is based on a C++ API called OLE DB (which betrays its family heritage from ODBC, written in C). Because ADO is a component technology, it is highly extensible, tying ADO to Microsoft's programming paradigm for the next millennium.

Objects versus Components

The Active Server is a component of the Internet Information Server. Specifically, it is an Internet Server Application Programming Interface (ISAPI) filter. This means that it is a Dynamic Link Library file that becomes part of IIS as soon as the operating system starts it running. This modular design of everything Microsoft publishes these days is a model for the way an ASP developer should write applications.

By exposing key ASP resources to the scripting engine running on the server (e.g., VBScript, JavaScript, Perl, and others), the Active Server enables the ASP developer to extend the functionality of the Active Server itself.

Objects are the first internals available to the ASP developer. The functions exposed by objects are the most common functions required by Active Server Pages. Examples include creating instances of server components (which you will read about next), manipulating text strings with URL and HTML encoding, and many other advanced functions that you will read about in the rest of this part of the book.

Components have a similar function; namely, to extend the functionality of the Active Server, but they have one fundamental difference: They are .dll files that run separately from the Active Server, but in the same address space as the server. Microsoft wrote these .dll files, but you can create your own components in any language that produces code compliant with the Component Object Model (COM) specification. By creating .dll files (and not .exe files that execute in their own address space), you give your components maximum speed.

Active Server components (both those components intrinsic to ASP and those you create yourself) do not have a user interface. Indeed, if you forget this and design a server component with a msgbox or inputbox function, you will hang the server. This is because the program (namely, your errant server component) that is running is waiting for user input that never comes, because the user interface is invisible. In addition, server components need to support only three interfaces (IUnknown, IDispatch, and IClassFactory).

Finally, VBScript does not have a type library, so if you want to use variable types other than Variant, write a component. For example, if you want to extend the Active Server's mathematical power, you DO NOT want to use the Variant data type; it will slow your mathematical processing to a crawl. Instead, create a program in Visual Basic, and compile it as an in-process .dll file; register it with the operating system, and call it in your Active Server Pages.

Down 'n Dirty

Remember, almost all new developments in computer programming today are innovative uses of objects. Whether you program in Visual Basic 4.0 or in Active Server Scripting, you are object-centric. Get ready to relax your brain—you're going to need a lot of mental flexibility as the section proceeds.

To start, here's a simple example. Say that, using the `TextStream` component, you treat a file as an object. That's not hard to imagine. One of the methods exposed by this component is `OpenTextFile`; again, fairly straightforward. But what happens in your brain when you think of data as an object? Treating a file as an object is simple—there's an object, a single object, and it's called a file. It's not a file that's part of a bigger file (unless you take the idea of a folder literally); it's just a file.

But data? A single data (okay, *datum*) is trivial, and ADO is far from trivial. You probably have to think of a data *source* in order to feel comfortable with the concept of data being an object. And what about queries and stored procedures? They result in recordsets that can range from zero rows to the total number of rows in the data source. One of the first things that we recommend you do when you start working with the ADO is stop thinking of database tables literally. Instead, think of them as abstract objects with their own collections, properties, and methods.

Most Access developers already are familiar with a data object model, which is exactly what the Access Data Access Object (DAO) model is. These developers should recognize nearly all the terms used in ADO, other than the `Connection` Object. The name is different, but the functionality is familiar; ADO's `Connection` Object basically provides the same functionality as the `Workspace` Object in Access.

Familiarity, however, won't prepare even seasoned Access developers for some of the stumbling blocks that they'll confront in ADO. For example, if your programming career developed as ours did, you went from an ISAM world like FoxPro to the DAO world of Access, and the first thing you gave up was the record number. In Access (and ADO), the record number doesn't exist. Access introduced developers to the *bookmark*, instead. ADO follows this tradition, with its own twist: *pages*.

Absolute pages are navigated in ways allowed by the nature of the underlying recordset. That is, some recordsets can be navigated freely, up and down; others permit only row-wise, forward movement. You'll see examples of both in a moment. For now, be aware that there are subtle nuances lurking in ADO, and the Active Server developer might need to take great care in specifying how and from where recordsets are fetched. As you'll see shortly, the other new demand of ADO programming for those without SQL Server experience is having to understand new terms; for example, *cursor*. (If you don't know it now, that's okay; you will in a moment.)

ADO and *Server* Objects

Using ADO, perhaps more than any other server component, highlights the symbiosis between `Server` Objects and components. The main reason for this interdependence is that, because Web applications are based on individual HTML pages, these applications can be problematical for the Active Server developer. The problem arises because, while on one hand, the application moves freely and easily between several forms or instances of the same form (as you will see demonstrated later), at the same time, a stable substrate of data underlies the dynamic interplay of user interface. The developer's challenge is to keep this data substrate available to any and all pages that need it.

There are two specific issues facing the ADO developer—performance and reference. Performance issues arise because you cannot spare the bandwidth to make repeated calls to server data stores for the same recordset (just because different pages need it). All pages should refer to the same fetched data.

Reference issues are similar to performance issues but different, because pages often will have to exchange data entered by the user; even more often, they will have to exchange data with one another (whether the data was fetched or entered). One or more pages needs to know what that data is and must be updated if that data is changed by another page in the application.

Figure 15.3 depicts these inter-relationships. A database contains information needed by an ASP application. The Active Server makes the call to fetch the data. If you use `Session` properties, discussed in the next section, you have to fetch this data only once; all the Active Server Pages will reference this copy of the data as necessary. If you do not use `Session` properties, then every time an .asp file needs the data, it has to requery the data provider. Also note in the figure that data can "trickle down" from one page to several others. This data may affect and be affected by the data in the original database.

FIG. 15.3

The problem of ADO programming centers in repeated calls to a data provider for data.

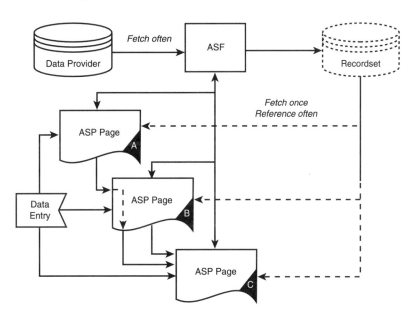

ASP has something for just this purpose, `Session` properties. Remember that VBScript is not yet able to reference a type library at design time and perform early binding. Therefore, all variables in VBScript are of type `Variant`. The performance issues that normally attend the exclusive use of variants usually are not issues in Active Server programming, because the client apps tend to remain thin. Intelligent design of server components enables the high-performance processing of variable data.

At any rate, Session properties can be created simply by setting them to a value. For example, a RecordSet Object can be created as a Session property simply by stating the following:

```
Session("rstAuthors") = rstAuthors
```

The ADO Object Model

As mentioned, of all the server components that ship with ASP, ADO is the most complex and the one with the most long-term impact on the future of programming. In this chapter, we focus on the highest level of the object model and highlight some of the key properties and methods necessary to make ADO work at its most basic level. A key objective of this chapter is to stress that understanding the relationships between features of ADO is more important than an understanding of its parts.

Exposed Objects

ADO exposes three primary objects to the developer: the Connection Object, the Command Object, and the RecordSet Object. For all practical purposes, the RecordSet Object is the most important; the Connection and Command Objects serve to enable the RecordSet Object's creation.

> **N O T E**   With version 1.0, everything in OLE DB exists so that data providers can present their data in tabular form (later versions of OLE DB might be able to output object-oriented data and semistructured data). From the perspective of Active Server Pages, the RecordSet Object is the key to the new level of interactivity that data-driven HTML enables. ■

The *Connection* Object   ADO's advantage comes from its ability to work in stateless environments. The Connection Object is responsible for recording the necessary information about the data provider from which the RecordSet Object will be created. ADO needs to inform the Windows NT server of the existence of an ODBC data provider by citing a Data Source Name (DSN). Recall that each DSN receives a name; the Connection Object refers to that name with its Open method and records the name in its ConnectionString property. The Open method also needs optional UserID and Password values, should the DSN require them.

Another feature of Connection Objects will be familiar to Access and SQL Server programmers. Like its predecessors, ADO can exploit the I/O efficiency of transactions using the BeginTrans, CommitTrans, or RollbackTrans methods. These methods—at least, in Access—are part of the Workspace Object, and you can see how it and the Connection Object exist for the same reason. Think of the Connection Object as the telephone and circuits that enable you to call your mother; they don't do the talking, but without them, there's no conversation.

If the Connection Object is like the telephone, then its Open method is like placing a call, and its Execute method is like opening your mouth. Actually, there are several ways to create a RecordSet Object. Essentially, you can do it with the Connection, Command, or even the

`RecordSet` Object itself. For the moment, we remain focused on the `Connection` Object. Listing 15.1 shows how you instantiate a `Connection` Object from the Database Access Component (identified by the `ADO` progID). You open this object by assiging it to the DSN named `"Blotter."` And you create a new recordset by invoking the `Execute` method (in this instance, you fetch all the records in a table named `"tblBlotter"`).

Listing 15.1   CH15.ASP— Using the *Connection* Object to Create a Recordset

```
Set objConn=Server.CreateObject("ADO.Connection")
objConn.Open("Blotter")
Set objRst=objConn.Execute "tblBlotter"
```

As mentioned, the `Execute` method takes a given SQL command and interrogates the DSN with it. Success yields a `RecordSet` Object that is created with the VBScript `Set` command. Using this approach creates an implicit `RecordSet` Object, by the way. This means that ADO has given you a minimalist `RecordSet` Object; more important, it generates the least powerful cursor. Specifically, the resulting cursor is the row-wise, scroll-forward, read-only variety. ADO, like good programmers, is profoundly lazy (the good kind of laziness, the kind that enables programmers to write great code).

The *Command* Object   The `Command` Object provides the second way to create a `RecordSet` Object. This object also creates a minimal cursor, but it was designed to exploit a key concept in database management: passed parameters. Parameters are variables stored inside queries and stored procedures. Think of queries, and especially stored procedures, as mini-programs compiled by the data provider. Like normal programs, these objects can accept data at runtime that affect how the object behaves. Queries designed like this are called "parameterized queries." For example, if you want to list only certain records from a given table, you pass the name of the field and the value of interest to the parameterized query, and it filters out all other records from the resulting recordset.

Of course, you can always do this by stuffing variables into the SQL statement, but this can be very time-consuming and frustrating, especially when you have to contend with embedded double and single quotes. A thorough discussion of the implementation details for parameters is covered in Chapter 16, "Working with ADO's `Connection` and `Command` Objects." For now, Listing 15.2 demonstrates the simplest way to open a recordset with the `Command` Object.

Listing 15.2   CH15.ASP—Opening a Simple Recordset with the *Command* Object

```
Set objCmd = Server.CreateObject(ADODB.Command)
objCmd.ActiveConnection ="intranet"
objCmd.CommandText="qryPhoneMessagesFor"
Set objRst = objCmd.Execute
```

▶ **See** "Utilizing Command Objects to Their Full Potential" for more information about Command
Objects, **p. 325**

As you can see, the structure of these commands is very similar to those used by the
Connection Object. In order to execute a Command Object, you need to tell it which connection
to use and what SQL statement to use. In Chapter 17, you will see that there are many other
ways to implement these basic requirements, but in all cases, the result is the same as that in
Listing 15.2.

N O T E You have a choice when it comes to creating recordsets with the Connection Object and
the Command Object: Refer to database objects such as queries, stored procedures, or
table names; or use explicit SQL statements such as "SELECT * FROM tblBlotter." Referring to
objects can yield dramatic improvements in performance because they can exploit all the processing
power of the data provider. However, using a SQL statement makes your code self-documenting; i.e.,
you can tell exactly what your program is doing as it interacts with the data provider. In most cases, this
advantage of self-documenting code is more than offset by the loss in performance; and besides, you
can always explicitly document calls to database objects. ▨

The *RecordSet* Object   When you use the RecordSet Object to *create* a recordset, you are
using the CreateObject method of the Server Object to instantiate an explicit RecordSet
Object. This means that you are responsible for specifying all the properties of the resulting
recordset (unless you accept default values). Alternatively, you can create a recordset implicitly
by using a Connection Object or the Command Object—but then you have no control over properties. If you need a dynamic cursor that is fully scrollable and permits batch updates, by using
the RecordSet Object, that's exactly what you'll get.

N O T E Cursors and related constructs are important in ADO, because the ADO developer has
complete control over details that can be overlooked safely when using DAO. We focus on
cursors as follows, and at the end of this chapter we provide a useful applet that demonstrates the
interplay between cursors and concurrency and how both are controlled with RecordSet Object
properties. ▨

At this point, you have made the call, connected with the other end, and are ready to start
talking. In the same way that a conversation is full of words, recordsets are full of data. To fill
the recordset with data, then, you don't use an Execute method; you use the Open method. Like
the Execute method, the Open method in a Connection Object context is different from the
Open method with the RecordSet Object. With the Connection Object, the Open method opens
a channel permitting data to flow; with the RecordSet Object, the Open method fills a recordset
with data.

By now, code like Listing 15.3 should be familiar. Regardless of the object and method you use
to create a recordset of data, you always need to tell ADO where the database is stored and
which table you need to manipulate. Again, the primary syntactical difference with the
RecordSet Object is that it is populated with the Open method, not the Execute method.

Listing 15.3   CH15.ASP—The Code Necessary to Create a *RecordSet* Object

```
Set objRst = Server.CreateObject("ADO.Recordset")
objRst.Source = "qryBlotterByDate"
objRst.ActiveConnection="Blotter"
objRst.Open
```

Each RecordSet Object contains a Fields collection of all the Field objects that are in the recordset. By manipulating the Fields collection, you change the structure of the underlying database table. That is, by referring to the Fields collection, you can construct SQL commands to update or otherwise modify the structure of the underlying tables at the data provider.

The real meat of the RecordSet Object, however, is in its methods and properties. To the extent that you do any serious database management by using an HTML user interface, your ADO programs probably will use all those methods at one time or another.

N O T E   Remember, the mission of ADO's underlying interface, OLE DB, is to be able to work with any data provider. Therefore, you would expect a rich set of methods and properties to accommodate all the different flavors, dialects, and technologies used to store data. OLE DB is designed to eventually embrace all formats from data streams to text files to object stores—an ambitious mission.

Properties might see less widespread use than methods (unless you find yourself immersed in such relational arcana as heterogeneous joins). Why? Because some ADO properties are not supported by some data providers. For example, not all data providers support bookmarks—Access does; FoxPro does not—nor do all Access cursors support bookmarks.

Methods

We selected the methods and properties in the following sections from the entire ADO object model because they are used in the demo program in the "Database Programming" section at the end of this chapter. Nearly all the ADO code that you write will use them. The chapters that complete this part of the book give more ambitious treatment of ADO coding, and we defer discussion of subjects such as *pages* and of methods such as AddNew, GetRows, and Move to those chapters.

N O T E   At the end of this section is a table that summarizes the list of methods and properties for each object.

Abandon   The Abandon method applies to Active Server Session Objects. Sessions are created as soon as a user opens an .asp file in a virtual directory of the Internet Information Server. This session stays open until one of two things happens. Either there is no activity from the user for 20 minutes (or the interval specified in the Timeout property of the Session Object) or an Abandon method is invoked.

If you need access to any connected database before the session expires (for example, to back up the database), you need to `Abandon` it first.

CreateObject The `CreateObject` method applies to the `Server` Object. This method creates instances of server components (such as `TextStream`) and ADO objects (such as `Connection` and `RecordSet`). The similarity with this method to its namesake in Visual Basic is that the `Server` Object must be part of the call; namely, `Server.CreateObject()`, not merely `CreateObject()`.

Open The `Open` method applies to `Connection` and `RecordSet` Objects. With the `Connection` Object, the method opens a connection—a channel of communication—to a server; specifically, to a Data Source Name. When invoked by a `RecordSet` Object, this method opens a cursor in a table in the DSN. The cursor is a current row-pointer within the recordset created with the `Open` method.

Requery The `Requery` method applies to the `RecordSet` Object created with the `Open` method. Its function is to refire the query that populated the recordset, fetching the current—perhaps updated—values from the underlying database table.

Update The `Update` method also is used by the `RecordSet` Object. It moves the data in the copy buffer to the `RecordSet` Object. Until this event occurs, the underlying table can have one value and the `RecordSet` Object another; after the `Update` method, they have the same data— unless something interfered with the routine processing of updates. Examples include incompatible combinations of `CursorType` and `LockType` properties (such as keyset cursors with batch updating in Microsoft Access).

> **N O T E** One of the design goals of ADO was to make coding more efficient for programmers. One of the first thing ADO changes is the old `Edit` method. In ADO, if you want to change a field's value, you simply change it; you no longer need to explicitly invoke the `Edit` method first (it's implied). The `AddNew` method, however, is still required, for there is no other way for ADO to know your intentions.

Properties

As with methods, we discuss more sophisticated ADO properties in Chapter 16 and Chapter 17. The properties in the following sections are listed in alphabetical order.

ActiveConnection The `ActiveConnection` property tells ADO where the data is and how to access it. `ActiveConnection` functions like a telephone connection in that it enables communication but does not communicate directly. Some ADO connections are like station-to-station long distance. Others are more restricted, like a person-to-person call, limiting data access to only certain people with specific passwords.

CursorType `CursorType` is an important property that applies to the `RecordSet` Object. It determines how hard the data provider has to work to make the records it stores available to your ADO program. The simplest cursor is a forward only, row-wise, read-only cursor. Other data providers can provide dynamic cursors that keep track of the status of underlying data.

LockType   The `LockType` property applies to `RecordSet` Objects and controls what results when the `RecordSet` Object executes its `Open` method. This property is important because it tells the data provider how to handle concurrency issues, should they arise.

Name   The `Name` property applies to the `Field` Object of the `RecordSet` Object.

Source   The `Source` property applies to `RecordSet` Objects. Usually, this is a text string of SQL commands to fetch data from the data provider. A shortcut is to use the name of the table alone; this is quicker than typing **SELECT * FROM tblBlotter**. Note, however, that if you want only a selected group of records or set of fields, you will have to use a SQL command, a query, or a SQL `Server` stored procedure.

Essential ADO

In this final section of this overview of ADO, you will take a quick look at some database theories, and you will see the source code for the demo program, ch15.asp, that you can download off the book's Web site.

ON THE WEB

http://www.quecorp.com/asp   Go to this book's Web site to download the demo program, ch15.asp.

Preliminaries

To help you come to terms with recordsets, we take a brief detour into the world of relational database management. The comments that follow are for those who have had little use for databases until now or those who have used database systems but didn't have a need to get into the theories of database management. More experienced readers can safely skip this section. You will read even more about concurrency control in Chapter 17, "Working with ADO's *Recordset* Object."

I Thought a Cursor Was Only Needed for the Screen

All of you are familiar with a cursor. Nearly all are aware of the feeling of panic and helplessness that comes when the cursor becomes invisible or freezes in its (mouse) tracks. Cursors tell you where you are and tell the computer what you want to do next.

In relational database management systems, and in SQL-based systems especially, cursors have a similar but deliberately invisible role to play.

Structured Query Language is called *set-based* and is fundamentally different from the *row-based* method used by business applications. It is small wonder that the spreadsheet was the first business application created for the personal computer. Virtually everything done in business can be best expressed in columns and rows.

continues

continued

There's more to life for SQL than business. SQL experiences the world with *sets*. Granted, the underlying tables of data that SQL uses may be stored in rows and columns—though not always—but the results of combining certain rows and columns results in a set. If you remember Venn diagrams from high school, you know that intersecting sets are the product of combining other sets. Those result sets were the areas where two or more circles overlapped or intersected.

Cursors originally were conceived to bridge the gap between these two worlds of sets and rows. They are a logical entity that *represents* the sets that SQL produces in a structure that business applications can manipulate. Without them, ADO wouldn't exist.

Concurrency and Locking Issues   There is an adage as old as the Internet that goes something like "Information yearns to be free." In the database business world, there is a related truism: Data needs to be changed. The subject of this word play raises two serious problems for database developers.

On one hand, displayed data (especially when more than one row is being displayed) often needs to be up-to-date. This means that when someone adds or deletes a record, all other displays of data from that table need to reflect the change.

On the other hand, when the value of one or more fields of an existing record gets changed by more than one person and at the same time, there is a potential conflict, a collision of wills. The DBMS must be able to sense these collisions and manage them effectively.

Cursors play a part in both of these situations. More precisely, different cursor types play different roles in these different circumstances. Cursors have two primary flavors—static and dynamic. Static cursors, as their name suggests, can't see additions and deletions made by other users. For example, if a business application that works with only one record at a time is being built, it need not concern itself with the need to update the number of rows in a recordset. This is the kind of recordset that ADO creates by default. Other times, a dynamic cursor is needed. Dynamic cursors sense, on their own, when the number of rows or the content of fields changes.

N O T E   Not all data providers support dynamic cursors.

The ASP developer also needs to address the issue of concurrency and the related issue of locking. Locking techniques fall into two categories: optimistic and pessimistic. Optimistic locking is relatively easy for the DBMS to implement, for it assumes that collisions and conflicts will be rare and doesn't activate locks until just before updating, and only if a conflict exists. Pessimistic locking assumes the opposite, and locks on data are required before processing a record can even begin. Again, not all DBMSs support both, and when some do, they don't give you a choice between the two.

N O T E In one sense, these issues make coming to terms with relational databases a little easier. The choice isn't whether to use optimistic or pessimistic locking; it's whether to buy Microsoft Access (where locking is automatic and both types are supported) or to use an old version of FoxBase+ (where pessimistic locking must be done manually in code) as your DBMS. The point is, if your database engine doesn't support a relational feature, you have to design around that limitation or pick another engine. ■

▶ **See** "Understanding Concurrency Control" for more information about concurrency and locking, **p. 338**

Keys, Indexes, and Bookmarks   Relational Database Management Systems always work more efficiently if they can uniquely identify individual records. They also work more efficiently if certain fields are indexed; that is, put in order, such as last names in alphabetical order. Tables need keys to do both these things. Indexes sort records based on the values of these key fields; if these values are unique, they serve double duty—they sort and uniquely identify records. In addition, if a SQL Server table has a key, it can have a keyset cursor. Access isn't as picky; a table of two fields and no indexes does not return an error when a dynaset (the closest thing to a keyset cursor that Access has) is created and updated.

In the demo program in the next section, you will see for yourself the effect on the underlying database table when you combine the `CursorType` and `LockType` properties with an Access database.

One more concept: bookmarks. Bookmarks are to cursors what cursors are to recordsets—they are placeholders. Some DBMSs (like FoxPro) keep track of record numbers. The Jet engine in Access and ADO do not. Instead, they rely on bookmarks to move the cursor to a previous location in a recordset. As you might guess, bookmarks are not supported by all cursors. Remember that dynamic cursors get updated when records are added or deleted. As a result, bookmarks aren't supported (in part, because the row that they used to represent may be gone). Only static and keyset cursors (and dynasets in Access) support bookmarks.

So, if you are working on recordsets with more than one record, and you need to be able to wander around this recordset as if it were a spreadsheet, you need to choose your cursor type carefully.

 T I P   SQL can get complex quickly; it was not designed to be read by humans. You can write your own SQL code by hand, if you want, but we don't recommend it. We recommend that you create SQL code in your application of choice. Our favorite is Microsoft Access; its QBE grid is the most amazing piece of code that we have come across in our years of programming. Perhaps SQL Server or something else works better for you. Regardless of the modeling method, when you have a SQL command that does what you need, cut the SQL code and paste it into your .asp file.

As this book was going to press, Microsoft's Visual InterDev application was coming out of beta testing. One of its most important features is modeled after, and significantly extends, the QBE grid of Access.

A Demonstration Program

We discuss the following demo program in three sections: initialization code, form processing, and database programming. This program has the great virtue of simplicity, and at this stage, clarity is more important for you than virtuosity.

ON THE WEB

http://www.quecorp.com/asp   The entire .asp file, ch15.asp, is available for download from this book's Web site.

N O T E   One of the greatest virtues of publishing on the Web is that we can make changes quickly and often with almost zero cost of production. For that reason, the actual code you download from the Web will be named ch15.asp, but it might not look exactly like the code printed in the book. If the Web code is different, it's because it's better. If you think it can be improved yet again, by all means let us know. ■

Initialization Code   Listing 15.4 describes what the Chapter 15 demo program is for. It includes the standard HTML code for the beginning of HTML files.

Listing 15.4   adoBasics.asp—Describes the Function of the .asp File and Sets Up the First Part of an HTML File

```
'********************************************************************
' Description:
'      An Active Server Program (ASP) file that demonstrates
'      many of the tips and techniques discussed in the book.
'      Most importantly, it illustrates the effect of the interaction
'      of two key recordset properties: CursorType and LockType.
'      It also demonstrates the reliance these properties have on the
'      underlying database management system (i.e., some DBMSs
'      do not support all CursorType or LockType values. In the context
'      of a cosmopolitan programming world like ADO, this is important
'       information.
' Arguments:
'      This program calls itself so when the txtCursorType and
'      txtLockType fields have value, they are passed back into the
'      program.
' Returns:
'      Nothing
' Modified:
'      Michael Corning 10/20/96. Final preparations for publication.
'********************************************************************
<HTML>
<HEAD>
</HEAD>

<BODY BGCOLOR="#EEEEEE" TEXT="#000000" LINK="#CC0000" ALINK="#FF3300"
➡VLINK="#330099">
<FONT FACE="Verdana" SIZE=2>
```

Next, some housekeeping chores. The two ways of indicating a comment in VBScript are shown in Listing 15.5, as well as a test to see if you need to abandon an ADO session.

Listing 15.5 adoBasics.asp—The Two Ways to Comment VBScript Code

```
' Note: using apostrophe for comments only works if they
' are inside the vbs tags (which you cannot use inside comments
' like this). Compare below using HTML comment.
REM You can also use the explicit REM statement instead of the
REM apostrophe.

REM When you're done, abandon the session so that you can
REM backup, move, or otherwise manipulate the underlying database
REM file. The session will abandon in 20 minutes, otherwise.
If Request("cmdQuit") ="Close" Then%>
        <FONT COLOR="Red">Closing connection</FONT><P>
        <%Session.Abandon
Else
        If IsObject(Session("SessionConnection")) Then
                Set objConn = Session("SessionConnection")
        %>
                <FONT COLOR="Green">Using the Cached Session connection</FONT><P>
        <% Else
                Set objConn = Server.CreateObject("ADO.Connection")
                objConn.Open("Blotter")
                Session("SessionConnection") = objConn
                ' Since we are experimenting with different Recordset
                ' Objects in this ASP file, we have moved the
                ' instantiation of it to the code block below that
                ' sets the recordsets
                ' properties for use by its Open method.
                ' Set objRst = Server.CreateObject("ADO.Recordset")%>
                <FONT COLOR="Yellow">Opening the Connection</FONT><P>
        <% End If

        ' Following two code blocks are necessary if you want to
        ' be able to use a default value
        ' AND be able to maintain your field entries between
        ' successive ASP file calls.
        If Request("txtCursorType") ="" Then
                intCursorType = 3
        Else
                intCursorType = Request("txtCursorType")
        End If
        If Request("txtLockType") ="" Then
                intLockType = 3
        Else
                intLockType = Request("txtLockType")
        End If
        %>
```

Form Processing   Listing 15.6 continues from the previous listing. It is simple, straightforward HTML form code. The only things that differ from standard HTML are in the beginning of this section: The form action calls the same file (namely, adoBasics.asp) that contains itself. This is similar to recursion but without the overhead or risk of running out of stack space. The second difference from orthodox HTML code is that values for form controls are variables (and, in Listing 15.5, are passed between calls to the adoBasics.asp file).

Listing 15.6   adoBasics.asp—How to Set Up a Form in an .asp File

```
<FORM ACTION="adoBasics.asp" METHOD="POST">
<TABLE CELLPADDING=3 BORDER=1 CELLSPACING=0 WIDTH=600>
        <TR>
                <TD COLSPAN=2>Cursor Type:
                <!--
                        Remember to use HTML comment delimiters when you are
                        commenting outside the vbs delimiters.  Remember to
                        put "=" before the Request object so that its value
                        is returned for the default value of the TEXT box.
                -->
                <INPUT TYPE="TEXT"
                        NAME="txtCursorType"
                        SIZE=3
                        VALUE="<% =intCursorType %>"></TD>

                <TD COLSPAN=2>Lock Type:
                <INPUT TYPE="TEXT"
                        NAME="txtLockType"
                        SIZE=3
                        VALUE="<%= intLockType %>">

                <!--
                        These command buttons have a name,
                        so the subsequent calls to this ASP file
                        can tell when they've been pushed. Without a
                        name, a command button serves only to fire the
                        form.
                -->
                <INPUT TYPE="SUBMIT"
                        VALUE="Edit"
                        NAME="cmdEdit">

                <INPUT TYPE="SUBMIT"
                        VALUE="Close"
                        NAME="cmdQuit"></TD>
        </TR>

        <TR>
                <TH><FONT SIZE="1">CursorType</TH><TH><FONT SIZE="1">
                        Description</TH>
                <TH><FONT SIZE="1">LockType </FONT></TH><TH><FONT
➥SIZE="1">
                        Description</FONT></TH>
```

```
                        </TR>
                        <TR>
                                <TD><FONT SIZE="1">0 </FONT></TD>
                                <TD><FONT SIZE="1">Keyset</FONT></TD>
                                <TD><FONT SIZE="1">-1 </FONT></TD>
                                <TD><FONT SIZE="1">Provider determines (usually read-
➥only)
                                </FONT></TD>
                        </TR>
                        <TR>
                                <TD><FONT SIZE="1">1 </FONT></TD>
                                <TD><FONT SIZE="1">ForwardOnly</FONT></TD>
                                <TD><FONT SIZE="1">1 </FONT></TD>
                                <TD><FONT SIZE="1">Read-only</FONT></TD>
                        </TR>
                        <TR>
                                <TD><FONT SIZE="1">2 </FONT></TD>
                                <TD><FONT SIZE="1">Dynamic</FONT></TD>
                                <TD><FONT SIZE="1">2 </FONT></TD>
                                <TD><FONT SIZE="1">Row-by-row pessimistic locking
                                        </FONT></TD>
                        </TR>
                        <TR>
                                <TD><FONT SIZE="1">3 </FONT></TD>
                                <TD><FONT SIZE="1">Static</FONT></TD>
                                <TD><FONT SIZE="1">3 </FONT></TD>
                                <TD><FONT SIZE="1">Row-by-row optimistic locking
                                        </FONT></TD>
                        </TR>
                        <TR>
                                <TD><BR></TD>
                                <TD><BR></TD>
                                <TD><FONT SIZE="1">4 </FONT></TD>
                                <TD><FONT SIZE="1">Optimistic batch updates</FONT></TD>
                        </TR>
                </TABLE>
                </FORM>
```

Database Programming   This final section, Listing 15.7, is the important stuff. A few things are worth emphasizing. First, in all ADO code there is no Edit method for the RecordSet Object. When you want to change a recordset field value, just change it. The Update method takes care of the rest of the overhead.

Second, the Requery method flushes out the data of local storage and attempts to permanently change the underlying database cursor. If everything worked as expected with the Update method, the Requery results in the new value.

Also note that we use a compiled query stored in the Access DSN. This provides any performance gains that might be invested in a cleverly designed Jet query. Finally, note the use of variables for setting the values of the key properties, CursorType and LockType. The user of the HTML form specifies these variables.

Listing 15.7   adoBasics.asp—Real Database Programming in an .asp File

```
<%
If intLockType  < -1 Or intLockType > 4 Or intLockType = 0  Then
        Response.Write("Select a lock type value between -1 and 4 (but
➥not 0)")
        ElseIf intCursorType  < 0 Or intCursorType  > 3 Then
                Response.Write("Select a cursor type value between 0 and 3")
        Else
                ' When ASP first called, Edit button has null value.
                If Request("cmdEdit") = "Edit" Then
                        Set objRst = Server.CreateObject("ADO.Recordset")
                        objRst.LockType = intLockType
                        ' Pick up the entered type
                        objRst.Source = "qryBlotterByDate"
                        objRst.CursorType = intCursorType
                        Set objRst.ActiveConnection=objConn
                        objRst.Open%>
                        <TABLE CELLSPACING=0 BORDER=1 WIDTH=600>
                        <TR>
                                <TD><BR></TD><TH>Before</TH><TH>After</TH>
                        </TR>
                        <%For i=1 to objRst.Fields.Count-1%>
                        <TR>
                                <TD ><FONT SIZE="2">
                                        <%If objRst(i).Name="Rep" Then%>
                                                <B>Does Rep field value change?</B>
                                        <%else
                                                =objRst(i).Name
                                        End If%>
                                </FONT></TD>
                                <TD>
                                        <FONT SIZE="2"><%=objRst(i)%></FONT>
                                </TD>
                                <% If objRst(i).Name = "Rep" Then
                                        ' oldRep used below to see if the update
                                        ' succeeded
                                        oldRep = objRst("Rep")
                                        ' We're hard coding the field change here.
                                        ' Normally, the field data is edited
                                        ' with forms; but since there are no data
                                        ' bound HTML form controls, getting
                                        ' these new values into the recordset and
                                        ' the cursor at the data provider is
                                        ' not trivial. We take up the challenge in
                                        ' Chapter 17.
                                        objRst("Rep") = objRst("Rep")+1
                                        objRst.Update
                                        ' Note: If you don't requery the recordset
                                        ' after a failed update then the recordset
                                        ' value remains changed, but the underlying
                                        ' cursor is not.
```

```
                              objRst.Requery
                    End If %>
                    <TD>
                    <% If objRst(i).Name = "Rep" Then
                              ' See if the correct combination of
                              ' CursorType and LockType properties
                              ' were selected for the Access database.
                              ' If so, the new value will be on
                              ' the screen and in the cursor. SQL Server
                              ' and other data providers may
                              ' respond differently than Access using
➡the
                              ' same property values.
                              ' Caveat developer.
                              If oldRep = objRst("Rep") Then%>
                                      <FONT SIZE="2"><%=objRst(i)%>
➡<B>NO</B></FONT>

                              <%Else%>
                                      <FONT SIZE="2"><%=objRst(i)%>
➡<B>YES</B></FONT>

                              <%End If
                    Else%>
                              <FONT SIZE="2"><%=objRst(i)%></FONT>
                    <%End If%>
                    </TD>
              </TR>
              <%next%>
              </TABLE>
          <%End If
      End if
End If%>

</FONT>
</BODY>
</HTML>
```

For Your Part We encourage you to try the .asp file for yourself. Experiment with it and keep track of the combinations of property values and outcomes. Remember that you are using an Access database and that other data providers might produce different results.

We also encourage you to make a working copy of this file on your own hard drive and experiment with other DSNs or tables in the referenced Access database. The program is fairly generic (except for the explicit field name, Rep), so relatively few changes will be necessary for you to use it with other Access tables, SQL Server, or other DBMSs.

From Here...

This chapter introduced what might be the most important part of the Active Server: ActiveX Data Objects. ADO is the next generation of database technology from Microsoft. It retains all the power of the OBDC specification but extends this power to the Internet. Combined with

DCOM to access data providers in widely dispersed locations, ADO will be even more powerful than RDO.

Also in this chapter, you explored some of ADO's most fundamental aspects and saw some of its most important points in a demonstration program. As exciting as this is, it still isn't "real database programming." We still haven't discussed what you can do with this new power.

For that, turn to the following:

- Chapter 16, "Working with ADO's *Connection* and *Command* Objects," introduces a diagramming method well suited to the nature of ADO. It also covers the `Connection` Object and the `Command` Object in great detail.
- Chapter 17, "Working with ADO's *RecordSet* Object," covers more database management theory and focuses on most of the methods and properties of the `RecordSet` Object.

Working with ADO's *Connection* and *Command* Objects

Chapter 15, "Introducing ActiveX Data Objects," was devoted to the significance of the ActiveX Data Object (ADO) innovation. We hope that you now feel as strongly as we do that ADO changes everything about how Internet programming will evolve and who will be doing most of it. Specifically, we believe that full-scale *n*-tier client/server programming will be adopted widely. Further, we believe that more of this kind of programming will be done by power users than could ever be done with traditional client/server development tools.

Knowing that something incredibly important has come along can be frustrating, though, if you don't know enough about it to get involved in the revolution. This chapter's mission is to ensure that you know which of ADO's dozens of features are the most important and why. The chapter was written for the ASP developer who wants to understand ADO, not merely use it. In Chapter 17, "Working with ADO's *RecordSet* Object," you will see a similar bifurcation: There is more to database programming than throwing code at an application. If you don't know what you're doing, it will be your undoing.

The strategy in this chapter, then, is to cover ADO's key features, the ones you will use all of the time. You might apply to this chapter the old scholastic truism that "Nothing is taught but for example." You will read text that describes the objects and their constituencies and that provides practical examples of how they work, as well.

Finally, in the chapter we use a powerful graphical formalism to model the model. The tools offered are for the developer who not only needs to know how one object works but also how that object affects all other ActiveX Data Objects.

You are about to enter a doorway to a new world on the Web. Many of those who have been on the Internet for some time have been waiting for this moment. Your day has come. ■

Introducing IDEF0, a Modeling Language for ADO

This chapter steps to the next level of complexity in the presentation of ActiveX Data Objects. Because there are three intrinsic objects in ADO, you will learn about the ADO object model from the perspective of each intrinsic object: `Connection`, `Command`, and `RecordSet`. The ADO object model is huge, and the application of it to the various data providers is so rich that to cover it exhaustively would mean writing a separate book.

To make this part of the book as practical as possible, we introduce a specific modeling formalism that is particularly effective at modeling relationships. The ASP documentation discusses each item in the ADO model individually, and there is a place for this. In this chapter, however, we take a different approach. While you literally will see ADO in all its complexity, you will not be overwhelmed by it. The key to making this possible is Integration Definition For Function Modeling (IDEF0).

> **N O T E**   IDEF0 was named by someone in the United States Government. We're at a loss to explain why its acronym doesn't better match its full name, nor can we explain why zero was added (except to distinguish the formalism from other IDEF standards such as IDEF1X). ■

IDEF0 is the public domain version of a graphical formalism developed by Doug Ross and his crew at SoftTech, Inc. in the '70s. In this section, you learn the handful of key points needed before you can fully utilize this powerful modeling tool.

ON THE WEB

http://nemo.ncsi.nist.gov/idef/standsp/idef0.html   The complete documentation for IDEF0 can be found at this Web site.

> **N O T E**   The IDEF0 diagrams in this chapter were created with Visio 4.1, using stencils and templates that we developed specifically for IDEF0. The Visio models are interactive; that is, you can double-click various parts of the diagrams to navigate their hierarchical structure. Further details are available on the 4GWeb site. ■

Selecting a Frame of Reference

The first thing that IDEF0 does is constrain a system to a well-defined frame of reference. The primary means to this end is in carefully selecting the system activities that are key to the person the model is meant to serve. You can see from the activities depicted in Figure 16.1 (namely, the labels of each box) that the model is built to serve the ASP developer, not the user.

FIG. 16.1

This overview of ADO provides the reader with a visual frame of reference.

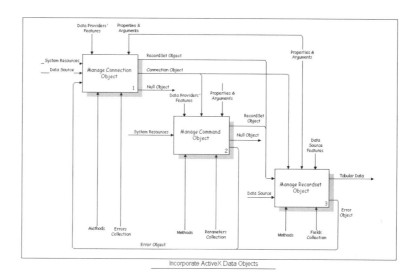

Incorporate ActiveX Data Objects

The Components of an IDEF0 Model

After the activities are specified, IDEF0's second most important feature is its identification of the *constraints* controlling those activities. Figure 16.1, these constraints are depicted by arrows entering from the top of each box. Constraints are like inputs, except they always contain information necessary to properly complete the activity.

> **N O T E** All activity boxes must have at least one constraint. Be careful to properly model each input to an activity: If the input contains information or instructions, the input is a constraint; otherwise, it is merely an input.

Simple inputs to activity boxes, such as data, are depicted in Figure 16.1 as arrows entering from the left. A specification such as HTTP/1.0, on the other hand, is data, too, but HTTP/1.0 is also a protocol. For that reason, HTTP/1.0 is a constraint, and form data is an input. Recordsets are considered input. However, the CursorType is a property and is therefore a constraint, not an input.

Arrows leaving the activity box from the right represent outputs. As with the inputs, they tend to be things. Outputs can be inputs to other boxes or can be constraints, depending on their nature. Outputs also can be inputs to the same activity, though this is rare. In ADO, outputs often are objects; for example, an intrinsic object such as a `Connection`, `Command`, or `RecordSet` or an implicit object such as `Error`, `Parameter`, or `Field`.

Arrows entering an activity box from below are called *mechanisms* and are anything that helps you complete an activity. In ADO, this most often is a method or a collection.

IDEF0 Models Heirarchy

The final important point about IDEF0 is that it is hierarchical; that is, each box can be further refined in its own box in a separate diagram. You will see this feature in action throughout the chapter. Wherever there is a shaded box, it means that there is at least one more level to explore. As an exercise, study these boxes, moving into ever greater detail; all the arrows at an upper level also must appear (with new ones, as well) on lower levels. This way, you leave no details behind as you move into greater complexity.

That's all you need to know to start using the IDEF0 methodology. There is, of course, more to say about the technique, but that's beyond the scope of this book.

Managing *Connection* Objects

You gain access to ActiveX Data Objects through the Database Access component and gain access to the constants used by ADO through the adovbs.inc file. Between the two, you won't believe what you can do on a Web page!

 TIP Each file that needs access to constants needs to include the adovbs.inc file. If you use a text editor that permits creating templates, add the #INCLUDE directive to the top of your ADO template.

The adovbs.inc file is stored in \inetpub\aspsamp\samples\ directory when IIS 3.0 is installed. You might find it helpful to make a copy of this file in either your own application directory or the subdirectory off it where you store your include files. If you left it in the installed directory, the syntax for including the constants file would look like this:

`<!--#INCLUDE VIRTUAL="/ASPSAMP/SAMPLES/ADOVBS.INC"➡`

As you can see from Figure 16.1, ADO consists of three intrinsic objects; that is, an object that must be created outside itself. `Connection`, `Command`, and `RecordSet` all are instantiated with the `Server.CreateObject` method (the only ADO objects that are). All other ADO objects are created from these three primary ones. Refer to the "Methods" label entering each box in Figure 16.1. When you go down a level in the diagrams for each of those boxes, as in Figure 16.2, for example, you see the actual `Server.CreateObject` statement that you will use to create each of these intrinsic ADO objects.

FIG. 16.2

These are the activities necessary to manage Connection Objects.

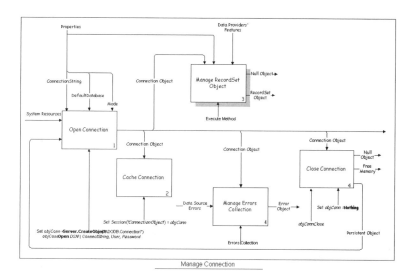

Creating and Maintaining *Connection* Objects

As Figure 16.2 shows, there isn't a lot going on with the Connection Object. There basically are three activities: creating and maintaining Connection Objects, using them to manage RecordSet Objects, and managing errors.

N O T E Notice a few typographical conventions used in all the IDEFO diagrams in this book. Italicized characters are given as examples; you can use any characters or conventions you prefer. Bold characters highlight the reserved words used by ADO. Normal text is used for literals. ▪

Variable Naming: In Matters of Style, There is No Argument

Variable-naming is always a matter of personal style. We happen to appreciate the extra information contained in a variable named objConn, for example; it serves as a reminder that this is both an object variable and a Connection Object. Should you need to give this variable a value, you likely would remember to use the Set statement to do so, because you know that the variable is an object.

In other places, we use txtWho to identify a text box control and to create its counterpart, strWho, to identify the memory variable that we use to test and set the default value of the form control.

The point is to take the time to think about your variables. Einstein once said that "A well-phrased problem is half answered." Likewise, a well-named variable is half self-documented. (If it's good enough for Albert, it's good enough for us.)

For those who want to argue about such matters, remember something else the ancients taught: *De gustibus non disputandum est*—in matters of taste, there is no argument.

Part

IV

Ch

16

Creating the *Connection* Object   Think of the `Connection` Object in the context of a phone conversation. When you want to make a call, you lift the receiver, perhaps push a button, and then wait for a dial tone. Once you hear that tone, you enter the address—oops, phone number—of the person—or machine—with whom you want to talk. Pretty simple. The `Connection` Object isn't much more complicated than that.

The first step, then, is to get your "dial tone." The `Server` Object and its `CreateObject` method provide this dial tone. Look in the lower-left corner of Figure 16.2, where the statement listed is the following:

```
Set objConn = Server.CreateObject("ADODB.Connection")
```

Once the Connection Object has been instantiated on the server and you have your dial tone, the object must obtain a value. This value is retrieved from a given Data Source Name (DSN). Recall from Chapter 2, "Understanding Windows NT and Internet Information Server," that you need to tell the operating system how to connect to an ODBC data source, and you must give the operating system a System DSN identity.

N O T E   Remember that ASP expects a System DSN, not a User DSN or a File DSN. What's the difference? As the name implies, a System DSN is available to all users on the NT Server, including NT System Services (such as ADO). Only you or your machine, however, can access User DSNs. Finally, a File DSN tells anyone with the same drivers installed how to access any given ODBC data source. ▪

At this point, you have a couple of choices: Refer to an installed DSN by name, or use a detailed connection string. In either case, you give the `Connection` Object its most important property, `ConnectionString`. This property is like a phone number. Without it, all you get is a dial tone. With it, you can talk to any database on the Internet (well, almost).

Maintaining Connections with *Application* and *Session* Objects   The most popular thing to do with `Connection` Objects is store them as `Application` Object or `Session` Object properties. This has the same effect as something called "connection pooling," but as you will see at the end of this section, scoping connections is not as efficient as connection pooling. At any rate, the easy part of scoping properties is creating the property itself. The hard part is deciding when and where to create it and how to check if the property currently exists.

First, see how easy it is to set a `Session` property? This example came out the source code from Figure 16.2:

```
Set Session("ConnectionObject") = objConn
```

N O T E   Because it's so easy to forget, we wanted to remind you again: Use the `Set` statement when assigning values to object variables. ▪

Now let's review some of the issues to keep in mind when you set properties this way. First, how should you scope this property: at `Application` scope or `Session` scope?

`Application` scope means that one instance of an object or property is stored in the `Application` Object and is available to all sessions currently running. `Session` scope means that each ASP session has its own copy of whatever was cached.

When making decisions like this one, it's important to remember that as soon as you create these properties, you turn your ASP application into a database—even if you don't use any ActiveX Data Objects. For example, if you choose to give your property `Application` scope, you introduce a type of issue that database programmers have to worry about: concurrency.

Concurrency issues are managed with locking mechanisms in databases, and so it is with `Application` Object properties. When anyone needs to access that property, the server must use the `Application` Object's `Lock` and `Unlock` methods. Otherwise, someone can change the property before or after access and introduce the threat of unexpected outcomes into your code.

Part

IV

Ch

16

Threading Models and Scoping Properties

Another concurrency issue applies to an instance of a component's object stored with `Application` scope; i.e., stored on the `Application` Object. Remember that the `Application` Object can be accessed by more than one user at a time; that is, accessed concurrently. Only one user, on the other hand, may use `Session` Objects, though there may be many simultaneous instances of the `Session` Object in the Active Server's memory at one time. The terms simultaneous and concurrent are not synonymous. If you don't keep the distinction straight, you will probably be confused by any discussion of threading models, such as the one you are in the middle of right now.

Okay, for an instance of a component object to be granted `Application` scope, it must be marked in the Windows Registry as *Both*, meaning such ActiveX objects can be used in either apartment-threaded or free-threaded modes. Objects marked Both permit access to the object by more than one thread, protect their data from thread collisions, and do not contain thread-specific data. By the way, collisions are what component threading and database management have in common. Single-threaded and apartment-threaded models can only be accessed by a single thread—something inconsistent with a multi-user environment like Active Server Pages with concurrent accesses to a single `Application` Object. So, if your component was created using either single-threaded or apartment-threaded models (and Visual Basic 4.0 components all are single-threaded), they cannot obtain `Application` scope at all.

The final issue to think about when scoping components is whether you need access to the server's built-in ASP objects (namely, `Response`, `Request`, and `Server`). This access is gained through pointers to interfaces exposed by these objects whenever someone requests the page that your component is on. The `OnStartPage` and `OnEndPage` events don't fire for objects with `Application` scope. `OnStartPage` and `OnEndPage` are special methods that ASP calls when an object is created on a page.

Scoping your objects to the level of the `Application` Object might look inviting, because there's only one instance of it, regardless of how many sessions are running concurrently; still, you cannot make this decision with impunity. Again, you must *understand* Active Server Pages (and ActiveX Data Objects) to effectively build applications that meet your needs.

You might have noticed that this discussion of scoping has focused on the `Application` Object. The reason is that this object is more tempting than the `Session` Object, and the consequences of cavalier use are more pernicious. By comparison, the `Session` Object is less problematic. However, like the Sirens of Odysseus, you must be wary of their allure.

The problem with caching database connections is that most of the time a user is on a page, the connection to the database is idle. That is, the `Connection` Object is needed to populate a recordset on the Active Server for the user, and one is needed to update the recordset in the event of an appended or deleted record or edited fields. The rest of the time, the `Connection` Object isn't necessary.

It's one thing to persist a recordset in a `Session` Object so that the user's data moves through all the pages of the application as the user moves. The `Connection` Object need not move too. Use the `Session` Object to cache recordsets; don't use it to cache the `Connection` Object (unless you're designing a low traffic intranet). Use "connection pooling" instead.

Pooling Your Resources   When the Active Server is installed on your computer, version 3.0 of the ODBC manager is installed as well. One of the key features of this version of ODBC is something called "connection pooling." Connection pooling means that open database connections in all sessions are managed in a pool. If a session's connection is idle for longer than 60 seconds, it is closed automatically. Before a new connection is opened, the pool of connections is checked for a temporarily idle connection first. If one is found, it is used. This strategy can have a dramatic improvement on throughput of the application.

N O T E   Connection pooling is disabled by default. To turn it on, change the registry entry
`StartConnectionPool` to 1. ■

> **CAUTION**
>
> Use extreme care when modifying the Windows Registry. If you make a mistake you run the risk of disabling your computer. If you have recently made an emergency backup disk for Windows NT or Windows 95, then you can always restore your system after such a disaster. You have made the emergency disk lately, haven't you?

> **CAUTION**
>
> If you use Microsoft Access in your ASP applications, be sure to install Windows NT Service Pack 2 (SP2) *before* you enable connection pooling. If you don't, you might crash your system when you shut down IIS. If the only database you use is SQL Server, then you can ignore this caution.

N O T E   You can tell which Service Pack is currently installed by looking at the first line you see on
the blue screen when Windows NT first boots. ■

To implement connection pooling, we recommend you store the `ConnectionString` property of the `Connection` Object in the `Session` Object. Since this property is itself a simple string, there is no harm in making it persistent in this manner.

First, in the `global.asa` file, assign the connection string to the `Session` Object in the `Session_OnStart` event handler. As an example (use your own values for the `ConnectionString` arguments):

```
Session("ConnectionString")="DSN=MyDSN;UID=master;PWD=slave"
```

Each .asp file that needs to access this database needs to have something like the following line in it:

```
<OBJECT RUNAT=Server ID=objConn PROGID="ADODB.Connection"></OBJECT>
```

You can also use the alternative syntax

```
Set objConn =Server.CreateObject("ADODB.Connection")
```

You open the `Connection` Object by invoking its `Open` method and passing the `Session` property you set previously as its only argument.

```
objConn.Open Session("ConnectionString")
```

N O T E We also recommend that you do not store an instance of the Database Access component in the `Session` Object. Instantiate it from each page separately. In this way, you can avoid the threading issues discussed earlier. If you must persist the component, and you *never* use Microsoft Access, however, then be sure you mark the threading model for ADO to *both* in the Windows Registry.

The safer bet is to use connection pooling as described in this section. ▨

Closing Connections

Closing a `Connection` Object does not destroy the object any more than hanging up the phone means you cannot turn right around and make another call. There are two reasons for using the `Close` method on a `Connection` Object.

First, if you are using connection pooling (described in the previous section), close the connection at the end of each page. Remember that ODBC will close your connection for you if it is idle for 60 seconds. After the recordset you need is fetched, often you can close your connection until you need to update or change the underlying database table.

The second reason for using the `Close` method is that those properties that are writeable are writeable only when the `Connection` Object is closed. Again, it's exactly the same for phone calls: All you get when you dial another number when you already have a listener on the other end is an irritated listener.

If you need to free up system resources and memory, and if you're sure you won't be needing the `Connection` Object (or `Command` and `RecordSet` Objects that may be attached to the connection), you can do so by setting the `Connection` Object to `Nothing`.

When you call the `Close` method on a `Connection` Object, its `ActiveConnection` property (and the `ActiveConnection` property of any `RecordSet` Object that uses the connection) becomes null, any parameters collection is emptied, and fields may lose data or report an error. Table 16.1 summarizes what happens to `Command` and `RecordSet` Objects when you tweak the `Connection` Object.

Table 16.1 Consequences of Closing Connections

Object	Property	Status	Comment
Command	ActiveConnection	Null	The `Command` Object persists but is dissociated with any `Connection` Object.
Parameter	All	Collection is emptied	If `ActiveConnection` is changed from one open `Connection` Object to another, the `Parameters` collection remains intact.
RecordSet	ActiveConnection	Null	Data and exclusive access are released.
Field	Value	Error (during immediate updates)	Call `Update` method before `Close`.
Field	Value	Lost (during batch updating)	You can save previous batch edits if you call `Update` before `Close`.

Managing Databases

The designers of ADO did a great job distributing power to each of the three intrinsic ADO objects. The `Connection` Object gets to control a very important function in database management, and this is especially important when it's done on the not-always-reliable Internet (you'll see why in the "Programming By Trial and Error" section). Later in this chapter, you will explore the power of parameters using the `Command` Object.

▶ **See** "Creating *RecordSet* Objects" for more information about the subtle properties of concurrency control, **p. 342**

Taken as a "Gang of Three," ADO is a potent system for database development. Never before in our years of database development have we encountered this degree of power at this level of usability.

Other than transaction methods (which you will learn about in the "Transactions with a Huge Return on Investment" section), how much data management can you do with the Connection Object? As you can see in Figure 16.3, not that much; but then, there are times when that's just enough.

FIG. 16.3

Manage Recordset Objects.

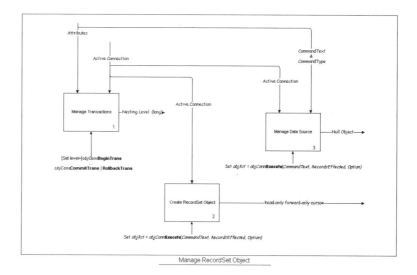

Quick and Dirty Data Retrieval   Using the Connection Object to retrieve a recordset gives you an "economy class" cursor. ADO figures that if you're using only the Connection Object, you aren't very picky about what you want, so you get what you pay for: a read-only, forward-only cursor, sometimes called a *"firehose"* cursor. These little guys are great when you need access to database records but don't need to change their values. With a forward-only cursor, you can move only from the current record to those later in the recordset (unless you cache the records). Therefore, if you need to know what a previous value was, you have to Requery the base table and start over.

▶ **See** "Navigating Among Records" for more information about caching recordsets, **p. 351**

Basic Batch Operations   The Connection Object uses the Execute method to create recordsets and work batch operations such as delete and append on the recordset's base table. The function syntax of the Execute method (e.g., when the method results in a recordset) is:

```
Set objRst=objConn.Execute(CommandText,RecordsAffected,Options)
```

When no result is returned, such as when an action query like an update is executed, use the subroutine syntax:

```
objConn.Execute CommandText,RecordsAffected,Options
```

The difference, of course, is that there is no Set statement and no parentheses, just like a VBScript subroutine.

The three arguments are simple. The CommandText argument is where you pass the SQL statement to the Execute method. The second argument is a variable whose value the data provider returns. In the case of the function syntax, this value is always –1. The Sub syntax is more interesting; the data provider returns the numbers affected by the batch operation. After calling the Execute method, refer to this value to ensure something happened, or the expected number of records were affected. The final argument helps squeeze the last bit of performance from this method. Select from the options in Table 16.2 to help the data provider find the fastest way to implement the Execute CommandText.

Table 16.2 Options for the *Execute* Method, Called by a *Connection* or *Command* Object

Value	Constant	CommandText is:
1	adCmdText	textual
2	adCmdTable	a table name
4	adCmdStoredProc	a stored procedure or querydef
8	adCmdUnknown	unknown; data provider resolves identity

N O T E These Option argument values apply to the Execute method when invoked by the Command Object, as well. ■

Performance is Everything

Using the Option argument in the Execute method is very important with the Connection Object—perhaps even more so than with its more powerful cousins, Command and RecordSet Objects—if you want maximum performance from your query or stored procedure.

Both queries and stored procedures are compiled by the data provider and optimized in the process. When you use the Option argument to tell the provider that the CommandText argument is either a query or a stored procedure you shave a few milliseconds off the processing time. Remember what the good Senator said: "A [millisecond] here, a [millisecond] there, and pretty soon, you're talking about real [time]!"

On the other hand, if you have to embed parameters in the CommandText argument, you give up performance, because you're sending raw, uncompiled text to the data provider. Still, in a world where a second is like a thousand years, telling the provider that a SQL string is coming saves it the time of figuring that out for itself.

Programming by Trial and Error

The Connection Object collects errors. This makes sense, because all access to the data provider is through the Connection Object, and it's the data provider that returns the errors in the first place. In each of the IDEF0 models, you probably will see at least one activity that outputs an `Error` object. We take editorial license with that, intentionally sending you to the "Roadmap" documentation (that was copied to your system when you installed Active Server Pages) to find out under what circumstances you create the error.

In Chapter 9, "Calling Procedures: Functions and Subroutines," you saw the basic error-handling mechanisms provided by VBScript. Nothing's different in ADO; you're still limited in what you can do when an error occurs. What ADO does give you is a rich `Errors` collection that helps you pinpoint what went wrong and why.

A Note from the Authors

Many years ago, one of this book's authors made a trip to a small community outside Saint Charles, Illinois, to perform a rite of passage. Every member of the Arthur Andersen & Company's Management Information Consulting Group had to prove his or her mettle at Computer Fundamentals School (not to learn about disk drives and keyboards, to learn IBM's Assembler language).

There are two things the author never will forget about that experience. The first is that, because the students used an IBM mainframe in those days (1980–1981), they ran their Assembler programs from punch cards. Processing cycles were so precious that students weren't allowed to develop their assigned payroll program using the venerable method of trial and error.

The second thing is that each student's program had to match the answer key, byte for byte—you worked on your code till there wasn't a single error left. A blank, a zero-length string, and `Null` all were different; in the answer key, only one was correct.

For warhorses like this author, ADO's `Errors` collection is more than extremely useful—it's liberating, as well. We will hazard a guess that most readers of this book have never programmed with punch cards. This vignette underscores the value of modern technology, especially debugging features—something we all (including the warhorses) tend to take for granted.

Before getting into the ADO `Errors` collection, be aware that there are several kinds of errors. VBScript returns either *compile-time errors* or *run-time errors*. You see compile-time errors when you execute any errant Visual Basic scripts. The ASP page tells you that the error is a compile-time error and halts the program. You also can tell it's a compile-time error if your ASP page uses a background color, because then you won't see that color. Instead, the code halts and is displayed with a little marker indicating where you need to look.

Run-time errors, on the other hand, run the .asp source code until the errant line is attempted. Again, the compiler will display hints about the problem. For example, here's our favorite: If you try to use the `Object` tag to instantiate a `Connection` Object with `Session` scope in your .asp file, here's what the compiler will display:

```
Active Server Pages error 'ASP0121'

Invalid Scope in object tag

/lab/_error.ASP, line 1
```

The object instance `objConn` cannot have `Application` or `Session` scope. To create the object instance with `Application` or `Session` scope, place the `Object` tag in the Global.asa file.

ADO errors, however, are the only ones collected in the Errors collection. That is, only errors *returned by a data provider* trigger the ADO Error collection system. Other errors, including some errors sent by the ADODB component, are handled by the compiler or the Visual Basic Err object. The unique thing about ADO errors is that the collection can have more than one Error object in the Errors collection. These multiple errors are created by the data provider. Multiple errors can be much more helpful in tracking down complex database management errors.

ON THE WEB

http://www.quecorp.com/asp   Enumerating the Errors collection is like enumerating the other collections you have encountered in this book. An example code snippet is taken from ch16.asp (available for download from this book's Web site) and shown in Listing 16.1.

Listing 16.1   ch16.asp—Enumerating the *Errors* Collection

```
If objConn.Errors.Count > 0 Then
    For each error in objConn.Errors
        Response.Write("Error Nr: " & Error.Number &"<BR>")
        Response.Write(Error.Description & "<BR>")
        Response.Write("Source: " & Error.Source & "<P>")
    Next
End If
```

Transactions with a Huge Return on Investment

Transactions are a big thing in the database world, and if Microsoft's Transaction Server is a success, they're going to get bigger. We leave the high-tech transaction stuff to another book. In ADO, as in DAO before it, transactions can make an enormous difference in performance.

Several years ago, one of this book's authors incorporated database transactions into the Retirement Capital Modeling software he built with Access. He shaved an order of magnitude off the processing time; that made it ten times faster.

Even more amazing, he had to add only a couple of lines of code to his existing module. Listing 16.2 borrows a little from Listing 16.1 and adds three statements of its own. Essentially, that's all there is to implementing database transactions.

Listing 16.2   ch16.asp—Adding Transaction Processing

```
objConn.BeginTrans
[database processing]
If objConn.Errors.Count = 0 Then
    objConn.CommitTrans
Else
    objConn.RollbackTrans
End If
```

What accounts for this easily tapped power? RAM is faster than the hard drive. When a transaction is pending, any disk I/O is suspended until a `CommitTrans` method is invoked. Should there be an error, the `RollbackTrans` method puts any changes back in their original state and ends the transaction. As long as the transaction is open, the disk is buffered by memory.

> **N O T E** In Listing 16.2, [`database processing`] (the second line) is where you insert your normal ADO code. Because you already may have such code written, you might want to think of transaction code as a wrapper around your routine database programming. This emphasizes the fact that you can retrofit nearly all your database access commands with transactions and see an immediate increase in performance. This increase will be especially impressive when your code is like the code that we originally started using transactions to improve: writing a temporary table to disk. The bigger the table, the better the performance.

The `Attributes` property of the `Connection` Object effects what happens after the transaction is closed. If the `Attributes` property is set to `adXactCommitRetaining`, ADO automatically starts another transaction after the `CommitTrans` method is finished. The same thing happens after a `RollbackTrans` method is done, if the `Attributes` property is set to `adXactAbortRetaining`. The bottom line on database transactions—you won't get better bang for your ADO buck with anything else.

Utilizing *Command* Objects to Their Full Potential

The next object in the ADO "Gang of Three" is the `Command` Object. As with the other two intrinsic objects, you create instances of the `Command` Object with a call to the ADO `Server` Object:

```
Set objCmd = Server.CreateObject("ADODB.Command")
```

The `Command` Object was created to optimize performance of queries and stored procedures, especially when parameters are used. After you get the hang of the `Parameters` collection, you never will go back to hassling with embedded parameters in SQL strings. Now see what else you can do with the `Command` Object.

Opening Connections

One of ADO's more interesting innovations is that it has abandoned a strict adherence to object hierarchy. If you have come to ADO from Microsoft Access, you know that you had to instantiate a database object before you could instantiate a `QueryDef` or a `RecordSet` Object. With ADO, this no longer is required. One of the benefits of this design policy is that your ADO programs are thinner than their DAO relatives—they contain a little less code. This is most obvious when the `Command` Object and `RecordSet` Object create their own `Connection` Object; for example, when the `ActiveConnection` property is assigned to the `Command` Object and during the `Open` method for the `RecordSet` Object.

Figure 16.4 gives you an overview of the Command Object. Refer to Figure 16.1 to see how the Command Object fits in with the other three intrinsic ADO objects. In this section, you learn about the first two boxes in Figure 16.4. The section "Opening Recordsets" drills down into box 3 of Figure 16.4 (this will be "Node A123," and it renders the detail of box 3 in Figure 16.4).

FIG. 16.4

Managing Command Objects.

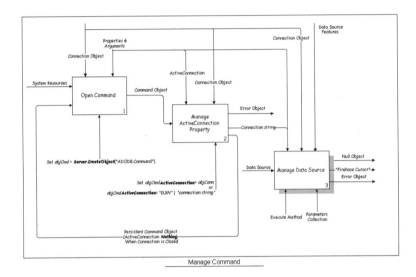

Now take a closer look at how to get a Command Object ready to create a recordset or otherwise operate on a base table (for example, update or delete records, modify table structures, and so on).

With *Connection* Objects   In the previous section, "Managing *Connection* Objects," you saw how a Connection Object was created and the advantages to creating persistent Connection Objects. If you want to take advantage of these features, merely assign the Connection Object to the ActiveConnection property of the newly created Command Object, like this:

```
Set objCmd.ActiveConnection = objConn
```

Next, tell the Command Object where the SQL statement is. You can use a simple table name (to fetch all the records of the table), a query name (which is important when this section discusses parameters), or a raw SQL string (when you use the INSERT INTO statement). For present purposes, use a parameterized query:

```
objCmd.CommandText="qryPhoneMessagesFor"
```

That's all there is to setting up a Command Object. After you next see a comparison of Connection Objects to connection strings, you will learn that getting the Command Object to do something useful remains fairly straightforward.

Without *Connection* Objects   If you don't need the overhead of a cached, persistent `Connec-tion` Object, ADO permits you to create a `Command` Object with a private `Connection` Object. The first of three options to create a new `Connection` Object is to assign the `ActiveConnection` property a DSN; the second option uses a connection string. The advantage of the latter is that you can override the default values in the DSN. The third option permits you to create a DSN "on-the-fly."

Here's the first version:

```
objCmd.ActiveConnection ="intranet"
```

Here's the second alternative, a connection string that specifies the arguments for the new connection:

```
objCmd.ActiveConnection ="dsn=intranet; database=intranet;uid=sa;pwd=;"
```

N O T E   Note the use of semicolons in the preceding line of code. When ADO sees the equal signs in the string, it knows that a connection string—and not a DSN—is being used. You don't use the `Set` statement when you use your own private `Connection` Object, because the object hasn't yet been created; it's implicit in the use of the connection string. That is, when ADO sees the connection string, it creates a new `Connection` Object on its own. You don't have to tell it to do so with the `Set` statement. ▨

And finally, here's the real trick: a DSN with no muss, no fuss:

```
objCmd.ActiveConnection="DRIVER={Microsoft Access Driver (*.mdb)};
➥ DBQ=c:\data\lab\intranet.mdb"
```

 T I P   If you are programming in a large shop and you're not the system administrator, using this last alternative enables you to get to a database without troubling the network administrator for a hard-wired DSN.

Okay, ADO understands where the data provider is and how to connect to it, as well as what you want to do with the data stored in that location. Now how do you activate this command? The answer is in the following section.

Opening *RecordSets*

The `RecordSet` Object is the ADO "workshop." You get nearly all of your database manage-ment tasks accomplished there. However, when your objective is not to retrieve data but in-stead to directly modify it or modify its structure, a recordset is not returned from the data provider. In this case, a `Null` object reference is returned along with any `Error` objects, should an error occur during command execution.

Figure 16.5 shows the overview of these scenarios and how each plays out in turn. Even though the "Manage Parameters" activity box appears first in the diagram, it is discussed last. As you will see, there's a good reason for this delay. When you're finished reading this chapter, you also will appreciate why "Manage Parameters" appears first in Figure 16.5.

FIG. 16.5

Manage recordsets with
Command Objects.

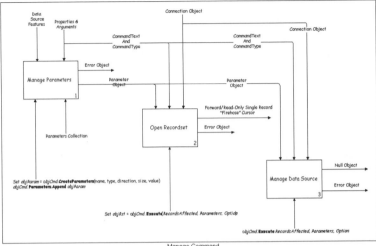

Manage Command

Returning Cursors   Cursors represent records stored in base tables. They are like shadows of data—not the real thing but nonexistent without the real thing. Likening a cursor to a shadow, however, presents only a partially accurate metaphor. It highlights (pun intended) the fact that, in a sense, cursors are separate from data, but while shadows are two-dimensional, cursors come in many varieties.

We give an in-depth discussion of concurrency issues in Chapter 17, "Working with ADO's *RecordSet* Object." For the moment, we stratify cursor types into two layers: safe and risky. Safe cursors do not permit changes, so concurrency issues are moot. Risky cursors are those in which more than one user can access or change the same underlying base table record at the same time. That is, when two different cursors represent the same real record, and when these two cursors can be used to change the real data stored in that real record, you run the risk of conflicting changes to data.

Both the Connection Object and the Command Object produce safe cursors. If you try to change a record in one of these cursors, you get an error. So what good are these cursors?

They excel at displaying base table data. Because Web pages originally were read-only, routinely using this kind of cursor was fine. With the advent of ADO, Web pages now are capable of all the dynamic features of desktop applications. If you stick to intrinsic controls on ADO-enabled Web pages, you still are fairly safe using the safe cursors of Connection Objects and Command Objects. Remember this, though: safe cursors do not lock records; they merely fetch data in the state it's in at the instant that it is accessed. The data is subject to change by other users while being viewed by one user, without that user knowing of the modifications. This particular process goes by the rather earthy description of "dirty reads."

This isn't a serious problem, just something to be careful about. Perhaps nothing more than a warning to users that the data they are viewing is subject to change is all that's necessary to minimize confusion. Indeed, viewers might need to make changes themselves. This is where the RecordSet Object comes in handy.

For now, remember that safe cursors are made for displaying data. Connection Objects do it with minimal code and are extremely useful when you want to see everything in a table. The Command Object is more flexible, because it can handle parameters with ease, and you can optimize Command Object performance by minimizing the amount of "conversation" between the data provider and the ASP program. You'll see the details of this optimization in the section "Using Parameters."

Part
IV
Ch
16

You create a RecordSet Object (using a Command Object to access a compiled query or stored procedure that does not need parameters) with a statement like the one shown here:

```
Set objRst = objCmd.Execute(RecordsAffected,,adCmdStoredProc)
```

Operating on Tables Without Cursors   When you need to execute a batch operation on data or to modify the structure of tables in a database, the Command Object is really in its element. Here, none of the issues surrounding concurrency plague you. The data provider manages the only locking issues that arise due to your changing data. You don't even have access to the CursorType and LockType properties when you execute action queries.

To execute batch operations with the Command Object, there are two places where you need to make changes: at the data provider (to set up queries or stored procedures) and in ADO (to configure the Command Object and its Parameters collection, if necessary). You're on your own when it comes to exactly what to do in your data provider to create the query or stored procedure. After you create the query or stored procedure, you need its name and parameter information when you create the Command Object and Parameters collection in ADO.

 TIP   It's all too easy to misspell long query or stored procedure names. After creating ours, we go to the object and select the Rename option. Then we copy the file name to the Clipboard and cancel the Rename operation. Back in ADO, we merely paste the name in the appropriate place in the source code and eliminate the occurrence of this all too common error message: "Invalid SQL statement."

After all of the housekeeping is done at the data provider, you need to inform ADO of the details. In the case of a simple query or stored procedure, all you need to do is set the CommandText property to the name of the query that you created in your data provider. For example:

```
objCmd.CommandText="qryPhoneMessages"
```

At this point, all that's left is to execute the query. The general syntax of the Execute method when invoked by the Command Object for batch operations (without parameters) is the following:

```
objCmd.Execute RecordsAffected,,adCmdStoredProc
```

Adding the two arguments, RecordsAffected and adCmdStoredProc, takes no time to complete. If you use an editor like HomeSite, you can create keyboard macros that do your typing for you. For the marginal effort, the RecordsAffected and adCmdStoredProc arguments give you both information (in the RecordsAffected variable that is returned by the data provider) and performance (by instructing the data provider to look for a query or stored procedure) in exchange.

ON THE WEB

http://www.dexnet.com/homesite.html   You can download a shareware version of HomeSite from this Web site.

The RecordsAffected argument is a long variable that tells you how many records were affected by the command. This can be very helpful to your user, and if zero is returned as an unexpected result, you might want to explore the reason. The adCmdStoredProc argument simply informs the data provider that the named query or stored procedure is a query or stored procedure. Without this information, the data provider needs to take the time to find the name.

> **N O T E** We have noticed that when we use the arguments in the Execute method, we may get slightly more lucid error messages from our data provider than at other times. This makes sense, because we took the time to help the data provider look for the object. ■

Passing the adCmdStoredProc argument in the Execute method is kind of like including your phone number when you leave a message on a friend's answering machine. He knows who you are and may even remember where he keeps your number, but why make him work that hard? Give him the number—and give your data provider the identity (and therefore the location) of your command. This works fine when your batch operations are simple, but what about when you want to update only a few records or fields?

Using *Parameters*

One of the ADO methods that make ADO simple to program is the AddNew method. We recommend that you use this method only when you have a good reason to do so. Instead, we suggest that you use Command Objects and their Parameters collection.

Remember a motto of this book: *De gustibus non disputandum est* (in matters of taste, there is no argument). When we offer a personal stylistic preference, don't assume it's the only way to do things.

The *Parameters* Collection   If you retrace the hierarchical path from Figure 16.2 to Figure 16.3, you see that the Parameters collection belongs to the Command Object, so any reference to this collection must be preceded by the object variable assigned to the appropriate Command Object (again, our favorite is objCmd).

Because you just created a query or stored procedure in your data provider, all the `Parameter` metadata is stored there. To populate the `Parameter` collection of the `Command` Object, you have two choices: interrogate the data provider (assuming that it can hear you and can respond—Microsoft Access can't; SQL Server can) or hardwire the metadata into your .asp code yourself.

We recommend that you choose the latter. The `Refresh` method of the `Parameters` collection interrogates a data provider at runtime, but you should use the `objCmd.CreateParameter` method, instead. You'll see why at the end of this section.

> **N O T E** You can let ADO interrogate the data provider at runtime, but this usually is a waste of time because query and stored-procedure designs tend to be static. There's a compromise between sloth (relying on run-time interrogation) and working too hard at design time (especially if there's a long lag between designing a query and using it in ADO code, i.e., if the lag is long enough to have forgotten how the query was designed). Create an Active Server custom component that interrogates the data provider at design time and reports the latest facts about the data provider's object. Not surprisingly, these are called design-time controls.

Actually, the `objCmd.CreateParameter` method is one of a pair of twins. Its counterpart is the `objCmd.Parameters.Append` method. We prefer keeping each of the two on its own line. Look closely at Listing 16.3 for the specifics of this coding strategy.

> **T I P** Another matter of taste is selection of a text editor. Our hands-down favorite is Nick Bradbury's HomeSite, version 2.0.
>
> Our number one favorite feature is HomeSite's capability to store keystrokes in toolbar buttons. We have a slew of macros. Perhaps the most productive is the one that generated Listing 16.3.

Listing 16.3 CH16ACTION.ASP—Creating and Appending a Parameter to a *Command* Object's Parameters Collection

```
' Begin parameter configuration...
strName="whom" 'enter name of parameter
lngDirection=adParamInputlngType =adVarChar
lngSize = 3 ' enter string length or else remove it from argument list
varValue = "mpc" 'enter parameter value
Set objParam = objCmd.CreateParameter(strName, lngType, lngDirection,
➥lngSize, varValue)
' ...end parameter configuration.

objCmd.Parameters.Append objParam
```

Notice again how picky we are about naming variables. The variable names include their type, and the constants selected are either default (for example, `adParamInput`) or most common (for example, `adVarChar`). The advantage of this technique is that you don't have to worry about the argument list in the `CreateParameter` method. The single exception is when you are not using a parameter that requires a `Size` argument (for example, `adInteger`); in that case, you need to delete the `lngSize` argument from the list (you can leave the memory variable alone, though).

Table 16.3 was taken from the ADO documentation that ships with Active Server Pages. It lists all the permissible values for the `Type` property of the `Parameter` object.

Table 16.3   Constants Available to Define a Parameter's *Type* Property

Constant	Value	Description
adBigInt	20	An 8-byte signed integer
adBinary	128	A binary value
adBoolean	11	A Boolean value
adBSTR	8	A null-terminated character string (Unicode)
adChar	129	A String value
adCurrency	6	A currency value (8-byte signed integer scaled by 10,000)
adDate	7	A date value
adDBDate	133	A date value (*yyyymmdd*)
adDBTime	134	A time value (*hhmmss*)
adDBTimeStamp	135	A date-time stamp (*yyyymmddhhmmss* plus a fraction in billionths)
adDecimal	14	An exact numeric value with a fixed precision and scale
adDouble	5	A double-precision floating point value
adEmpty	0	No value was specified
adError	10	A 32-bit error code
adGUID	72	A globally unique identifier (GUID)
adIDispatch	9	A pointer to an IDispatch interface on an OLE object
adInteger	3	A 4-byte signed integer
adIUnknown	13	A pointer to an IUnknown interface on an OLE object
adLongVarBinary	205	A long binary value (`Parameter` object only)
adLongVarChar	201	A long String value (`Parameter` object only)
adLongVarWChar	203	A long null-terminated String value (`Parameter` object only)

Constant	Value	Description
adNumeric	131	An exact numeric value with a fixed precision and scale
adSingle	4	A single-precision floating point value
adSmallInt	2	A 2-byte signed integer
adTinyInt	16	A 1-byte signed integer
adUnsignedBigInt	21	An 8-byte unsigned integer
adUnsignedInt	19	A 4-byte unsigned integer
adUnsignedSmallInt	18	A 2-byte unsigned integer
adUnsignedTinyInt	17	A 1-byte unsigned integer
adUserDefined	132	A user-defined variable
adVarBinary	204	A binary value (`Parameter` object only)
adVarChar	200	A String value (`Parameter` object only)
adVariant	12	An OLE Automation Variant
adVarWChar	202	A null-terminated Unicode character string (`Parameter` object only)
adWChar	130	A null-terminated Unicode character string

Part

IV

Ch

16

TIP Be sure to use the `#INCLUDE` directive in any .asp file that uses Visual Basic or ADO constants.

"Parsimonious Processing"   Programmers who practically grew up writing desktop applications need to remember to do two things when ADO calls them to the big leagues of client/server programming. First, give the client/server database management system very precise instructions—don't make it waste a nanosecond of its time. Remember, the DBMS is serving perhaps thousands of people at once. Gone are the days when the only database traffic to worry about was between your hard drive and your CPU.

Second, because the DBMS is designed to do all the processing on the server side and sends back to the client only the results of those operations, make sure it sends back the smallest amount of data that will meet your needs.

You might call this "parsimonious processing." When you use a `Command` Object and its `Parameters` collection, you're being as parsimonious as possible—good for you. This might make your programming job a bit more challenging, but you're developing Active Server Pages now. You have arrived. You can do it.

Now take a close look at what happens when you wisely use the `Command` Object but relax your diligence and revert to the `objRst.AddNew` method.

Say that you opened a recordset by referring only to the table name, something like this:

```
Set objRst.Open "tblPhoneMessage", objConn, adOpenDynamic, adLockPessimistic
```

What you did was ask the data provider to produce a cursor as rich as can be, to work as hard as is capable to preclude interference between concurrent accesses. Add to this overhead your request for all the records in the table, just so you can insert one more, and you're an accident waiting to happen.

Discussion of concurrency and isolation levels comes in Chapter 17, "Working with ADO's *RecordSet* Object." At this point, we lobby for an alternative to editing your new record, one field at a time (depicted in Listing 16.4).

Listing 16.4   ch16insert.asp—Using the *AddNew* Method

```
objRst.AddNew
objRst("for")="mpc"
objRst("caller")="katy"
objRst("message")="The check just arrived!"
objRst.Update
```

N O T E   When you see consecutive commas in argument lists, it means the missing argument is optional, and you are skipping it. ▮

Using a `Command` Object (and an abbreviated version of parameter assignment), your code might look like Listing 16.5.

Listing 16.5   ch16insert.asp—Using a *Command* Object and Parameters

```
objCmd.CommandText="INSERT INTO tblPhoneMessage (for, caller, message)
➥VALUES(?,?,?)"

Set objParam=objCmd.CreateParameter(, adVarChar, , Len(strFor), strFor)
objCmd.Parameters.Append objParam
Set objParam=objCmd CreateParameter(, adVarChar, , Len(strCaller),
➥strCaller)
objCmd.Parameters.Append objParam
Set objParam=objCmd.CreateParameter(,adVarChar, , Len(strMessage),
➥strMessage)
objCmd.Parameters.Append objParam

objCmd.Execute RecordsAffected,,adCmdText
```

Using the `Len(variable)` in Listing 16.5 is a shortcut to referring to your database schema for the size of variable-length fields. The risk that you run using this technique is in coming across a string that's longer than the field in the base table. Should this happen, this code raises an error. Besides, using the `Len()` function betrays the message that we have preached throughout this chapter: Know your database schema before you start writing ADO code.

Purists among you, then, will want to hardwire the field length in the fourth argument. You be the judge.

Did you catch the three important differences between Listing 16.5 and Listing 16.3? If you miss any one of them, you'll see errors. Listing 16.5 has the following:

- No Set statement
- No parentheses
- A new constant in the Option argument that now says adCmdText (because you're sending a raw SQL statement to the data provider)

Before our closing argument for parsimonious processing with parameters, here are a few more points to note about Listing 16.5:

- There is no necessary order for the fields at the beginning of the listing (but each field in that list must be a valid field name in the base table).
- There needs to be an equal number of fields and question marks in the VALUE() argument at the end of the CommandText property.
- The order of the CreateParameter Append method pairs will mirror the order of the fields in the CommandText property.

As you can see, precious little server activity is called for using Listing 16.5. You don't have to create a cursor, make repeated INSERT calls to the data provider for each field that you edit, or invoke the Update method. Even your brain takes a rest in Listing 16.5, because you don't have to think about what kind of cursor you want to create or evaluate different record locks.

The data provider handles all of those details with a sagacity that most programmers never will attain. That's why they're called client/server database management systems.

Listing 16.5 comes to the data provider on its terms. The results of this and all other examples of data access covered in this chapter are nothing short of dramatic. You're off to a good start in an ADO programming career, don't you think?

From Here...

This chapter was your first step from Chapter 15, "Introducing ActiveX Data Objects," where you learned about what made ActiveX Data Objects unique and innovative. This chapter also is a bridge to Chapter 17, "Working with ADO's *RecordSet* Object." In this chapter, you concentrated on the contributions that two intrinsic ADO objects, the Connection Object and the Command Object, make to Active Server Pages technology. You saw that ADO was a break with tradition, not adhering to a strict hierarchy of objects. You also learned how to maximize performance using Command Objects and their Parameters collection. You now know that from simple cursors to complex batch operations, Connection Objects and Command Objects can do a lot of work for you.

■ Chapter 17, "Working with ADO's *RecordSet* Object," moves you into the heart of the `RecordSet` Object. You will learn more about concurrency control, about how to create sophisticated cursors, and about how to navigate their records. You will also learn the finer points of adding and deleting records and of batch updates.

■ Chapter 18, "Epilogue: Looking to a Future with Active Server Pages," explores what you might be able to do with something as revolutionary as ADO. Predicting the future might be risky business—or the greater risk may be not being imaginative enough—but ADO is too compelling and exciting to resist trying.

## CHAPTER 17

Working with ADO's *RecordSet* Object

You have almost reached the end of your journey in preparing for Active Server Pages development. After one more topic and a case study, we cut you loose.

In this chapter, you will explore the vast world of the RecordSet Object. Everything in ADO leads you to this place; now you will learn what to do when you get there. Fully 50 percent of the ADO documentation that ships with Active Server Pages is devoted to the RecordSet Object and its collections, methods, and properties. This is not surprising, because that's where all the data is. Sure, you can access limited cursors with the Connection Object and the Command Object, and you've got the Parameter objects. But in all these cases, data is aloof. In this chapter, you will get into the thick of the bits and bytes of your databases. Roll up your shirtsleeves and take a deep breath. ■

Come to terms with concurrency control

Concurrency control is the only database theory you will be exposed to in this book. This is necessary, because an extremely important part of ADO deals explicitly with cursors and certain kinds of cursors create circumstances that harbor potential concurrency conflicts.

Create *RecordSet* Objects, the workhorse of ADO

RecordSet Objects create recordset cursors. Careful creation of recordset cursors is a key performance factor. Learn how to do it properly.

Get around in a recordset

The main advantage of recordsets is that you can wander around in them; you're not limited to a single pass as you are with the Connection Object and the Command Object.

Learn how to manipulate recordsets

Using standard ADO record-manipulation methods can get you up and running quickly. Discover the methods' pros and cons.

Understanding Concurrency Control

One advantage of a well-designed desktop application like Microsoft Access is that it shields the user from most of the really arcane aspects of database management. The most trouble Access ever caused its users was by refusing to update tables accessed with queries that couldn't modify data; for example, when two tables were joined on a field with a one-to-many relationship. In ADO, the developer has a finer level of control over issues normally handled behind the scenes by an application such as Access. But with this new power comes new responsibility, and responsibility is always served by knowledge.

In this section, you delve deeper into database management theory. The result should be an understanding that lets you create recordsets consistent with your needs. Spend a little time here, and you will save a lot of time at your computer. You will understand how cursor types, lock types, and isolation levels all affect your RecordSet Object's behavior.

Learning About Locks

ADO enables you to create robust client/server database applications quickly. By definition, this means that more than one person will have access to your databases at the same time. This feature of client/server systems is called *concurrency*. Concurrent access to data means a large organization can have one repository of data and many people reading and changing it as if they were the sole owner. That is, the database management system assumes responsibility for the accuracy of the data stored in its files. This is a defining difference between manual systems and automated ones. With an increase in power of this order of magnitude come other issues of at least another order of magnitude. Database theory, then, must solve a problem called *interference*.

Interference introduces corruption into your database and delays in data access. Quantum mechanics has its fabled "Uncertainty Principle" (namely, one cannot know the precise position *and* momentum of a subatomic particle at the same time). Database management systems have their own version of this principle: You cannot maximize concurrency and minimize interference at the same time. Unlike physics, however, we have some latitude in our Uncertainty Principle. In physics, you choose one or the other property to observe; in database management, you move between a range of tradeoffs. To the extent that you minimize interference by maximizing locks on database records, you lose some concurrency and, therefore, some performance. To the extent you make the cursors as fast as possible by using no locks at all, you open yourself to the threat of interference. To design ADO applications that meet your expectations with the fewest downstream surprises, you must understand concurrency and interference issues and how they play off one another.

As an ADO developer, you do not have to be concerned with the concurrency control implementation strategy used by your data provider. You do need to know what your options are when you define your RecordSet Object.

Optimistic Locking Some data providers give you, the developer, a major say in how a database application operates. After all, you're the one who understands the operating environment of your application. If your ASP application is running on a small intranet, it's unlikely that concurrency and interference keep you up nights. *Optimistic locking* mechanisms assume that this is true, so database processing continues with updates stored in a temporary buffer until an order to update is given by the user. The base table is locked the instant before the update is applied to its records, and the lock is released immediately after the update succeeds. If there are conflicts (e.g., someone else has a record lock on the record being updated), the transactions are rolled back and the conflicts are resolved separately from further processing.

Sometimes, data providers permit more than one record to be edited at the same time, and the data providers update all records virtually simultaneously. This is like a second layer of concurrency, but it usually raises no additional concurrency issues, because the records usually don't interact with one another. When two people access the same record at the same time, however, this might not be true; for example, one person changes the value of Field B based on the value of Field A, but at the same time, someone else changes Field A.

At any rate, in batch updating, this is not an issue. Under conditions of high concurrency, however, permitting batch updates might aggravate the problem of interference, because one person is changing more than one record at the same time. It's up to you to balance the advantage of increased speed due to batch processing (arising from the relatively lower disk access required for batch updates) with the increased risk of interference.

Pessimistic Locking   Optimistic locking might work well on an intranet, but an application running on the Internet might have thousands of concurrent accesses and edits. To ensure data integrity under these conditions, data processing might need to obtain locks on records as soon as editing begins. Performance might suffer under heavy loads, but if data integrity is important, this might be a price you have to pay. Optimistic locking, by contrast, suffers from none of the problems discussed next.

Care must be exercised when using pessimistic locks. Because whole records, or a 2K page of records in Microsoft Access, are locked before the update occurs, concurrency is seriously curtailed. If there are inordinate delays during the edit process (e.g., someone starts an edit and then goes to lunch before he finishes editing his record) or a catastrophe at the user's end (e.g., a power outage or General Protection Fault), there can be serious consequences to the usability of the affected record(s).

Of course, there are times when all records in a database must be locked pessimistically. You can't have people updating a table when you need to execute a batch operation on the table's records. Table updates such as marking a given field in all records with given value, massive deletes such as removing all records for a departing employee, or any other operation that must look at all records in a file all require this kind of lock. This is usually not a problem because these batch operations usually take only seconds to complete, and such maintenance work is usually scheduled for the least busy hours of the day.

There is one other caveat worth noting about pessimistic locking. On an intranet, database processing is not that much different from traditional client/server processing. Intranets are stateless, but there are relatively few things that interfere with routine HTTP transactions. On the Internet, however, almost anything can happen; and at any given time, somewhere on the network, it is happening. Pessimistic locking in these circumstances is even less attractive on the Internet than it is on intranets.

There is one other issue beyond the threat of network interruption: latency, the natural delays inherent in a packet-switched network. For ADO development, this means that any temporal issues attached to pessimistic locking are heightened when used on the Internet. Until we realize the promise of the all-fiber network, this is a fact of network life.

Understanding Isolation Levels

Strictly speaking, the topic of isolation levels belongs to a discussion of transactions, such as you read about in the "Transactions with a Huge Return on Investment" section of Chapter 16, "Working with ADO's *Connection* and *Command* Objects." Because isolation levels also are related to locking policy, however, we include the topic here. Isolation levels combine lock types with lock duration, and they give tacit recognition to the needs of the cursor.

N O T E You will read more about cursors when you learn about the fine points of opening recordsets in the section, "Creating *RecordSet* Objects." In the context of isolation levels, cursors come into play when the data provider makes transaction decisions that minimize disruption of the data contained in existing cursors during concurrent data access. ▨

An important objective in concurrency control is *serializable interleaved execution.* The term might sound a little pretentious, but it accurately describes what every good database administrator wants to see: two transactions operating on the same data whose individual outcomes leave the other's outcomes unaffected. In other words, the results of concurrent processing were the same as if the two (or more) transactions had been executed serially (instead of concurrently).

There are three kinds of problems that interfere with creating serializable transactions:

- *Dirty Reads*: This is a common problem that results when a transaction is permitted to see changes made by other transactions that have not yet been committed to an update. For example, two users are accessing customer data. Transaction 1 is in the process of updating a customer's address. Before the edit is committed, another user accesses the same customer with Transaction 2 in order to print an invoice. While the invoice is printing, the user of Transaction 1 decides he is on the wrong client so he rolls back the changes to the address. Too late for the user of Transaction 2; they are going to get an angry phone call from a customer who owes them no money but is getting an invoice nonetheless.

- *Nonrepeatable Reads*: This kind of interference is less frequent than dirty reads and, in fact, is the opposite of a dirty read. With a dirty read, there was an edit in process, another use was put to the uncommitted data, and then the transaction was abandoned. With nonrepeatable reads, you look up data, another transaction commits changes to it, and when you look up the data again, it's different. In our previous example, Transaction 1 is working on a new order from a customer. The customer screen shows this customer is very close to her credit limit, but it looks like her current order will be approved.

Transaction 2 comes in and completes another order for the same customer before Transaction 1 can be committed to the database. Transaction 2 has used up all available credit, leaving a problem for the person entering Transaction 1.

■ *Phantom Records*: This kind of error is similar to the one exemplified by the non-repeatable reads example. If a data point is derived from the values of records (as is something like available credit), then you can get into trouble if the number or value of those records changes while a transaction is in process that relies on that recordset being intact and unchanged.

When you create a Connection Object, you also define its level of isolation. If you don't do this explicitly by assigning the value from Table 17.1 to the Connection Object's IsolationLevel property, ADO assigns the constant for you. The default constant is about midrange and is set at adXactCursorStability. This means that transactions processed on a default connection can view changes made on other connections only after those changes have been committed. As the name adXactCursorStability implies, this policy ensures that cursors capable of viewing other cursors (set independently with the CursorType property in the RecordSet Object's Open method) don't change until they need to.

Part

IV

Ch

17

Table 17.1 Isolation Levels

Constant	Value	Description
adXactUnspecified	-1	If the provider is using a different IsolationLevel than specified but which cannot be determined, the property returns this value.
adXactChaos	16	Indicates that you cannot overwrite pending changes from more highly isolated transactions.
adXactBrowse	256	Indicates that from one transaction you can view uncommitted changes in other transactions.
adXactReadUncommitted	256	Same as adXactBrowse.
adXactCursorStability	4096	Indicates that from one transaction you can view changes in other transactions only after they've been committed. (Default.)
adXactReadCommitted	4096	Same as adXactCursorStability.
adXactRepeatableRead	65536	Indicates that from one transaction you cannot see changes made in other transactions, but that requerying can bring new recordsets.
adXactIsolated	1048576	Indicates that transactions are conducted in isolation of other transactions.
adXactSerializable	1048576	Same as adXactIsolated.

N O T E   The information in Table 17.1 was taken from the documentation for the `Supports` method in ADO. This method interrogates the data provider to determine if a given function is supported. Care should be exercised in its use; sometimes support is indicated in general but might fail in particular circumstances. For example, a `RecordSet` Object might support the `Update` method, but the particular update query might not be updatable; e.g., a crosstab query. ■

Other transactions can be made more or less isolated. A personal favorite (due to the avocation of chaos theory) is `adXactChaos`, which is the lowest level of isolation. From here, you can see everything that's going on, but you can change nothing (in more highly isolated transactions). The highest level of isolation is `adXactSerializable`. At this level, your transactions are so isolated (and concurrency is so low) that none of the errors listed previously can occur. This is the most pessimistic kind of locking. (For more information about isolation levels and transactions, see Chapter 10, "Inserting, Updating, and Deleting Rows" in the book, *Special Edition: Using ODBC2,* by Robert Gryphon, et al., beginning on p. 181.)

Creating *RecordSet* Objects

As a point of clarity: Recordsets are merely data; `RecordSet` Objects give us access to data through recordset cursors they create. Strictly speaking, recordsets have no properties and no methods; they are merely data. `RecordSet` Objects, on the other hand, encapsulate data and programming in their properties and methods, respectively.

Recordsets are important for two reasons: They move data from a storage system like Microsoft Access or SQL Server, and they accept changes we make to that data so that the data store can be updated for subsequent use. This seemingly simple functionality masks a complexity with few peers. A Database Management System (DBMS) is among the most complex software systems ever devised. As you can see from our all too brief discussion of concurrency control, there is much that goes on with recordsets that we take for granted.

Figure 17.1, the same figure as Figure 16.1 in Chapter 16, "Working with ADO's *Connection* and *Command* Objects," puts the `RecordSet` Object in context. This chapter is devoted to the activity in box 3 of Figure 17.1, "Manage `RecordSet` Object," and all the children of box 3; viz., all the other activities modeled by the figures in this chapter.

Figure 17.1 depicts the interrelationships between the three primary activities of ADO programming. The inputs to the activity we focus on in this chapter, "Manage `RecordSet` Object," can be either data directly fetched from a data provider, or it can be data marshaled by one or both of the other intrinsic ADO objects, the `Connection` Object or the `Command` Object.

The primary constraints on `RecordSet` Object management are the `Connection` Object and the features present in the data provider. The `Connection` Object is independent of any recordset that might have been created by a `Connection` Object and passed as input to this activity. In terms of constraints, the `Connection` Object tells the `RecordSet` Object we are managing where its data comes from. Data provider feature sets are a constraint to managing `RecordSet` Objects because not all features included in ADO are supported by all data providers.

Implementing `RecordSet` Object management tasks is the function of the object's methods and its only collection, the `Fields` collection. Output is always tabular data. A special kind of data is error data returned by the data provider, and this data is input for the "Manage `Connection` Object" activity in box 1 of Figure 17.1.

FIG. 17.1

The context of managing the *RecordSet* Object is defined by its interaction with the other ActiveX Data Objects.

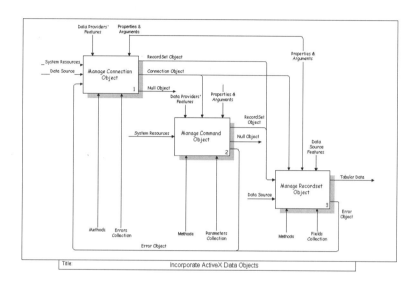

Opening Recordsets

As you can see from Figure 17.2, data provided from a source is packaged as a `RecordSet` Object using the `Server.CreateObject` method. However, if you don't have an open `Connection` Object before you invoke this method, you produce an `Error` object at the data provider. Barring this oversight, you must assign the `Source` and `ActiveConnection` properties with appropriate values, and you might need to override default values of the other properties to produce the kind of cursor that you need. Once the recordset exists, a *tabular* representation of base table data is created for you to edit, browse, and navigate by using user interface controls of your choice.

N O T E   Your choice of data controls has the same implications as all the other choices you face in your Internet development efforts. The same spectrum is there in all cases. For example, once you have a recordset and a cursor, you must choose between the intrinsic HTML FORM controls and HTML TABLEs at one end of the spectrum and data-bound ActiveX controls at the other end. Again, these choices boil down to the primary goal: Reach the broadest audience or provide the richest experience. ▨

N O T E   The tabular nature of the cursor is emphasized because ADO is capable of accessing non-ODBC data, such as text files and e-mail messages. There, semi-structured data stores are not inherently tabular. For ADO's purposes, they must be represented to your ASP application in tabular form. ▨

FIG. 17.2

Manage *RecordSet* Objects.

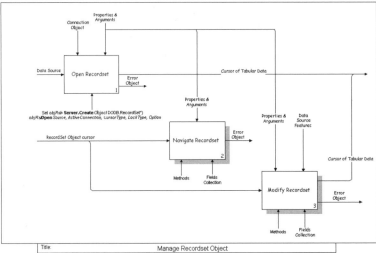

Take a look at Listing 17.1, a code snippet from the Phone Message application available for download from the Working Active Server Pages Web site. The technique used in the listing requires a lot of coding but also makes the code virtually self-documenting. For the purposes of this discussion, it helps highlight important nuances that would be lost in denser code. For example, we deliberately created a rich cursor (i.e., one that you can navigate and can edit with the "firehose" cursor of Chapter 16, "Working with ADO's *Connection* and *Command* Objects") to demonstrate several important features of the RecordSet Object. Had we used more elegant code, you might have missed our specifically choosing a cursor type and lock type that gave us the richness we needed.

Listing 17.1   ch17.asp—Creating a *RecordSet* Object

```
Set objConn = Server.CreateObject("ADODB.Connection")
objConn.Open "intranet"
Response.Write(objConn &"<P>")

Set objCmd = Server.CreateObject("ADODB.Command")
Set objCmd.ActiveConnection = objConn
objCmd.CommandText = "tblPhoneMessage"
objCmd.CommandType = adCmdTable

Set objRst = Server.CreateObject("ADODB.RecordSet")
' Type mismatch if you forget to use the Set statement when assigning
' an object to the Source property
Set objRst.Source = objCmd
objRst.CursorType = adOpenKeyset
objRst.LockType = adLockOptimistic
objRst.Open
```

ON THE WEB

http://www.quecorp.com/asp   You can download the entire Phone Message application from the Active Server Pages Web site.

> **CAUTION**
>
> Remember, if you decide to use a `Command` Object for the `RecordSet` Object's `Source` property, be sure to assign this property a value with the `Set` statement. Failure to do so results in a "Type mismatch" error. (Do we sound like the voice of experience?)

Before we continue with a detailed look at cursors, we must compare them to recordsets. To help clarify the relationship, consider a `Select` query in Microsoft Access. Specifically, when you execute a query in Access, you see as many records as will fit inside the query window. You might see 30 records, but there might be 3,000 records in the recordset. In one sense, the 30 records out of 3,000 available represent the cursor of the recordset. To be sure you get this, think about the table that the query was built on; imagine that the table had 30,000 records in it. In all three cases, the same essential thing is happening: We reduce available data. The query fetched only those records of interest; the cursor displayed only those records that would fit in a window.

Sometimes, a cursor is intended to mean a pointer to the current row of a recordset. To avoid confusion, think of this interpretation of the meaning of cursor to be the end result of the process we just described. That is, this minimalist cursor is the last reduction of data, from the set of rows that fits in a window to the single row of data we want to read or edit.

All right, then, you're now ready to dive into the details of what makes cursors tick and how to create the kind of cursor that will meet your needs as you master the art of ADO programming.

More on Cursors

Because you just created your first industrial-strength cursor in Figure 17.1, now is a good time to reflect on what you did. So you can appreciate the significance of your accomplishment, we quickly review the so-called "firehose."

▶ **See** "Managing *Connection* Objects" for more information about "firehose" cursors, **p. 314**

Both `Connection` Objects and `Command` Objects have primary responsibilities in the world of ADO. Creating cursors is a secondary duty for them. Cursors created from those two objects are meant to be used for purposes that require neither record edits nor recordset navigation. Reporting is the chief function of such cursors; use them frequently when that's all you need to do. In the `PhoneMessage` system, for example, a lot of reporting is done, so the `Command` Object is ideal for those purposes. It creates a compact cursor, and its `Parameters` collection makes quick work of filtering the base table to display only specific individuals' messages.

What about editing an existing record—or, for that matter, new ones? If you want, you can use a keyset cursor and the `AddNew` method of the `RecordSet` Object. For low-volume applications,

Part
IV
Ch
17

that's acceptable. For high-volume Internet applications, you need to do a better job of working with your data provider. When performance is at stake, use the Command Object to send a SQL INSERT INTO statement to the server, altogether bypassing the need for a cursor. You saw an example of this technique in Chapter 16, "Working with ADO's *Connection* and *Command* Objects," Listing 16.6. In that listing you take memory variables from a filled out on-line form and use their values in the Command Object's Parameters collection. Because the form was originally blank, there was no cursor needed to fill in the form. To edit an existing record, however, you do need a cursor because you need to know what the old data is before you can change it.

Taking an Inventory of Cursors   Table 17.2 provides an inventory of available ADO cursor types and lists their features. Depending on what you need your application to do, you can select the correct cursor type to meet your needs.

Table 17.2   Cursor Types and Features

Cursor Type	Supports Method Constants
adOpenForwardOnly	None (this is Cursor Type's default value)
adOpenKeyset	adBookmark, adHoldRecords, adMovePrevious, adResync
adOpenDynamic	adMovePrevious,
adOpenStatic	adBookmark, adHoldRecords, adMovePrevious, adResync

A Library of Cursors

Dynamic cursors can see everything: Edits, additions, deletions made by other users are all visible. This is because, if they are supported by the data provider, they automatically re-fetch data from base tables at specified intervals. All movement through dynamic cursors is supported. Bookmark movement (viz., the capability to move to specific records and jump over intervening records) is supported by dynamic cursors if the data provider supports bookmarks.

Keyset cursors are almost as powerful as dynamic cursors. For example, keyset cursors can see changes made by others, and navigation is as flexible. However, records added and deleted by other users are not visible to the user in keyset cursors.

Static cursors are snapshots of data. Navigation is forward and backward, and by bookmark if supported by the data provider, but unlike the keyset cursor, static cursors cannot see changes to data made by other users.

The *default cursor*—the forward-only kind—behaves just like the static cursor except that it can't go backward. Because this cursor doesn't have to keep track of other users' added, deleted, or changed records, and because it has to "drive" only on a one-way street, this cursor is optimized for reporting. That's why it's the cursor of choice for the Connection Objects and Command Objects.

You might find that more than one cursor type is needed for any given recordset in a single ASP application. Once a recordset is open, you cannot change the CursorType property. However, you can invoke the Close method on the RecordSet Object, change the CursorType property, and then reopen the RecordSet Object, without error.

Some data providers, such as SQL Server 6.5, support *server-side cursors*. Chapter 15 of *Special Edition: Using Microsoft SQL Server 6.5* (Branchek et al., Que, 1996) provides an excellent discussion on this topic. As you might guess, the key advantage to server-side cursors is the absence of networking overhead. In addition, server-side cursors can take advantage of the power of the server hardware and database software.

Moving Through Cursors with Bookmarks   In the old days, the database management system kept track of record numbers. With graduation to Microsoft Access came giving up record numbers for *bookmarks*. Bookmarks support the same functionality as record numbers, but each exists in a different world. Indexed Sequential Access Method (ISAM) file managers have physical rows that they can reference (that's why they're called *sequential*); ODBC data stores don't. Structured Query Language is a set-based language, with no rows in a set. Cursors and bookmarks were invented to transform sets into rows and columns. So, whereas the order of record numbers in an ISAM file is the order in which the records were entered, cursors are in the order created by the WHERE and ORDER BY clause of the SELECT statement that created the recordset.

You have seen how cursor types define the behavior of the SQL cursor and that implementing the level of concurrency control dictated by the cursor type is not trivial. Concurrency control is such a complex process that volumes are written about it. Database designers needed flexibility in defining how this concurrency control was exercised, so that resource deployment more closely matched business needs.

Cursors are to behavior as bookmarks are to position. Keeping track of a record's position is no small matter; consequently, not all data providers support bookmarks. When they do, ADO returns a Variant array of Byte data to uniquely identify each record in the recordset. Bookmarks are a column in the recordset, column 0, and their value is usually in the key of the keyset cursor. This key is usually taken from a key field in the underlying table or from a unique index if one exists.

Setting and retrieving bookmarks is similar to doing the same thing with Session properties and Cookies. However, because not all recordsets support bookmarks, it's a good idea to wrap some error prevention code around the use of the Bookmark property, as is done in Listing 17.2. This listing first tests for support of the Bookmark property for a given RecordSet Object.

N O T E   When properties or methods are discussed, the RecordSet Object is the appropriate focus of the discussion. When values in columns and rows are of interest, the recordset is germane. ■

Note that this RecordSet Object variable could be using any cursor type. You might have an .asp file that uses a firehose cursor in one use and a keyset cursor in another. Both cursors could define the behavior of objRst.

Part
IV

Ch
17

If bookmarks are supported, the value of the bookmark for the current record is assigned to a memory variable. Later, say after you have enumerated all the records in your recordset, you can return to the specific record whose bookmark is stored in varBookMark simply by assigning the Bookmark property of the RecordSet Object to the value of that variable.

In this way, you can navigate around the recordset at will; you don't have to simply move one record at a time, either forward or backward. You can skip any number of records in the recordset and go directly to a record of interest.

Listing 17.2   ch17.asp—Using the *Bookmark* Property

```
fBookMarkOK = objRst.Supports(adBookmark)
If fBookMarkOK Then
Response.Write("CursorType " & objRst.CursorType & " <B>supports</B>
➥ Bookmarks<BR>")
varBookMark=objRst.Bookmark     ' this stores the bookmark
Response.Write("<B>Currently on ID:  " & objRst("id") & "</B><P>")
➥Else
     Response.Write("CursorType " & objRst.CursorType & " does <B>not</B>
➥ support Bookmarks<P>")
End If
[Other recordset programming goes here...]...
If fBookMarkOK Then
     objRst.Bookmark = varBookMark      ' this resets the current record
     Response.Write("<B>Returned to ID:  " & objRst("id") & "</B><BR>")
End If
```

Using Pages

This section describes the basic mechanism in ADO that manages recordsets one page at a time. That is, any given recordset can be partitioned into any arbitrarily sized group of records called pages. The most common use of recordset pages is for displaying data, much like a spreadsheet. Buttons are provided on the form so the user can page up or down in the recordset as necessary.

Listing 17.3 is responsible for managing the recordset of data to be displayed by Listing 17.4. The cursor created is the keyset variety, which means your display can be updated with values entered by other people. The updating will happen automatically as you move from page to page; or if you know someone else has changed data, or you want to confirm that the page you see has only the most current data, then you can select the Requery button to manually refresh the cursor.

The property that controls the position within the cursor is the AbsolutePage property. Changing this value tells ADO which page to go to, and it will display data beginning on whatever record is first on the indicated page. The other important property is the PageSize property. You specify it on the form, and whatever value you use becomes the denominator of a fraction that returns the number of pages that will fit with your specified page size. If a recordset has six records and you specify a PageSize of two, you will have three pages to display. If you selected a page size such as four, you would still get two pages in the PageCount property (the

PageCount property is also displayed on the form). The PageSize property can be changed at any time during the life of the RecordSet Object.

Listing 17.3 CH17ABSOLUTE.ASP—Managing the Recordset

```
<%

strAction = Request.Form("cmdMove")
intPageSize = CInt(Request.Form("txtPageSize"))

If intPageSize=0 Then
      intPageSize = 3
End If


If strAction="Requery" Then
  Set objRst = Session("objRst")
      objRst.Requery
ElseIf Not (strAction = "PgUp" Or strAction = "PgDn") Then
      Set objConn = Server.CreateObject("ADODB.Connection")
  objConn.Open "guestbook","sa",""
  Set objRst = Server.CreateObject("ADODB.Recordset")
  objRst.Open "qryGuestbookListingDesc", objConn, adOpenKeyset,
➥adLockReadOnly, adCmdStoredProc
      objRst.PageSize=intPageSize
  objRst.AbsolutePage = 1
  Set Session("objRst") = objRst
  ' Store page in session var because AbsolutePage is Write-only
  Session("pg") = 1
Else
  Set objRst = Session("objRst")
      objRst.PageSize = intPageSize
  Select Case strAction
      Case "PgUp"
      If Session("pg") > 1 Then
      Session("pg") = Session("pg") - 1
                            objRst.AbsolutePage = Session("pg")
                  Else
                            Session("pg") = 1
        objRst.AbsolutePage = Session("pg")
                  End If
            Case "PgDn"
      If objRst.AbsolutePage < objRst.PageCount Then
      Session("pg") = Session("pg") + 1
        objRst.AbsolutePage = Session("pg")
      Else
       Session("pg") = objRst.PageCount
        objRst.AbsolutePage = Session("pg")
      End If
            Case Else
       Session("pg") = 1
      objRst.AbsolutePage = Session("pg")
       End Select
End If
%>
```

Listing 17.4 has two sections. The top section is a FORM used to specify the size of the recordset's page. It is put at the top of the window so that it stays in place as the size of the display area changes with the PageSize property of the RecordSet Object. This FORM also includes a command button that calls the Requery method on the underlying database table. The second section displays the data for a specified page. Note the enumerating loop to display field names and later field values for all records on the current page.

Listing 17.4   CH17ABSOLUTE.ASP—Displaying the Data from the Recordset

```
<BODY>
Page Count: <%= objRst.PageCount %> Record Count: <%= objRst.RecordCount %><BR>
Current Page: <%= Session("pg") %>
<P>
<FORM ACTION=ch17absolute.asp METHOD="POST">

Enter number of records per page: <INPUT TYPE="TEXT" NAME="txtPageSize"
➥VALUE="<%= intPageSize %>" SIZE=5>
<%
If Session("pg") > 1 Then
 'Only show buttons that are appropriate %>
  <INPUT TYPE="Submit" Name="cmdMove" Value="PgUp">
<%
End If
If Session("pg") < objRst.PageCount Then %>
  <INPUT TYPE="Submit" Name="cmdMove" Value="PgDn">
<% End If %>
<INPUT TYPE="Submit" Name="cmdMove" Value="Requery">

</FORM>

<TABLE BORDER=1 CELLSPACING=0 CELLPADDING=3>
<TH>REC#</TH>
<%

For Each x in objRst.Fields %>
      <TH><%= UCase(x.Name) %></TH>
<%
Next

' Enumerate the fields collection
' within a loop that increments through the recordset's rows.
For j = 1 to objRst.PageSize %>
  <TR>
      <TD VALIGN="Top"><%= j %></TD>
  <% For Each x in objRst.Fields %>
    <TD VALIGN=TOP><%= x.Value %></TD>
  <% Next %>
  </TR>
      <%
objRst.MoveNext
If objRst.EOF Then
    ' Don't try to print the EOF record.
  Exit For
```

```
   End If
 Next
%>
</TABLE>
</BODY>

</HTML>
```

Navigating Among Records

ADO is alluring. It packs an incredible amount of functionality in a comparatively simple language. It does several things for you without your even asking; e.g., it updates current edits as soon as you move the current record pointer with the `Move` method. Its methods and properties are elementary and straightforward. And it's a lot of fun to code.

Part IV

Ch

17

If you're waiting for the other shoe to drop, here it comes: If you're a programmer, ADO could lure you into complacency. If you're not a programmer, ADO could mislead you into forgetting that performance still comes from solid understanding—not from taking shortcuts.

In some respects, programming in ADO is too easy, at least at first. That is, if you're looking for the mythic Edit method, stop—it doesn't exist (although that didn't stop two of this book's authors from searching for it!). If you expect to call the `Update` method every time you call the `AddNew` method, don't bother (unless you're passing arguments to the `Update` method, in which case you need to call `UpdateBatch` instead). ADO is smart. If you start editing a record and then move that record's pointer, ADO doesn't abandon the edit (as Microsoft Access does); it calls `Update` for you to complete the transaction. After a while, you start feeling like Colonel Blake from "M*A*S*H*" when his orderly, Corporal "Radar," would always finish the colonel's commands before the colonel could; that is, Radar would have the results for the colonel before the colonel was finished asking for it.

At the other extreme, you might be beguiled by the `Filter` property—there's just so much you can do with it, and you never have to get near SQL Server. But just try using a `Filter` on a client/server data provider (even the `AddNew` method is problematic in this regard). Again, you have something so easy and direct; when it even calls the `Update` method for you, well, it's almost like the program is coding itself. But when used on a busy Internet site, the true cost of this kind of effortless coding comes back to haunt you. ADO's methods can choke under pressure.

Finally, you might be tempted to rely on a method like `Supports`. It's wonderful when you need information such as what a data provider can do for your program and which features the data provider supports, but this doesn't reduce your responsibility for knowing two things at design time: your database schema and your data provider's capabilities. What we call this *design-time design* means design your program at design time, not at runtime. If your data provider supports bookmarks, it always will do so. After you know that, don't test for it in your code.

Having warned you of their dangers, we now advise you to capitalize on the assets just described. Use these features to get to know your data provider and your new program's design.

But when you go into production, strip out the fluff and get ruthless with bandwidth. Until we're all 100 percent fiber, we have no choice. We have a moral obligation to be as efficient as we possibly can.

Now let's get on with navigating recordsets. Figure 17.3 expands on the activity depicted in box 2 of Figure 17.2. It consists of three activities—reducing, caching, and moving records. Filtering records is one way to reduce a recordset to a smaller number of records. Filtering the recordset of a RecordSet Object is constrained by the value of the RecordSet Object's Filter property.

Caching records is only germane when you are dealing with a forward-only cursor. The only constraint on this activity is the value of the CacheSize property of the RecordSet Object. Updating the cursor with the new number of records is accomplished by the Requery method. This new cursor can be an input to the last activity in Figure 17.3.

FIG. 17.3

These are the activities involved in navigating a recordset.

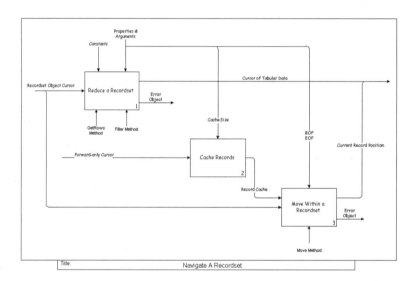

Movement within a recordset is constrained only by the beginning and end of the recordset. That is, you cannot move to a record previous to the beginning of the recordset or past the end of the recordset. You can, however, write VBScript code to sense the BOF and EOF properties of the RecordSet Object and then move to the last record (when BOF is true) or the first record (when EOF is true), accordingly.

Filtering Records

When the technology is appropriate (for example, a small intranet hosted by Microsoft Access), few ADO methods can match the protean power of the Filter property. The Delete, UpdateBatch, Resync, and CancelBatch methods can use it. You can filter a recordset to include only those records that were edited but uncommitted. You can filter recordsets for records that you have never seen or touched, and it can filter records you can see in your Web client based on their `Bookmark` property. It's fast and easy to use. It just can't be used with impunity.

There are two different groups of filters you can use in your programs. First, there are filters that use a criterion constant. These filters are used to reduce a recordset by some current attribute; e.g., records you have edited in batch mode but have not yet sent to the server. For instance, you might need to delete dozens of detail records from an invoice. You will probably want to confirm that those you deleted are those that need to be deleted, so you could filter your customer's invoice recordset to show only deleted records. That way, if you see a mistake, you can fix it before the server updates the underlying table. ADO offers you three filter constants, and they are listed in Table 17.3; you can only select one criterion at a time.

The second group of filters uses a criteria string. These filters are used to reduce a recordset to one that matches one or more attributes. For example, you can filter for all invoice records whose stock status is "back-ordered" or all records whose quantity is greater than 3 and whose value exceeds $100. You can select as many attributes as necessary.

Part
IV

Ch
17

Keep these two kinds of `Filter` properties separate. Though you can filter filtered recordsets successively, don't expect to do that if, for example, you filter a recordset with a criteria string and then filter that cursor (namely, the result of a filter) by using a criterion constant. You won't get the result you expect.

Filtering with Criterion Constants Filtering recordsets with constants usually is done in the context of one of the methods included in the Comment column of Table 17.3. In this section, you will see the code snippets that set up the filter. The code that uses it is listed in each of the following sections related to each method.

Table 17.3 Criterion Constants for the *Filter* Property

Constant	Value	Comment
`adFilterNone`	0	Removes all filters from a recordset. Equivalent to a zero-length string.
`adFilterPendingRecords`	1	Views only records changed in batch mode and not yet sent to the server.
`adFilterAffectedRecords`	2	Views only records changed with `CancelBatch`, `Delete`, `Resync`, or `UpdateBatch` methods.
`adFilterFetchedRecords`	3	Views only records in local memory from the cache of the last database fetch.

The first new property you need to become familiar with when filtering is the recordset's `CacheSize` property. The unusual thing about this property is that it is read/write even when the recordset is open. Most properties can be set only on a closed object.

N O T E   Setting the CacheSize property affects only the next filter. That is, the contents of the
current filter are unaffected by changing CacheSize. ▓

What Is a *Cache*?

When you open a RecordSet Object, the data provider retrieves data from the data source and
buffers this data in an area of memory called a cache. This is the local memory available to ADO that
contains the actual cursor of data. The current record pointer tells the data provider when it's time to
go back to the RecordSet Object and get more data for the cursor. Forward-only cursors restrict this
fetch to one direction.

All this happens behind the scenes. The process becomes important, however, when you're navigating
a recordset, because the cache size determines how far you can roam.

N O T E   Changes made concurrently by other users are invisible to your cache (the other user has
his or her own cache). That is, if someone else changes data in the table that your cache
came from, you won't see it automatically. To update your cache, tell the data provider to refresh the
underlying RecordSet Object's contents with a call to Resync or Requery. ▓

Note that Listing 17.5 is interesting for several reasons. The cursor returned by the Connection
Object—the firehose cursor—is forward/read-only, and its default CacheSize property is equal
to 1. However, as with a statistical sample, a filter of 1 is no filter at all—you need more records.
You get them by increasing the CacheSize property. Because you can't set the CacheSize prop-
erty of a Connection Object recordset before it is opened, you set it afterward and then
Requery the database to get the records that you want.

Listing 17.5   ch17AddNew.asp—The *CacheSize* and *Filter* Properties

```
<%
set objConn = Server.CreateObject("ADODB.Connection")
objConn.Open "driver ={Microsoft Access Driver
(*.mdb)};dbq=c:\data\intranet\intranet.mdb"
set objRst = objConn.Execute("tblPhoneMessage")
objRst.CacheSize = 10
objRst.Requery
objRst.Filter = adFilterFetchedRecords
%>
```

The point of this exercise is to show how the filter that is set by using the
adFilterFetchedRecords gets its contents. You can see that whatever is in the last batch of
fetched records is represented by the adFilterFetchedRecords criterion constant. Remember,
this makes sense only in the context of a batch operation such as deleting or updating records.
For the rest of the story, tune in to the next section.

N O T E Another interesting feature of Listing 17.5 is that it uses what Kyle Geiger calls a "DSN-less" connection. All that's required to get ADO to talk to a database is using the two arguments included on the listing's second line. It's better to go to the trouble of setting up system DSNs—but it's nice to know how to avoid the trouble. ▪

Each of the other criterion constants in Table 17.3 can replace the one in Listing 17.5, but the filter for them is set after a batch operation such as deleting records, not after fetching records from a data provider, as is the case in Listing 17.5.

N O T E If you try to use the `adFilterAffectedRecords` or `adFilterPendingRecords` constants with the `Update` method, you'll raise an error. These criterion constants can be used only with the `UpdateBatch` method, and then only when the `Filter` property is assigned one of the criterion constants listed in Table 17.2. ▪

Filtering with a Criteria String   Filtering for a given set of records by using a criteria string is really no different than specifying a SQL statement. It is a bit more limited, though. You can use any or all of the following comparison operators: `=, <>, >=, <=, LIKE`.

N O T E If you use the `LIKE` operator, you must limit yourself to the asterisk (`*`) and percent sign (`%`) wild cards, and they must be used at the end of the string. Field names that contain spaces must be surrounded by square brackets(`[ ]`). Surround text with single quotes (`' '`) and dates with pound signs (`##`). ▪

To filter a recordset to include only phone messages to `mpc` received today, you would use the following criteria string:

```
objRst.Filter = "for = 'mpc' AND on = " & Date & "#"
```

Filtered recordsets can be filtered even further by applying another filter to the recordset. For example, if the filter that you just applied had too many records, you could use the criteria string `"caller = 'Katy'"` to reduce the set to only those calls made today by Katy.

Getting Rows of Records

You also can use the `GetRows` method to fetch records. Records fetched by `GetRows` go into an array, not a recordset. Therefore, you "navigate" the recordset indirectly. Each row and column in the array represent a record and field. This technique can be especially handy when you want to grab and display a lot of records from a database. Another advantage of the `GetRows` method is that the "records" are more persistent than a cursor. You can pass them around between VBScript functions or subroutines, for example. By using the optional `Fields` argument, you can select a given set of fields, as well as records. Listing 17.6 is an example from the PhoneMessage ASP application, which you can download from the Working with Active Server Pages Web site, **http://www.quecorp.com/asp**.

Listing 17.6   msgupd8.asp—An Example of the *GetRows* Method

```
Dim aFields(6)
aFields(0)="ID"
aFields(1)="FOR"
aFields(2)="ON"
aFields(3)="CALLER"
aFields(4)="OF"
aFields(5)="PHONE"
aFields(6)="MESSAGE"
aMessages = objRst.GetRows(adGetRowsRest, ,aFields)%>
<TABLE BORDER=0 CELLSPACING=2 CELLPADDING=3>
<TR   BGCOLOR="#800000">
    <% For Each col in aFields %>
        <TH><FONT SIZE="2" COLOR="#FFFFFF" FACE="Arial">
        <%= col %>
        </FONT></TH>
    <% Next %>
</TR>
<%For row = 0 to UBound(aMessages,2)%>
<TR>
    <%For col = 0 to UBound(aMessages,1)%>
        <TD VALIGN="Top">
            <FONT SIZE="2" FACE="Arial">
            <% If col=0 Then%>
                <A HREF="phonemsg.asp?ID=<%= aMessages(col,row) %>">
                <%= aMessages(col,row) %></A>
            <% Else %>
                <%= aMessages(col,row) %>
            <% End If %>
            </FONT>
        </TD>
    <% Next %>
</TR>
<% Next %>
</TABLE>
```

Moving the Current Record

The Move method family completes this section's discussion on methods. These methods all are simple. Here's the basic syntax:

objRst.**Move** *Delta StartBookmark*

The Delta argument can be any positive or negative number. If you move past the beginning or end of a recordset, you generate an error. Remember that the beginning of the recordset is one position *before* the first record, and the end of the recordset is the one position *after* the last record. These positions return the BOF and EOF properties, respectively.

The StartBookmark argument tells the Move method where to begin the move operation. You can pass this argument only if the RecordSet Object supports the Bookmark property. If it does, then the Move method first goes to the record whose bookmark equals the current value of the RecordSet Object's Bookmark property. From there, the Move method goes forward or backward the number of records given with the Delta argument.

TIP Forgetting to append the object variable to the Move method generates a "Type mismatch" error.

The other Move methods are simplified versions of the general case. In their cases, instead of passing arguments, you append the qualifier to the name of the method. For example, objRst.MoveFirst puts you on the first record. You can guess for yourself where the MoveLast, MovePrevious, and MoveNext methods take you.

NOTE Don't let these descriptors mislead you into thinking that there are record numbers in ADO. The best way to emulate the function of a record number here is with bookmarks (if the data provider and cursor type support them). ▪

TIP Astute use of the CacheSize property on a recordset gives you the cached cursor that you read about in the previous section. Even a forward-only cursor can move backward if the Move –n method is called. That is, you can use a negative delta on a firehose cursor to move backward.

Modifying Data

In this section, you'll learn about the easy-to-program features that ADO offers the ASP developer, making recordset modification as simple as possible. Given the demands of client/server programming and the virtues of the Command Object's Parameters collection, we contend that using these features without careful thought does not serve your long-term programming interests. After you've read this book, you'll know enough about the ASP programming and Internet development environments to make this judgment on your own.

With that disclaimer made, it's time to complete your lessons in ADO database programming. Figure 17.4 provides the details of activity box 3 in Figure 17.2. The task of modifying the recordset falls into four activities: adding, editing, deleting, and updating records. These activities are all fairly straightforward, being constrained by their respective Filter property and the feature set of the data provider.

FIG. 17.4

These are the activities used to modify a recordset.

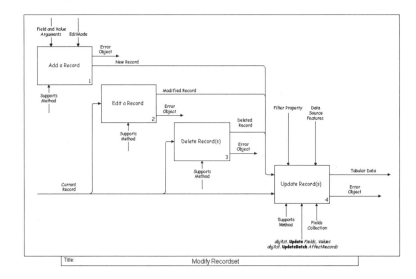

Editing

If you come from almost any other programming environment, you're accustomed to having some command or method that gets a recordset ready to accept new values. Before the idea for writing this book came about, one of its authors sent an e-mail to another one saying, "Hey, David, we're both working too hard! ADO simply forgot to include an Edit method!" If you want to change a field in a record, don't just sit there—change it!

But how? Once again, your first decision is whether to use data-bound controls or not. Intrinsic FORM controls like the TEXT and SELECT tags are not linked to any data source. The contents of these and other controls must be matched up with fields in the recordset. Each field, then, is modified directly in code like this:

```
objRst("message")=Request.Form("message")
```

One way to automate the updating of a recordset is to enumerate the recordset's fields, assigning their value from the Form collection of the Request object. The code snippet in Listing 17.7 shows you how.

Listing 17.7   MSGUPD8.ASP—Automatically Updating a Recordset with *Form* Variables

```
<%For Each x in objRst.Fields
        ' This test assumes an autoincrement field is named "ID"
If x.Name<>"ID" Then
        x.Value=Request.Form(x.Name)
        End If
Next%>
```

There is one requirement, and one warning about Listing 17.7. In order for it to work, the name of the FORM element must equal the name of the Field object. The warning is that you cannot change an AutoIncrement number in a Microsoft Access database. If you exploit that feature of Access, be sure you know the name of the field and insert it in place of "ID" in Listing 17.7. Only fields with names other than the primary index will be edited.

A related warning is if you have some other kind of field acting as a unique index, you need to add a function that tests for the uniqueness of field values for new records. If this field is also serving as a primary key, you will not be able to change it without violating the referential integrity of your database. This restriction is relaxed if you have a data provider that uses cascading deletes and edits and you have constructed your database schema to take advantage of those features.

Adding

Luckily for die-hard Access programmers, ADO retained the AddNew and Update methods. The AddNew method has the following syntax:

```
objRst.AddNew Fields, Values
```

NOTE The Fields and Values arguments have nearly the same form and exactly the same function as the INSERT INTO statement in Listing 16.6 (Chapter 16, "Working with ADO's *Connection* and *Command* Objects"). Read about using these arguments in the next section.

One difference between ADO's and Access's implementations of AddNew is that Access abandons any new record edit if the current record changes before the Update method is called. ADO calls the Update method for you to complete the transaction.

Another new twist on the AddNew method is that if you pass the Fields and Values arguments to the AddNew method, you don't need to invoke the Update method. ADO does this automatically (provided you have not set the LockType property of your RecordSet Object to adLockBatchOptimistic, in which case you would have to *explicitly* call the UpdateBatch method to commit the edits to the database).

 TIP When arguments are passed to AddNew, be sure that, if you have defined your RecordSet Object's LockType property with the adLockBatchOptimistic constant, you update your new records with the UpdateBatch method, not the Update method.

Once successfully added, a new record remains the current record until the record pointer is deliberately moved. If the recordset supports bookmarks, the new record remains visible and is placed at the bottom of the recordset. Without bookmarks, the new record might be invisible. If so, the record can be brought back into the cursor with the Requery method or by invoking the Close and Open methods in succession (clearly, Requery is easier).

EditMode is an interesting recordset property related to the AddNew method. When you add a new record, this property is set to adEditAdd and indicates that the current record is in the copy buffer only and has not been added to the database. EditMode is important when the editing operation is interrupted (by a fire drill, lunch, or a meeting) and your code needs to know if the Update method should be called.

Updating

The record-updating operation relates to the earlier discussion of concurrency control and record locking in the "Understanding Concurrency Control" section at the beginning of this chapter. Some data providers support batch updates of data to improve throughput or minimize network traffic. The choice of using the Supports method to test for data provider support versus knowing your software's capabilities in advance dictates how you implement this feature.

Except for using Update instead of AddNew, the syntax for the Update method is identical to that of the AddNew method:

```
objRst.Update Fields, Values
```

The two arguments passed to this method (and to the AddNew method) are Variants. They can be single variables or Variant arrays of data containing field names and values, respectively. Listing 17.8 is a code block that demonstrates how to create two arrays, populate them with values, and pass them as arguments to the Update method.

Listing 17.8—Using Arrays with the *Update* Method

```
Dim aVarFields(2), aVarVals(2)
aVarFields(0)="for"
aVarFields(1)="caller"
aVarFields(2)="on"
aVarVals (0)="mpc"
aVarVals (1)="Katy"
aVarVals (2)=Date
objRst.AddNew
objRstUpdate aVarFields, aVarVals
```

N O T E Note the size with which the arrays were declared and the absence of parentheses when these arrays were included as Update arguments in Listing 17.8. An array of size two has three elements because all arrays in VBScript are currently zero-based. A common mistake when using arrays with the Update and AddNew methods is to include their parentheses (as you do in the Dim statement in Listing 17.8). If you include the parentheses in Listing 17.8, you will raise an error. ■

If you use the UpdateBatch method instead of the immediate Update method, be sure that you have specified the adLockBatchOptimistic LockType property for your RecordSet Object, and use the UpdateBatch syntax; it's different from the immediate Update method of Listing 17.8:

```
objRst.UpdateBatch AffectedRecords
```

N O T E You cannot use the `Fields` and `Values` arguments with the `UpdateBatch` method. ▪

The `AffectedRecords` argument can take one of the three constant values shown in Table 17.4.

Table 17.4 The *UpdateBatch* Constants

Constant	Value	Comment
AdAffectCurrent	1	Sends pending changes from the copy buffer to the server.
AdAffectGroup	2	Updates only records currently filtered.
AdAffectAll	3	(Default) writes all records to the base table, including any that might be filtered.

Issues with Updating

If you need to update a record, be sure you do not use the default value for a recordset's `LockType` property, which is read-only. If appropriate, use `adLockOptimistic`. If you have the `LockType` set properly and still have an error when attempting to update the record, be sure you are not trying to update an `AutoNumber` field in Microsoft Access.

Finally, you also might encounter a "legitimate" update failure; that is, your data provider has found something wrong with your new data. Usually, this is caused by referential integrity or index violations. If you suspect this, move to your database program and try doing the update there. At the least, the error messages you get there probably will be more helpful.

Deleting

By default, the `Delete` method affects the current record in a recordset. Alternatively, you can instruct the `Delete` method to remove all currently filtered records in the recordset. The default argument is `adAffectCurrent`, and the other option is `adAffectGroup`.

Here is an example code block that deletes a filtered group of records.

```
StrFilter = "for = 'mpc' And on = #" & Date & "#"
objRst.Filter = strFilter
obj.Rst.Delete adAffectGroup
```

You also can use the `Delete` method on the `Parameters` collection. `Delete` is the opposite of the `Parameters` collection's `Append` method, so the syntax looks familiar. The difference is that the `Delete` method accepts only the name of the parameter. For example:

```
objCmd.Parameters.Delete "fax"
```

N O T E The name of the parameter is the first argument that you gave the method when you appended it to the `Parameters` collection. ▪

CAUTION

Remember that the deleted record remains the current record until you call one of the Move methods. If you delete a record, be sure that you move off the current record before attempting to read any fields. Moving off the current record causes the deleted record to disappear. Attempting to read data in a deleted record raises an error.

If you get nervous when writing code that deletes records, there are two ways to hedge your bets: Use transactions or use batch updates. Of course, your data provider must support at least one of these techniques (Microsoft Access and SQL Server support both). If it does, you can use the Connection Object's RollbackTrans method to undo the deletes; to change your mind using batch updates, you can use the RecordSet Object's CancelBatch method. Because both techniques work in the copy buffer, it's no big deal to them to undelete a record. The original wasn't changed in the first place.

 Using the CancelBatch method works even if you have moved the pointer to the current record after the delete. After you call CancelBatch, immediately move the pointer to the current record to some specific location in the recordset; for example, call objRst.MoveFirst. This way, the recordset doesn't lose its bearings.

From Here...

You made it through the chapter (and probably the book), so pat yourself on the back—you've covered a lot of material.

In Part I, you took the lay of the development land; you saw the highlights of almost all the different kinds of software development currently in use. From HTML to component programming to client/server development, they all come together in Active Server Pages, and ASP brings something important and unique to each of those disciplines.

In Part II, you were introduced to the basics of VBScript and HTML. You learned how to construct dynamic Active Server Pages replete with functions and subroutines. You learned how to improve the performance of your HTML forms with VBScript on the client side, and how to extend that power and performance with VBScript on the server side.

In Part III, you learned about all the objects and components that make up the Active Server. You saw how on the one hand, these components extended your reach with whatever programming language you felt best met your programming needs; and on the other hand, how those components pointed the way to the future of Internet programming. That way is marked by the Component Object Model (COM) and Distributed COM (DCOM). You saw how you could follow that example and extend the Active Server with components of your own design.

In Part IV, you met perhaps the most challenging feature of this new world of Internet development: database programming. A whole book could easily be devoted to this material alone, but

Part IV served to introduce you to the issues involved in bringing database technology to the Web and to the basics of one of the most important innovations ever to come out of Microsoft: ActiveX Data Objects. You learned how to exploit the power of the intrinsic objects in ADO: the Connection Object, Command Object, and the RecordSet Object, and how to implement the features of common database applications.

Believe it or not, there still are things we had to leave out of this book. Please refer to the fine print in the ASP/ADO documentation if you need more information.

ON THE WEB

http://www.quecorp.com/asp   In the meantime, we suggest that you add the Web site, "Working with Active Server Pages," to your Internet Explorer Favorites folder. The Web is the best source for new material (and corrections to errors you might have found in this book). As we move from writing a book about ASP to doing full-time ASP development, we will find things we might have done differently and better here. The Web gives us the distribution channel we need to keep this reference work as up-to-date as possible.

Please participate in this process by sending e-mail and telling us your pioneering stories, as you move from the pages of this book to a land of new opportunity. For that's what you are, a pioneer, and we don't know a better way to describe what awaits developers as they bring HTML, good design, and component-based client/server database programming into reality as fourth-generation Web sites.

Good luck.

Part
IV

Ch
17

## CHAPTER 18

Epilogue: Looking to a Future with Active Server Pages

We hope you find the Active Server platform as exciting as we do, and if you have not yet grasped the fundamental importance of this set of tools, then we encourage you to search out other resources on this technology. One exciting upcoming book covers Microsoft's Commercial Internet System published by Que. We have covered the importance of Active Server, including both in-depth evaluation of some areas, and broad exposure to others. We hope that, minimally, we have illustrated the range of technologies that come together to provide an Internet/intranet application. The many technologies—from Networking and NT Servers, to Visual Basic and HTML coding—all coexist to enable the redefined client/server world presented in this book. Key technologies include:

▬ Where are we?

The Internet development world of Active Server covers a lot of ground and so have we, from Visual Basic Scripting to building COM Objects.

▬ What did we want to cover?

In the Web development world, the current happenings you should be following include emerging development tools, methodologies, and integration with diverse Internet protocol standards.

▬ What's next?

In trying to understand what's happening next, take a glimpse at Viper, Falcon, and the third-party COM market.

▬ What's in the future?

Active Server and the development community this platform helps nourish will lay a foundation for new types of application development.

TCP/IP-based networking with Windows NT Server

The Internet Information Server as a Web server gateway to your system servers and data

Active Server scripting with HTML as the evolution of programming on the Web

COM objects, both prebuilt and bundled, as well as custom-developed

TCP/IP-based networking with Windows NT Server lays the foundation for all Internet/intranet development with Active Server. The importance of this infrastructure is often overlooked but dare not be forgotten by programmers. Like the freeways that we take for granted and only give negative attention to when they are jammed with cars or are blocked off with construction, so, too, is the network.

Building a strong infrastructure is the key to a successful application. As we have been in the business of hosting applications, which we have also developed for the Internet, the importance of a strong infrastructure has been particularly clear to us over the last couple of years. When clients report that the application is broken, most often the code works just fine, but the server has crashed or we have dropped off the Net. Unfortunately, although we try to explain this to clients or end users, they simply see that the application does not work. To them, the application is broken! And to a certain extent, they are absolutely correct.

The Web server, like the network, forms your infrastructure. Interestingly enough, the job of a Web server is actually pretty basic. All it really does is reply to very simple file requests. With Active Server, like the CGI-based applications before it, the Web server takes on an increasingly powerful role in the overall Internet application landscape. Microsoft has pinned its Internet plans on the HTTP protocol or Web client/Web server interface as the key to Internet applications. Although the Internet could support countless different record layouts and application transport approaches, Microsoft and many others have focused on the standards provided by the HTTP Web browser-based approach. With this emphasis, the Web server becomes the gate to your kingdom of data and services. Because of the Web server's incredibly important role, you must take careful measures to ensure that this relatively simple server application runs correctly.

So, now that we have agreed upon this Internet network standard and accepted the Web server as our gateway, we can focus on Active Server Scripting and COM objects to begin building powerful new applications. With server-sided Visual Basic scripting and development tools starting to take shape, you can begin to build applications. Active Server Pages, unlike previous Visual Basic application development environments, becomes a beginning rather than a stopping point in the Web development area, with future products and Active Server Pages upgrades holding exciting possibilities. Like the development of the VBX third-party market before it, COM objects, as well as the objects available in Active Server, enable developers to view VBScripting as the glue to tie powerful prebuilt components together for rapid application development.

As has been discussed in varying degrees of detail, components and Active Server objects greatly extend the power of this new application development medium. Developers can now easily integrate a range of functionality into their applications, from database access to file input/output. Keep your eyes on the developing third-party market for server-side COM objects to continue the empowerment of this emerging development platform. ■

What Did We Want to Cover?

We tried to provide you with the basics of application development by Working with Active Server pages. Unfortunately, in a topic this rich, this book is actually the starting point for what probably will be a series of books on this exploding new development platform. With that in mind, we wanted to highlight some of the areas discussed and some of the areas we wanted to cover but simply had to defer to later efforts. Some specific areas that did not get the coverage that they deserve include:

- Development tools for creating Internet/intranet applications
- A development methodology for leveraging the Internet in an innovative multi-developer model
- A closer look at integrating your HTTP-based application with other Internet standard protocols

While Active Server Pages is in its early stages, development work does not have to be limited to a text-only authoring tool as this book might have lead you to believe. At the time this book was written, a text editor like notepad was the development tool of choice, but even as we neared completion, tools like Microsoft's Internet Studio have reached their first public beta. It stands to reason, then, that development tools will rapidly become available to further hasten the development of Active Server applications. Minimally, you now have access to a WYSIWIG HTML editor that integrates Visual Basic debugging and help for writing Active Server script as well as integrating COM objects.

Perhaps our biggest regret is that we didn't explore more thoroughly the multi-developer project management and source code management opportunities provided by this new development platform. Although the implications of this development platform are just beginning to become known, it clearly offers transformational opportunities to integrate multiple, geographically dispersed developers as well as end users into a more efficient development model. In part, a methodology for leveraging these opportunities did not get explored in this book due to our own limitations in understanding how to take advantage of this New World. At this point, it has only become clear that opportunities exist, and we must leave it to future books or perhaps to you in the development community to help implement new methodologies and approaches to take full advantage of this opportunity.

Finally, with respect to moving beyond the HTTP world, this book did not fully introduce the capability to leverage other Internet standards such as Mail (SMTP), Chat (IRC), Telnet, News (NNTP), and others into the application development process. Although the case study in the appendixes shows a few token examples of integrating an e-mail component into your application, we hope you will not take this book's oversight as a statement that these alternative standards don't matter. In fact, nothing could be further from the truth. Seamlessly utilizing Mail, FTP, and other standard protocols with your Active Server-based application provides a valuable mechanism for extending the use and effectiveness of your application. You should definitely consider how these other widely used standbrds might play a key role in your application. Consider exploring Que's upcoming book on Microsoft's Commercial Internet System for some of these additional features.

What's Next?

So what's next? If this is such a fundamental tidal wave in the application development world, where should you watch for the waves to crash? A key area to watch includes the Viper and Falcon technologies, which provide a real-time message queuing capability to NT Server. COM objects can easily leverage these messaging technologies for many purposes, such as connecting to IBM mainframes. One example of this is the recently announced product from Level8Systems for integrating your Viper/Falcon-based Windows NT application into IBM's MQSeries product on the mainframe.

However, in addition to real-time messaging and queuing technology, probably the single most important development will be the exploding COM market for reusable components. We predict an exciting new third-party market taking shape that will exceed by an order of magnitude the VBX market that preceded it. The implications to the development community can be predicted by just a couple of the early entrances that were being discussed at the computer show in Las Vegas that goes by the simple name of "COMDEX 96." A couple of varied examples that can provide a flavor include:

- Microsoft Exchange Server Components
- RUMBA's COM objects for accessing an AS400 and more
- Citrix's WinFrame COM objects for accessing an NT Server

Microsoft Exchange Server Components

The SMTP COM object originally slated for release with the Active Server product in IIS3.0 was pulled early in the beta process, to the disappointment of many developers. Fortunately this type of COM object and others have already re-emerged, coming from the Exchange Server group and (at the time of this book) were being promoted, even though not yet released, on the Microsoft Web page at **http://www.microsoft.com/exchange/**. A simple SMTP COM for sending messages provides only the first in what will be a series of objects to leverage the entire messaging architecture provided by Microsoft's Exchange Server.

RUMBA's COM Objects

RUMBA has provided a combination of OCX client-side objects and server-side COM objects to enable the easy access of AS400 database systems via a standard Web browser. The OCX offers terminal emulation of an AS400 application to the browser while the COM object enables an Active Server application to directly query an AS400 database. ODBC drivers for the AS400 can provide another alternative, and as always, performance is a key concern. However, this type of capability creates exciting opportunities for companies trying to reinvent the way users interact with existing systems.

WinFrame COM objects

Many network administrators have been following the hype surrounding Citrix's WinFrame product. This product, which comes as an altered version of Windows NT Server, supports multiple users from remote locations (even 28.8 dialed-in users) logging into one NT Server machine. With an early adoption of COM standards, they have taken this flexibility one step further. Again, with a combination of OCX objects and COM server-side objects, Citrix is leading the way in providing Active Server developers with flexible alternatives to meet their application development needs.

What's in the Future?

One of the aspects of Internet development, and more specifically, Active Server, that continues to amaze, is its transformation of the application development process. Unlike previous application development experiences, working with Active Server engages the prospective users and other laymen in the application development process like never before. The interactive nature of the Internet and the capability to expose your pages to the general user community very early in the development process has fundamentally changed the development process.

The process of developing the introduction service spotlighted in the case study found in the appendixes of this book provides the perfect example of this point. From the very first prototyped pages of the new account sign-up process, the client became actively involved in testing the pages. Even before we notified him of new pages becoming available, we noticed him in the pages, providing e-mail-based feedback on problems and concerns. At the time, we found his continuous inquiries and comments annoying and distracting from what we considered our job to be. We believed he was slowing the process down by constantly interrupting our development efforts with feedback.

We had come to believe that our job was to take the design specification that we had painstakingly worked to create and then to build the application from that specification. What we later came to understand was that this new development tool had also brought a new development methodology or model into existence. Quite unbeknownst to us, we had embarked on a totally new way of developing applications. This evolving site became a living application the day the first .asp file was placed on the server. Suddenly, the client's friends and prospective end users were logging on and testing our pages at the same time we were completing the features for them.

The results of this unprecedented level of client involvement became a thorough, ongoing test of the developing application by the intended end user community. Bug reports continuously flowed into our e-mail boxes. Although this process did give rise to the dreaded "feature creep," on more than one occasion, it also saved us from fundamental design flaws that were detected very early in the process. As the applications neared completion, we found that the code had been thoroughly tested and required very little reworking later on in the process. Though it took some time in the beginning to align the end user expectations or to make sure that they understood what it meant to be testing pages that were truly alpha code, the user community loved the opportunity to be involved in the process.

> **N O T E** Feature Creep, for those that have been lucky enough to have never faced it, represents the adding of new features into a previously designed and partially completed application. ■

This experience led us to our current views for the future of application development. I see a transformation occurring that thoroughly integrates the end users and development community. Although the experience highlighted the education that needs to take place for both of these groups, it also touched me with the power and understanding that will result. Users will be 100 percent accountable when the site goes into a beta testing phase, and they will be involved and will gain unprecedented understanding of the challenges and opportunities faced by application developers. This change has already begun as the Internet has provided an immediate mechanism for distributing applications to groups more efficiently and, as a result, more frequently. But this development model will further this trend in a way currently only imagined by the most forward-thinking among us.

A Final Thought

You have reached the end of hundreds of pages of information about information. You have seen how Active Server Pages make the dynamic acquisition and display of information very, very easy.

Most of our readers are probably interested in applying ASP technology to business. Indeed, ASP, in our view, will revolutionize many business processes and models. But that is nothing compared to the larger impact this technology will have.

In this book you have seen that the Web accomplished what thousands of very talented information specialists could not do: It got an unlimited variety of computers and software to work together with some semblance of coherence. In the process, the Web liberated information. It made it more public than could scarcely be imagined only a few years ago.

This was the first great step into the new world of computer technology. This is a cosmopolitan world of information, incredibly rich and accessible. At the same time that Active Server Pages was released, Microsoft was also shipping its commercial and personalization Servers: highly capable and scalable systems required if electronic commerce is to be more than good press.

But the genius of ASP is that it's small. Everything you need to create fourth-generation Web sites is right there, right in front of you, *every one of you*, right now. It's in there; it's in the Active Server.

You're ready. Go for it. Change the world...

Appendixes

Case Study: Building an Interactive Product

The time has come to bring together the objects, components, and scripting capabilities provided by Active Server Pages to build a comprehensive Web-based business. The tools you have read about to deliver features from user tracking to database access come together to enable the construction of a comprehensive product or service-based business site. This chapter introduces you to the creation of an Introduction Service currently in operation on the Internet at **http://www.1st-site.com**. As you explore this Internet-based site, you will apply Active Server Pages to enable the development of the core components necessary in implementing any Internet- or intranet-based business.

Bringing it all together

Now that you have an understanding of how to use Active Server Pages, bring together the database capabilities and other Active Server tools to deliver a complete interactive site.

A review of the hardware, software, and performance issues

Though addressed in Chapter 2, when you create a site, the hardware resources, software components, and performance monitoring features of a site should not be overlooked.

Our case study model: an Introduction Service

Our case looks at an Introduction Service currently in use on the Internet to understand the ways Active Server tools come together to create a business on the Internet.

Bringing It All Together

Bringing together the technology provided by Internet Information Server 3.0's Active Server Pages to construct a business site offering products and services involves the same type of design and development steps found in more traditional client/server application development processes. Critical steps in this process include the development of an intuitive client application to support the user, the implementation of a secure, flexible and scalable server, and the effective use of database tools for managing information.

The Client

With Active Server Pages, the browser becomes the client. Active Server Pages allow the use of a browser that only understands displaying HTML pages. Active Server Pages as discussed in this book focus almost entirely on the tools, which rely entirely on the server for any processing other than standard HTML requests and posts. While this allows applications to be developed that support the widest possible number of browsers, the browser client can also enhance the Active Server application by including client-side features. These features can include Netscape Plug-ins, Client-Side Java Script, or VBScript, as well as Client-Side ActiveX Controls.

The Server

The server-based services make up the heart of Active Server Pages. With Active Server, certain tools are required in the server implementation such as a Windows-based operating system and Web server. This book focuses on Windows NT Server, though Windows 95 and Windows NT Workstation can also serve Active Server Pages. With the selection of Windows NT Server and Internet Information Server as the operating system and Web server, the choice of hardware used and additional components and services utilized must be determined, depending on the amount of traffic and specific site features selected.

Database Tools

While much of this book focuses on Microsoft Access, sometimes this type of ODBC-compliant and user-friendly tool does not provide sufficient performance or stability for Active Server applications. ODBC-compliant drivers enable you to utilize database servers from Microsoft SQL Server on Windows NT, to UNIX-based tools from Informix to Oracle. When your application requires high traffic loads and extensive database reliance, be careful not to overlook the need to utilize high performance databases.

N O T E Open DataBase Connectivity (ODBC) refers to the Microsoft-promoted standard for accessing databases in Windows NT. With the release of 3.0 and future planned enhancements, this has become the standard for enabling programs to communicate with databases. For more information visit **http://www.microsoft.com**.

Often, high performance database servers can become an integral part of your application by introducing extended features. For example, in this case study, you will see the use of Microsoft's SQL Server for SMTP message delivery.

N O T E Simple Mail Transport Protocol (SMTP) has become the messaging or electronic mail standard of the Internet. Microsoft Exchange Server, Microsoft SQL Server, and countless other applications continue to extend the methods for leveraging this standard for delivering information.

Generally, your key Windows NT Services include the Web server, which executes your Active Server Pages, a database server to execute your SQL queries, and perhaps an e-mail server to support integration of mail features into your application.

A Review of the Hardware, Software, and Performance Issues

This book focuses on the task of utilizing Active Server Pages to develop interactive Web-based environments. However, we must also address enabling the robust and flexible processing of these pages through the proper selection of hardware and software. In addition to these selections, the monitoring and general maintenance of acceptable performance levels can become critical, as the traffic volumes of your site begin to grow. The key issues that can often be overlooked in the development process include:

- Security of your site and its information
- Flexibility of the software and services you implement
- Scalability of your Web-based application
- Real-time monitoring and tracking of usage

Secure Server

The Windows NT operating system provides some degree of security, but don't be lulled into a false sense of comfort by the name and all of the C2 security-level hype. Windows NT Server is not secure just out-of-the-box. Although the level of security often demands balancing acceptable cost and risk tolerances, any implementation team minimally should understand the issues involved in the security question. Most companies, for example, make certain assumptions before evaluating what measures to take with respect to security, such as whether or not the physical servers are secure from malicious attack; generally, if physical access to your servers is compromised, any sufficiently sophisticated attacker can disable your site, if not actually get access to your data. Let's face it, a sledge hammer, if nothing else, can usually disable a computer. Once your basic assumptions have been set, you can begin to evaluate the necessary level of security needed.

At a minimum, consider the network access and NT security features. The network security can be managed by a range of hardware- and software-based Firewall products that create proxies to limit access to IP addresses and packet filtering. At the NT server, control over users and their file, directory, and application execution-related permissions can be controlled.

> **CAUTION**
>
> Please review current articles on NT security holes. Some of the known problems include the use of protocols like NetBIOS over TCP/IP. The ability to execute .bat files, the everyone group, and the guest account.

Flexibility in Your Server

Building flexibility into your site relates to how and which services become critical to your application. If you select services that have an upgrade path from a third-party vendor or have an object model that allows easy maintenance, supporting your application's forward move will be a much easier task. One effective approach to building flexibility is the use of DCOM components. DCOM components can extend your ability to quickly expand features by creating callable functions that can easily be reused in the development of new or the modification of existing features. Components developed in-house and an increasing number of third-party components that provide upgrade paths for your applications without costly investments in custom software development should be considered.

N O T E   Distributed Component Object Model (DCOM), similar to Component Object Model (COM), can be thought of as a simple evolution of the Object Linking and Embedding (OLE) standards before them. In short, DCOM represents an OLE object without any user interface, and some exciting new features.

In addition to the selection components, applications often will rely on additional NT services such as database and e-mail services. The application services you select to support the Active Server pages can dramatically affect the flexibility to change and enhance your application.

Scalability

N O T E   Scalability, second perhaps only to "open" as a buzzword in application development, provides one key measure of the quality designed into an application.

Ensuring a scalable application in the Internet area becomes incredibly important. Unlike an Intranet application in which user communities and transaction volumes can be accurately estimated, the Internet offers the possibility of rapid volume increases. Understanding what hardware and software resources will become bottlenecks and knowing how to address these problems is vital during the application development process.

N O T E In our experience, most planners vastly overestimate traffic volumes; occasionally, however, you hit upon a huge success, and you need to know how you can respond to changes in traffic. ▪

The key resource problems a Web-based application can run into include the following areas:

Computers: how many, and what roles they play

Each computer's Random Access Memory (RAM)

Each computer's Central Processing Unit (CPU)

Simple Web servers love RAM. They run well on a slower Central Processing Unit (CPU), provided adequate RAM is present. Active Server Pages require both RAM and execution resources on the CPU. Similarly, databases often focus much more on the RAM for caching than on the CPU. In addition to RAM and CPUs, network bandwidth and disk I/O can also become a bottleneck.

With Active Server Pages, database servers, and DCOM objects, resources can often be distributed across multiple computers, creating alternatives to implementing servers with gigabytes of RAM and multiple CPUs. These issues, however resolved, should not be overlooked in the design and development stages of the site.

Real-Time Monitoring and Tracking of Usage

While real-time monitoring and usage tracking can sometimes be handled by network administrators or service providers, be certain that you have adequate tools in place to ensure acceptable performance and uptime levels. If a network administrator assure you that this area is under control, ask some key questions:

- What type of usage statistics can you access?
- Do you continually monitor the Web Server?
- If the Web site goes down, what steps are taken to correct the problem?
- How does the server reach the Internet? (e.g., T1 to what provider? What monitoring do they have?)
- Who provides Domain Naming Services (DNS) for the site? (This is a key reason users can't access a site.)

N O T E Domain Naming Services (DNS) will probably not be an application that you manage or support directly. DNS servers, coordinated by the InterNIC, run at many locations across the Internet, cooperatively providing name resolution for Web sites such as your **www.yourcompany.com** to a unique Internet address like **205.171.129.2**. ▪

Regardless of the assurances a network administrator gives you or your decision to monitor the site yourself, consider a program such as IPSWICTH's WhatsUp monitoring services. These services can ping your site and others on the Net at set intervals and page, e-mail, or beep you when failure occurs. Also, consider an external off-site such as RedAlert to ping your server (**http://www.redalert.com**). This company can provide a valuable safeguard if your monitor goes down or a problem develops that you can't detect from your monitoring computer.

Our Case Study Model: An Introduction Service

The following appendixes explore the specific functionality enabled in the **Love@1st-site.com** Introduction Service. This case study focuses on the key features and elements of the site that will be required by many businesses that attempt to build a community and deliver a service over the Internet for a fee.

The site provides a fee-based subscription service that enables the member to search the member database and to request introductions in a controlled and secure environment. The site effectively uses the Web's capability to provide in-depth information and search features to members who are reviewing other members' profiles.

To aid your understanding of the case study, Table A.1 provides an index of all the ASP pages used and of the overall table layout for the site. The .asp files reside in two directories. The root directory controls the Active Server Pages used for managing the membership communities' experience and includes:

Table A.1   Complete List of .asp Files in Root Membership Directory

File Name	Size	Purpose
abandon.asp	82 bytes	Testing tool to abandon Sessions
archive.asp	667 bytes	Frame Set for Archive area
archive_left.asp	2K	Left window of Archive
archive_right.asp	2K	Right window of Archive
archive_top.asp	521 bytes	Top window of Archive
billingupdate.asp	4K	Billing processing code
billingupdate2.asp	4K	Billing processing code
confirm.asp	382 bytes	Confirmation page for New Member sign up process
confirmactivate.asp	2K	Members reactivating
confirmbillupdate.asp	3K	Members updating their billing information
confirminactivate.asp	2K	Confirmation of taking deactivation for a member
edit3_top.asp	250 bytes	Members editing information
editacct1.asp	6K	Members editing information

File Name	Size	Purpose
editacct1_frame.asp	670 bytes	Members editing information
editacct2.asp	17K	Members editing information
editacct2_frame.asp	683 bytes	Members editing information
editacct3.asp	7K	Members editing information
editacct3_frame.asp	688 bytes	Members editing information
editacct5.asp	8K	Members editing information
editacct5_frame.asp	673 bytes	Members editing information
editacct_bot.asp	599 bytes	Members editing information
editacctupdate.asp	11K	Members editing information Processing
editprofile.asp	730 bytes	Frame set for members editing information
global.asa	1K	Application control routines
inactivate.asp	1K	Initial deactivation page for members
logon.asp	2K	Core logon page
logoncheck.asp	4K	Processing for logon
logonsearch.asp	1K	Alternative search for logon
logonsearchrun.asp	2K	Processing for alternative search for logon
newacct1.asp	4K	New Account signup process
newacct2.asp	13K	New Account signup process
newacct3.asp	13K	New Account signup process
newacct4.asp	5K	New Account signup process
newacct5.asp	9K	New Account signup process
newacct6.asp	11K	New Account signup process
profile.asp	722 bytes	Frame Set for reviewing Member Profile
profile_bot.asp	2K	Bottom of profile review frame
profile_display.asp	9K	Core page of profile review frame
profile_evaluate.asp	3K	Processing page of profile review
profile_process.asp	2K	Processing page of profile review
profile_top.asp	2K	Top of profile review frame

continues

App

A

Table A.1 Continued

File Name	Size	Purpose
reactivate.asp	728 bytes	Member reactivation process
scan.asp	4K	Page for detailing picture scanning process
scanaction.asp	684 bytes	Page for detailing picture scanning process
search.asp	5K	Criteria selection for search frame
search_top.asp	578 bytes	Top of search frame
searchframe.asp	665 bytes	Frame Set for search criteria
searchrun.asp	8K	Processing for search features
start.asp	657 bytes	Frame Set for member after logon
start_left.asp	2K	Left home page for members after logon
start_right.asp	2K	Right home page for members after logon
start_top.asp	769 bytes	Sat Nov 16 12:26:12 1996
validate.asp	596 bytes	Validation include for top of all pages
validatenew.asp	753 bytes	Validation include for top of all New Account signup pages

The secure administrative area resides in a separate directory, secured by Windows NT's file- and directory-level permissions included in Table A.2.

Table A.2 List of .asp Files in Secure Administrative Directory

File Name	Size	Purpose
adminparamadd.asp	905 bytes	Processing to add parameter
adminparamdetail.asp	1K	Review detail value of parameter
adminparamhead.asp	908 bytes	Top level review of value for parameters
adminparamupdate.asp	1K	Processing to update parameter
adminprofileupdate.asp	1K	Processing to update member profile
adminroute.asp	341 bytes	Router for managing administrative area

File Name	Size	Purpose
adminsearch.asp	3K	Search criteria for finding members
billingtypes.asp	784 bytes	Display billing plans
billingtypesadd.asp	1K	Add new billing plan
billingtypesdetail.asp	1K	View detail of existing billing plan
billingtypesupdate.asp	2K	Update existing billing plan
download.asp	3K	Initiate download to accounting system
referredby.asp	794 bytes	Display top level referral parameters
referredbyadd.asp	691 bytes	Add new referral parameter
referredbydetail.asp	1K	View details of referral parameters
referredbyupdate.asp	1K	Update referral parameter
toggledownload.asp	577 bytes	Process download to accounting system

Finally, the database responsible for enabling the site includes 6 tables. You explore the individual tables and their relationships in more detail as you explore the specific features they enable. For now, the tables include:

- *Members Table*: contains all member-specific information
- *Selections Table*: maintains tracking on all relationships between members
- *AdminParameters Table*: stores system-wide parameters
- *States Table*: stores a list of U.S. states
- *Billing Table*: tracks credit card and individual payment information
- *PaymentPlans Table*: stores billing options available on the site

The overall table layout and relationships are illustrated in Figure A.1.

FIG. A.1

This shows the table layout for database-enabling the Introduction Service site.

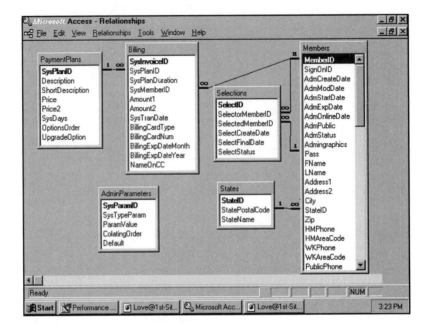

Establishing a Membership-Based Community

Building a membership-based community immediately demands certain features and functionality requirements that should be provided as part of the site. These features almost always require a database and generally include a New Account sign-up process, logon/validation, and a series of account maintenance and administrative features.

You should begin the design process by assessing the membership database required for collecting the necessary membership information and for tracking user activity. The membership-related database tables will store user information for customizing the user's experience at the site, for evaluating current status and permissions, and for assessing appropriate billing. These critical features highlight the importance of proper design. The design decisions will ensure that the required fields of information are available and the performance requirements for the database are met.

Designing a database: Member table

Due to the importance of a database in managing a membership-based community, starting with a careful design of the information to be collected proves invaluable in the subsequent development steps.

Establishing a New Member

Establishing a New Account means implementing a New Account sign-up process and recording the information necessary to track that New Member.

Managing logon and validation

In developing a membership-based Web site, it is critical that you provide an efficient method to log a user onto the site and to validate a user's membership status.

Users maintaining their own account information

To manage a membership-based site without incurring unreasonable administrative expenses, the site must provide facilities that enable users to maintain their own account information.

> **N O T E**   Generally, membership means a database. Any other method of tracking membership-related information is unreasonably costly and inefficient. ▓

After a well-designed data structure has been established, the following sections detail the features necessary to manage the membership-based environment including the New Account sign-up process, logon/validation features, and user's account maintenance. Establishing a New Account sign-up process provides a good starting point, as it often highlights required features that may have been overlooked in the initial design process. The logon and account validation code should have a focus on efficiency and security for the site. The logon and validation components primarily focus on controlling which aspects of the site users can reach, and they provide an important mechanism to ensure that security and fee collection features of the site are properly enforced.

As you turn your development activities toward managing account status and history tracking, as well as account maintenance and administrative activities, your focus turns toward automating the administrative activities involved in account upkeep and reporting requirements. ▓

Database Design—Membership Tables

The database design process for creating the Membership table provides a system for defining various types of information to be used by the system. Minimally, the information collected should include a unique ID to track the various members. In practice, additional information will be collected in several categories:

- *System Status information*: unique ID, account status, date stamps, and more
- *Administrative information*: billing-related information and other account management information
- *Profile-related information*: information updated by the members themselves

In the Love@1st Site Introduction Service (Service), we undertook a comprehensive design phase, involving the key constituencies involved in creating, financing, and using the site to determine the necessary information to track about the user community. The information includes system information, administrative information, e-mail services, related flags, Member Profile data, and a profile of the member's Ideal Mate.

> **CAUTION**
>
> The table information illustrated as follows shows field information based on a Microsoft Access table; this maintains consistency with the presentation of this book and was the environment used during testing of the site. The production version of this site is Microsoft SQL Server.

System Information

From the system level, we determined a series of fields of information we had to collect to manage the member at the site. The specific fields of the Membership table, which can be found on the book's Web site at **http://www.quecorp/asp,** are listed in Table B.1:

Table B.1   The Database Structure of the Primary System Information of the Membership Table

Field Name	Data Type	Size	Description
MemberID	Number (Long)	4	Core account number—hidden from user
SignOnID	Number (Long)	4	Session ID—temporary value for tracking
Download	Number (Long)	4	Flag for downloading information to accounting system
ReferredBy	Text	25	Information on accounts referred from partner Web sites
InactivateReason	Number (Long)	4	Reason flag for inactive status
CompletedProcess	Yes/No	1	Flag to show successful completion of New Account sign up and billing process

Some of fields utilized for system-related functionality are classified as Administrative fields to illustrate that they can be updated by site administrators through Active Server Pages. Together, System and Administrative fields form the set of information used by the system to manage members. System information is updated only by the core program itself and not by members or administrative users of the site.

Administrative Information

Administrative information, like System information, provides key data for tracking and managing the member, the key distinction being that Administrative information can be edited by administrative users of the site. Allowing key membership-related information to be administered by site users is a fundamental method for distributing control and management tasks away from the code writer to the site users. This creates the mechanism for avoiding continual upgrades to code. The key administrative fields for the Membership table are listed in Table B.2.

N O T E   The key value of editable information will be demonstrated in more depth in the administrative Appendix, as you note the parameter-driven nature of core features ranging from drop-down box options to billing structures. ▪

Table B.2   The Database Structure of the Primary Administrative Information of the Membership Table

Field Name	Data Type	Size	Description
AdmCreateDate	Date/Time	8	Initial account creation data
AdmModDate	Date/Time	8	Date account last modified
AdmStartDate	Date/Time	8	Date paid membership began
AdmExpDate	Date/Time	8	Date valid membership status expired
AdmOnlineDate	Date/Time	8	Date user last logged on to site
AdmPublic	Yes/No	1	Flag denoting searchable account
AdmStatus	Number (Long)	4	Status of member account, i.e., active, inactive
Admingraphics	Yes/No	1	Graphic images submitted for display by member, a prerequisite for active account status

Profile and General Demographic Account Information

The profile information displays information entered by the users themselves for other members to view. The profile information enables the searching features of the site and allows members to get to know each other while deciding whether or not to introduce themselves. The specific information includes all the fields illustrated in Table B.3.

Table B.3   The Database Structure of Profile and General Demographic Information of the Membership Table

Field Name	Data Type	Size	Description
Pass	Text	50	Password for secure access
FName	Text	30	First name
LName	Text	50	Last name
Address1	Text	150	Address line one
Address2	Text	150	Address line two
City	Text	50	City
StateID	Text	2	State
Zip	Text	20	Zip code
HMPhone	Text	30	Home phone number
HMAreaCode	Text	3	Home area code (for searching)

Field Name	Data Type	Size	Description
WKPhone	Text	30	Work phone number
WKAreaCode	Text	3	Work area code (for searching)
PublicPhone	Number (Long)	4	Flag denoting phone number can be released
Email	Text	50	E-mail address
PublicEmail	Yes/No	1	Flag denoting e-mail address can be released
Maiden	Text	50	Mother's maiden name for validation if password is lost
ProfSex	Yes/No	1	Male or female
ProfPrefID	Yes/No	1	Preferred sex (cannot be altered)
ProfRaceID	Number (Long)	4	Ethnic/racial background
ProfRlgnID	Number (Long)	4	Religion
Profdob	Date/Time	8	Date of birth for custom birthday notes and user validation
ProfHeightF	Number (Long)	4	Member height (feet)
ProfHeightI	Number (Long)	4	Member height (inches)
ProfBodyID	Number (Long)	4	Member body type
ProfStatusID	Text	50	Marital status (married is not an option)
ProfEdID	Number (Long)	4	Education level
ProfOcc	Text	150	Occupation description
ProfChldNum	Number (Long)	4	Number of children
ProfChldExist	Number (Long)	4	Flag whether or not member has children
ProfChldNew	Number (Long)	4	Interest in having children
ProfSmkgID	Number (Long)	4	Smoking status
ProfDrkgID	Number (Long)	4	Drinking status
ProfEyeID	Text	15	Member's eye color
ProfHairID	Text	15	Member's hair color
ProfAct	Memo	-	Member general entry of activities they enjoy
ProfMovie	Text	100	Favorite movies
ProfMusic	Text	50	Multiple selection list for music IDs
ProfBook	Text	100	Last book read

App

B

continues

Table B.3   Continued

Field Name	Data Type	Size	Description
ProfWhat	Memo	-	What are you looking for in a relationship question
ProfQ1ID	Number (Long)	4	ID of second parameter-driven question
ProfQ1Info	Memo	-	Answer to parameter-driven question

This profile and demographic information is used to dynamically build profile pages for display to users interested in learning more about a certain member that they find in a search or who requests their introduction.

Automated E-Mail Services Flag Information

The Service provides extensive e-mail features for its membership community as a method of communication between members. Members may generate e-mails to other members through the system without the identity of either member being released. And based on profiles and flag selections, the system may automatically generate an e-mail message to notify a member of an introduction request or that someone matching her Ideal Mate profile has joined the membership community. The flags in the Membership table that manage this set of features are included in Table B.4.

Table B.4   The Database Structure of Automatic E-Mail Services Flags in the Membership Table

Field Name	Data Type	Size	Description
Eselect	Yes/No	1	Send me a message when another member selects me.
Eaccept	Yes/No	1	Send me a message when a member I have selected accepts my request.
EGenie	Yes/No	1	Send me a message if a member matching my Ideal Mate profile joins.
EGen	Yes/No	1	Send me general site announcements of events.
EOK	Yes/No	1	Allow members to send me notes after they have selected me.

Microsoft SQL Server's "send mail stored" procedure drives these e-mail services that are executed through database calls by Active Server Pages through the ActiveX Data Object (ADO) component.

Ideal Mate Profile Information

The Ideal Mate-related profile very closely mirrors the Member Profile information and enables a member to customize the search utilities to the profile that she will use most often when searching the system. In addition, the Ideal Mate profile provides a mechanism that enables the system to attempt matching New Members with members already in the system. This automated matching feature sends users e-mail notifications that encourage them to return to the site and provides them with value-added services to facilitate members finding members. The specific fields associated with managing these features are illustrated in Table B.5.

Table B.5   The Database Structure of Ideal Mate Profile Information in the Membership Table

Field Name	Data Type	Size	Description
idlRaceID	Number (Long)	4	Ideal Mate race
idlagehigh	Number (Long)	4	Ideal Mate age range (high)
idlagelow	Number (Long)	4	Ideal Mate age range (low)
idlRlgnID	Number (Long)	4	Ideal Mate religion
idlHeightFlag	Number (Long)	4	Ideal Mate height above or below flag
idlHeightF	Number (Long)	4	Ideal Mate height (feet)
idlHeightI	Number (Long)	4	Ideal Mate height (inches)
idlSmkgID	Number (Long)	4	Ideal Mate smoking status
idlDrkgID	Number (Long)	4	Ideal Mate drinking status
idllocflag	Yes/No	1	Ideal Mate location flag, i.e., is location relevant?
idllocarea1	Text	3	Ideal Mate area code if relevant
idllocarea2	Text	3	Ideal Mate area code, number two if relevant

Establishing a New Member

With the table design completed for the Membership table, developing a member sign-up process becomes the first step of site creation. This enables the testing users to enter members and to work with the site almost immediately, leading to a clarification of missing information that has to be added to the site. The New Account sign-up process results in five separate Active Server Pages or .asp files. The initial development of the pages focused entirely on functionality, with graphic design and general look enhancement taking place at the very end of the development process.

The five-step New Account process walked the prospective member through the entering of Ideal Mate, Profile, demographic information, billing selection, and payment choices. Whereas the final two steps relating to billing are dealt with extensively in a later appendix, at this point we will explore the creation of a New Account.

New Account: Step 1

The initial page shown in Figure B.1 largely presents standard HTML, providing information within a standard form that enables users to enter data and to select options. The only significant use of Active Server Pages features includes the lookup of parameters to populate drop-down lists and the Server-Side Include of a validation .asp file, which will be explored in more detail later in this chapter. This page, however, initiates the session and collects the Ideal Mate information used to initially insert a New Member record in step 2.

FIG. B.1

The initial New Account page collects beginning information prior to inserting a New Member record.

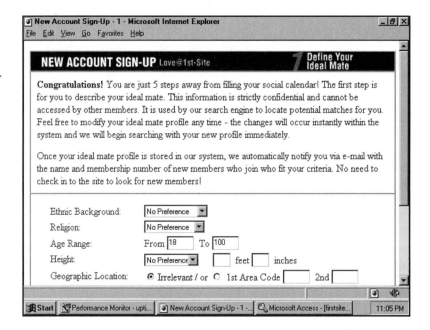

Listing B.1 illustrates the Server-Side Include feature and the defaulting of drop-down values for ethnic background.

Listing B.1   NEWACCT1.ASP—First Page in the New Account Sign Up Process

```
<!--#include file="validatenew.asp"-->
<%
  Set Conn = Server.CreateObject("ADODB.Connection")
```

```
'
'  --------------------------------
'  --------------------------------
'  Output HTML Area
'  --------------------------------
'  --------------------------------
%>
...

<tr><td width=20%><font color="#0000A0">
Ethnic Background:</font></td><td width=50%>
<select name="idlraceid" size=1 >
<option checked value="0"><font color="#0000A0">No Preference</font></option>
<%
    Set RS = Conn.Execute("SELECT * FROM AdminParameters where (systypeparam = 1)
➥ order by colatingorder;")
    Do While Not RS.EOF
%>
<option value="<%=rs("sysparamid")%>"><%=rs("paramvalue")%></option>
<%
    RS.MoveNext
    Loop
    RS.Close
%>
</select></td></tr>
...
```

The code illustrated in Listing B.1 includes an example of how a parameter table can be used for populating options in the system. This parameter table can then be maintained by site administrators through standard Active Server Pages.

New Account: Step 2

During step 2, shown in Figure B.2, the initial account record is created with the add new method. In addition to the Server-Side Include validation in step 1 and the parameter-driven populating of drop-down boxes illustrated in step 1, step 2 checks logon status to ensure that the current user has not already inserted the initial record; then step 2 either does a database insert or simply redisplays the account ID, depending on the logonstatus of the session ID. Listing B.2 illustrates the database insert and user validations done in step 2.

Listing B.2 NEWACCT2.ASP—Inserting the Initial Record with Ideal Mate Information from Step 1 and System/Administrative Defaults for the New Account

```
<!--#include file="validatenew.asp"-->
<%
    Set Conn = Server.CreateObject("ADODB.Connection")
    Conn.Open("firstsite")
```

continues

Listing B.2   Continued

```
Select Case session("logonstatus")

Case 3 ' Already Past this insert step
      msg = "<blink>Please Record your New Member ID:</blink>" &
session("memberid") & " "

Case 2 ' Proper Status for Insert of New Account


    set rsInsert = Server.CreateObject("ADO.RecordSet")
    'Conn.BeginTrans
    rsInsert.Open "Members", Conn, 3, 3

    rsInsert.AddNew
    rsInsert("SignOnID")          = session.sessionid
    rsInsert("AdmCreateDate")  = Date()
    rsInsert("AdmModDate")  = Date()
    rsInsert("AdmStartDate")   = Date()
    rsInsert("AdmOnlineDate")  = Date()
    rsInsert("AdmPublic")     = 0
    rsInsert("AdmStatus")     = 0
    rsInsert("publicphone")    = 0

    'Testing Uncertain Values

    heightF = request.form("idlHeightF")
    heightI = request.form("idlHeightI")

    if heightF = "" then heightF = 0
    if heighti = "" then heightI = 0

    rsInsert("idlRaceID")      = request.form("idlRaceID")
    rsInsert("idlAgeHigh")     = request.form("idlAgeHigh")
    rsInsert("idlAgeLow")      = request.form("idlAgeLow")
    rsInsert("idlRlgnID")      = request.form("idlRlgnID")
    rsInsert("idlHeightFlag")    = request.form("idlHeightFlag")
    rsInsert("idlHeightF")    = heightf
    rsInsert("idlHeightI")    = heighti
    rsInsert("idlSmkgID")     = request.form("idlSmkgID")
    rsInsert("idlDrkgID")      = request.form("idlDrkgID")
    rsInsert("idlLocFlag")    = request.form("idllocflag")
    rsInsert("idlLocArea1") = request.form("idllocarea1")
    rsInsert("idlLocArea2") = request.form("idllocarea2")
    rsInsert("download")          = 0
    rsInsert("stateid")      = "CA"

    rsInsert.Update
    'Conn.CommitTrans
    rsInsert.Close

    sql = "SELECT Members.SignOnID, Members.memberid, Members.AdmCreateDate FROM
➡Members WHERE(((Members.SignOnID)=" & session.sessionid & ") AND
➡((Members.AdmCreateDate)=Date()));"
```

```
    Set RS = Conn.Execute(sql)
    msg = "<blink>Please Record your New Member ID:</blink> " & rs("memberid") &
" "

    '   ------------------------------------
    ' Set Session Object with memberid value
    '   ------------------------------------
    memval = rs("memberid")
    session("memberid") = memval
    session("logonstatus") = 3
    rs.close
End Select
'   --------------------------------
'   --------------------------------
' Output HTML Area
'   --------------------------------
'   --------------------------------
%>
...
```

App

B

FIG. B.2

This is a sample of the form fields present in step 2 of the New Account sign up process.

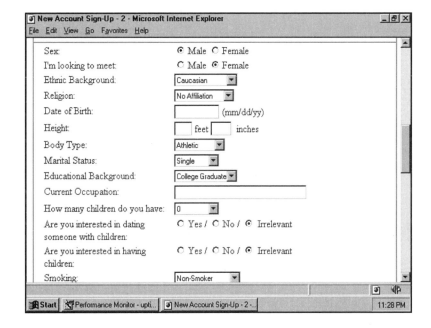

New Account: Step 3

Step 3 (see Figure B.3) provides an update SQL statement to add additional profile information to the New Members record. To update the record, step 3 performs a series of data evaluations and manipulations to prepare the information for the update statement. Conditional processing such as If/Then statements and For/Next loops are used to evaluate form-based information, and in addition to simple evaluations, a callable string function is invoked for modifying various fields to strip out single and double quotation marks, which can affect the SQL-based update statement.

FIG. B.3

Step 3 of the New Account process updates the newly inserted record with the additional profile information entered in step 2.

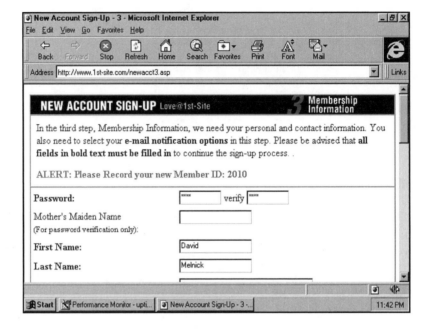

The code in Listing B.3 illustrates several important features associated with the update of an existing account. In addition to the update of the account record in the database, Listing B.3 also illustrates callable functions and variable testing.

Listing B.3   NEWACCT3.ASP—The Use of a Callable Function, Variable Testing, and Update SQL Statement

```
<!--#include file="validatenew.asp"-->
<script language=vbscript runat=server>
Function StripChars(txtstring)
    tempstring = ""
    length = Len(txtstring)
    For i = 1 To length
        singlechar = Mid(txtstring, i, 1)
        If singlechar = Chr(34) then
            tempstring = tempstring & Chr(180) & Chr(180)
        ElseIf singlechar = Chr(39) then
            tempstring = tempstring & Chr(180)
        Else
            tempstring = tempstring & singlechar
        End If
    Next
    StripChars = tempstring
End Function
</script>
```

```asp
<%
  Set Conn = Server.CreateObject("ADODB.Connection")
  Conn.Open("firstsite")
  'Set Conn = Session("Conn")
' ------------------------------------------
' Update based on member id in session object
' ------------------------------------------

'Testing Uncertain Values
'------------------------
OCC = request.form("profocc")
act = request.form("profact")
movie = request.form("profmovie")
music = request.form("profmusic")
book = request.form("profbook")
what = request.form("profwhat")
Q1Info = request.form("profQ1Info")
heightF = request.form("profHeightF")
heightI = request.form("profHeightI")
dob = request.form("profdob")
profhairid = request.form("profhairid")
profeyeid = request.form("profeyeid")

if occ = "" then occ = "NA"
if act = "" then act = "NA"
if movie = "" then movie = "NA"
if music = "" then music = 0
if book = "" then book = "NA"
if what = "" then what = "NA"
if Q1info = "" then Q1info = "NA"
if HeightF = "" then HeightF = 0
if Heighti = "" then HeightI = 0
if dob = "" then dob = "01/01/01"
'----------------------

if request.form("profsex") <> "" then
sql = "UPDATE Members SET"
    sql = sql & " Members.ProfSex =" & request.form("profsex") & ","
    sql = sql & " Members.ProfPrefID =" & request.form("ProfPrefID") & ","
    sql = sql & " Members.ProfRaceID =" & request.form("profRaceID") & ","
    sql = sql & " Members.ProfRlgnID =" & request.form("profRlgnID") & ","
    sql = sql & " Members.Profdob =#" & stripchars(dob) & "#,"
    sql = sql & " Members.ProfHeightF =" & stripchars(HeightF) & ","
    sql = sql & " Members.ProfHeightI =" & stripchars(HeightI) & ","
    sql = sql & " Members.ProfBodyID =" & request.form("profBodyID") & ","
    sql = sql & " Members.ProfStatusID ='" & request.form("profStatusID") & "',"
    sql = sql & " Members.ProfEdID =" & request.form("profEdID") & ","
    sql = sql & " Members.ProfOcc ='" & stripchars(occ) & "',"
    sql = sql & " Members.ProfChldNum =" & request.form("ProfChldNum") & ","
    sql = sql & " Members.ProfChldExist =1," '& request.form("ProfChldExist") & ","
    sql = sql & " Members.ProfChldNew =1," '& request.form("ProfChldNew") & ","
    sql = sql & " Members.ProfSmkgID =" & request.form("ProfSmkgID") & ","
    sql = sql & " Members.ProfDrkgID =" & request.form("ProfDrkgID") & ","
    sql = sql & " Members.ProfEyeID ='" & ProfEyeID & "',"
    sql = sql & " Members.ProfHairID ='" & ProfHairID & "',"
```

continues

Listing B.3   Continued

```
        sql = sql & " Members.ProfAct ='" & stripchars(act) & "',"
        sql = sql & " Members.ProfMovie ='" & stripchars(movie) & "',"
        sql = sql & " Members.ProfMusic ='" & stripchars(music) & "',"
        sql = sql & " Members.ProfBook ='" & stripchars(book) & "',"
        sql = sql & " Members.ProfWhat ='" & stripchars(what) & "',"
        sql = sql & " Members.ProfQ1ID =" & request.form("ProfQ1ID") & ","
        sql = sql & " Members.ProfQ1Info ='" & stripchars(Q1Info) & "' "
        sql = sql & " WHERE (((Members.AdmCreateDate)=Date()) AND"
        sql = sql & " ((Members.memberID)=" & session("memberid") & "))"
        Set rsupdate = Server.CreateObject("ADO.Recordset")
        rsupdate.Open sql, Conn, 3
end if

Set rsStates = Conn.Execute("SELECT StatePostalCode FROM States;")
' -------------------------------
' -------------------------------
sql = "SELECT * FROM Members WHERE MemberID=" & session("MemberID") & ";"
Set rs = Conn.Execute(sql)
%>
```

Recap of New Account Sign-Up Process

The New Account sign-up process involves the creation of a New Account record; a prospective member's data is carefully entered into the database, tracked, and evaluated for potential matches as the prospective member moves through a series of screens that guides the entry of information. Some of the key Active Server features invoked include:

- Session ID for tracking state during the initial insert and retrieval of a member record
- Request Object for gathering data entered in form fields
- VBScript for the conditional processing related to data validation and manipulation
- ADO Component for the active use of a database to store information entered

Managing Logon and Validation

Once a New Member Profile has been successfully created and activated by whatever administrative process has been created, a logon process must be created to validate a user's identity. In addition, with a membership paradigm, users who attempt to open an .asp file without logging on must be trapped and routed to a logon screen for validation. At first glance, this process seems to require the use of Windows NT Server's User Manager. After a quick review, however, it becomes clear that managing the authentication process through a database has many benefits over the user manager from maintainability and efficiency perspectives. As a result, I leave the user manager for highly sensitive security issues such as site administration and immediately rely on database lookups for membership authentication.

The components of an effective Logon and Validation model include a logon screen, which can set a `Session` variable for tracking the logon status, and a validation .asp file, which is included at the top of every page and which redirects users to the logon screen if they do not pass a simple check of the logon session variable. These components immediately provide much better security than most solutions found on the Web today. One of the benefits of a `Session` variable is that it only resides at the server. Rather than writing a status with a `Cookie`, which can be "spoofed," the logon status relates to a given Session ID on the browser and, therefore, does not get directly passed over the Internet.

 T I P | Generally, on the Internet, spoofing refers to creating a transaction where the one computer pretends to have the address, or identity, of another computer. We use this imagery because with a faked `Cookie`, a computer could send a transaction to the Web server that would lead it to mistakenly assume it was a different computer.

The Logon Process

The logon process can be more or less complicated, depending on your method for authenticating the member. The logon screens should also be candidates for two types of security measures. First, the field in which a password or other type of information is entered should be set as a password so that asterisks are displayed in the browser in place of the data entered by the user; second, this screen may also be used with an SSL socket (i.e., **HTTPS://** reference) to ensure the encryption of password information as it passes over the network. These security decisions depend on the level of security required at your site.

Secure Sockets Layer (SSL)

SSL provides the most widely used mechanism for securing Web-related information in transit on the Internet. In summary, SSL provides an encryption standard for Web browsers and Web servers to securely share information.

The initial logon page simply requires a form field for the entry of whatever validation information needs to be submitted. For our Introduction Service, Figure B.4 displays the logon screen and all required information captured, including the MemberID and a Password.

In addition to the basic data entry fields, our Service displays a system message that explains why the user ended up at this page. The appropriate message string is set to a `Session` property and subsequently displayed if a failed logon attempt occurs or if the user gets routed to the logon screen from a validation in some other .asp file. In addition, if the `Session` property used for storing messages is left empty, then the current session is abandoned to enable the user to log on again. Listing B.4 illustrates the code used at the top of the .asp file to check the `Session` property containing the message and either display the message, if the logon attempt failed, or abandon the current session and allow a new logon to occur.

FIG. B.4

This is the Logon Entry Screen used to submit member ID and password information.

Listing B.4 LOGON.ASP—Illustration of Message Display at the Top of the Logon Page

```
<%  msg = session("msg")
'-----------------------------------'
Output HTML Section
'-----------------------------------
%>
<html><head><title>
Love@1st Site - Interactive Introductions-Logon
</title></head><body bgcolor="#FFFFFF">
<%=msg%>
<%
  If session("msg") = "" then
     session.abandon
  End If
  session("msg") = ""
%>
```

Once the initial logon request is submitted, the Service begins a comprehensive set of evaluation routines to identify whether or not the logon attempt authenticates the user, and if not, to determine why the authentication attempt failed.

The logon.asp invokes the logoncheck.asp file, which directly outputs nothing. The authentication file simply evaluates the logon attempt and either redirects a successful logon to the start.asp page or sets a message to the session (msg) variable and redirects the user back to the logon.asp page. If a successful logon occurs, the logoncheck.asp also writes an update back to the Membership table to change to the current date/time, the date/time field used for tracking the last time the user logged on to the Service.

The code illustrated in Listing B.5 shows the process for authenticating the user on the Service. The code also handles the different failure conditions that can result by carefully reviewing all possible failures followed by a comprehensive message back to the user.

N O T E The logoncheck.asp cannot directly write HTML output because the redirect feature does not function once HTTP headers have been sent (see format of HTTP record for more details about what the headers include). Headers are sent as soon as a `response.write` event occurs. ▪

App

B

Listing B.5   LOGONCHECK.ASP—Authentication Process for Logon

```
<Script Language=VBScript runat=server>
Function redirect()
  Response.Redirect "logon.asp"
end function
</script>

<%
 Set Conn = Server.CreateObject("ADO.Connection")
 Conn.Open("firstsite")


 '--------------------------------------------------
 '--------------------------------------------------
 'Level 1 Basic Validation Testing
 '--------------------------------------------------
 '--------------------------------------------------


 'Test for Entry of Member ID prior to Running Search
 '--------------------------------------------------
 if request.form("memberid")="" then ' No Member ID Entered
   session("msg") = "<h3><center>Oops! The Member ID# didn't work.  Try the
Member ID# search below.</center></h3>"
   Redirect 'Call Function to Exit Back to Logon Screen

 'Run Search
 '--------------------------------------------------
 else 'Run Database Lookup
   sql = "SELECT members.admonlinedate, Members.MemberID, members.pass,
➥Members.FName, Members.LName, Members.AdmExpDate, Members.AdmStatus,
➥Members.InactivateReason, Members.AdminGraphics, Members.AdmCreateDate FROM
➥Members "
   sql = sql & "WHERE (((Members.MemberID)=" & request.form("memberid") & "));"
   set rs = conn.execute(sql)
 end if


 '-------------------------------------------
 '-------------------------------------------
 'Level 2 Validation Testing
```

continues

Listing B.5 Continued

```
'-----------------------------------------
'-----------------------------------------

If not rs.eof then
    test = rs("memberid")
    session("memberid") = test
End If


'Member ID Entered Now Run Search for Record
'-----------------------------------------
If rs.eof Then 'No Record Found Bad ID
   rs.close
   session("msg") = "<h3><center>Oops! We couldn't find Member ID# <em>" &
➥request.form("memberid") & "</em>. Please try again or use our Member ID#
➥Search below.</center></h3>"
   Redirect 'Call Function to Exit Back to Logon Screen


'Customer Record Found Now Check Password
'-----------------------------------------
elseif not request.form("password") = rs("pass") then
   rs.close
   session("msg") = "<h3><center>Oops!  Your ID# is okay, but the password didn't
➥work.  (Remember it is case sensitive) Try again.</center></h3>"
   Redirect 'Call Function to Exit Back to Logon Screen

'Check for inactive status
'-----------------------------------------
elseif rs("admstatus") = 0 then

   if rs("CompletedProcess") = 0 then
      rs.close
      session("msg") = "<h3><center>Not Active or Expired Account</center></h3>"
      Redirect 'Call Function to Exit Back to Logon Screen
   end if

'Password OK now check to see if pictures arrived.  They have 30 days.
'-----------------------------------------------------------------
elseif (rs("admingraphics") = 0) and (rs("admcreatedate") + 30 < date()) then
   session("msg") = "<center><font color=" & """" & "#FF0000" & """" & ">
➥<strong>We have not received your photos yet.  You are not able to
➥access Member Services until we receive your photos.</strong></font></center>"
   session("scanaction") = "lockout"
   Response.Redirect "scan.asp"

'See if pictures arrived.  After 15 days they get a warning message.
'-----------------------------------------------------------------
elseif (rs("admingraphics") = 0) and (rs("admcreatedate") + 15 < date()) then
   session("msg") = "<center><font color=" & """" & "#FF0000" & """" & "><strong>
➥We have not received your photos yet.  If we do not receive your photos prior
➥to " & rs("admcreatedate") + 15 & ", we will remove your access to Member
➥Services.</strong></font></center>"
```

```
        session("scanaction") = "warning"
        Response.Redirect "scan.asp"
    '--------------------------------------------------
    '--------------------------------------------------
    ' Step 3. Success Logon Approved
    '--------------------------------------------------
    '--------------------------------------------------
    else
        session("logonstatus") = 1
        session("AdmOnlineDate") = rs("AdmOnlineDate")

        sql = "UPDATE Members SET"
            sql = sql & " Members.AdmOnlineDate = #" & Date() & "#"
            sql = sql & " WHERE Members.MemberID=" & request.form("memberid") & ";"
            set rs2 = conn.execute(sql)

        response.redirect "start.asp"
    end if

    rs.close

%>
```

App

B

The Validation Checks

Two discrete validation .asps are used in the Service. The first validate.asp file is used in every page with the exception of the New Account pages, while the second validatenew.asp is used on all New Account pages. Both validation pages rely on the Session property named logonstatus.

The New Account validation pages use the logon status Session property extensively to monitor what point in the New Account process New Members have reached. This file relies on the Select Case statement to evaluate all possible statuses of the logon status Session property. Currently only Case 0 and 1 are in use. Listing B.6 illustrates the code of the Select Case statement used to evaluate the Logon Status on New Account Pages.

Listing B.6   VALIDATENEW.ASP—The Select Case Evaluation of the Logon Status Variable for Users in the New Account Pages

```
<%
  'Set ADO Object variable for use in remainder of page processing
  Set Conn = Server.CreateObject("ADODB.Connection")
  Conn.Open("firstsite")

Select Case session("logonstatus")
Case 0 'New Session No Status
      session("logonstatus") = 2

Case 1
      session("logonstatus") = 2
```

continues

Listing B.6   Continued

```
Case 2 'New Member in Sign Up Process first page
Case 3 'New Member in Sign Up Process Record Created
Case 4 'New Member in Sign Up Process Error Status
End Select
%>
```

The standard validate.asp file, which is invoked with a Server-Side Include statement on all other pages, provides evaluations very similar to the validatenew.asp file, with one minor exception: It only takes action if a logon status is 0. Every other status qualifies either as a New Member in process or as a properly logged on member account. The code for this evaluation is illustrated in Listing B.7.

Listing B.7   VALIDATE.ASP—Validation File Included in All *.asp* Files Other than the New Account Pages

```
<%
 Set Conn = Server.CreateObject("ADODB.Connection")
 Conn.Open("firstsite")

Select Case session("logonstatus")
Case 0 'New Session No Status
      session("msg") = "<h3><center> Your are currently not logged in or your
➡login has timed out </center></h3> Please logon to continue your session,
➡sorry for any inconvenience</h4>"
      Response.Redirect "logon.asp"

Case 1 'Authenticated User Properly Logged On
Case 2 'New Member in Sign Up Process first page
Case 3 'New Member in Sign Up Process Record Created
End Select
%>
```

Recap of Logon and Validation Process

The Logon and Validation process requires a small amount of code and only a couple of .asp files, but based on Server-Side Includes, these files find their way into every single Active Server Page processed for delivery to the client. Although not complex in implementation, this file provides the heart of membership security features and should be carefully put into effect. Some of the key Active Server features invoked include:

- Custom `Session` Variable for tracking logon status
- `Response.Redirect` feature for rerouting users from any page to the `logon.asp`
- VBScript for the conditional processing related to authentication
- ADO Component for the active use of a database to look up account information

Users Maintaining Their Own Account Information

Implementing a cost-effective, fee-based subscription service requires automating the costly administrative responsibilities that can develop due in part to member account maintenance and site enhancement. As one effective step in controlling these costs and at the same time empowering the user community with additional control and convenience, a site should place as much maintenance responsibility as possible with the end user community. The Introduction Service places extensive maintenance features in the hands of the members, as illustrated on the primary maintenance screen in Figure B.5. From Ideal Mate settings to billing information, the member has control.

App

B

FIG. B.5

This is the primary maintenance screen for a member to administer his account information.

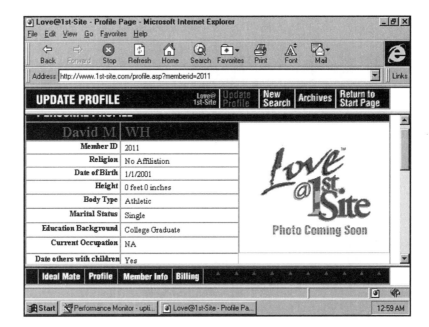

Enabling members to edit these pages simply involves taking the New Account pages and adapting them for update. The primary change involves defaulting all values in the form fields to be populated with a member's currently set information. In addition, these pages will be updated out of order rather than linearly as with the New Account process. Without going into repetitive detail with the editacctX.asp files, in Listing B.8 we will illustrate just the editacct3.asp, which contains Member Information. The key task involves looking up the customer record and ensuring that the member ID of the currently logged on user matches the one used to look up customer information so that no other user can accidentally edit another member's account.

Listing B.8   EDITACCT3.ASP—Member Editing of Account Information Based on Defaulted Form Field Values

```
<%
  Set Conn = Server.CreateObject("ADODB.Connection")
  Conn.Open("firstsite")

  sql = "SELECT * FROM Members WHERE MemberID=" & session("MemberID") & ";"
  Set rs = Conn.Execute(sql)

  Set rsStates = Conn.Execute("SELECT StatePostalCode FROM States;")

'Testing Uncertain Values
'------------------------
OCC = request.form("profocc")
act = request.form("profact")
movie = request.form("profmovie")
book = request.form("profbook")
what = request.form("profwhat")
Q1Info = request.form("profQ1Info")
heightF = request.form("profHeightF")
heightI = request.form("profHeightI")
dob = request.form("profdob")

if occ = "" then occ = "NA"
if act = "" then act = "NA"
if movie = "" then movie = "NA"
if book = "" then book = "NA"
if what = "" then what = "NA"
if Q1info = "" then Q1info = "NA"
if HeightF = "" then HeightF = 0
if Heighti = "" then HeightI = 0
if dob = "" then dob = "01/01/01"
%>

<html>
<base href="http://www.1st-site.com/">
<head>
<title>Edit Membership Information</title>
</head>
<form action="editacctupdate.asp" target="_top" method="POST">
<body bgcolor="#FFFFFF" text="#0000A0">
<table border=1 cellpadding=8 cellspacing=0 width=604>
<tr><td>
<p>Changed your home or e-mail address? Want to change
 your password? Care to change your e-mail notification
 preferences? Modify your information and preferences
 below, then click on the Update button. Your changes
 will take effect immediately.
</p>
</td>
</tr>
<tr>
<td align="center">
<br>
```

```
<br>
<table width=100%>
<tr><td width=30% valign="top">Password:</td><td
 colspan=2 width=40% valign="top"><input type=password
 size=10 maxlength=10 name="pass"
 value="<%=rs("pass")%>"></td></tr>
...
```

All edit files invoke the one editaccountupdate.asp file illustrated in Listing B.9. This file centralizes all of the update statements into one file to isolate the code associated with updating accounts. This process of organizing .asp files in an intuitive manner for managing your code can provide invaluable support when you need to edit your code. The editaccountupdate.asp simply executes an update SQL statement based on the fields entered.

Listing B.9   EDITACCOUNTUPDATE.ASP—Centralized .asp for Updating Member Accounts Based on Member-Initiated Updates of Their Member Information

```
...
    sql = "UPDATE Members SET"
        if request.form("fname") <> "" then
            sql = sql & " Members.fname ='" & stripchars(request.form("fname")) &
➥"',"
        end if
        if request.form("lname") <> "" then
            sql = sql & " Members.lname ='" & stripchars(request.form("lname")) &
➥"',"
        end if
        sql = sql & " Members.pass ='" & stripchars(pass) & "',"
        sql = sql & " Members.address1 ='" & stripchars(address1) & "',"
        sql = sql & " Members.address2 ='" & stripchars(address2) & "',"
        sql = sql & " Members.city ='" & stripchars(city) & "',"
        sql = sql & " Members.stateid ='" & request.form("stateid") & "',"
        sql = sql & " Members.zip ='" & stripchars(zip) & "',"
        sql = sql & " Members.hmareacode ='" & stripchars(hmareacode) & "',"
        sql = sql & " Members.hmphone ='" & stripchars(hmphone) & "',"
        sql = sql & " Members.wkareacode ='" & stripchars(wkareacode) & "',"
        sql = sql & " Members.wkphone ='" & stripchars(wkphone) & "',"
        sql = sql & " Members.publicphone =" & request.form("publicphone") & ","
        if request.form("email") <> "" then
            sql = sql & " Members.email ='" & stripchars(request.form("email")) &
➥"',"
        end if
        sql = sql & " Members.publicemail =" & request.form("publicemail") & ","
        sql = sql & " Members.maiden ='" & stripchars(maiden) & "',"
        sql = sql & " Members.ESelect =" & request.form("eselect") & ","
        sql = sql & " Members.Eaccept =" & request.form("eaccept") & ","
        sql = sql & " Members.EGenie =" & request.form("egenie") & ","
        sql = sql & " Members.EGen =" & request.form("egen") & ","
        sql = sql & " Members.download = 1,"
        sql = sql & " Members.AdmModDate = #" & Date() & "#,"
```

continues

Listing B.9 Continued

```
        sql = sql & " Members.EOK =" & request.form("eok") & " "
        sql = sql & " WHERE Members.memberID=" & session("memberid") & ";"

        Set rs = Server.CreateObject("ADO.Recordset")
        rs.Open sql,Conn,3

End If

newpage = "profile.asp?memberid=" & session("memberid")
response.redirect newpage
%>
```

The process of managing account information follows the pages used for creating a New Account very closely. Although these pages can be fairly easily copied over and modified for use, I recommend that you leave these edit account pages until late in the development process because changes in the New Account pages and Member table have cascading impact on the Edit Account pages. Most test users have little need to manage accounts and can easily live without this set of features until late in the development process.

Summing Up

Establishing a membership-based community relies upon effective management of the New Account process, logon and account validation, and effective distribution of account maintenance into the membership community. However, if the community sponsor intends to charge fees for products and services, providing a compelling and interactive user experience coupled with effective administration and a convenient billing/payment service will determine the overall effectiveness of the site as a business venture.

Appendix C, "Delivering an Interactive Introduction Service," explores delivering an interactive service, followed by a look at the administrative and payment services included in the Introduction Service site. ●

Delivering an Interactive Introduction Service

To deliver an interactive Web-based environment with Active Server Pages the developer must enable Web site users to play active roles in determining how dynamic pages are generated. Generally, enabling users to play active roles requires the use of a database or some other method of enabling the Web site to track choices made by users. After the site tracks choices or decisions made by users, this information can be integrated into layout and information displayed on dynamic pages.

The Introduction Service case study delivers this interactivity by enabling users to search through a database of other users, followed by a structured process for interacting with other users that they selected for an introduction. This appendix discusses the methods used to enable users to search for each other, followed by a review of how the users participate in the interactive introduction process. In addition to the purely Web-driven interactivity, this appendix explores the capability to integrate other services such as e-mail into the interactive process. ■

Database design: Selections table

The process of managing users' experiences at the site focuses largely on utilizing membership information; however, tracking how one user communicates with another user requires an additional data table named Selections.

Finding other members

A well designed site should provide comprehensive search features that enable members to find each other within the site.

The introduction process and the Start page

A key success factor for the Introduction Service is providing site routing, security, anonymity, and accountability.

E-mail-driven introduction features

A distinguishing factor for current Web sites relates to leveraging mail to facilitate site features, specifically in this case, integrating database and mail services.

Database Design: Selections Table

The Selections table provides a structure for tracking members in relation to other members. When a member requests an introduction or responds to a request for an introduction, the Selections table tracks the user's choices. This table provides a mechanism for tracking the status of an evolving introduction as it moves from an anonymous request from one member to an acceptance or unfortunate rejection from another member.

The Selections table enables the Active Server Pages to evaluate and dynamically display different pages for members, depending on the status of current introductions in the process for a particular member. This information defines both the information displayed to a member and the toolbar options available at any given time for that member. The table structure for managing the status and history of introductions turns out to be quite simple; in fact, the entire table is made up of only the 6 fields shown in Table C.1.

Table C.1   Selections Database Design Specification, Including Field Level Information

Field Name	DataType	Description
SelectID	Number (Long)	Primary key
SelectorMemberID	Number (Long)	Member ID of initiating member
SelectedMemberID	Number (Long)	Member ID of receiving member
SelectCreateDate	Date/Time	Date of initial selection
SelectFinalDate	Date/Time	Date of completed/final response
SelectStatus	Number (Long)	Current/final status of selection

Finding Other Members

The process of searching for members involves, not only the searching of active members based on criteria in their profiles, but also the active use of the Selections table to automatically filter out the members who have been previously selected. This filtering process prevents a member from having to continually scroll through a history of their past rejections or failed love connections. The key components utilized in a search include the Ideal Mate information, which enables the Service to automatically default information into the search criteria for a member; the Member Profile, which provides the information evaluated during the search; and the Selections table, which filters to limit the results returned.

The Search Pages involve a series of three .asp files that are dynamically created, including the Initial Search page, the resulting summary display of results, and the Member Profile, which allows members to request introductions.

Initial Search Page

The Initial Search page displayed in Figure C.1 defaults the Ideal Mate information and enables the member to customize the search criteria to either broaden or narrow the types of members that will be returned for display and possible selection.

FIG. C.1

The Initial Search page enables the member to begin a search of the member database.

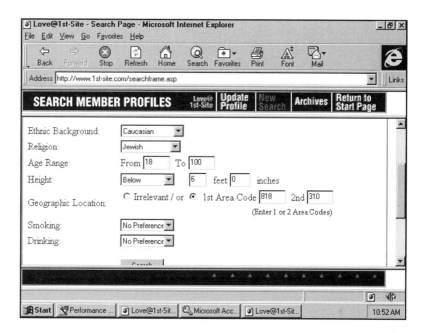

The Service automatically filters out past rejections to save the member redundancy in the search process. And the search will also automatically include specific constraints based on the member's profile to avoid finding members of the wrong gender.

The Active Server Page for searching looks up the current member, based on his logged-on session variable, which stores his member ID and uses the Ideal Mate information to populate defaults into the search criteria. As illustrated by the session (nextmemberid) variable, the system also limits the number of selections displayed on the results page and allows the user to move through subsequent pages to display additional members. This next page technology, while not trivial to implement, allows you to manage the volume of data downloaded to any single page. The next page functionality becomes increasingly important in services like this one in which graphic images are displayed for each record found in the database. Listing C.1 illustrates the code utilized to provide the searching user with default values automatically populated into the selection parameters they can set.

Listing C.1 SEARCH.ASP—Initial Search Page

```
<!--#include file="validate.asp"-->
<%
  Set Conn = Server.CreateObject("ADODB.Connection")
  Conn.Open("firstsite")
  session("nextmemberid") = 0
  membernum = session("memberid")
  sql = "SELECT * FROM Members WHERE MemberID=" & membernum & ";"
  Set rs = Conn.Execute(sql)
  Set rsRace = Conn.Execute("SELECT * FROM AdminParameters where (systypeparam = 1)
➥order by paramvalue;")
  Set rsReligion = Conn.Execute("SELECT * FROM AdminParameters where
➥(systypeparam = 2) order by paramvalue;")

  Session("SearchPagesDisplayed") = 1
%>

<html><head>
<title>Search for your Ideal Mate</title>
</head>

<body bgcolor="#FFFFFF" text="#0000A0">
<table border=1 cellpadding=5 cellspacing=0 width=604>
<tr><td>
Our search wizard works within your constraints to help
 you find exactly who you are looking for.  Search
 with as many or as few criteria as you like.
...
 we let 90's technology work to your advantage.<p>

<form action="searchrun.asp" target="_top" method="POST">
<input type=hidden name="profprefid" value="<%=rs("ProfPrefID")%>">
...
```

Executing the Search and Displaying a Result Set

The Active Server Page named searchrun.asp either executes a direct search if a member ID was directly entered, or it runs a parameter-based search of the member table based on the more comprehensive criteria entered. The searchrun.asp also manages the next page feature, which allows members to display additional records if their searches return too many members. The display of the page allows the member to drill into a detailed Member Profile page by clicking any photo displayed in the results page.

The execution of the searchrun.asp performs a database search, resulting in, not only a listing of the top 10 members found, but also a complete list of members found, enabling the user to page back and forth through the complete result set. Building a custom SQL statement requires a series of tests and field validations, based on the form data passed in by the search.asp page. The comprehensive logic illustrated in Listing C.2 details the complicated construction of a custom SQL statement for processing.

Listing C.2   SEARCHRUN.ASP—Section of the searchrun.asp file, Which Constructs the Custom SQL Statement for Execution

```
<!--#include file="validate.asp"-->
<%
    Set Conn = Server.CreateObject("ADODB.Connection")
    Conn.Open("firstsite")

'Tracking next page feature
' ----------------------------------------------
If (not isempty(request.form("btn"))) or (Session("SearchPagesDisplayed") > 4) then
    session("nextmemberid") = 0
End If


' ----------------------------------------------
' Don't mix gay/hetero, set appropriate sql
' ----------------------------------------------
sql = "SELECT ProfSex, ProfPrefID FROM Members WHERE MemberID=" & session
➥("MemberID") & ";"
Set rs2=Server.CreateObject("ADO.Recordset")
rs2.Open sql, Conn,1

ProfPrefID = rs2("ProfPrefID")
If rs2("ProfSex") = rs2("ProfPrefID") Then
 sqlsex = " AND (Members.ProfSex = Members.ProfPrefID) "
Else
 sqlsex = " AND (Members.ProfSex <> Members.ProfPrefID) "
End If

rs2.close

'------------------------
'Test Direct or Full Lookup
'------------------------
if request.form("direct") <> "" then
'------------------------
'Direct Check
'------------------------
sql = "SELECT Top 10 Members.MemberID, Members.FName, Members.LName,
➥Members.City, members.admingraphics FROM Members "
if isnumeric(request.form("direct")) = -1 then
  sql = sql & " WHERE ((members.profsex =" & request.form("profprefid") & ")
➥AND ((Members.memberid)=" & request.form("direct") & ") AND
➥((Members.memberid)<>" & session("memberid") & ") AND ((Members.AdmStatus)=1) AND
➥((Members.AdmPublic)=Yes))" & sqlsex & " Order By Members.MemberID;"
else 'First Name Search
  sql = sql & " WHERE ((members.profsex =" & request.form("profprefid") & ")
➥AND ((Members.FNAME)='" & request.form("direct") & "') AND
➥((Members.memberid)<>" & session("memberid") & ") AND ((Members.AdmStatus)=1)
AND ((Members.AdmPublic)=Yes))" & sqlsex & " Order By Members.MemberID;"
end if
```

App

C

continues

Listing C.2 Continued

```
else
'.........................
'Full Search
'.........................
sql = "Select Top 11 members.admingraphics, members.fname, Members.LName,
➥members.memberid, members.city from members where "
  if request.form("idlRaceID") > 0 then
      sql = sql & " Members.profRaceID =" & request.form("idlRaceID") & " and "
  end if
  if request.form("idlRlgnID") > 0 then
      sql = sql & " Members.profRlgnID =" & request.form("idlRlgnID") & " and "
  end if
  select case request.form("idlheightflag")
    case 0
    case 1
      sql = sql & "((Members.profHeightf * 12) + (Members.profHeightI))
➥<= " & ((request.form("idlHeightF") * 12) +
➥request.form("idlHeightI")) & " and "
    case 2
      sql = sql & "((Members.profHeightf * 12) + (Members.profHeightI))
➥>= " & ((request.form("idlHeightF") * 12) +
➥request.form("idlHeightI")) & " and "
  end select

  if request.form("idlSmkgID") = 1 then
      sql = sql & " Members.profSmkgID =" & "0" & " and "
  end if

  if request.form("idlDrkgID") = 1 then
      sql = sql & " Members.profDrkgID =" & "0" & " and "
  end if

  if not request.form("idlagelow") = "" and not request.form("idlagehigh") = "" then
      doblow = date - (request.form("idlagelow") * 365)
      dobhigh = date - ((request.form("idlagehigh") + 1) * 365)

      sql = sql & " (Members.profdob between #" & dobhigh & "# and #" & doblow &
➥"#) and "
  end if

'Insert SQLsex or Gender Criteria portion of SQL
  sql = sql & " ((members.profsex =" & request.form("profprefid") & ")
➥ AND (Members.memberid<>" & session("memberid") & ")
➥and (Members.AdmStatus=1) AND (Members.AdmPublic=Yes)" & sqlsex

  if request.form("idllocflag") <> 0 then
      sql = sql & " and ((Members.HMAreaCode = " & "'"
➥ & request.form("idllocarea1") & "'" & ") or "
      sql = sql & "(Members.HMAreaCode = " & "'" &
➥request.form("idllocarea2") & "'" & "))"
  end if

  sql = sql & " and (Members.MemberID >= " &
➥session("nextmemberid") & ")) Order By Members.MemberID;"
```

```
end if
' ------------------------------
'Execute Search
' ------------------------------
Set rs=Server.CreateObject("ADO.Recordset")
rs.Open sql, Conn,1
%>
...
```

Once the SQL statement has been constructed and executed, the task now turns to displaying the results. Using graphic images stored in a predefined directory and given names based on the IDs in the Member Profile, providing the capability to page through the search results is a deceptively difficult challenge. Listing C.3 illustrates the creation of the display page and record tracking feature to enable the paging logic.

The key aspects of the paging logic include the assumption that records are sorted by ID number, and, therefore, by searching for ID numbers greater than the last one displayed, you will return additional non-overlapping records. In addition, a Session property is utilized as a counter to determine which page or set of records the member currently is displaying. Finally, the page defaults a series of hidden form fields to the values that have been input for the search. Defaulting the values to hidden form fields enables the page to rerun itself, retrieving all of the information for rebuilding the search directly from the form fields. Other approaches for optimizing this type of paging logic might include storing the RecordSet as a Session property and retrieving a full RecordSet at the initial search.

Listing C.3   SEARCHRUN.ASP—Display Section of the searchrun.asp file, Which Manages the Next Page Feature

```
<html><head>
<title>Search Results Profile</title>
</head>

<body bgcolor="#FFFFFF" text="0000A0">
<form action="searchrun.asp" TARGET="_top" method="POST">

<table border=1 cellpadding="0" cellspacing="0" width=600>
<tr><td colspan=5><img src="images/searchrun.gif"
 align=bottom width=600 height=30></td></tr>

<tr>
<%
'----------------------
'Display first ten results
'----------------------
  i=0
  Do While (Not RS.EOF)
  i = i + 1
  if i < 11 then
     if rs("admingraphics") = 0 then
        imagename = "Default.tn"
```

continues

Listing C.3   Continued

```
     else
        imagename = rs("memberid") & ".tn"
     end if
%>
     <td align=center>
     <a href="profile.asp?id=1&memberid=<%=rs("memberid")%>">
<img src="/images/profile/<%=imagename%>.jpg"
 align=bottom border=0 width=100 height=85></a><br>
     <% line1 = rs("fname") & " " & left(rs("lname"),1)Â & " </strong> " &
rs("memberid") %>
     <font size=1><strong><%= line1 %><br><%=rs("city")%></font></center>
     </td>
<%
     if i/5 = int(i/5) then response.write "</tr><tr>"
  Else
     'Set next page memberID
     session("nextmemberid") = cint(rs("MemberID"))
  End If
  RS.MoveNext
  Loop
  RS.Close
%>
</tr>

<%
'---------------------
'O Results found in search
'---------------------
If i = 0 then %>
   <tr><td colspan=5 width=600><b>No members met your
search criteria.  You may wish to try a less specific
 search criteria.</b></td></tr>
<% End If %>

<%
'---------------------
'Add Next Page feature
'---------------------
 If (i = 11) and (Session("SearchPagesDisplayed") < 4) then %>
   <MAP NAME="nextpage">
   <AREA SHAPE="RECT" COORDS="20,1 147,20">
   </MAP>
   <tr><td colspan=5 width=600><INPUT NAME="submit"
➥ INPUT TYPE="IMAGE" SRC="/images/nextpage.gif" BORDER=0
➥ USEMAP="#nextpage"></tr></td>
<% Else %>
   <% Session("SearchPagesDisplayed") = 0 %>
   <tr><td colspan=5 width=600><img src="/images/blackbar.gif"
➥align=bottom width=600 height=24></td></tr>
<%'---------------------
End If %>

</table>
```

```
<%If ProfPrefID = 0 then%>
   <center><img src="gclikani.gif" width=300 height=80 border=0></center>
<%Else%>
   <center><img src="bclikani.gif" width=300 height=80 border=0></center>
<%End If
'----------------------
'Store hidden values for page feature
'----------------------%>
<INPUT NAME="direct" VALUE="<%=request.form("direct")%>" TYPE=HIDDEN>
<INPUT NAME="profprefid" VALUE=<%=request.form("profprefid")%> TYPE=HIDDEN>
<INPUT NAME="idlraceid" VALUE=<%=request.form("idlraceid")%> TYPE=HIDDEN>
<INPUT NAME="idlrlgnid" VALUE=<%=request.form("idlrlgnid")%> TYPE=HIDDEN>
<INPUT NAME="idlheightflag"Â VALUE=<%=request.form("idlheightflag")%>
➥TYPE=HIDDEN>
<INPUT NAME="idlheightf" VALUE=<%=request.form("idlheightf")%> TYPE=HIDDEN>
<INPUT NAME="idlheighti" VALUE=<%=request.form("idlheighti")%> TYPE=HIDDEN>
<INPUT NAME="idlsmkgid" VALUE=<%=request.form("idlsmkgid")%> TYPE=HIDDEN>
<INPUT NAME="idldrkgid" VALUE=<%=request.form("idldrkgid")%> TYPE=HIDDEN>
<INPUT NAME="idlagelow" VALUE=<%=request.form("idlagelow")%> TYPE=HIDDEN>
<INPUT NAME="idlagehigh" VALUE=<%=request.form("idlagehigh")%> TYPE=HIDDEN>
<INPUT NAME="idllocflag" VALUE=<%=request.form("idllocflag")%> TYPE=HIDDEN>
<INPUT NAME="idllocarea1" VALUE="<%=request.form("idllocarea1")%>" TYPE=HIDDEN>
<INPUT NAME="idllocarea2" VALUE="<%=request.form("idllocarea2")%>" TYPE=HIDDEN>

</form>
</body>
</html>
<%end if%>

<%Session("SearchPagesDisplayed") = Session("SearchPagesDisplayed") + 1 %>
```

App

C

Displaying an Individual Member for Introduction

Once a user has identified and selected a suitable member by clicking a photograph from the Search Results page, a Member Profile is displayed with a custom toolbar. The Member Profile page is invoked from a number of sources, and so the toolbar varies quite dramatically from one use to the next. When the Member Profile is displayed as the result of a search, the options primarily include the capability to request an introduction. The request creates a selection record with initial status, which displays the member on the Start page of both the selected and selecting member.

The basic Member Profile page includes comprehensive profile information about the member, but the last name, phone number, and mail information is not displayed at this point. That information is displayed only after both members have approved the introduction process.

The Active Server Pages used to generate the Member Profile page and navigation toolbar become a little more complicated because of the use of frames. Frames are used extensively throughout the Service site, and although they do not fundamentally change the way Active Server Pages are used, you must understand that multiple independent pages are being requested and executed for the display of a single request.

Frames and Active Server Pages

Frames involve a Frame Set page that manages which pages are called; although ASP execution properly works on all frames, they are independent pages, and therefore, you must be careful in your scoping of request-based variables.

Profile Display Frame Set (Manager)   The initial page call requests the profile.asp page, which manages the calling of other .asp files and the passing of request-based variables into those pages. The additional pages called include:

■ profile_top.asp displays custom Service-wide toolbar options.

■ profile_display.asp displays requested Member Profile information.

■ profile_bot.asp displays custom introduction-specific selection options.

Many features of the site rely on an initial call to a Frame Set as illustrated in the sections for Editing, Archiving, and more. Listing C.4 illustrates the basic setup of a Frame Set.

Listing C.4   PROFILE.ASP—Frame Manager .asp File Responsible for Calling All Individual Frame .asp Files

```
<!--#include file="validate.asp"-->
<HTML>
<TITLE>Love@1st-Site - Profile Page</TITLE>

<%session("id")=request.querystring("id")%>

<FRAMESET ROWS="41, *, 33">
<FRAME SRC="profile_top.asp" NAME="toolbar" MARGINWIDTH=0 NORESIZE
➥SCROLLING="no">
<FRAME SRC="profile_display.asp?memberid=<%=request.querystring("memberid")%>"
➥NAME="bottom" NORESIZE MARGINWIDTH=0 SCROLLING="auto">
<FRAME SRC="profile_bot.asp?memberid=<%=request.querystring("memberid")%>"
➥NAME="top" MARGINWIDTH=0 NORESIZE SCROLLING="no">
</FRAMESET>
<NOFRAME>
This page requires Netscape 2.0 or higher, Microsoft
 Explorer 3.0 or  AOL 3.0.
<p>
Please download one of the previously mentioned
 browsers to view this page.
</NOFRAME>

</HTML>
```

The Top and Bottom frames provide toolbar/navigation features whereas the Center frame ignores the logic associated with providing custom toolbars and focuses on the more standardized display of a member's profile.

Center Frame—Profile Display   The profile display relies upon the selected member ID request variable passed into the page and then uses the session variables to determine what options have been enabled on the current page display; i.e. if this represents a mutually consented introduction display, additional information including last name, phone number, and mail may be displayed.

The code from the `profile_display.asp` illustrated in Listing C.5 provides the lookups and evaluations conducted prior to generating the custom HTML-based display. The following SQL statement and evaluations highlight the lookups to populate the HTML page and the rule-based evaluations based on a session variable to determine how much confidential information to include on this page. The session variable is configured when this page call begins from the Start page, reflecting, not a new introduction request, but an introduction request that already has been created and assigned a status flag.

Listing C.5   PROFILE_DISPLAY.ASP—Format and Display of the Requested Member's Profile Information by the Profile Display

App
C

```
<!--#include file="validate.asp"-->
<%
  Set Conn = Server.CreateObject("ADODB.Connection")
  Conn.Open("firstsite")
  sql = "SELECT * FROM Members WHERE MemberID=" & Request("MemberID") & ";"
  Set rs = Conn.Execute(sql)


'-----------------------
'Request display values from AdminParameters
'-----------------------
sql="SELECT ParamValue From AdminParameters WHERE SysParamID=" & s("ProfRaceID")
Set rsRace = Conn.Execute(sql)

sql="SELECT ParamValue From AdminParameters WHERE SysParamID=" & s("ProfRlgnID")
Set rsReligion = Conn.Execute(sql)

sql="SELECT ParamValue From AdminParameters WHERE SysParamID=" & s("ProfBodyID")
Set rsBody = Conn.Execute(sql)

sql="SELECT ParamValue From AdminParameters WHERE SysParamID=" & rs("ProfEdID")
  Set rsEduc = Conn.Execute(sql)

sql="SELECT ParamValue From AdminParameters WHERE SysParamID in (" &
➥rs("ProfMusic") & ")"
  Set rsMusic = Conn.Execute(sql)

  sql = "SELECT ParamValue From AdminParameters WHERE SysParamID in (" &
➥rs("ProfQ1ID") & ")"
  Set rsQuestion = Conn.Execute(sql)

'-----------------------
```

continues

Listing C.5   Continued

```
    If rs("AdminGraphics") = 0 then
        PictureHead = "default.hd.gif"
        PictureFull = "default.fl.gif"
    Else
        PictureHead = rs("MemberID") & ".hd.jpg"
        PictureFull = rs("MemberID") & ".fl.jpg"
    End If
'........................

    Set DBConn=Server.CreateObject("ADODB.Connection")
    DBConn.Open("firstsite")
    sql = "SELECT ProfAct, ProfQ1Info, ProfWhat FROM Members WHERE MemberID=" &
Request("MemberID") & ";"
    Set rsMemo=Server.CreateObject("ADODB.Recordset")
    rsMemo.Open sql, DBConn,3


'........................
'Determine what confidential info to display
'........................
    If session("lookupstatus") = 3 then 'Accepted
        fullname = rs("Fname") & " " & rs("Lname")   'Variable named Fullname
        If rs("publicphone") = 1 then
            homephone = rs("hmareacode") & " " & rs("hmphone")
            workphone = "Not Available"
        ElseIf rs("publicphone") = 2 then
            homephone = "Not Available"
            workphone = rs("wkareacode") & " " & rs("wkphone")
        ElseIf rs("publicphone") = 0 then
            homephone = rs("hmareacode") & " " & rs("hmphone")
            workphone = rs("wkareacode") & " " & rs("wkphone")
        End If
    Else
        homephone = ""
        workphone = ""
        fullname = rs("Fname") & " " & Left(rs("Lname"), 1)
    End If
'........................
%>
...
```

Top Frame—Service-Wide Toolbar   The Top frame or `profile_top.asp` evaluates session status variables to determine what toolbar options to display. This evaluation includes a wide variety of possibilities because the profile.asp Frame Set can be called for many purposes, ranging from a member maintaining her own profile to a member getting access to a profile from a search. The specific values are less important than the idea that statuses are used to custom generate different toolbar options. In Listing C.6, many of the options are actually the same for the Introduction Service, but the graphics displayed vary.

Listing C.6 PROFILE_TOP.ASP—Top Frame, Providing System-Wide Navigation Options

```
<HTML>
<BODY BGCOLOR="#ffffff">
<table cellspacing=0 cellpadding=0 border=1 width=600>
<tr><td><LEFTMARGIN=0>

<%If session("comingfrom") = "1" then%>
   <MAP NAME="b_select">
<AREA SHAPE="RECT" COORDS="319,1 381,30"
HREF="profile.asp?memberid=<%=session("memberid")%>" TARGET="_top">
<AREA SHAPE="RECT" COORDS="384,1 439,30" HREF="searchframe.asp" TARGET="_top">
<AREA SHAPE="RECT" COORDS="444,1 506,30" HREF="archive.asp" TARGET="_top">
<AREA SHAPE="RECT" COORDS="511,1 597,30" HREF="start.asp" TARGET="_top">
   </MAP>
   <IMG SRC="b_select.gif" BORDER=0 USEMAP="#b_select">

...

<%Else%>
   <MAP NAME="update">
<AREA SHAPE="RECT" COORDS="319,1 381,30"
HREF=Â"profile.asp?memberid=<%=session("memberid")%>" TARGET="_top">
<AREA SHAPE="RECT" COORDS="384,1 439,30" HREF="searchframe.asp" TARGET="_top">
<AREA SHAPE="RECT" COORDS="444,1 506,30" HREF="archive.asp" TARGET="_top">
<AREA SHAPE="RECT" COORDS="511,1 597,30" HREF="start.asp" TARGET="_top">
   </MAP>
   <IMG SRC="update.gif" BORDER=0width=600 height=30  USEMAP="#update">
<%End If%>

<%session("comingfrom")=""%>

</td></tr></table></BODY></HTML>
```

App

C

Bottom Frame—Introduction Specific Options   The bottom frame or `profile_bot.asp` evaluates session status variables to determine what toolbar options to display in the top toolbar; however, the set of options provides choices that are specific to the introduction process rather than choices that enable Service-wide routing. This frame manages, not only the introduction process options, but also the member's personal profile editing options as well. Listing C.7 provides a comprehensive look at managing custom toolbar options.

Listing C.7 PROFILE_BOT.ASP—Introduction-Specific Navigation Options for the Member

```
<HTML><BODY BGCOLOR="#ffffff">
<table cellspacing=0 cellpadding=0 border=1 width=600><tr><td>
<%
if cint(request("memberid")) = cint(session("memberid")) then
'-----------------------------------------
' Option 1 - Editing Profile
```

continues

Listing C.7   Continued

```
'............................................
%>
<MAP NAME="ud_menu">
<AREA SHAPE="RECT" COORDS="20,1 93,24" HREF="editacct1_frame.asp" target="_top">
<AREA SHAPE="RECT" COORDS="97,1 148,24" HREF="editacct2_frame.asp" target="_top">
<AREA SHAPE="RECT" COORDS="150,1 237,24" HREF="editacct3_frame.asp" target="_top">
<AREA SHAPE="RECT" COORDS="241,1 289,24" HREF="editacct5_frame.asp" target="_top">
</MAP>
<IMG SRC="ud_menu.gif" BORDER=0 USEMAP="#ud_menu">
<%
else
Select Case session("lookupstatus")
'............................................
Case 0   ' Initial Selection , Allows Request Introduction
'............................................
%>
<MAP NAME="request">
<AREA SHAPE="RECT" COORDS="20,1 147,30"
HREF="profile_process.asp?decision=0&memberid=<%=request("memberid")%>"
➥target="_top"></MAP>
<IMG SRC="request.gif" BORDER=0 USEMAP="#request">
<%
'............................................
Case 1  ' Checking on Status of Selection, Allows Email
'............................................
%>
<MAP NAME="sendbott">
<AREA SHAPE="RECT" COORDS="20,1 147,20"
HREF="profile_process.asp?decision=4&memberid=<%=request("memberid")%>"
➥target="bottom"></MAP>
<IMG SRC="sendbott.gif" BORDER=0 USEMAP="#sendbott">
<%
'............................................
Case 2 ' Time to make a decision, Allows Yes, No, Not at this time
'............................................
%>
<MAP NAME="yesno">
<AREA SHAPE="RECT" COORDS="20,1 54,24"
HREF="profile_process.asp?decision=1&choice=1&memberid=<%=request("memberid")%>"
➥target="_top">
<AREA SHAPE="RECT" COORDS="56,1 163,24"
HREF="profile_process.asp?decision=1&choice=3&memberid=<%=request("memberid")%>"
➥target="_top">
<AREA SHAPE="RECT" COORDS="166,1 191,24"
HREF="profile_process.asp?decision=1&choice=2&memberid=<%=request("memberid")%>"
➥target="_top">
<AREA SHAPE="RECT" COORDS="195,1 287,24" HREF="start.asp" target="_top">
</MAP>
<IMG SRC="yesno.gif" BORDER=0 USEMAP="#yesno">
<%
```

```
'----------------------------------------
Case 3 ' Yes Disply, Enhanced Information
'----------------------------------------
%>
<IMG SRC="startbot.gif" BORDER=0>
<%
End Select
end if
session("lookupstatus") = 0
%>
</td></tr></table></BODY></HTML>
```

The Introduction Process and the Start Page

The heart of the Introduction Service is the process by which members introduce themselves to other members. This Introduction Process involves extensive logic to manage the various stages: from the initial request for introduction, to the acceptance or rejection by the selected member, to the acknowledgment of the answer by the selecting member. In the previous search area, we explored the mechanism that members use for the initial request for introduction. From that point on, a member manages the process from her Start page, which has a custom display that is based on the selections she has made and the requests for introduction that other members have made to that member. The basic flow of the Introduction Process after the initial selection goes to the Member Profile page where a member can either accept or reject an introduction request.

The Start Page, Controlling the Introduction Process

Like the profile area, frames drive the Start page area. Also like the profile area, the frames provide navigation toolbars and specific introduction-related choices. The roles of the specific frames include:

- `Start_top.asp` provides Service-wide navigation options.
- `Start_left.asp` provides displays and options for responding to other members' requests for introduction.
- `Start_right.asp` provides displays and options for tracking the status of a pending request for introduction.

The start.asp file provides Frame Set control in a similar way to the profile.asp. This includes very little use of Active Server Pages features other than the Server-Side Include and processing of the validate.asp page. The individual frames deliver all of the dynamic page content. The Top frame does not currently vary by member, and while important differences exist for the member between the left and right page, the code is surprisingly similar.

Start Top: Service-wide Navigation   The Top frame displays a standard set of options, which, at this time, do not vary by user; therefore, no specific processing takes place in the Top frame other than initializing several request variables in hyperlinks for use on subsequent page requests.

App
C

Start Left: Other Member's Requests In contrast to the top, the start left does a lookup based on member ID to identify all of the records in the Selections table with an active status for display on the user's Start page. Depending on the status of a user's particular selection record, the member has the capability to change the selections status.

The left page executes a search that is driven primarily by a join between the Member table and the Selections table as illustrated in Listing C.8. The filtering of this SQL statement is based on the member ID selected and the record's current status. Following the execution of the query, the processing page invoked evaluates the status of the introduction to determine whether to return to the Start page or to display the Profile page.

Listing C.8 START_LEFT.ASP—Frame for Displaying a Graphic Image and Information on Members that have Selected the Logged-on User

```
<html><head><title>left</title></head>
<body bgcolor="#FFFFFF" text="0000A0"><LEFTMARGIN=0>
<table border=1 cellpadding=0 cellspacing=0 width=296 align-"right">
<%
  Set Conn = Server.CreateObject("ADODB.Connection")
  Conn.Open("firstsite")
  sql = "SELECT Top 40 selections.SelectCreateDate, selections.SelectFinalDate,
➥selections.selectid, selections.SelectStatus, selections.SelectorMemberID,
➥Members.Admingraphics, Members.FName, Members.LName, Members.City, * FROM
➥Members INNER JOIN selections ON Members.MemberID = selections.SelectorMemberID
➥WHERE (((selections.SelectStatus)<5) AND ((selections.SelectStatus)<>2) AND
➥((selections.SelectStatus)<>3) AND ((selections.SelectedMemberID)="
  sql = sql & session("memberid") & ")) ORDER BY selections.SelectFinalDate DESC;"
Set RS = conn.Execute(sql)
If RS.EOF Then
        Response.write "<center><b>No members have selected you.</b></center>"
  End If

  Do While Not RS.EOF

  line1 = rs("fname") & " " & left(rs("lname"),1) & " " & rs("selectormemberid")
➥& "<br> " & rs("city")

%>
<tr><td align=center width=192>
<font size=2><strong><%=line1%><br></strong>
<%
'---------------------------------
'Display Message Depending on Status
'---------------------------------
Select Case rs("selectstatus")
Case 0 'Open Selection
  msg = "Selected On " & rs("selectcreatedate") & " <br> Status Open"
Case 1 'Yes Response
  msg = "Responded Yes on " & rs("selectfinaldate")
Case 2 'No Response
  msg = "Responded No Thank You <br>on " & rs("selectfinaldate")
```

```
Case 3 'Not at this time
  msg = "Responded Not at this time <br>on " & rs("selectfinaldate")
Case 4 'Went Inactive
  msg = "They went Inactive <br>on " & rs("selectfinaldate")
End Select

  Response.write msg
'--------------------------------
%>
</font></td><td width=102>
<%
  if rs("admingraphics") = 0 then
     imagename = "Default.tn"
  else
     imagename = rs("selectormemberid") & ".tn"
  end if
%>
<a
href="profile_evaluate.asp?selectid=<%=rs("selectid")%>
➥&status=<%=rs("SelectStatus")%>&id=3&memberid=<%=rs("selectormemberid")%>"
➥target="_top"><img src="/images/profile/<%=imagename%>.jpg"
➥align=top border=0 width=100 height=85></a>
</td></tr>

<%
  RS.MoveNext
  Loop
  RS.Close
%>

</table></body></html>
<%Conn.Close%>
```

Start Right: Member's Pending Requests   The right page illustrates the status of member selections made by the logged-on member. Like the left page, the right page builds a query that is based on a join of the member table. But in this case, the join is on the selector member ID and the selected member ID. The query also filters, based on status. Listing C.9 illustrates the code to execute the query and to generate the list of selected members customized by each member's current status.

Listing C.9   START_RIGHT.ASP—Frame for Displaying a List of Members that have been Selected by the Logged-on Member

```
<html><head><title>Right</title></head>
<body bgcolor="#FFFFFF" text="0000A0">
<LEFTMARGIN=0><div align=left>
<table border=1 cellpadding=0 cellspacing=0 width=300>
<%
  Set Conn = Server.CreateObject("ADODB.Connection")
  Conn.Open("firstsite")
  sql = "SELECT Top 40 selections.SelectCreateDate, selections.SelectFinalDate,
```

continues

Listing C.9 Continued

```
➥selections.selectid,  selections.selectfinaldate, selections.SelectStatus,
➥selections.SelectedMemberID, Members.FName, Members.LName, Members.City,
➥Members.Admingraphics, * FROM Members INNER JOIN selections ON
➥Members.MemberID= selections.SelectedMemberID WHERE
➥(((selections.SelectStatus)<5) AND ((selections.SelectorMemberID)="
sql = sql & session("memberid") & ")) ORDER BY selections.SelectFinalDate DESC;"
  Set RS = Conn.Execute(sql)

  If RS.EOF Then
      Response.write "<center><b>You have not made any selections.<br>(Click on
➥<font color=#FF0000>New Search</font> button above)</b></center>"
  End If

  Do While Not RS.EOF

  line1 = rs("fname") & " " & left(rs("lname"),1) & " " & rs("selectedmemberid")
➥& "<br> " & rs("city")
%>
<tr><td width=100>
<%
  if rs("admingraphics") = 0 then
      imagename = "Default.tn"
  else
      imagename = rs("selectedmemberid") & ".tn"
  end if
%>
<a
href="profile_evaluate.asp?selectid=<%=rs("selectid")%>&status=
➥<%=rs("SelectStatus")%>&id=2&memberid=<%=rs("selectedmemberid")%>"
➥target="_top"><img src="/images/profile/<%=imagename%>.jpg"
➥align=top border=0 width=100 height=85></a>
</td><td align=center width=192>
<font size=2><strong><%=line1%><br></strong>

<%
'--------------------------------
'Display Message Depending on Status
'--------------------------------
Select Case rs("selectstatus")
Case 0 'Open Selection
  msg = "Selected On " & rs("selectcreatedate") & "<br> Status Open"
Case 1 'Yes Response
  msg = "Responded Yes on " & rs("selectfinaldate")
Case 2 'No Response
  msg = "Responded No Thank You <br>on " & rs("selectfinaldate")
Case 3 'Not at this time
  msg = "Responded Not at this time <br>on " & rs("selectfinaldate")
Case 4 'Went Inactive
  msg = "Member went Inactive <br>on " & rs("selectfinaldate")
End Select

  Response.write msg
'--------------------------------
%></font></td></tr>
```

```
<%
  RS.MoveNext
  Loop
  RS.Close
  Conn.Close
%>
</table></div></body></html>
```

The Evaluation Page

Once any graphic from either the left or the right page is clicked, it invokes the profile_evaluate.asp page, which can be thought of as a pre-processor of the status information, prior to redirecting the user into the profile area. The evaluation logic determines which options to provide members when they reach the profile_bot.asp, as well as what information to display. In fact, if the status denotes rejection, the profile evaluate page actually redirects the member back to the Start page while updating the Selections table status to remove that member from the displayed list.

The profile_evaluate.asp file illustrated in Listing C.10 demonstrates the extensive use of the Redirect feature to provide security and stability. The Redirect feature also enables the .asp files to be designed in a more module approach. If the status updates and redirection of the evaluation page were included on the display page, a refresh of the page would risk incorrect updates being applied to the Selections Status table.

TIP Separating the update SQL statements from the display pages and using a response. The Redirect feature can protect your system from refreshes and other unanticipated and hard to trap events that could cause invalid updates to your tables.

Listing C.10 PROFILE_EVALUATE.ASP—Evaluation of Selection Status to Determine Necessary Selections Status Updates and Member Routing

```
<%
  Set Conn = Server.CreateObject("ADODB.Connection")
  Conn.Open("firstsite")

  '.......................................................
  '.......................................................
  Session("lookupid") = cint(request.querystring("selectid"))
  If request.querystring("id") = "2" then
     session("comingfrom") = "r"  'user clicked left side picture
  ElseIf request.querystring("id") = "3" then
     session("comingfrom") = "l"  'user clicked right side picture
  End If


  '.......................
  'Evaluate Status of request
  '.......................
```

continues

Listing C.10   Continued

```
select case request.querystring("status")

Case "" 'No status, either edit profile or initial search results
  session("lookupstatus") = 0 'No Selection Yet

'-----------------------
Case "0" 'Open Status No Choice Made Yet
'-----------------------
  If request.querystring("id") = "2" then 'Selector

    'Check to see if profile selected has allowed email to be sent to him/her
sql="SELECT EOK FROM Members WHERE MemberID = " & request.querystring("memberid") & ";"
    Set rs = Conn.Execute(sql)
    if rs("EOK") = -1 then
      session("lookupstatus") = 1 'OK to send email
    else
      session("lookupstatus") = 4 '4 indicates don't allow email to be sent
    end if
    '------------------------------------------------
  elseif request.querystring("id") = "3" then ' Selected
    session("lookupstatus") = 2 'Checking to make decision
    '------------------------------------------------
  End If

'-----------------------
Case "1" 'Yes In Process Status - Selector acknowledges Yes
'-----------------------
  if request.querystring("id") = "2" then
      'set conn = session("conn")
      sql = "UPDATE Selections SET"
      sql = sql & " selections.selectstatus = 7"
      sql = sql & " WHERE selections.SelectID=" & Session("lookupid") & ";"
      Set rs = Server.CreateObject("ADO.Recordset")
      rs.Open sql,Conn,3
  end if

  session("lookupstatus") = 3
  session("lookupstatus2") = 2 'Flag for enhanced disply info
    '------------------------------------------------


'-----------------------
Case "2" ' No In Process Status
'-----------------------
  'Update to Status 5
      'set conn = session("conn")
      sql="UPDATE Selections SET"
      sql=sql & " selections.selectstatus = 5"
      sql=sql & " WHERE selections.SelectID=" & request.querystring("selectid") & ";"
      Set rs = Server.CreateObject("ADO.Recordset")
      rs.Open sql,Conn,3
  response.redirect "start.asp"
```

```
'------------------------
Case "3" 'Not at this time In Process Status
'------------------------

   'Update to Status 6 if ID 2 or Selector
           'set conn = session("conn")
           sql="UPDATE Selections SET"
           sql=sql & " selections.selectstatus = 6"
           sql=sql & " WHERE selections.SelectID=" & request.querystring
➥("selectid") & ";"
           Set rs = Server.CreateObject("ADO.Recordset")
           rs.Open sql,Conn,3
   response.redirect "start.asp"


'------------------------
Case "4" 'Inactive In Process Status
'------------------------
 'If request.querystring("id") = "3" then 'Selector
           'Delete Record if ID 2 or Selector
           sql="Delete * from Selections"
           sql=sql & " WHERE selections.SelectID=" & request.querystring
➥("selectid") & ";"
           Set rs = Server.CreateObject("ADO.Recordset")
           rs.Open sql,Conn,3
   'End IF
   response.redirect "start.asp"


'------------------------
Case "5" ' NO Final Status
'------------------------

   'This case should never be invoked ERROR
   response.redirect "start.asp"


'------------------------
Case "6" ' Not at this time Final, Searching OK and selected bys Archive
'------------------------
 'From Archive of Selected
   session("lookupstatus") = 0


'------------------------
Case "7" ' Yes Final, no Search but both have archive
'------------------------
 'From Archive Selector or Selected
   session("lookupstatus") = 3
   session("lookupstatus2") = 2 'Flag for enhanced disply info

End Select
'------------------------
'------------------------

redirectpage = "profile.asp?memberid=" & request.querystring("memberid")
response.redirect redirectpage

Conn.Close

%>
```

Mail-Driven Introduction Features

In addition to the features that members manage themselves in order to control the introduction process, the Service site has several mail features. These features enable the system to use logic to generate batch mail messages to members at various times and for different reasons. The key mail features include:

- E-mail to notify a member that they have been selected
- E-mail to notify a member that a new member matching his Ideal Mate profile has joined the system

This type of automated communication between the Internet site and the member community can facilitate going beyond the Web server to integrate other servers and services into the site's interactive experience.

From Here...

After having built an understanding of how to approach constructing a membership-based community and exploring the Introduction Service's example of building interactivity into the site experience, we need to now turn to the administrative and fee collection side of an Internet/intranet based business site.

The following two appendixes begin a discussion of how to manage the fee collection process and how to enable site administrators to control the membership community and to maintain the site.

Managing the Membership: Maintenance, Security, and Monitoring

The capability of Active Server Pages to use a database for dynamically generating Web pages provides opportunities for creatively managing the process of site maintenance. Site maintenance, security, and monitoring mechanisms play key roles in the success or failure of a Web-based application and should not be overlooked in the development process. An often overlooked feature of building a database-driven application is the capability to parameterize key maintenance aspects of the site.

The following pages explore some of the methods for parameterizing the maintenance of a Web application. This appendix provides only a starting point, illustrating some methods that might be applicable for your Web-based application. The key takeaway points are an understanding of the possibilities provided by monitoring mechanisms, security, and site maintenance tools and techniques for building an interactive database-driven, Web-based application. ■

Database design: AdminParameters table

Controlling site-wide parameters involves creative use of data tables for both efficiency and ease of maintenance.

Managing members and site-wide parameters

Setting up a site that can effectively control its membership and site-wide options without the need of costly custom coding for labor intensive data entry is a key success factor in any Active Server application.

Communicating with the membership

Mail messages and custom site postings should provide efficient and low-cost methods for delivering information to your membership community.

Security and monitoring

With extended administrative features and increased membership reliance on your Active Server site, ensuring high availability and effective security is a priority.

Database Design: AdminParameters Table

In the overall database design, the AdminParameters table does not directly relate to any one table except that it provides the values that can be used to populate drop-down boxes. In fact, the entire purpose of the AdminParameters table is to provide site administrators the capabilities to vary the values in drop-down boxes throughout the system without having to alter HTML or Active Server Pages. Figure D.1 illustrates the tables used by the Introduction Service and shows how they relate to each other.

FIG. D.1

This shows an overview of Introduction Service table design and relationships.

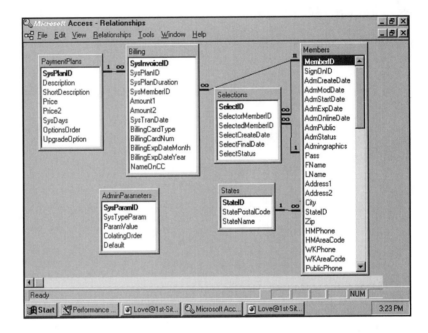

The AdminParameters table provides a method for enabling one table to act as a container for many categories of small lists such as religious choices and ethnic options. Table D.1 illustrates the fields in this table such as text descriptions and unique IDs. In addition to storing categories of values, the table also enables you to specify a collating order and a default value within a given category of values. This method proves invaluable for enabling site administrators to rapidly make changes to their sites without involving a programmer in the process. A specific example of a category of values that might be included in this table is ethnic background, which includes Caucasian, Hispanic, Asian, and others that can be changed and added over time.

Table D.1   Administrative Parameters for Use Throughout the System

Field Name	Data Type	Size	Description
SysParamID	Number (Long)	4	Primary Key
SysTypeParam	Number (Long)	4	Category of parameter

Field Name	Data Type	Size	Description
ParamValue	Text	150	Actual text display value
ColatingOrder	Number (Integer)	2	Value for sorting within category
Default	Yes/No	1	Default value within category

Managing Members and Site-Wide Parameters

Managing a site often requires several levels of security, allowing site administrators various levels of information access and update capabilities. At this time, the Introduction Service has only one level of security, allowing users access to a series of query and update features for information throughout the site. The areas of management fall into two primary categories. The first category of management is the editing of specific members' information as well as site-wide parameters like the AdminParameters table values. This first category makes up the majority of features included in the Introduction Service. The second category represents money-related or accounting-related areas of the Server and includes all administration related to accounting, billing, and fee collection. Whereas we cover money issues in great detail in Appendix E, "Implementing Billing and Payment Mechanisms," at this time we focus on the functionality surrounding administration of membership account information and site-wide information parameters.

App
D

Managing Member Information

Unlike the screens used by the members to manage their own information, for the Site Administrator, managing user information involves finding the user or member he intends to modify and then starting a process to edit information on that user's record. We will focus on the administrative access to the user account, based solely on member ID (though search facilities also exist on the site to find a member by first and last name). This initial member screen illustrated in Figure D.2 does a lookup on the member ID entered and returns a page partially filled with read-only display information and partially filled with form fields that are defaulted to current member values and are ready for editing.

The resulting display page or adminsearch.asp page (see Listing D.1) provides an editing environment in which site administrators can edit specific administrative flags on the account, including expiration date, password, availability of graphics, gender settings, and more. The Active Server Page involves a very straightforward lookup and display. And because Windows NT Server security has been enforced to isolate the secure directory from normal members and guest users, no validation pages are required.

FIG. D.2

The Membership editing screen enables site administrators to update user profiles.

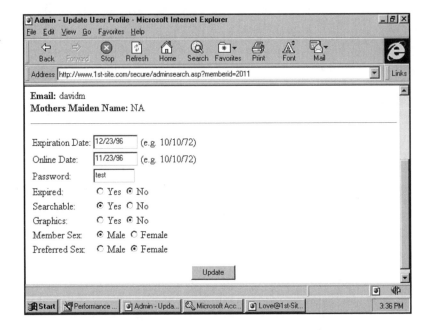

Listing D.1 ADMINSEARCH.ASP—Lookup and Display Page for Administering a User's Account

```
<%
  Set Conn = Server.CreateObject("ADODB.Connection")
  Conn.Open("firstsite")

  If request.querystring("memberid") = "" then
     memberid = 0
  Else
     memberid = request.querystring("memberid")
  end if

  sql = "SELECT * FROM Members WHERE Members.MemberID=" & memberid & ";"
  Set rs = Conn.Execute(sql)

  If rs.EOF then
     newpage = "index.htm"
     response.redirect newpage
  End If
%>
<html><head><title>Admin - Update User Profile</title></head>
<body bgcolor="#FFFFFF">
<form action="adminprofileupdate.asp" method="POST">
...
```

Once any and all changes have been made, the administrators can update the member account by executing the adminsearch.asp file. The Update page or adminprofileupdate.asp completes all the validations and testing necessary to build and execute the update SQL statement on behalf of the administrative user as illustrated in Listing D.2.

Listing D.2   ADMINPROFILEUPDATE.ASP—Administrative Routine for Updating Member Account Information

```asp
<%
    Set Conn = Server.CreateObject("ADODB.Connection")
    Conn.Open("firstsite")

    'Testing Uncertain Values
    '-------------------------
    admexpdate = request.form("admexpdate")
    admonlinedate = request.form("admonlinedate")
    If admexpdate = "" then admexpdate = "01/01/96"
    If admonlinedate = "" then admonlinedate = "01/01/96"

    sql = "UPDATE Members SET"
        sql = sql & " Members.admexpdate =#" & admexpdate & "#,"
        sql = sql & " Members.admonlinedate =#" & admonlinedate & "#,"
        if request.form("pass") <> "" then
            sql = sql & " Members.pass ='" & request.form("pass") & "',"
        end if
        sql = sql & " Members.admstatus =" & request.form("admstatus") & ","
        sql = sql & " Members.admpublic =" & request.form("admpublic") & ","
        sql = sql & " Members.admingraphics =" & request.form("admingraphics") &
➥","
        sql = sql & " Members.profsex =" & request.form("profsex") & ","
        sql = sql & " Members.download = 1 ,"
        sql = sql & " Members.AdmModDate = #" & Date() & "#,"
        sql = sql & " Members.profprefid =" & request.form("profprefid")
        sql = sql & " WHERE Members.memberID=" & request.form("memberid") & ";"
        Set rs = Server.CreateObject("ADO.Recordset")
        rs.Open sql,Conn,3

    if request.form("admstatus") = 0 then
        sql2 = "UPDATE Selections SET"
        sql2 = sql2 & " Selections.SelectStatus = 4,"
        sql2 = sql2 & " Selections.SelectFinalDate = #" & Date() & "#"
        sql2 = sql2 & " WHERE (Selections.SelectedMemberID=" &
➥clng(request.form("memberid"))  & ") AND (Selections.SelectStatus <> 7);"
        Set rs2 = Conn.Execute(sql2)
    end if

%>
<html><head><title>Confirm Admin Update</title></head>
<body bgcolor="#FFFFFF">
<h3><center>Your update has been processed</center></h3>
<p><a href="http://www.1st-site.com/secure/index.htm">
Return to Admin Homepage</a></p></html>
```

Managing Site-Wide Parameters

Site-wide parameters stored in the AdminParameters table offer the administrative user (non-programmer) a mechanism for updating the site without knowing Active Server syntax and without the risk of adding new code, which could cause damage to the overall functioning of the site. Determining what information should be hardcoded into the pages and what information to set up as lookups in a table like the AdminParameters table requires careful consideration and should be a focus of your work in the design phase of any site development project. Overuse of administrative parameters can unnecessarily slow down the site and can cause extra traffic on the database. The balance point must be set on a case-by-case basis. On the Introduction Service, we chose to implement parameters for many of the choices that members made while building their profiles. The importance of these choices stemmed from the search engine features and how those features relied on profile information during the search process. Figure D.3 shows the categories that can be controlled on the Introduction Service.

FIG. D.3

Administrators can edit a variety of profile parameters.

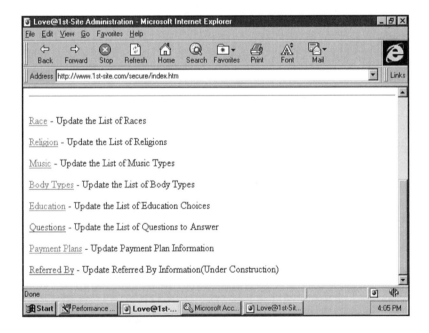

Once an administrator selects a given category, the parameter lookup page or adminparamHead.asp executes a search for all values in the AdminParameters table, based on that category. To prevent removing values that a user currently has selected in her profile, the administrative user can update or add but can not delete records. A series of four .asp files provides all functionality for the lookup, add, and update of administrative parameters:

- adminaramhead.asp for lookup
- adminparamdetail.asp for editing
- adminparamadd.asp for adding
- adminparamupdate.asp for inserting or updating information

The adminparamhead.asp provides a simple lookup and list of the values, based on category ID. In addition, a link is created to the adminparamadd.asp for a new entry and a hyperlink to the adminparamdetail.asp for editing an entry. The code generating this page is illustrated in Listing D.3.

Listing D.3   ADMINPARAMHEAD.ASP—Simple Display of Category-Based Information in the AdminParameters Table

```
<%
  Set Conn = Server.CreateObject("ADODB.Connection")
  Conn.Open("firstsite")
  sql = "SELECT * FROM AdminParameters WHERE systypeparam = " &
➥request.querystring("Type") & " ORDER BY ColatingOrder;"
  Set rs = Conn.Execute(sql)
%>
<html><head><title>Administration - Parameter List</title></head>
<body bgcolor="#FFFFFF">
<h1><center>Administration - Admin Parameters</center></h1>

<%'----------------------
'Add Feature
'----------------------%>
<p><a href="http://www.1st-site.com/secure/
➥adminparamadd.asp?Type=<%=rs("systypeparam")%>">[Add Value for this Param
➥eter]</a></p>

<%'----------------------
'Editing Feature
'----------------------
Do While Not rs.EOF%>
    <p><a href="http://www.1st-
➥site.com/secure/inparamdetail.asp?Type=<%=rs("systypeparam")%>&value2=<%=rs
➥("sysparamid")%>"><%=rs ("paramvalue")%></
➥a></p>
    <%rs.MoveNext
Loop%>

<center><p><a href="http://www.1st-site.com/secure/index.htm">Return to Admin
➥Homepage</a></p></center>
</body></html>
```

App
D

Whether the hyperlink for editing a specific item is selected, invoking the adminparamdetail.asp, or the link enabling the adding of a new item is selected, invoking the adminparamadd.asp, the resulting page displayed to the Site Administrator is virtually identical. Only two differences exist between the adminparamdetail.asp and adminparamadd.asp options. The first difference is a flag set identifying whether to add a new record or edit an existing record. The second difference is that when an existing record is selected, the values in the HTML form fields are populated based on the currently set values in the database. Figure D.4 illustrates the adminparamdetail.asp display, which shows an existing record with values populated from the database. Listing D.4 illustrates the code used to generate the page.

FIG. D.4

adminparamdetail.asp display for editing of the Admin Parameters.

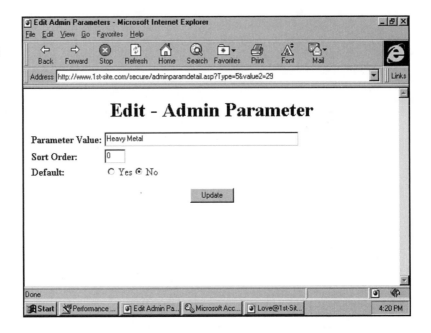

Listing D.4 ADMINPARAMDETAIL.ASP—Detail Display of Individual Record from the AdminParamaters Table for Editing

```
<%
  Set Conn = Server.CreateObject("ADODB.Connection")
  Conn.Open("firstsite")
  sql = "SELECT * FROM AdminParameters WHERE sysparamid =" & request("value2")
  Set rs = Conn.Execute(sql)
%>
<html><head><title>Edit Admin Parameters</title></head>
<body bgcolor="#FFFFFF">
<form action="adminparamupdate.asp" method="POST">
<h1><center>Edit - Admin Parameter</center></h1>
<table>
<tr><td width=20%><b>Parameter Value:</b></td><td>
<input type=text size=60 maxlength=150 name="paramvalue"
➥value="<%=rs("paramvalue")%>"></tr></td>

<tr><td width=20%><b>Sort Order:</b></td><td>
<input type=text size=3 maxlength=3 name="colatingorder"
➥value="<%=rs("colatingorder")%>"></tr></td>

<% If rs("Default") = -1 then %>
   <tr><td width=20%><b>Default:</b></td><td>
<input type=radio name="default" checked value=-1>
Yes<input type=radio name="default" value=0>
No</tr></td>
<% Else %>
   <tr><td width=20%><b>Default:</b></td><td>
<input type=radio name="default" value=-1>
```

```
Yes<input type=radio name="default" checked value=0>
No</tr></td>
<% End If %>

</table>
<p><center><input type=submit name="btn" value="Update"></center>
<INPUT NAME="value" VALUE=<%=request.querystring("value2")%> TYPE=HIDDEN>
</form></html>
```

The final step in the administrative area for maintaining a value in the AdminParameters table involves the Active Server Page for executing the insert or update of the value. This Active Server Page or adminparamupdate.asp file provides a simple conditional evaluation to determine whether to update or insert and then uses the request variables passed in from the form to execute the SQL statement as illustrated in Listing D.5.

Listing D.5   ADMINPARAMUPDATE.ASP—Insert or Update of Value in the AdminParameters Table

```
<%
    Set Conn = Server.CreateObject("ADODB.Connection")
    Conn.Open("firstsite")

    colatingorder = request.form("colatingorder")
    if colatingorder = "" then colatingorder = 0

'------------------------
'Update Feature
'------------------------
    if request.form("btn")="Update" then
        sql = "UPDATE AdminParameters SET"
            sql = sql & " AdminParameters.paramvalue ='" &
⮡request.form("paramvalue") & "',"
            sql = sql & " AdminParameters.default =" & request.form("default") &
⮡","
            sql = sql & " AdminParameters.colatingorder =" & colatingorder
            sql = sql & " WHERE AdminParameters.sysparamID=" &
⮡request.form("value") & ";"
        Set rs = Server.CreateObject("ADO.Recordset")
        rs.Open sql,Conn,3
'------------------------
'Add Feature
'------------------------
    else
        set rsInsert = Server.CreateObject("ADO.RecordSet")
        Conn.BeginTrans
        rsInsert.Open "AdminParameters", Conn, 3, 3
        rsInsert.AddNew
        rsInsert("systypeparam")        = request.form("systypeparam")
        rsInsert("paramvalue")          = request.form("paramvalue")
        rsInsert("colatingorder")       = request.form("colatingorder")
        rsInsert("default")             = request.form("default")
        rsInsert.Update
```

continues

Listing D.5 Continued

```
      Conn.CommitTrans
      rsInsert.Close
   end if
'------------------------
%>
<html><head><title>Confirm Admin Update</title></head>
<body bgcolor="#FFFFFF">
<h3><center>Your update has been processed</center></h3>
<p><a href="http://www.1st-site.com/secure/index.htm">
Return to Admin Homepage</a></p></html>
```

The series of four Active Server Pages and one table, which provides the site parameters features, can be invaluable to all site development efforts and can be easily plugged into different sites.

Communicating with the Membership

In a Web-based environment driven by Active Server Pages, the challenge of maintaining active communication with the membership can appear at first to be difficult. In the same way that members no longer having to communicate directly with customer service or other types of support personnel has lowered the cost of delivering an interactive service, the amount of direct contact the service provider has with the membership also has been limited. However, with the effective use of dynamic page-generation capabilities and the integration of mail services, the service provider can also creatively deliver information to the member in a very convenient, consistent, and unobtrusive manner.

The primary methods of communication utilized in the Introduction Service include the capability to provide custom information on the Start page as a user logs into the system and batch mail to the community through database-driven mail delivery.

Posting Information on the Start Page

Unlike a bulletin board or banner at the front of a physical location, the custom-generated Start page empowers the service provider to deliver specific messages to a particular user. For example, because the system knows the birthday of every member, when a member logs on whose birthday equals the current date, a custom system birthday greeting or promotion can be provided. This type of custom message delivery, which can be driven by any information stored about the member, provides a flexible method of communicating with a membership. In fact, its flexibility actually leads to a design problem as you try to limit the site to a set of features that can be set as parameters for the site.

The specific components necessary to implement a rule-based approach to delivering this type of custom messaging includes setting up a database table like the one illustrated in Table D.2, followed by logic to generate the message display and administrative pages to edit the messages and rules.

Table D.2   SysMessage Table for Storing and Administering Messages

Field Name	Data Type	Size	Description
SysMessageID	Number (Long)	4	Primary Key
MemberFieldName	Text	75	Name of field in member table to evaluate
SysOperator	Number (Long)	4	Value to represent =,>,< for evaluating rule
MatchingValue	Text	150	Value to compare to value in members field specified based on operator selected
SysMessage	Memo	-	Actual text display value or message
SysActive	Yes/No	1	Value to assign whether this rule-based message is currently active

A birthday message would be a specific example of a rule that could be set up in the data table illustrated in Table D.2. This would include a data record such as the one illustrated as follows.

```
MemberFieldName        SysOperator    MatchingValue    SysMessage
memdob                 =              Date()           <b>Happy Birthday <b>
```

The information included would be the name of the Date of Birth field in the member table, a matching operator like the equal sign (=), a matching value like a function providing the current date (Date()), and finally a message that can be used for display. Once you set the table structure for assigning the rule-based evaluation and add the necessary values to the table, the two remaining components to implement include:

- Incorporating the rule-based logic into your Start or Home page
- Providing an administrative environment for updating, inserting, and deleting the messages provided

The administrative environment will closely follow what has already been illustrated with administrative parameters in the section "Managing Site-Wide Parameters." Listing D.6 provides a sample of how you integrate the rule-based messaging template into your Start page as a Server-Side Include.

Listing D.6   TEST_MESAGE.ASP—Custom Message Delivery Mechanism for Providing Users with Start Page Greetings and Other Communication

```
<%
'Assume Member information is available under in rs recordset
'-----------------------------
Set Conn = Server.CreateObject("ADODB.Connection")
Conn.Open("firstsite")
```

continues

Listing D.6 Continued

```
sql = "SELECT * FROM SysMessage WHERE SysActive = -1"
Set rsMessage = Conn.Execute(sql)

Do While Not rsMessage.EOF
    'Evaluate logical operator with select case
    Select Case rsMessage.sysoperator
    Case 1
    if rs(rsMessage.memberfieldname) = rsMessage.matchingvalue then
        response.write rsmessage.sysmessage
    end if
    Case 2
    if rs(rsMessage.memberfieldname) > rsMessage.matchingvalue then
        response.write rsmessage.sysmessage
    end if
    Case 3
    if rs(rsMessage.memberfieldname) < rsMessage.matchingvalue then
        response.write rsmessage.sysmessage
    end if
    End Select
rsMessage.MoveNext
  Loop
  rsMessage.close
%>
```

Batch Mail Delivery to Membership

Similar in principle to the custom messages delivered to the Start page for your membership, mail can provide a mechanism for delivering a custom message to a subset of your membership community. The mail functionality provides an important complement to the Start page bulletin board-type posting, much like a company mailing complements a flyer in the break room.

With the batch mail delivery, the focus returns again to the administrative pages provided to a site administrator, who is responsible for membership communication. Although maintaining a mail distribution list for sending broadcasts to a membership community hardly appears as something new, the value added by combining a Microsoft SQL Server delivery engine with Active Server Pages is in the capability to target the messages based on membership information stored in the database.

N O T E The mail capability described in "Batch Mail Delivery to Membership" requires Microsoft's SQL Server product. Currently, this site primarily operates based on Microsoft Access, which does not currently have the SendMail extended stored procedure capability. ■

The primary components to delivering this type of content do not include an additional data table as in the Start page message delivery, because message creation and delivery will be based on an administrator actively using Active Server Pages. Instead, the primary modules needed for this communication include only Active Server Pages in the administrative area, which provides search criteria to build a list for distribution and then a message area for typing in the appropriate message.

N O T E   As an additional approach or feature, a new table could be created to set up rules for delivering system-generated mail messages, based on a scheduled stored procedure in Microsoft SQL Server. ■

The first administrative page involves defining the group of members to receive the mail message. This involves implementing a search process similar to that used in the members search process described in Appendix C. Figure D.5 illustrates this first administrative page.

FIG. D.5

This is a search screen for building a list of the Introduction Service's membership for custom mail message delivery.

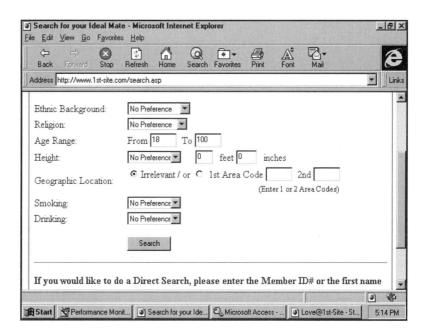

App D

Once the query has been run, a summary report should be provided that enables the site administrator to ensure they have properly run the search criteria that they wanted. At this point, a simple subject line and text area for delivering the message must be provided.

CAUTION

Be careful if your messages exceeds 255 characters because this may cause a problem with the standard SendMail extended stored procedure provided with Microsoft SQL Server.

Security and Monitoring

As with any site, security and performance monitoring play important roles in the overall success or failure of a site. Based on the NT Server platform, a series of tools and features can be implemented to ensure a secure and robust site. The specific focus of this section is to provide an overview of the steps taken in the rollout of the **http://www.1st-site.com** Introduction Service, based entirely on Active Server Pages. The key points for discussion include ensuring:

- Security of your network and computer servers
- Monitoring of the load and overall performance of your site
- Monitoring to ensure your site remains on the Net

We need to preface this discussion by saying that we are engaging upon a big topic, and an entire book can easily be dedicated to the issues surrounding security on the Internet/intranet. We will not attempt to provide that type of treatment here but will instead only share the steps that were taken with respect to the Introduction Service. Along the way, however, we will highlight red flags that you should pursue. Whether the areas highlighted as red flags fall under your direct responsibility or not, you should be armed to ask questions. Don't let a network administrator ignore your inquiries because the chances are good that they also are trying to understand all of these risks. With that said, here is a quick tour of the procedure we took in bringing up *Love @ 1st Site*.

Security of Your Network and Computer Servers

For the Introduction Service, security fell into two areas: the ability of an outsider to penetrate our network or one or more of our servers (we run Microsoft SQL Server, Microsoft Exchange Server, and Microsoft IIS 3.0 on three different machines), and the risk of someone intercepting a transmission across the Internet that might include credit card numbers, passwords, or other sensitive information.

Information in Transit on the Net   The issue of information in transit impacted the use of both the Web Server and the FTP Server. Both of these products are combined in IIS 3.0, but they provide different levels of security in the way they move information.

With respect to the FTP server, basically we were out of luck. All FTP information is transmitted as plain text that includes NT Server usernames and passwords. Somehow we had to enable administrators to move member pictures into the Web server directories, but by compromising the FTP logon, any hacker could immediately log into our administrative pages. We considered creating limited, separate, FTP-only accounts but still faced the risk of unauthorized access to our art work. This would have been the solution if a working version of Microsoft's Point to Point Tunneling Protocol (PPTP) had not become available in the commercial release of Windows NT Server. Though it required an NT machine at both ends (because NT provides the only current client platform), PPTP enabled us to map drives across the Internet with Windows NT's fully enabled authentication model, including encrypted authentication.

Point to Point Tunneling Protocol (PPTP)

The complete specification can be found at the Microsoft home page, currently **http://www.microsoft.com/ntserver/communications/pptp.htm**. One of the features enabled by the PPTP standard is the ability to access file sharing services on a Windows NT Server, which has enabled PPTP filtering in the Network Control Panel.

OK, so what about the Web server? The traditional response in this area is Secure Sockets Layer (SSL). By using an SSL certificate provided through Verisign (**http://www.verisign.com**), we were able to provide encryption of data moved between the two locations.

Secure Sockets Layer (SSL)

The SSL standard provides a method for encrypting communication between a Web server and Web browser. For additional information on SSL, visit **http://www.versign.com**, a leading provider of signed SSL keys for use by Web servers.

N O T E   We will discuss SSL in more detail in Appendix E on billing and payment issues

But at this point, we have achieved only an acceptable level of confidence with respect to information in transit from one place to another. The far greater threat involves direct penetration of our network and servers.

App
D

Network Security and "The Firewall"   Any self-respecting network today should be insulated from the outside world by some form of firewall. This word is used quite loosely and actually reflects a series of services, including Proxy Servers and packet filtering. Microsoft's Proxy Server, now in final release, provides the capability to hide your computer IP address from the outside world by establishing a group of IP addresses for the outside world and a separate set of IP addresses for your internal network that the Proxy Server maps to enable internal computers to talk with external computers. Another important feature that we evaluated, packet filtering, limits the type of traffic that can make it through your firewall onto the internal network.

While implementing these features seems like an obvious precaution, at the time of this book's release, we were still determining the firewall-related features we would implement (have mercy on our defenseless network). We have been involved in many bad implementations in which, by default, too much network security was implemented and applications appeared to be down to the outside world. We hope to have this up and running before street date to ensure that no one out there decides to teach us a lesson. The key message here is DO IT—add these features—just be careful not to bring down your application in the process.

Server Security: "The NT Myth"   Everyone that we talk to seems to think that out-of-the-box, NT Server provides that oft talked about C2 government security level. Actually, out-of-the-box, NT has a lot of holes. If you are responsible for network security, you need to understand the risks inherent in NT. Check out the October 1996 issue of Windows NT Magazine for more information.

I won't go ad nauseum through all of the steps we have had to take to secure the Introduction Service, but here are some cautions you should heed:

- Be careful about enabling Netbios over TCP/IP.
- Disable your system Guest account.
- Disable your Everyone group (very, very **carefully**).
- Consider removing permission for the execution of .cmd and .exe files.
- Separate, as much as possible, sensitive company data onto separate devices from your Web data, including system files.
- Don't use FTP if at all possible.
- Take care, for the list does go on...

Monitoring the Load/Performance of Your Site

While being careful not to burden your system with excessive monitoring, you will need some monitoring and logging to provide useful information for determining when you need to add RAM and CPU resources. The performance monitor and your Web server statistics can provide this type of valuable information. Take some time to figure out how you can take the hundreds of thousands of records accumulated by these monitoring tools and turn them into meaningful information. Your Web administrator should be exploring commercial products and creative uses of database queries to help in this process. From a development perspective, you may also want to integrate a custom logging feature into your Active Server Pages, i.e. set up insert statements to create log records in a table, based on different types of key activity.

Most people limit the monitoring of their systems to a passive role. However, you also should consider carefully how to use the Alert mode of the performance monitor to launch different types of notification programs. In addition to the performance monitor, you should assess the other types of NT services running in your environment and determine how they can help. For example, Microsoft Exchange Server can monitor any of your running services and generate Mail notifications. SQL Server can also provide monitoring capabilities that result in running stored procedures that send Mail or execute command line programs.

For our Introduction Service, we focused on the alerting capabilities of the Performance Monitor to launch batch programs that work in conjunction with a product called WinBeep. This provided an effective method of generating pages. We also are using our nationwide PageNet service, which accepts mail messages and routes them automatically to electronic paging devices. This has been a very cost-effective notification strategy that has only one major limitation. If you go off of the net or if your mail server is down, you will never know it. This limitation highlights the need for redundancy in your notification strategy.

Monitoring to Ensure Your Site Remains on the Net

We have already begun to discuss the need for monitoring to ensure your site remains live, but now we take a slightly more structured look at the areas you should focus on to ensure that your site is up. Nothing is worse than clients or customers who can barely turn on a computer calling to let you know that your site is down. Specific focus areas include:

- Internal monitoring of your server services
- Internal monitoring of the outside world
- An external third-party monitoring of your key services

Internal Monitoring of Your Server Services   Finding a stable product to monitor your internal services may be the single most important step we took to ensure that our site has the highest possible amount of up time. The product from IPSwitch (**http://www.ipswitch.com**), called WhatsUP and illustrated in Figure D.6, provides a highly reliable method for, not only monitoring, but also for providing flexible notification services.

FIG. D.6

This illustrates a standard network grid view within IPSwitch's WhatsUP network monitoring product.

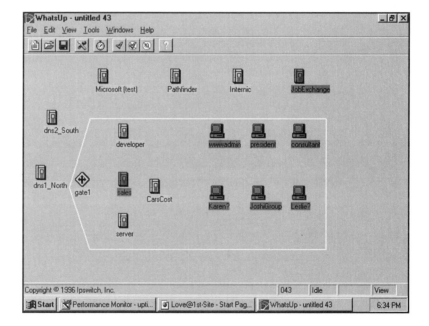

App

D

The services that can be monitored and the types of notifications available are partially illustrated in Figure D.7. They include mail, pager, and beeper notifications, based on failures of any service monitored. We have been very pleased with the flexibility and stability of these low-cost methods of monitoring a site.

FIG. D.7

The illustration displays the administrative screens of WhatsUP network monitoring product.

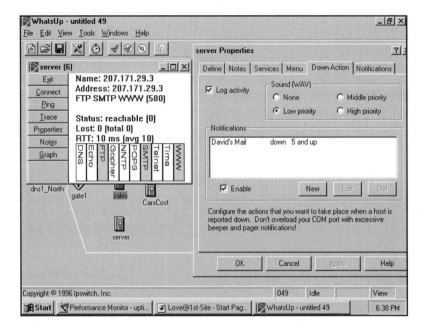

In addition to monitoring with notifications, we have taken it one step further with our use of the Performance Monitor to actually restart services when they stop or when the thread count for the service drops below one. This type of active monitoring has proven invaluable, especially during the early Beta stages, as Active Server Pages evolved from a DBWeb product into Denali into ActiveX Server and then finally into IIS 3.0's Active Server Pages. The Performance Monitoring alert illustrated in Figure D.8 launches a batch file when the thread count of the InetInfo.exe or IIS drops below one.

Windows NT Server Thread Count

In order for a program to be running, it has to have had at least one thread running. When a thread count drops from some number greater than 0 to 0, it is analogous to the program terminating.

The batch file is not complicated; just be careful in the Performance Monitor setup. The complete content of the batch file took the form of:

```
net stop "world wide web publishing service"
net stop "ftp publishing service"

net start "world wide web publishing service"
net start "ftp publishing service"
```

FIG. D.8
This is a view of the Performance Monitoring settings to kick-off the Batch file necessary to restart the Web server.

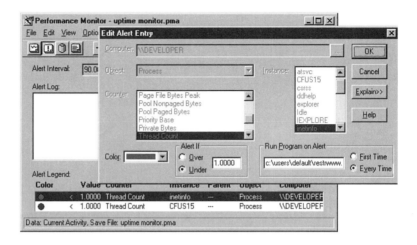

Batch File

A Batch file in Windows NT Server, similar to Batch files in Dos, is just a simple text file with a .bat file extension which contains commands executable at the command prompt.

Internal Monitoring of the Outside World   The WhatsUp described previously provides the capability to ping high up-time sites on the Internet such as **http://www.microsoft.com** and the **http://rs.internic.net**.

Although the practice of systematically querying other sites on the Internet is discouraged due to its tendency to create unnecessary Internet traffic, pinging other Internet sites can provide invaluable warnings to a Site Administrator. By pinging another Internet location, you can provide a high level of confidence that your site can be reached by other locations on the Internet as well. When another site does not respond to a ping or other query, it provides a good indication that your site may be having problems reaching the Internet.

An External Third-Party Monitoring of Your Key Services   Many companies, like RedAlert, now offer the service of pinging your server from an outside source periodically and generating a page, mail message, or other type of notification in the event of several failures. These services are often fairly inexpensive and can help detect DNS or other problems that may not be obvious from inside your internal network.

 Don't throw the panic button if you miss one check with your ping; this often results from a time-out due to ordinary traffic or load issues.

Bringing It All Together

At this point, we have thoroughly reviewed the processes of building a membership community and of providing members with an interactive environment. We have also finished

App

D

reviewing some important administrative issues involved in monitoring and securing your site, as well as providing an effective, efficient, and low-cost maintenance infrastructure.

As you move into the final appendix of the case study, your attention turns to the bottom line. The process of charging fees and effectively tracking and collecting those fees in a secure and efficient manner requires careful planning. From on-line authorizations to the implementation of an accounting system, creating a business based on Active Server technologies requires the ability to manage the money. ●

Implementing Billing and Payment Mechanisms

This appendix takes you through all aspects of the Introduction Service site that are related to securely and efficiently setting payment options, collecting money, and downloading information to an off-line database. Further, this chapter introduces additional systems and vendor issues regarding electronic commerce transactions on the Internet. While you explore the approach taken for the Introduction Service, take note of the alternative options presented, as well as standards described for enhancing the approach, detailed in this appendix. Overall, this appendix serves as a hands-on introduction to dealing with money on the Net. ■

Database design: billing and PaymentPlans tables

Tracking customer payments and available payment plans requires tables that should be separate from your standard member information tables.

Payment plans setup and management with Active Server Pages

Whenever possible, business sites should enable flexible administrative control over billing options for the non-programming site manager.

Internet-based payment mechanisms

Internet commerce generally focuses on securely and efficiently authorizing credit cards, but you also should understand the standards and financial services infrastructure that is continuing to develop.

Database Design: Billing and PaymentPlans Tables

In the development of a database to manage the billing and payment features of a business Web site, two key types of information must be trapped. First, the payment options available to the site user, and second, the actual payment transactions that occur between an end consumer and the site.

The payment/billing options, or the payment plans can be hard coded into .asp files, but creating a table of values offers a much more flexible approach. With a PaymentPlans table, you can set parameters to control the range of options and the type of administrative flexibility built into the site. Key information includes, at a minimum, a description of the payment plan and the cost.

When users make selections from a set of payment plans, information regarding payment total and method of payment must be captured to a second table. This table could be part of the member's information table; generally, however, members will make payments over the life of their account, and, often, separating the payment information, such as the credit card number, from the member table can offer added security as well.

For the Introduction Service, we implemented two tables, including the Billing table for capturing individual transactions, and the PaymentPlans table for storing parameter-driven and administrator-controlled payment plan types.

Payment Plan Types

The PaymentPlan table contains 8 fields, enabling description and promotion options to be stored. This information is then used to dynamically generate HTML pages as users move through the billing section of the New Account sign up process. The PaymentPlans table layout is illustrated in Table E.1.

Table E.1 PaymentPlans Table for Providing Payment Plans, Which Could Be Edited by Site Administrators

Field Name	Type	Size	Description
SysPlanID	Number (Long)	4	Primary Key
Description	Text	125	Long description for display on Active Server Pages
ShortDescription	Text	25	Short description for display on Active Server Pages
Price	Currency	8	Price for initial promotional period
Price2	Currency	8	Price for membership after promotional period
SysDays	Number (Long)	4	Length of promotional period

Field Name	Type	Size	Description
OptionsOrder	Number (Byte)	1	Additional options selected
UpgradeOption	Yes/No	1	Flag to define as Upgrade option only

Billing Transactions Table

A billing transaction represents an actual payment plan selected by a member during either the New Account or Account Renewal process. The 12 fields trap credit card-related information, member ID, plan type, and time/date stamps. Specific fields are shown in Table E.2.

Table E.2   Billing Table for Capturing Member-driven Payment Information

Field Name	Type	Size	Description
SysInvoiceID	Number (Long)	4	Primary Key
SysPlanID	Number (Long)	4	Index Key to PaymentPlans table
SysPlanDuration	Number (Integer)	2	Days for use of Amount1 price field
SysMemberID	Number (Long)	4	Index Key to Member table
Amount1	Currency	8	Promotional price
Amount2	Currency	8	Regular price
SysTranDate	Date/Time	8	Date/Time flag
BillingCardType	Text	50	Type of credit card used
BillingCardNum	Text	50	Card number
BillingExpDateMonth	Number (Integer)	2	Expiration date, month
BillingExpDateYear	Number (Integer)	2	Expiration date, year
NameOnCC	Text	50	Name on credit card, defaulted to member name

App
E

Payment Plans Setup and Management with Active Server

Payment Plan Setup involves managing the administrative issues involved in offering parameter driven Payment Plan options to members. This does not concern so much the method of payment used such as Visa or MasterCard, but rather the services and prices that members choose from setup options maintained by site administrators. The section "Enabling Internet-Based Payment Mechanisms" dives into the issues and approaches used to capture payment information. In contrast, the current section deals with setting up a parameter-driven approach for offering members selections during the billing process.

Only four administrative pages drive this process. These are similar to the administrative parameters discussed in Appendix D. These pages include:

- List page for reviewing all current payment plans
- Detail page for seeing the current value of a specific plan
- Add page for entering new plan values
- Update page for updating an existing plan

Payment Options List Page

Figure E.1 displays a list page for looking up and displaying linked payment plan options for editing. This provides the first screen to the site administrator in editing the available payment plans set up for the site.

FIG. E.1

This displays a list page for looking up and displaying linked payment plan options for editing.

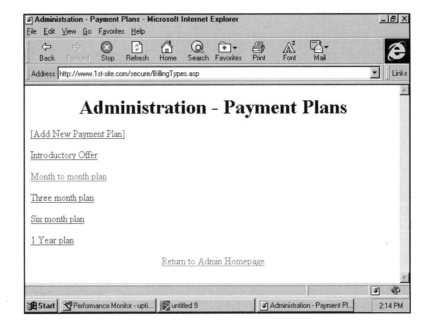

The list page (generated by the code illustrated in Listing E.1), much like simple lookup pages that we have dealt with many times up to this point, provides a database lookup of the PaymentPlans table and displays all current plans. The list page enables a site administrator to either begin editing an existing plan type or to add an entirely new plan type.

Listing E.1   BILLINGTYPES.ASP—List Page for Displaying Current Payment Plans in Use at the Site

```
<%
  Set Conn = Server.CreateObject("ADODB.Connection")
  Conn.Open("firstsite")
  sql = "SELECT * FROM PaymentPlans ORDER BY optionsorder;"
  Set rs = Conn.Execute(sql)
%>

<html><head>
<title>Administration - Payment Plans</title>
</head><body bgcolor="#FFFFFF">
<h1><center>Administration - Payment Plans</center></h1>

<p><a href="http://www.1st-site.com/secure/billingtypesadd.asp">
➥[Add New Payment Plan]</a></p>

<%Do While Not rs.EOF%>
   <p><a href="http://www.1st-site.com/secure/billingtypesdetail.asp?
➥value=<%=rs("sysplanid")%>"><%=rs("shortdescription")%></a></p>
   <%rs.MoveNext
Loop%>

<center><p><a href="http://www.1st-site.com/secure/index.htm">ÂReturn to Admin
Homepage</a></p></center>
</body></html>
<%Conn.Close%>
```

Payment Options Add and Detail Pages

Once the site administrator has selected an option from the current page, the site administrator will be moved to the .asp file displaying the payment plan details or displaying a blank form allowing the administrator to add new payment plans. Whether on the detail view page (billingtypesdetail.asp) or on the new plan add page (billingtypesadd.asp), the site administrator can then create a new payment plan or edit the existing plan she has selected. Figure E.2 displays the Detail or Add page. This page looks the same with the exception that if the detail of an existing plan has been selected, the form fields will be populated by existing values; in contrast, while adding a new plan, these fields will be empty.

The Add page varies from the Edit page in that it does not default the form fields with current data; other than that, these pages produce the same resulting HTML form. The example in Listing E.2 illustrates the code used for generating an HTML form when the site administrator is editing an existing payment plan defaulted with text and check box values from the existing PaymentPlans table values.

App

E

FIG. E.2

This shows the display for Add or Detail page of the Payment Options editing area.

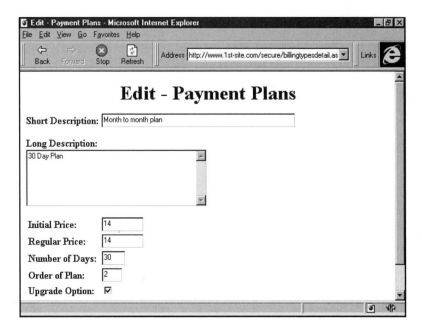

Listing E.2 BILLINGTYPESDETAIL.ASP—Display of Existing Payment Plan Values, Resulting from the List Page

```
<%
  Set Conn = Server.CreateObject("ADODB.Connection")
  Conn.Open("firstsite")
  sql = "SELECT * FROM PaymentPlans WHERE sysplanid =" & request("value")
  Set rs = Conn.Execute(sql)
%>
<html>
...
<form action="billingtypesupdate.asp" method="POST">
...
<p><b>Long Description:  </b><br>
<textarea name="description" rows=5 cols=60 max=255 wrap>
➥<%=rs("Description")%></textarea>
<P>

<table>
<tr><td width=20%><b>Initial Price:  </b></td><td>
<input type=text size=10 maxlength=10 name="price"
➥value="<%=rs("price")%>"></tr></td>
...
```

Payment Options Update Page

The Update page generated by the Detail or Add pages is illustrated in Listing E.3. This page conditionally determines what action has been selected, including update, add, or delete, and then implements the database action, based on values passed from the Detail or Add page.

Listing E.3   BILLINGTYPESUPDATE.ASP—Conditional Database Action to Either Insert, Delete, or Update the PaymentPlans Table

```
<%
   Set Conn = Server.CreateObject("ADODB.Connection")
   Conn.Open("firstsite")

...'Testing Uncertain Values

   '------------------------
...'Evaluate Update, Delete, Add condition
   '------------------------
   if request.form("btn")="Update" then

'Update
'-----------
sql = "UPDATE PaymentPlans SET"
sql = sql & " PaymentPlans.shortdescription ='" & shortdescription & "',"
sql = sql & " PaymentPlans.description ='" & description & "',"
sql = sql & " PaymentPlans.price =" & price & ","
sql = sql & " PaymentPlans.price2 =" & price2 & ","
sql = sql & " PaymentPlans.sysdays =" & sysdays & ","
sql = sql & " PaymentPlans.upgradeoption =" & upgradeoption & ","
sql = sql & " PaymentPlans.optionsorder =" & optionsorder & " "

Set rsUpdate = Server.CreateObject("ADO.Recordset")
rsUpdate.Open sql,Conn,3

   elseif request.form("btn")="Delete" then

'Delete
'-----------
sql = "DELETE FROM PaymentPlans WHERE PaymentPlans.sysplanid=" Â&
request.form("value") & ";"
Set rsDelete = Server.CreateObject("ADO.Recordset")
rsDelete.Open sql,Conn,3

   else

'Add
'-----------
   set rsInsert = Server.CreateObject("ADO.RecordSet")
   Conn.BeginTrans
   rsInsert.Open "PaymentPlans", Conn, 3, 3
   rsInsert.AddNew
   rsInsert("shortdescription") = shortdescription
```

continues

App

E

Listing E.3   Continued

```
        rsInsert("description")    = description
        rsInsert("price")          = price
        rsInsert("price2")         = price2
        rsInsert("sysdays")        = sysdays
        rsInsert("optionsorder")   = optionsorder
        rsInsert("upgradeoption")  = upgradeoption
        rsInsert.Update
        Conn.CommitTrans
        rsInsert.Close

    end if
%>
... 'HTML
<%Conn.Close%>
```

Enabling Internet-Based Payment Mechanisms

Once you implement the payment plan options by either using the method described in "Payment Plans Setup and Management with Active Server" or by using some other method, the next task is the accepting and tracking of member payment transactions. Active Server Pages with the ADO component enables members to make selections and submit payment-related information for storage in a database. The task of taking that stored information and then translating it into actual cash deposited in a checking account, however, still requires either custom components, third-party software, or human intervention.

The following sections, not only address both the Active Server Pages and ADO-based approach to capturing the payment information, but also go a step further by describing both the Introduction Service's approach and other options for collecting and tracking payments. When diving into Internet-based payment mechanisms, you need to cover:

- Dynamically presenting the user/member with payment options
- Validating the payment mechanisms used and storing the information provided
- Implementing infrastructure for providing the necessary accounting/tracking

Following the coverage of these tasks, you will be introduced to the evolving technologies, vendors, and standards in the electronic commerce area that you should watch for opportunities to offer enhanced methods for dealing with the "money" part of a business site.

Dynamically Presenting Payment Options

The first step in collecting money from a member of the Introduction Service occurs in both the New Account and Edit Account areas of the site. The process is virtually identical for both areas, and so the payment options section, which follows, looks at only one, the New Account sign up process. As we discussed in Appendix B, the user enters a 5-step process to sign up for a new account. In Appendix B, we carefully examined the first 3 steps involved in the set up of a new member record in the system. The final 2 steps involve, first, presenting payment options based on the PaymentPlans table, and second, validation and storage of the information that members provide.

Dynamically presenting payment plan options for the new member involves looking up information in the PaymentPlans table and displaying that information in an HTML forms-based format that enables the new member to select the options she wants and the related payment mechanisms and amounts that will be charged. Figure E.3 displays the first of two steps in the payment pages of the New Account sign up process, and Listing E.4 illustrates the code invoked to create the HTML page.

N O T E All payments accepted by the Introduction Service are based on the credit card as the payment mechanism. Other mechanisms such as checks, debit cards, and digital cash services are discussed briefly in "Emerging Payment Technologies, Vendors, and Standards." ▪

FIG. E.3
This displays the payment screen in step 4 of the New Account sign up process.

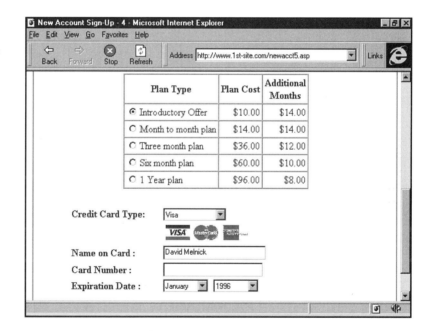

Generating the payment page in step 4 of the New Account sign up process involves a lookup and display with the support of a database similar to SQL statement lookups of databases which we have covered many times throughout this book. The necessary HTML forms-based options must be displayed for members to select a payment plan and to input credit card information.

N O T E A function enabling the formatting of a long integer as currency was required at the time this site was put into production. Since then, Active Server Pages has implemented masking or formatting-related features to allow the more easy display of numbers in a money format. ▪

Listing E.4   NEWACCT6.ASP—First Payment Plan Related Page in New Account Sign Up Process

```
<!--#include file="validatenew.asp"-->
<%
'Lookup of Payment Plans and Member Name
'-----------------------------------------
  Set Conn = Server.CreateObject("ADODB.Connection")
  Conn.Open("firstsite")
  sql = "Select * FROM PaymentPlans ORDER BY optionsorder;"
  Set rs = Conn.Execute(sql)
  sql = "Select LName, FName FROM Members WHERE MemberID=" ➥ &
session("MemberID") & ";"
  Set rsName = Conn.Execute(sql)
  name = rsName("FName") & " " & rsName("LName")
%>
...

'Function for converting number to currency
'-----------------------------------------
<script language=vbscript runat=server>
Function cvtdollars(price)
intlen = len(fix(price))
pricelen = len(price)
  if fix(price) = price then
     cvtdollars = "$" & price & ".00"
  elseif (pricelen - intlen) < 3 then
     cvtdollars = "$" & price & "0"
  else
     cvtdollars = "$" & price
  end if
end function
</script>

...
'-----------------------------------------
'Code not shown representing the
'table/form tags for displaying payment plans and
'credit card options, SEE CD ROM for complete source
'-----------------------------------------
```

Validating and Storing Payment Information

Once the Payment Plan selection and credit card information have been submitted via an HTML form, the system should validate and then store that information. Storing the information involves inserting the payment record into the Billing table for use in whatever accounting/tracking system may be in use.

▶ **See** "New Account: Step 2," for more information about inserting records in a database, **p. 391**

Validation, in contrast, can take on a large variety of forms. Without revisiting the steps involved in using VBScript to evaluate data entered, the focus of validation will instead center on the Introduction Service's acceptance of credit cards. With a focus on credit cards as the only accepted method of payment, a very specific set of validation steps emerge. Validation steps can be implemented up to and including the actual authorizations and capture of funds from the credit card's issuing bank. With all credit card transactions, the primary validation steps include:

1. Expiration date after today's date
2. Valid credit card number, based on check digit test
3. Authorization of credit card through interchange network
4. Capture of funds into merchant bank account

Credit Card Authorizations Process   Before continuing with a review of the Introduction Service, you need to understand what is involved in processing financial transactions. Processing of financial transactions involves institutions and computer networks that we have not discussed up until now. To review, the network-based communications that take place throughout the sections of the Introduction Service we have reviewed to this point include only the client browser, whether it is being used by a site administrator or a member, and the servers used for database, Mail and Web-serving activities. To perform a credit card transaction, a credit card number provided by the member to you, the merchant, must be submitted to the Merchant's bank, which then submits an authorization request to the credit card's issuing bank.

In the "real" world, a credit card authorization process can be illustrated by the following example of a consumer visiting a gas station to buy gas. The consumer stops and pumps the gas, just as a member of the Introduction Service uses the Service's features. The consumer then sees a billing amount on the pump, similar to the displayed payment plan options and amounts discussed in the previous section, "Dynamically Presenting Payment Options." The consumer then provides a credit card to the merchant. For the Introduction Service, the member submits the credit card for your current processing step. At this point, you, as the merchant, have two primary options for accepting this transaction—On-line or Batch authorizations of the credit card.

Batch is simlar to the consumer handing the card to the gas station attendant and having the attendant make a carbon copy of the card information with a simple mechanical card swiper. This batch approach, like the storing of the credit card in a database, enables the merchant to submit copies of the charges to the merchant bank at a later time for collection. The problem with this batch approach is that the credit card account may be closed, over its limit, or stolen. The merchant just doesn't know the status of the card at the time of purchase. This situation reflects the state of most merchants currently operating on the Internet.

In contrast, the gas station may have a direct electronic connection for authorizing credit cards, either through a machine at the pump, a smart cash register, or a small electronic device, probably from Verifone, plugged into a phone line by the cash register. With this direct connection, the gas station can process the credit card number, merchant identification number, and the transaction amount through a network that contacts the credit card's issuing bank for an

App

E

authorization. If a successful authorization is completed, the gas station's merchant bank receives the information necessary to allow the money to be transferred, probably ending up in the gas station's merchant account by the next business day. This capability to connect to an authorizing network or "interchange" for real-time point of sale authorizations and capture of money currently exists on the Internet. You will be introduced to the forms it currently takes in the section "Emerging Payment Technologies, Vendors, and Standards."

Introduction Service's Specific Validation Steps   In contrast to on-line authorizations, the Introduction Service stopped short of capturing funds at the point of purchase and chose instead to implement a batch processing of credit cards. The Introduction Service authorizations are completed off of the Internet through a dial-up software program.

N O T E   Although many Internet merchants today perform batch authorizations of credit cards, on-line authorizations have become increasingly easy to implement with the increase in vendor-provided software tools and the growing openness of banks to accept merchants processing Internet-based transactions. ▪

The gas station in the preceding batch processing example could only take a copy of the credit card for all processing to be done later. Unlike the gas station, the Introduction Service, (with the support of computer technology) at the point of purchase, can complete two levels of validation that might not normally be completed till the merchant bank attempted to deposit the funds. The two tests include a basic test that the expiration date of the card is greater than or equal to today's date, and the second, more important test, *check digit* validation. The check digit validation relies on published and well established standards supported across all credit card issuing banks for defining a valid number range.

From the entry of the credit card number on the HTML form in step 4 of the New Account sign up process, the information is processed through a check digit function. This function evaluates each number in the string of numbers provided and applies the check digit logic illustrated in Listing E.5

Listing E.5   BILLINGUPDATE.ASP—Check Digit Evaluation of Credit Card Information

```
<Script Language=VBScript runat=server>
Function validcard(CreditCard)
' Input is a credit card number in the form of a string.
' Validates numbers which use a "double-add-double MOD 10"
' check digit Output is False if not valid, True if valid.
'--------------------------
'Staring Evaluation of card
'--------------------------
ValidCard = False              'Assume invalid card
If (CreditCard <> "0") and (CreditCard <> "") then
  CC = Trim(CreditCard)        'Trim extra blanks
  CheckSum = 0                 'Start with 0 checksum
  Dbl = 0                      'Start with a non-doubling
```

```
'--------------------------
'Beginning backward loop through string
'--------------------------
For Idx = Len(CC) To 1 Step -1
  Digit = Asc(Mid(CC, Idx, 1)) 'Isolate character

If ((Digit > 47) And (Digit < 58)) or (Digit = 32) Then
  If Digit <> 32 Then
    Digit = Digit - 48        'Remove ASCII bias
    If Dbl Then               'If in the "double-add" phase
        Digit = Digit + Digit 'then double first
        If Digit > 9 Then
           Digit = Digit - 9  'Cast nines
        End If
    End If
    Dbl = Not Dbl             'Flip doubling flag
    CheckSum = CheckSum + Digit 'Add to running sum
    If CheckSum > 9 Then        'Cast tens
        CheckSum = CheckSum - 10'(same as MOD 10 but faster)
    End If
  End If
Else
  ValidCard = 0
  Exit Function
End If

Next
'--------------------------
  ValidCard = (CheckSum = 0)    'Must sum to 0
Else
  ValidCard = 0
End If
'--------------------------
end function
</script>
```

After the card number passes an expiration date evaluation and a check digit evaluation, additional code not illustrated in Listing E.5 is processed to insert the information into the Billing table as a valid billing transaction. At this point, the system assumes that the member has paid in full; if, however, in the accounting/tracking steps a site administrator identifies a credit card authorization failure, they will edit the member account to show they are no longer paid in full.

Implementing Accounting/Tracking

The final component of the Introduction Service involved in accounting/tracking primarily takes place off of the Internet without the assistance of Active Server Pages. The Introduction Service accounting system has been custom developed to track and maintain account information. For your site, you should consider open accounting systems if you do not already have an accounting system in place. If you have an accounting system or other database infrastructure in place, the challenge becomes integrating the Internet-based database services into your current system. Ideally you may directly connect the same systems you currently utilize in the development of your Active Server site. Because most major databases today have ODBC drivers that can be used, you may find connecting directly to your existing systems to be a viable and effective solution.

N O T E Open Accounting Systems means systems in which data is stored in a standard data structure that can be accessed by other programs. Prior to making an investment in an accounting system, carefully consider your ability to export or share accounting information with other computer programs ■

There are several reasons that you may find yourself required to connect two separate systems together in a batch mode like the Introduction Service:

- Your existing accounting system may not be ODBC compliant.
- You may need additional security assurances.
- You may need to host the Internet database at a remote location that can't connect directly to your accounting/tracking system.

Regardless, if you need to keep two systems in sync, first, you should evaluate the possibility of implementing a scheduled synchronizing process via a replication feature of the database servers or through a well-planned, automatic file download and upload process. If, like the Introduction Service, however, you need two separate systems, you may consider the approach implemented for this Service.

The Introduction Service keeps its off-line accounting/tracking system up-to-date with the Internet-based database through the manual use of administrative pages for generating a download file, which then gets imported into its accounting system. The Service's download process utilizes the TextStream Component to dynamically create a file on the server for download by an administrative user. The administrative interface has a very simple HTML forms page, which generates the download page illustrated in Figure E.4

After the file is successfully downloaded, the administrative user presses the update button, which flags the records as having been downloaded. Specific account information is downloaded any time a change occurs, which results in a new or modified account/members record. This process only involves two .asp files: one file for the streaming of all flagged records to a text file with an associated update to the records download flag, and a second file to toggle the download flag back, acknowledging that the information has been downloaded successfully. Listing E.6 illustrates the first .asp file or step in the download process.

FIG. E.4

This is the download page for updating the off-line accounting/tracking system.

Listing E.6 DOWNLOAD.ASP—File for Streaming Records to a Text File in a Set Format and Updating a Download Flag

```
<%
  Set Conn = Server.CreateObject("ADODB.Connection")
  Conn.Open("firstsite")

  session("filecounter") = session("filecounter") + 1
%>

<HTML>
<HEAD><TITLE>Download Page</TITLE><HEAD>
<BODY bgcolor="#FFFFFF">
<H1><CENTER>FileMaker Pro Download</CENTER></H1>

<%
  'set conn = session("conn")

  sql = "UPDATE Members SET"
  sql = sql & " Members.Download = 2"
  sql = sql & " WHERE Members.Download = 1;"
  Set rsupdate = Server.CreateObject("ADO.Recordset")
  rsupdate.Open sql, Conn, 3
```

continues

App

E

Listing E.6 Continued

```
  Set rs = Server.CreateObject("ADO.Recordset")
  sql = "Select * From Members Where Download > 0;"
  rs.Open sql, conn, 3
%>


<%
  set Txtfile = Server.CreateObject("Scripting.FileSystemObject")
  FileRoot = "download.txt"
  FileName = "c:\wwwarea\hotsites\wwwroot\1stsite\secure\" & cstr(FileRoot)
' Set to open for writing and to overwrite other files
  Set a=Txtfile.CreateTextFile(cstr(FileName),True)
'-------------------------------
' Load array with lines for file
'-------------------------------
    dim txtline
    Do While Not RS.EOF
       Set rs2 = Server.CreateObject("ADO.Recordset")
       sql2 = "Select Top 1 * From Billing Where SysMemberID=" & rs("MemberID")
➥ " ORDER BY SysTranDate DESC;"
       rs2.Open sql2, Conn, 3

       If not rs2.eof then
txtline = """" & rs("MemberID") & """" & ","
txtline = txtline & """" & rs("AdmStatus") & """" & ","
txtline = txtline & """" & rs("Maiden") & """" & ","
txtline = txtline & """" & rs("Pass") & """" & ","
txtline = txtline & """" & rs("FName") & """" & ","
txtline = txtline & """" & rs("LName") & """" & ","
txtline = txtline & """" & rs("Address1") & """" & ","
txtline = txtline & """" & rs("Address2") & """" & ","
txtline = txtline & """" & rs("City") & """" & ","
txtline = txtline & """" & rs("StateID") & """" & ","
txtline = txtline & """" & rs("Zip") & """" & ","
txtline = txtline & """" & rs("HMPhone") & """" & ","
txtline = txtline & """" & rs("HMAreaCode") & """" & ","
txtline = txtline & """" & rs("WkPhone") & """" & ","
txtline = txtline & """" & rs("WkAreaCode") & """" & ","
txtline = txtline & """" & rs("Email") & """" & ","
txtline = txtline & """" & rs("ProfSex") & """" & ","
txtline = txtline & """" & rs2("SysPlanID") & """" & ","
txtline = txtline & """" & rs2("SysPlanDuration") & """" & ","
txtline = txtline & """" & rs2("SysMemberID") & """" & ","
txtline = txtline & """" & rs2("Amount1") & """" & ","
txtline = txtline & """" & rs2("Amount2") & """" & ","
txtline = txtline & """" & rs2("BillingCardType") & """" & ","
txtline = txtline & """" & rs2("BillingCardNum") & """" & ","
txtline = txtline & """" & rs2("BillingExpDateMonth") & """" & ","
txtline = txtline & """" & rs2("BillingExpDateYear") & """" & ","
txtline = txtline & """" & rs2("NameOnCC") & """" & ","
txtline = txtline & """" & rs("AdmStartDate") & """" & ","
txtline = txtline & """" & rs("ProfPrefID") & """" & ","
txtline = txtline & """" & rs("ReferredBy") & """"
a.writeline txtline
```

```
End If
RS.MoveNext
Loop
RS.close
%>

Your file can now be downloaded by clicking below:<br>
<a href="<%=fileroot%>"><%=fileroot%></a><p><hr>
Once you have successfully saved your download file, press
the Update button below.  <b>It is imperative that you check
the data you saved before pressing this button.</b>  By
pressing the Update button, you are acknowledging that you
received your download correctly.

<FORM action="toggledownload.asp" method="POST">
<center>
<input type=submit name="btnUpdate" value="Update">
</center>
</FORM></BODY></HTML>
<%Conn.Close%>
```

After the file has been successfully downloaded, a second .asp file is executed to acknowledge the successful download and to flag all of the downloaded accounts back to their original status.

Emerging Payment Technologies, Vendors, and Standards

Although you have been introduced to the batch approach to accepting credit cards, you should be aware of the on-line authorizations approach as well. Several vendors currently provide mechanisms for accepting credit cards for on-line authorizations, but by far, the most well-known company is CyberCash. We have worked with Verifone and their vPOS system for Microsoft's Merchant Server, and we are currently working with CyberCash. Both approaches offer a very preliminary implementation of the Secure Electronic Transaction (SET) standard promoted by Visa, MasterCard, and a series of other companies.

App
E

Referring again to the gas station example to explain SET, the full implementation of SET would be like the gas station installing the mechanisms that authorize your credit card for payment at the pump prior to your pumping the gas. In this case, the gas station attendant never actually sees your credit card number and, instead, only gets the authorization code and transaction information. This is equivalent to the use of a "wallet" in your Web browser when full SET becomes available. This approach provides more security and accountability than you get today in most "real" world situations. Because the merchant never actually sees your card, the potential for fraud and other abuses is reduced dramatically. In addition, the direct nature of this transaction further reduces chance of error in the process. Unfortunately, the current implementation of SET more closely resembles the situation in which you hand your card to the gas station attendant and he swipes the card through an electronic reader or smart cash register. In this situation, the merchant has the opportunity to see and save your credit card number.

Developments to watch include the capability to do coin or small transactions, as well as debit cards, through CyberCash and other service providers. Also, CommercNet, a non-profit, member-driven company provides a good source of information on upcoming development. For more information on these companies visit **http://www.commercenet.com**, **http://www.cybercash.com**, and **http://www.visa.com**.

We have worked closely with Wells Fargo and, more recently, Bank America and are happy to note a complete turn in the position of these major banks. While Wells Fargo has been very progressive in many areas already, both banks have demonstrated a real commitment to facilitate commerce over the Net and no longer voice caution and doubt to would-be electronic commerce companies. This shift has made banks willing to issue merchant accounts for Internet-only companies, as well as to facilitate the rollout of the SET standard. This commitment comes from leading financial players, ranging from vendors like Verifone to the networks managed by Visa and MasterCard to the banks and clearinghouses like Wells Fargo and Bank America. A clear movement has begun, not only in the progressive technical companies, but also in the core institutions that act as the gatekeepers of commerce.

With the conclusion of this payment discussion, you should now be ready to implement a comprehensive business site with the capability to build and track a membership, manage an interactive service, provide a comprehensive administrative environment, and bill and collect payments. At this point, you just need to decide what you want to build. ●

A Quick Tour of HTML

Active Server Pages applications enable you to create powerful, data-driven, dynamic Web pages. Whereas scripting provides the engine that drives your applications, the language of the browser is HTML. For those of you who are new to creating HTML documents, this appendix provides you with the foundation and tools you need to begin. If you are already a seasoned Web developer, this appendix provides a useful reference of the HTML commands and syntax that you will integrate into your script. ■

An Introduction to HTML

The HyperText Markup Language, or as it is more commonly referred to, HTML, is the formatting language of the World Wide Web. It is derived from SGML (Standard Graphical Markup Language), a complex specification for marking up text. HTML is a series of instructions that the browser uses to display the content of the document being received. One of the main benefits of HTML is that it is platform independent. Any operating system/application combination that can display HTML-formatted documents can be a participant on the Web.

The HTML language is governed by the World Wide Web Consortium Standards Group, and the current revision level is 2.0. We will be covering a number of HTML tags from version 2.0 and some of the newer tags in the proposed version 3.2. For the most recent revision activity on the HTML standard, check out the W3C Web site at **http://www.w3.org/pub/WWW/ MarkUp**.

One key point about HTML development that you need to understand is, that in addition to the formatting attributes that you specify, you will also specify the logical connections or links between pages. This capability to hyperlink within and between documents enables you to seamlessly travel between related topics. This gave birth to the idea of *The Web*.

This quick tour is not intended to be a comprehensive HTML reference, but it will provide you with an introduction to the language and enable you to start creating HTML documents right away.

The Basics

The HTML language is composed of tags, elements, and attributes. You'll take a quick look at each of these components, and then move on to creating your first Web page.

Document Tags   The tags define a specific set of formatting instructions that apply to the content within the tag scope. A tag scope is defined as anything contained between the starting tag <TAG> and the ending tag </TAG>.

Formatting Elements   An element is a specific formatting instruction. For example, the <H1> tag contains the Heading One element.

Formatting Attributes   The attributes of an element are enclosed within the starting tag of the element. Attributes are additional parameters that provide extra formatting information for the browser. For example, in the tag <A NAME="TOP" TITLE="START">, the attributes associated with the element Anchor are NAME and TITLE.

The HTML Document

An HTML document is structured around three main formatting sections, or document structure *tags*. Start with Listing F.1 to illustrate the document tags, and then examine each tag individually.

Listing F.1   F1.htm—A Simple Web Document: Hello World

```
<HTML>
<HEAD>
<TITLE> My First Web Page </TITLE>
</HEAD>
<BODY>
Hello World!
</BODY>
</HTML>
```

The first thing that you notice are the funny looking delimiters around some of the text. Words enclosed within the < > delimiters are tags. These are the tags discussed previously, and they are instructions to the browser about how and, sometimes, where to display the content within the document. In this case, the content is Hello World!, as shown in Figure F.1.

FIG. F.1

A simple Web page can be created by using just a few tags.

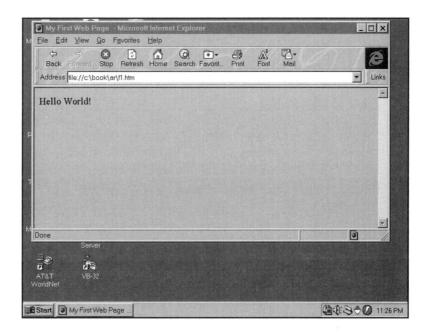

 TIP As a rule, tags should always be the same case. The industry standard is uppercase, but you might use upper- or lowercase, as long as you are consistent. So, for starting and ending tags, you might use <TAG></TAG> or <tag></tag>, but don't use <TAG>/<tag>. Using mixed case is inconsistent and will only cause confusion for the next developer who maintains your code.

App

F

Document Structure Tags

Document structure tags are used to break the document into functional pieces. They enable someone who is viewing your document source to quickly and easily understand the outline of the document, and its overall structure.

<HTML>   This is the document structure tag that is always at the top of your HTML page. Notice also that the end of the document will have a closing HTML tag as well </HTML>. Most tags have an opening and a closing tag. The closing tag is identified by the slash / in front of the tag name.

<HEAD>   This is another document structure tag that identifies the page heading in the document. You will find information about the document within the <HEAD> tags. The title for the page is usually placed in the head section as well.

<BODY>   The body section is the last of the document structure tags. The <BODY> tag is a notification that the body of the document (the content of the page) follows. Be sure to include the </BODY> tag at the end of the document, before the closing </HTML> tag.

N O T E You are not required to include the document structure tags in your HTML document. Most browsers display a page without document tags perfectly well. But, to ensure that your intent is clear and that you conform to the HTML specification, always include the document structure tags within your Web pages. ▨

Take a minute to see how the preceding sample code will look in *your* browser. Now, you have two choices to complete the next exercise. If you are currently connected to the Web, hop over to the on-line edition of this appendix at **http://www.quecorp.com/asp/appendixf**. From here, you can select Listing F.1, and it will open the document in your browser. For those of you who want to practice actually creating your first page, follow these simple steps:

1. Open up your favorite line-text editor (Notepad is a good one to use).
2. Type the preceding sample code from Listing F.1 into it.
3. Save the file as hello.htm in the directory of your choice.
4. Open the page in your browser.

For Internet Explorer users:

1. Select File, Open from the main menu.
2. Enter the path to your hello.htm file (ex: **c:\hello.htm**).

For Navigator users:

1. Select File, Open File from the main menu.
2. Enter the path to your hello.htm file (ex: **c:\hello.htm**).

You should now see your first Web page in your browser. It should appear similar to the page shown in Figure F.1. Good work!

<TITLE> The title tag is not a document structure tag, but it does reside within the <HEAD> tags. The title in most browsers shows up as the title on the browser window. This is also the text that is added to the *Favorite Sites* or *Bookmarks* when your users add the site to their personal site lists.

 TIP Be sure to make your document title short and unambiguous. It will be the first item that your users see and will also be their reference for the page in the future. As a painful example, consider the titles: *Mary and John's Wonderful Home Page, Which Describes Their Full And Exciting Lives* versus *Mary and John's Home Page.*

Text Handling and Formatting

There are a number of tags that enable you to format text and to apply a variety of styles to it. Take a brief look at the definition of these tags, and then move on to the additional examples.

<P> Paragraph Tag Use this tag to delineate paragraphs. It groups text into logical units and adds a carriage return to the document after the paragraph is displayed. This tag requires a </P> end tag when formatting text. When used alone to add a carriage return, no end tag is required.

```
<P>The very long road to the wizard's house happened to be
paved with yellow bricks. Am I on the road less traveled?</P>
```

The browser does not include the white space or the line-feeds between the lines of your HTML file. If you create multiple paragraphs without using the <P>aragraph tags, all the text will run together as one long paragraph. If you want to add blank lines between paragraphs, use the <P>aragraph tag without the closing </P> tag.

**
 Line Break Tag** This tag can be used within other tags to provide a line break between words or sections. The main difference between the line break tag and the paragraph tag is that the line break tag does not include an additional carriage return, as you can see in Figure F.2. The code is shown in Listing F.2.

App
F

Listing F.2   F2.htm—The Paragraph Tag Adds an Additional Carriage Return

```
<HTML><HEAD>
<TITLE>Paragraph and Line Break</TITLE>
</HEAD><BODY>
<P> I continue along the road of yellow bricks when <BR>
I happen to notice a straw filled shirt, puffy pants <BR>and a hat hanging in
➥what appears to be a wheat field</P>
<P>Now, I ask, are we in Kansas anymore?</P>
</BODY></HTML>
```

FIG. F.2

The paragraph tag adds a carriage return after the text.

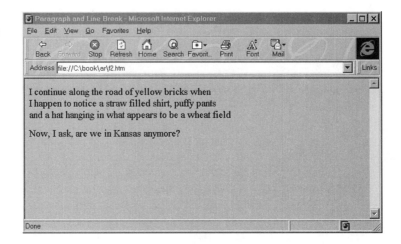

<BLOCK QUOTE> Block Quote Tag   The block quote tag is used to specify a quotation. You can freely use the <BR> tag within a block quote tag group.

```
<BLOCK QUOTE>Four score and seven years ago, our forefathers<BR>
brought forth on this continent a new nation, conceived in liberty<BR>
and dedicated to the proposition that all men are created
equal.</BLOCKQUOTE>
```

In addition to the text formatting tags, there are a number of tags that are used to change the appearance of selected characters, words, or text within a block. These formatting commands, found in Table F.1, apply a logical character style, which implies that the formatting is implicit within the browser, not explicitly stated in the tag.

Table F.1   Logical Formatting Tags

Tag	Characteristic	Description
<EM>	Emphasized	Emphasizes the text
<STRONG>	Stronger emphasis	Might be bold
<CODE>	Code sample	Formatted with a fixed font
<SAMP>	Similar to <CODE>	Used for samples
<KBD>	Keyboard commands	Instructs user input
<VAR>	Variable	Represents a variable
<DFN>	Definition	Explains a term or concept
<CITE>	A citation	Used for short quotations

All of the logical formatting tags require a start and an end tag. Here is an example of how you might use some of these tags:

```
<P><EM>Hey!</EM>he shouted as they walked away.<STRONG>Wait up</STRONG>
he said in an even louder voice.</P>
```

In addition to the logical styles, there are also physical styles that affect the displayed text, which are shown in Table F.2.

Table F.2   Physical Formatting Tags

Tag	Characteristic	Description
`<B>`	Bold	Applies the bold style to the text
`<I>`	Italic	Applies an italic style to the text
`<TT>`	Typewriter	Applies a mono-spaced typewriter font

All of the formatting tags in Table F.2 have specified suggestions to the browser about the format and style of the text. Figure F.3 shows how these styles will appear in a typical browser. Notice on the example line that you can nest logical and physical styles. To achieve a bold italic, you can enter the tags like:

```
<B><I>Wait Up</B></I>
```

FIG. F.3
You can apply logical and physical styles to document text.

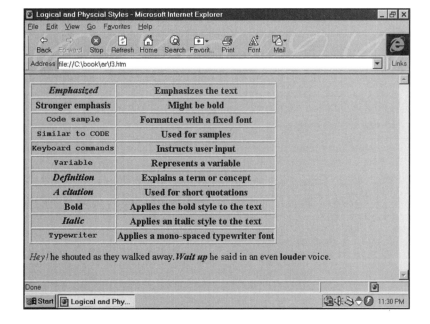

App
F

In Listing F.2, there is no explicit control over the white space between characters. To illustrate this ignoring of white space by the browser, consider the following two lines of HTML, which produce the exact same output on the browser.

```
<P>Here is a            paragraph     with      embedded        spaces</P>
<P>Here is a paragraph with embedded spaces</P>
```

The browser will remove all spaces between words after the first one encountered in the string. This ignoring of embedded spaces will happen within all the HTML tags except one.

The only formatting tag that requires the display to emulate the format of the content as it is passed in is the <PRE>Formatted text tag. Using this tag ensures that the white space around the characters is preserved. This tag is useful when you want the text to be formatted as typed in the HTML file. For example, if you want to create a picture from the text in your document, enclose it in the <PRE> tag to ensure that it will be displayed as input. For example,

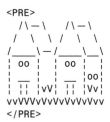

Just for fun, you might try enclosing the preceding picture in the paragraph tags <P> instead of the <PRE> tags. It will end up looking like one long line of characters. Not exactly the message that you are trying to convey!

Lists

There are a number of tags that you use to create lists of items, which is useful in a variety of situations. You can create ordered lists, numbered lists, lists of terms and definitions—almost any configuration that you can dream up. You can also nest lists of the same type and of differing types together.

<UL> Unordered List   The unordered list tag creates a list of bulleted items. The bullet is determined by the browser. Within each of the list tags, you enter list items with the <LI> tag. The <LI> tag *does not* include an end tag. For example,

```
<P>Guaranteed list for successful campfire meeting</P>
<UL>
    <LI>Marshmallows
    <LI>Hershey Bars
    <LI>Graham Crackers
</UL>
```

<MENU> Menu List   The menu list is the most basic list tag. It creates a list but does not include any indenting or bullets.

<OL> Ordered List   This tag creates an ordered list. Each of the list items will be sequentially ordered when the items are displayed. If you nest the ordered list, the numbering restarts at 1 for each nested group, as you can see in Figure F.4. For example,

```
<OL>
    <LI>Item 1, Group 1
    <OL> Group 2
        <LI>Item 1, Group 2
        <LI>Item 2, Group 2
    </OL>
        <LI>Item 2, Group 1
</OL>
```

FIG. F.4

Nested ordered lists start at 1 within each nested level.

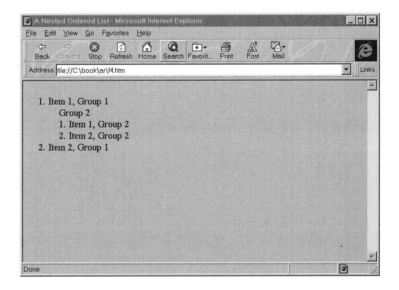

<DL> Glossary List   The glossary list tag creates a listing that has a list item and then a list description. It ends up looking like a glossary in your browser. Instead of list items, <LI>, a glossary list has matched pairs of <DT> terms and <DD> definitions. Here is what the glossary list looks like in action:

App

F

```
<DL>
<DT> macarena <DD> A new dance that my children have mastered,
                  but sadly, I have not
<DT> macaroni <DD> Dinner of choice for college students
    and recent grads
</DL>
```

You can also mix the list types by nesting the types together, as shown in the following code and illustrated in Figure F.5.

```
<OL>
    <LI>Flowers
        <UL>
            <LI>Sunflower
            <LI>Rose
        </UL>
    <LI>Dogs
        <UL>
            <LI>Poodle
            <LI>Retriever
        </UL>
</OL>
```

FIG. F.5

You can nest and mix list types within your documents.

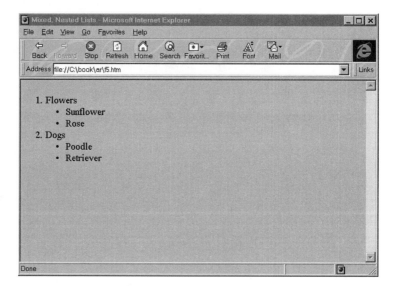

In each of the listings, we have indented the listings to separate the lists visually, as well as in the HTML document when it is displayed. There is no requirement for formatting the HTML; the browser even ignores extra blank spaces. By using intelligent spacing and comments, however, your code will be readable and easily maintainable.

Additional Notable Tags

The following tags do not fall into any of the categories outlined previously, yet are very important in their own right.

<!— —> Comments   In any development environment, you need to be able to add comments to your source code to enable you and those that work on the code after you to understand your intentions for the page. The comment tag enables you to add these notes for you and other Web developers. Incidentally, the comment tag is also used in scripting as the delimiters of the script code. For example:

```
<SCRIPT LANGUAGE="VBScript">
<!--
   Dim aVariable                'we have created a variant variable
   aVariable = "5"              'now it looks like a string
   aVariable = aVariable + 5    'now it looks like an integer with a value of 10
-->
</SCRIPT>
```

▶ **See** "Scripting and HTML" for more information about scripting and script tags, **p. 110**

<HR> Horizontal Line   The horizontal line is very useful for dividing the page into logical groupings. It does just what you think it would do: It creates a horizontal line all the way across the page.

Providing Links

The capability to click a topic or graphic and go to another related document is what makes the World Wide Web a *Web*. This simple functionality enables you to walk (or should we say surf) from document to document, just like following the strands of a Web toward your ultimate destination. Of course, many of us just surf without any particular destination in mind. To enable this movement within and between pages, there is a special tag that is used—the anchor tag.

The <A> link/anchor tag has a number of attributes that define the link or anchor that you want to jump to. An anchor is a location within a page. So, if you want to go to a location within the current page, you can link to an anchor on that same page. If you want to go to another document, you link to that document's URL. If you want to go to a document and a particular place within that document, you link to the URL and the anchor within the target document. Confused yet? Take a look at the link/anchor tag attributes and you will start to understand:

```
<A NAME="PROJECTS" HREF="HTTP://WWW.MELNICK.COM" TARGET="MAIN">
```

The HREF attribute specifies the location to jump to when the link is activated. The NAME attribute names this anchor so that it can be accessed or jumped to from another part of the same page or another page altogether. Here are some examples of links that will jump from the same page to this anchor:

```
<A HREF="#PROJECTS">
```

and from another page to this page and anchor:

```
<A HREF="HTTP://WWW.MELNICK.COM#PROJECTS">
```

Notice that to jump to an anchor, you precede the anchor name with a pound (#) sign.

The text for an anchor in the browser is highlighted with a color specified in the LINK attribute

App

F

within the BODY tag. After the link is selected, the color changes, so the client can see where he has been. This is referred to as an explored link. Even days later, if a page is still in the browser cache, and the page is requested again, the explored links will still be apparent.

In addition to linking to other pages, you can also use a special set of tags to provide an e-mail command that brings up a preaddressed e-mail form on the client's browser. The first additional tag is the <ADDRESS> tag. This formats the text with an address style. Along with the <ADDRESS> tag, you also want to change the protocol on the HREF statement from http to mailto:. Here is an example:

```
<A NAME="RETURNMAIL" HREF="mailto:Selfanbaum@worldnet.att.net">
<ADDRESS>Selfanbaum@worldnet.att.net</ADDRESS></A>
```

> **CAUTION**
>
> If you haven't already noticed, you can nest multiple tags. Just be sure that you always close the tags in order. If you are nesting three tags, be sure that their order is <T1><T2><T3></T3></T2></T1>. If you enter the ending tags in a different order, you are sure to get unpredictable and unwanted results.

There are a number of other attributes of the anchor tag not discussed here. You learn about some of the other attributes such as TARGET when you examine frames in the section "Working with Frames" later in this appendix. For a complete listing of the attributes of the <A>Anchor tag, please see the HTML specification or pick up one of the many available HTML reference books. You can view the HTML specification online at **http://www.w3.org/pub/WWW/ MarkUp/**.

Using Images

One of the most attractive and interesting features of browsing on the Web is the incredible variety of graphics that you come across: everything from classical art to new wave. These days, even the control buttons on the pages are colorful. To add images to your Web page, all you need to do is use the image tag.

The <IMG> image tag has a number of attributes, the most important one being the image source. You implement the image tag as follows:

```
<IMG SRC="myimage.gif"> or <IMG SRC="images\myimage.gif">
```

You can enter the image source in relative or absolute terms, relative to the location of the document, or an absolute path to the file. After you have the image, you can decide where you want to place it on the page, in relation to the last text that was put into the HTML stream. To tell the browser where to place the image, use the ALIGN attribute of the <IMG> tag.

```
<IMG SRC="myimage.gif" ALIGN=TOP>
```

The image alignment attribute can be set to TOP, MIDDLE, BOTTOM, LEFT, or RIGHT. The vertical image alignments are in relation to the text line in which the image is being displayed. When you use the LEFT or RIGHT alignment, this also instructs the browser to wrap any text immediately following the image tag around the graphic.

One of the most common activities that you will use images for is linking to other pages or to a higher-resolution image than the one being displayed. The image tags that you have seen so far have all been *in-line* images. These images show up within the page that is being displayed. If you place an image in an anchor tag (in the HREF attribute), that image file will be returned to the browser for display when the link is selected.

The first code line shown as follows illustrates an image linking to another document. The second line shows an image linking to a higher-resolution image for display in the browser.

```
<A HREF="http://www.melnick.com"><IMG SRC="melnick.gif"></A>
<A HREF="http://www.melnick.com/monet.jpg"><IMG SRC="monet.gif"></A>
```

Image Maps

One of the best ways to provide your users with a cohesive picture of the places they can jump to from a page is through the use of image maps. Image maps are just like using image tags with one important distinction: You can send the user to different places depending on *where* on the image they click. Imagine that you have a Web site illustrating a newly constructed home. You create an image map from a blueprint of the house. As a user clicks the different rooms of the house, he would be taken to additional images of those rooms. Image maps provide an easy and intuitive way to select a link.

Image maps can be implemented on the client side (CSI Maps), on the server side (SSI Maps), or on the client side with additional code to implement the map on the server if the browser does not support client-side mapping. The latest browsers from Microsoft, Internet Explorer 3.01, and Netscape Navigator 3.0 support client-side image maps. Client-side image maps provide a number of advantages over server-side maps. First, they can be created and tested locally, requiring only a browser. Second, they will reduce the number of hits on your server, always helpful at a busy site.

The first requirement when creating image maps is a program that will generate, or help generate, the map for you. For a good list of available image map utilities, check out the image maps section on Yahoo! at **http://www.yahoo.com/Computers/Internet/World_Wide_Web/ Programming/Imagemaps/**.

Creating Client-Side Image Maps   The <MAP> tag is used within your document to describe the client-side image map. Here is a quick example that will give you an idea of how it looks within a document:

```
<MAP NAME="imgmap">
 <AREA SHAPE="RECT" COORDS="100,15,191,74" HREF="/img/house.gif">
 <AREA SHAPE="RECT" COORDS="66,21,128,74" HREF="/img/car.gif">
 <AREA SHAPE="RECT" COORDS="22,21,55,74" HREF="/img/boat.gif">
</MAP>
<IMG SRC="/img/townmap.gif" USEMAP="#imgmap">
```

The <MAP> </MAP> tags define the image map named imgmap. When the image is added, the USEMAP attribute is set to the map name to use when processing the click on the image. Regions can be circles, rectangles, or complex polygons. Again, the easiest way to generate the mapping information is to use an image utility. One of our favorite tools for creating client-side image maps is Live Image version 1.1. It has a 14-day trial and is an easy-to-use, powerful program. Live Image can be found at **http://www.mediatec.com**.

All you need to do is insert the map into your document and provide an image with a reference to the map. The rest is handled by the browser.

T I P The best image maps are those with clearly defined regions. Picasso's pictures would be better than Monet's. A flowchart would be better than a patchwork quilt. Get the idea?

Creating Server-Side Image Maps   Server-side image maps involve creating a map file on the server. The map file is set as the reference for the image file within the <IMG> tag. When the image file is clicked, the map file is called, which in turn, calls a CGI or ISAPI program, passing in the coordinates of the click. Within the HTML file, the image map link is added as shown here:

```
< A HREF="http://www.yourhost.com/cgi-bin/imagemap/picmap.map">
<IMG SRC="/pic.jpg" ISMAP BORDER=0></A>
```

The first line sets the anchor and reference to the picmap.map mapping file. The image to be clicked is pic.jpg. The ISMAP attribute identifies the image as an image map. When the image is clicked, the image map processing program on the server will be invoked, and the new link will be launched.

On the server, the image map can be implemented using the CERN or NCSA standard. The image map processing CGI program that you are using on your site will determine which format to use. An example of an NCSA-type image map file that might support a product line image is shown here:

```
default /products/imap/default.htm
rect /products/imap/a.htm 35,80 135,160
rect /products/imap/b.htm 144,58 215,145
circle /products/imap/c.htm 10, 15 20
```

The points after the rectangle specify the top-left and bottom-right corners of the region. You specify a circle by selecting the center of the circular region, and then by specifying the radius in pixels. A polygon is defined by specifying a list of the connecting points, in order around the region.

Client-Side Maps with Server-Side Alternative   If your clients might have browsers that do not support client-side image maps, the best implementation is to provide support for client-AND server-side maps. For those browsers that do support client-side maps, it is one less hit against your server. To ensure that all your users can have access to the image map functionality, you will include a default for a server-side image mapping file. To do this, you include the

USEMAP attribute and the ISMAP attribute within the anchor. Those browsers that support CSI maps will process them within the browser. Those that don't will ignore the USEMAP attribute and call the server-side map. An example of this dual function usage follows:

```
<a href="/cgi-bin/imagemap/works/workman.map">
     <img src="workman.gif" USEMAP="#Work" ISMAP>
```

Backgrounds

There are two ways that you can set the background for the display of your Web pages. The first is by setting the background color attribute of the <BODY> tag.

```
<BODY BKCOLOR=#FFFFFF>
```

The background color attribute sets the background color to the RGB value that is specified in the attribute. The attribute accepts a six-position hexadecimal number in which the first two places represent the R(red), the second two the G(green), and the third, the B(blue) value. The values for each parameter can range from 0 to 255. If you are running Windows 95 or Windows NT, an easy way to get the RGB values for a color is to use the color option within the Display Properties dialog box. To invoke the dialog box:

1. Right-click anywhere on the desktop.
2. Select properties from the pop-up menu.
3. After the Display Properties dialog box is shown, select the Appearance tab, and then the color combo box.
4. Finally, select Other from the combo box choices, and the color selection wheel appears.

Each time you select a color on the wheel, the RGB values are shown. After you have found the right color, copy down the RGB values and add them to your BKCOLOR attribute. Just be sure to select Cancel from the color dialog box, or you might inadvertently change the background color of your Windows desktop!

The second way to enhance the appearance of the background is by specifying an image that will be tiled on the browser window. Once again, this is an attribute of the <BODY> tag.

```
<BODY BACKGROUND="tilepic.gif">
```

CAUTION

It is very tempting to create a brightly colored background or to use a busy image for the tiled background of your page. Just remember that even though you want your page to be aesthetically pleasing, the ultimate goal is to enable the user to view the content without being distracted by a noisy or busy page.

As you move from page to page on the Web, you will notice that the text within the pages you visit, as well as the links and explored links, have many different colors. You can specify the color for the TEXT, LINK, and VLINK (explored link) within your document, just as you selected the background color within the BODY tag, by adding additional attributes. For example:

App

F

```
<BODY BKCOLOR="FFFFFF" TEXT="#336699" LINK="#003366" VLINK="#0099cc">
```

The attributes BKCOLOR, TEXT, LINK, and VLINK set the color of the background, the text, the links, and explored links, respectively. A link initially has the color specified in the LINK attribute. When a link has been followed, its color changes to that specified in the VLINK attribute.

Creating Tables

The capability to create tables within your Web pages enables you to provide a wealth of informative content in an easy-to-read and easy-to-reference format. Before the table tags were supported by most browsers, you were stuck with manually formatting the table, using a combination of the <PRE> tag, and spaces within the HTML lines. A number of different vendors have added additional functionality (extensions) to the table specification, such as the support for variable size borders found in Netscape Navigator 2.0 and above, and Internet Explorer 3.0 and higher. The basic <TABLE> elements and attributes are covered as follows.

You have surely deduced this already, but a table is created by using the <TABLE> tag. Jump right into the following example, and then you can step back and examine the various attributes of the table element.

```
<HTML>
<HEAD>
<TITLE>Using Tables</TITLE>
</HEAD>
<BODY>
<TABLE BORDER>
<CAPTION ALIGN="TOP">Some Teams and Some Scores</CAPTION>
  <TR>
    <TH>Redskins</TH>
    <TH>Chiefs</TH>
    <TH>Colts</TH>
  </TR>
  <TR>
    <TD>13</TD>
    <TD>44</TD>
    <TD>12</TD>
  </TR>
</TABLE>
</BODY>
</HTML>
```

Once again, notice that the indents in the code do not affect the page display at all. It is just a way to help ensure that your start and end tags match, as well as to give you a sense of the logical nesting of the tags. In Figure F.6, you see the sample table as shown in a browser.

FIG. F.6

Tables are a good replacement for the *<PRE>* tag.

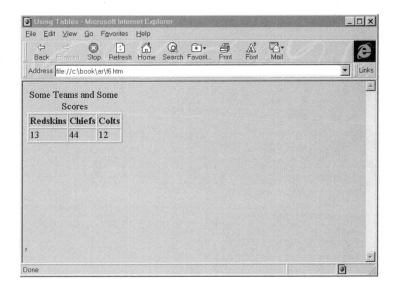

The table element has one attribute that we added within the <TABLE> tag, BORDER. This adds a border around the table. A table consists of rows and cells within a row. In a row, you can have heading cells and data cells (within which you can have images, lists—almost anything).

<TR> **Row.** The row tag encloses cell headings and cell data items. There is no requirement for all the rows to have the same number of cells. The browser compensates as best it can with odd numbers of cells within rows.

<TH> **Cell Heading.** Use these tags to denote the headings of the table. The headings might be across the top, down the left side, or on both axes.

<TD> **Cell Data.** The cell data tags surround data elements in the table. You can also specify images to reside in the cell. To insert an in-line image into a cell of a table, specify the tag as follows:

```
<TD ALIGN="CENTER"><IMG SRC="cellimg.gif"></TD>
```

Notice that we have also added another attribute of the cell data element, ALIGN. The cell data, as well as the cell heading, can be aligned horizontally or vertically. The horizontal alignment attribute is ALIGN, and the vertical alignment attribute is VALIGN. The default for both attributes is CENTER and MIDDLE, respectively. The values that you can use for ALIGN are TOP, CENTER, and BOTTOM. Valid values for the VALIGN attribute include LEFT, MIDDLE, and RIGHT. In Listing F.3, you can see that it is valid to place most any tag type within a table cell, even image tags.

App

F

Listing F.3 F3.htm—Adding Styles, Lists, and Other Tags to Table Cell Contents <HTML>

```
<HEAD>
<TITLE>Important Reminders</TITLE>
</HEAD>
<BODY>
<TABLE BORDER>
<CAPTION ALIGN="TOP">To Do Items This Week</CAPTION>
  <TR>
    <TH>Monday</TH>
    <TH>Tuesday</TH>
    <TH>Wednesday</TH>
    <TH>Thursday</TH>
    <TH>Friday</TH>
  </TR>
  <TR>
   <TD>Take out the trash</TD>
   <TD>Pick up Kids at School
     <UL>
        <LI>Danny at 3:00
        <LI>Joey at 3:45
     </UL>
   </TD>
   <TD>Dinner with Parents</TD>
   <TD>Library Book Sale</TD>
   <TD>Plan for Weekend
   <UL>
       <LI>Get Flowers
       <LI>Order Dinner
       <LI>Pick Up Tux
   </UL>
   </TD>
  </TR>
</TABLE>
</BODY>
</HTML>
```

Another useful formatting element is the COLSPAN attribute of the <TH> or <TD> tags. This forces the cell to span a number of columns. Listing F.4 shows how this is useful when grouping multiple columns together.

Listing F.4 F4.htm—The Colspan Attribute: Useful for Grouping Columns Within a Table

```
<HTML>
<HEAD>
<TITLE>Class Team Listing</TITLE>
</HEAD>
<BODY>
<TABLE BORDER>
<CAPTION ALIGN="TOP">The Teams and Their Scores</CAPTION>
```

```
<TR>
<TH COLSPAN=2>Blue Team</TH>
<TH COLSPAN=2>Red Team</TH>
<TH COLSPAN=2>Green Team</TH>
</TR>
<TR>
    <TH>Harrient</TH> <TH>Jordan</TH>
    <TH>Bobby</TH> <TH>Lisa</TH>
    <TH>Reggie</TH> <TH>Jonas</TH>
</TR>
<TR>
     <TD ALIGN="CENTER">25</TD> <TD ALIGN="CENTER">35</TD>
    <TD ALIGN="CENTER">25</TD> <TD ALIGN="CENTER">30</TD>
    <TD ALIGN="CENTER">20</TD> <TD ALIGN="CENTER">25</TD>
</TR>
<TR>
    <TD ALIGN="CENTER" COLSPAN=2>60</TD>
    <TD ALIGN="CENTER" COLSPAN=2>55</TD>
    <TD ALIGN="CENTER" COLSPAN=2>45</TD>
</TR>
</TABLE>
</BODY>
</HTML>
```

Figure F.7 shows the COLSPAN attribute in action. It is Listing F.4, displayed within a browser.

FIG. F.7

The COLSPAN attribute visually groups columns together.

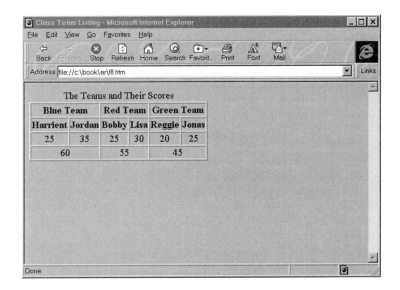

The ALIGN attribute and the COLSPAN attribute work very well together. You can nest most tags within other tags. You will surely encounter a number of pages with tables nested in tables nested in tables. If you are not sure whether a particular tag can be nested, give it a try. As you create pages with just HTML, it is very easy to save the file and load it from your browser to see if your code will work.

App
F

T I P When you begin to develop your Active Server applications, many times it is easier to create the framework for your pages by using HTML only, and then add the scripting code later. This could be considered a form of RAD (rapid application development). This way, you can show your users (client) the pages as they are being prototyped, and fill in the logic as the interface is signed off on.

As a general rule, you will want to test the appearance of your pages on at least a few (OK, two) of the major Web browsers, the latest revisions of Netscape Navigator and Microsoft's Internet Explorer. This will ensure that the vast majority of your users will have a rich and satisfying experience at your Web site.

Designing HTML Forms

Forms processing on the Inter/intranet is one of the most important pieces to the HTML puzzle. By using forms, you provide a structured interaction with your users. They can enter information into the forms for data update, request custom information, and generally interact on an individual level with your Web application.

Traditionally, forms processing was handled by CGI scripts that were written in a variety of languages. With the introduction of the Active Server Pages, you can process forms using the power of the Visual Basic Scripting code.

The server side of forms processing is discussed in Chapter 11, "Building a Foundation of Interactivity with *Request* and *Response* Objects." In this section, we will be focusing on the HTML commands and syntax that are used to create the forms within the browser. After you have a firm grasp on creating the form on the client, you can move into scripting the Request Object in the chapter referenced earlier, which processes the form on the server.

A form is created on a browser with the <FORM> tag. There are a number of attributes that you can use when creating a form. You can start with the short example found here:

```
<FORM  METHOD="POST"  ACTION="http://www.proc.com/form2.asp"> ... </FORM>
```

The METHOD attribute specifies how the form will be sent to the processing script or CGI application on the server. There are two values you can set the METHOD attribute to, GET and POST. The POST method returns the form data to the server on a separate data stream. The GET method puts the return data into an environment variable called QUERY_STRING, which the server can then parse. The ACTION attribute is the script/CGI program that is used to process the form.

There are a number of form interface elements that you can add to your forms such as entry boxes, combo boxes, list boxes, text areas, check boxes, radio buttons, and command buttons. Listing F.5 creates a sample form page that illustrates many of the form interface objects. Figure F.8, which follows the listing, shows the form as displayed within a browser.

Listing F.5   F5.htm—Interface Elements Found Within a Form: Input Boxes, Radio Buttons, and Check Boxes

```
<HTML>
<HEAD>
<TITLE>Fun With Forms</TITLE>
</HEAD>
<BODY>
<P>Please enter the required information so that your membership
➥application can be processed.</P>
<FORM METHOD="POST" ACTION="http://www.noserve.com/procform.asp">
<P>Last Name: <INPUT TYPE="Text" NAME="LastName" SIZE=40>
   First Name: <INPUT NAME="FirstName" SIZE=25>
</P>
<P> Address: <INPUT NAME="Address" SIZE=60> </P>
<P> City: <INPUT NAME="City">
    State: <INPUT NAME="State" SIZE=2>
    Zip Code: <INPUT NAME="ZipCode">
</P>
<P> Select a User Id: <INPUT NAME="UserId" MAXLENGTH=8> <BR>
    Select a Password: <INPUT TYPE="Password" NAME="UserPass" MAXLENGTH=8">
</P>
<P> Your Computer Type: <BR>
    <INPUT TYPE="RADIO" NAME="COMPTYPE" VALUE="IBM">IBM Compatible
    <INPUT TYPE="RADIO" NAME="COMPTYPE" VALUE="MAC">Apple Mac/Power PC
</P>
<P> What Computer Magazines are you receiving? (Check all that apply)<BR>
    <INPUT TYPE="CHECKBOX" NAME="PCMag" VALUE="UNCHECKED">PC Magazine<BR>
    <INPUT TYPE="CHECKBOX" NAME="InfoWorld" VALUE="UNCHECKED">Info World<BR>
    <INPUT TYPE="CHECKBOX" NAME="PCWeek" VALUE="UNCHECKED">PC Week<BR>
    <INPUT TYPE="CHECKBOX" NAME="Computerworld" VALUE="UNCHECKED">ComputerWorld
</P>
<P>How did you hear about our organization?<BR>
<SELECT NAME="HowHear">
<OPTION>Business  Associate
<OPTION>Magazine
<OPTION>Trade Publication
<OPTION>Your Mother
</SELECT>
</P>
<P>Any Additional Comments you might wish to make:<BR>
<TEXTAREA NAME="Comment" ROWS=15 COLS=45>
</TEXTAREA>
</P>
<INPUT TYPE="SUBMIT" VALUE="Submit Membership">
<INPUT TYPE="RESET"  VALUE="Reset Form">
</FORM>
</BODY>
</HTML>
```

App

F

FIG. F.8

A form within a browser resembles a data input dialog in any application.

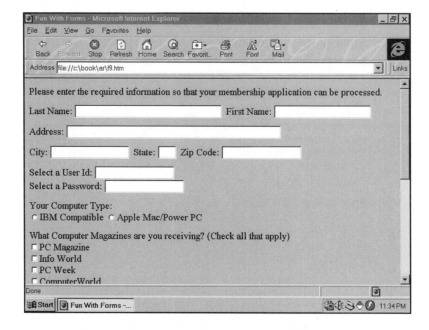

Now take a few moments to look at each of the new tags, which represent controls on your form. The tag that adds controls to a form is the <INPUT> tag. This tag has a number of attributes that govern the type, placement, size, and default value of the control.

The first attribute is TYPE. (See Table F.3.) The TYPE attribute specifies the type of control that is added to the form. The VALUE attribute specifies the default value of the control.

Table F.3   User Interface Control Types

Type Specifier	Widget Type	Value
"TEXT"	Entry Field	-
"RADIO"	Radio Button	Value returned when selected
"CHECK"	Check Box	True or False for check
"SUBMIT"	Submit Button	-
"RESET"	Reset Button	-

The next control that we encounter in our script is the combo box. This control is specified by using the <SELECT> tag. This tag also has a number of attributes, as well as <OPTION> tags, which are used to specify the items in the list.

The NAME attribute is the name of the combo box. You can also specify the MULTIPLE SIZE=N attribute, which displays the list in list box format with N items showing in the list.

There are numerous permutations and combinations that you can use when designing your forms. Although we are not going to look at all of the options for creating forms, you can specify colors, special fonts for headings, and a number of other attributes to make your forms more attractive. With the addition of Java Applets and ActiveX controls, the possibilities for forms processing have been greatly expanded.

 TIP A great way to align the text and entry boxes within a form is to put them into a table.

Working with Frames

Using frames in your Web pages enables you to create virtual windows within a single page. This enables you to provide links to multiple locations from within the same document that are independent from one another.

> **CAUTION**
>
> This powerful new frame functionality is not implemented in all browsers today, so if you are going to implement frames, be sure to also have a link to a non-frame version of your page.

In the wonderful world of frames, there are two types of documents that are used. The first is the layout document. This is the document that informs the browser how to divide the client window into logical rows and columns, and tells the browser which documents to place in each "frame." The second document in the frames world is the type that you have been learning about up to this point, a content document. The only real difference in the content documents that you have seen up to this point concerns where a followed link will be displayed within the framed page. First tackle the layout document, and then move on to the links within the content document.

To create a layout document, start with the generic HTML document tags template and replace the <BODY> </BODY> tags with <FRAMESET> </FRAMESET> tags. The <FRAMESET> tag alerts the browser that frame layout information follows. If a browser does not support frames, everything found within those tags will be ignored. Within the <FRAMESET> tag, you specify the number of rows and columns that create the frame. There are three ways that you can specify how the page is logically divided.

App

F

■ **Fixed Pixels**

The rows and columns are specified in pixel width and height. To create two rows of fixed 100 pixel height and one row that will be the size of the browser window minus 200 pixels, you would code the FRAMESET tag as follows: <FRAMESET ROWS="100,100, *". The * is a special symbol that means *the remaining space* on the page.

■ **Relative Size**

You can also specify the rows and columns, using a relative size. For example, you can create three columns, each one half as big as the next (for example, 100, 50, 25), with the syntax: `<FRAMESET COLS="2*, 2*, *"`

■ **Percentage**

The final type enables you to create the frames as a percentage of the page. To create two rows of equal height, you would specify the tag as `<FRAMESET ROWS="50%,50%">`.

Regardless of how you specify the logical frames, you must now add the content documents to the frames. The easiest way to understand this is to see it in action: Create a simple framed document. Using the following code, you create two columns, with a list of links on the left and a content window on the right.

```
Frames.htm
<HTML>
<HEAD>
<TITLE> Frames Are Easy</TITLE>
</HEAD>
<FRAMESET COLS ="25%,75%">
<FRAME src="left.htm" NORESIZE SCROLLING="NO">
<FRAME src="right.htm" SCROLLING="YES" NAME="main" BASE TARGET="_SELF">
</FRAMESET>
</HTML>
```

There are a few things to notice right away. You have divided the page into two columns. The documents are placed by using the `<FRAME>` tag in the order that they are declared. The first document, `left.htm`, will fill the first column, and the second document, `right.htm`, will fill the next. Take a look at the attributes of the `<FRAME>` tag in Table F.4

Table F.4   *<FRAME>* Tag Attributes

Attribute	Description
SRC	The source document for the frame.
NORESIZE	The frame will not be sized by the user.
SCROLLING	Yes or No, can or cannot scroll the frame window.
NAME	The name by which other frames reference this frame.
BASE TARGET	The target of the links. SELF points to the current frame; TOP removes all frames and loads a full page into the browser. You can specify a TARGET on the link if you do not set a BASE TARGET in the <FRAME> tag.
MARGINWIDTH	Width of the left and right margins in pixels, minimum value of 1 if used.
MARGIN HEIGHT	Same as MARGINWIDTH for height, minimum value of 1 if used.

Now look at the content documents within this simple frames document.

```
Left.htm
<HTML>
<BODY>
<A HREF="newright1.htm" TARGET "main">A New Main Frame</A><BR>
<A HREF="newright2.htm" TARGET "main">Another Main Frame</A><BR>
</BODY>
</HTML>
```

Notice that the target of the links are "main," which was the name given to the second column frame in the layout document frames.htm. This ensures that when the link is selected, the new page will be loaded into the second column frame. Continuing on:

```
Right.htm
<HTML>
<BODY>
<P>I am a content document within a frame.  Many times,
I have wished I could just <A HREF="newright1.htm">
<STRONG>replace<STRONG>
</A>myself</P>
</BODY>
</HTML>
```

In the right.htm, the link does not have a target. In the layout document, we set the BASE TARGET to SELF for the right.htm content document. This ensures that any links activated from this page will be loaded into the same frame that right.htm now occupies. Figure F.9 shows the completed frame document in action.

FIG. F.9

Frames are a quick and easy way to combine multiple pages within a single view.

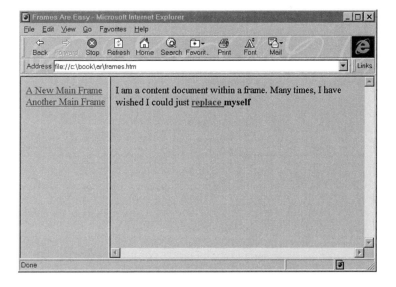

App

F

Parting Thoughts

You have taken "A Quick Tour" through the HTML language. As the language continues to mature and extensions today become the revisions of tomorrow, your accomplishments via HTML and the Active Server will only get better and more interactive. But until then, this short appendix should give you a sense of the HTML language, as well as a jump-start to get you up and running with Active Server.

There are a number of excellent HTML language books available at your bookstore. Any serious Web developer should own one. Even though much of the work is being done for us these days by HTML generators such as Microsoft's FrontPage 97, or Netscape Navigator Gold, it is always useful to understand what is going on behind the scenes. It will give you a better understanding of the environment and make you a better Web developer. ●

Index

Check Out Que® Books on the World Wide Web
http://www.quecorp.com

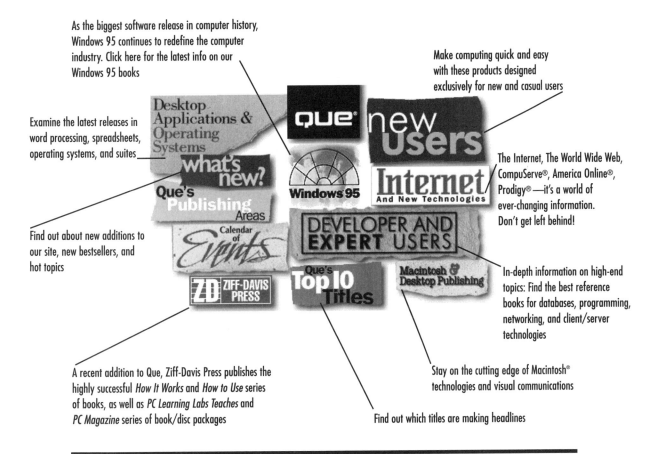

As the biggest software release in computer history, Windows 95 continues to redefine the computer industry. Click here for the latest info on our Windows 95 books

Make computing quick and easy with these products designed exclusively for new and casual users

Examine the latest releases in word processing, spreadsheets, operating systems, and suites

The Internet, The World Wide Web, CompuServe®, America Online®, Prodigy® —it's a world of ever-changing information. Don't get left behind!

Find out about new additions to our site, new bestsellers, and hot topics

In-depth information on high-end topics: Find the best reference books for databases, programming, networking, and client/server technologies

A recent addition to Que, Ziff-Davis Press publishes the highly successful *How It Works* and *How to Use* series of books, as well as *PC Learning Labs Teaches* and *PC Magazine* series of book/disc packages

Stay on the cutting edge of Macintosh® technologies and visual communications

Find out which titles are making headlines

With 6 separate publishing groups, Que develops products for many specific market segments and areas of computer technology. Explore our Web site and you'll find information on best-selling titles, newly published titles, upcoming products, authors, and much more.

- Stay informed on the latest industry trends and products available
- Visit our online bookstore for the latest information and editions
- Download software from Que's library of the best shareware and freeware

Copyright © 1997, Macmillan Computer Publishing-USA, A Viacom Company

MACMILLAN COMPUTER PUBLISHING USA
A VIACOM COMPANY

Technical Support:

If you need assistance with the information in this book or with a CD/Disk
accompanying the book, please access the Knowledge Base on our Web
site at **http://www.superlibrary.com/general/support**. Our most
Frequently Asked Questions are answered there. If you do not find the
answer to your questions on our Web site, you may contact Macmillan
Technical Support **(317) 581-3833** or e-mail us at **support@mcp.com**.

Complete and Return This Card
for a *FREE* Computer Book Catalog

Thank you for purchasing this book! You have purchased a superior computer book written expressly for your needs. To continue to provide the kind of up-to-date, pertinent coverage you've come to expect from us, we need to hear from you. Please take a minute to complete and return this self-addressed, postage-paid form. In return, we'll send you a free catalog of all our computer books on topics ranging from word processing to programming and the Internet.

Mr. ☐   Mrs. ☐   Ms. ☐   Dr. ☐

Name (first) ☐☐☐☐☐☐☐☐☐☐☐☐ (M.I.) ☐ (last) ☐☐☐☐☐☐☐☐☐☐☐☐☐☐☐☐☐

Address ☐☐☐☐☐☐☐☐☐☐☐☐☐☐☐☐☐☐☐☐☐☐☐☐☐☐☐☐☐☐☐☐☐☐☐

☐☐☐☐☐☐☐☐☐☐☐☐☐☐☐☐☐☐☐☐☐☐☐☐☐☐☐☐☐☐☐☐☐☐☐

City ☐☐☐☐☐☐☐☐☐☐☐☐☐☐☐☐☐☐ State ☐☐ Zip ☐☐☐☐☐ ☐☐☐☐

Phone ☐☐☐ ☐☐☐ ☐☐☐☐ Fax ☐☐☐ ☐☐☐ ☐☐☐☐

Company Name ☐☐☐☐☐☐☐☐☐☐☐☐☐☐☐☐☐☐☐☐☐☐☐☐☐☐☐☐☐

E-mail address ☐☐☐☐☐☐☐☐☐☐☐☐☐☐☐☐☐☐☐☐☐☐☐☐☐☐☐☐☐

1. Please check at least (3) influencing factors for purchasing this book.

Front or back cover information on book .... ☐
Special approach to the content .... ☐
Completeness of content .... ☐
Author's reputation .... ☐
Publisher's reputation .... ☐
Book cover design or layout .... ☐
Index or table of contents of book .... ☐
Price of book .... ☐
Special effects, graphics, illustrations .... ☐
Other (Please specify): _____ ☐

2. How did you first learn about this book?

Saw in Macmillan Computer Publishing catalog .... ☐
Recommended by store personnel .... ☐
Saw the book on bookshelf at store .... ☐
Recommended by a friend .... ☐
Received advertisement in the mail .... ☐
Saw an advertisement in: _____ ☐
Read book review in: _____ ☐
Other (Please specify): _____ ☐

3. How many computer books have you purchased in the last six months?

This book only .... ☐   3 to 5 books .... ☐
2 books .... ☐   More than 5 .... ☐

4. Where did you purchase this book?

Bookstore .... ☐
Computer Store .... ☐
Consumer Electronics Store .... ☐
Department Store .... ☐
Office Club .... ☐
Warehouse Club .... ☐
Mail Order .... ☐
Direct from Publisher .... ☐
Internet Site .... ☐
Other (Please specify): _____ ☐

5. How long have you been using a computer?

☐ Less than 6 months   ☐ 6 months to a year
☐ 1 to 3 years   ☐ More than 3 years

6. What is your level of experience with personal computers and with the subject of this book?

	With PCs	With subject of book
New	☐	☐
Casual	☐	☐
Accomplished	☐	☐
Expert	☐	☐

Source Code ISBN: 0-7897-1115-x

7. Which of the following best describes your job title?

Administrative Assistant .... ☐
Coordinator .... ☐
Manager/Supervisor .... ☐
Director .... ☐
Vice President .... ☐
President/CEO/COO .... ☐
Lawyer/Doctor/Medical Professional .... ☐
Teacher/Educator/Trainer .... ☐
Engineer/Technician .... ☐
Consultant .... ☐
Not employed/Student/Retired .... ☐
Other (Please specify): _____ ☐

8. Which of the following best describes the area of the company your job title falls under?

Accounting .... ☐
Engineering .... ☐
Manufacturing .... ☐
Operations .... ☐
Marketing .... ☐
Sales .... ☐
Other (Please specify): _____ ☐

9. What is your age?

Under 20 .... ☐
20-29 .... ☐
30-39 .... ☐
40-49 .... ☐
50-59 .... ☐
60-over .... ☐

10. Are you:

Male .... ☐
Female .... ☐

11. Which computer publications do you read regularly? (Please list.)

_____
_____
_____
_____
_____
_____
_____
_____
_____
_____

Comments: _____
_____
_____

Fold here and scotch-tape to mail.

BUSINESS REPLY MAIL
FIRST-CLASS MAIL PERMIT NO. 9918 INDIANAPOLIS IN

POSTAGE WILL BE PAID BY THE ADDRESSEE

ATTN MARKETING
MACMILLAN COMPUTER PUBLISHING
MACMILLAN PUBLISHING USA
201 W 103RD ST
INDIANAPOLIS IN 46290-9042

NO POSTAGE
NECESSARY
IF MAILED
IN THE
UNITED STATES